THE NOMADIC WOLF

ANNA ELLE

Copyright © 2025 by Anna Elle.

All rights reserved.

The characters and events portrayed in this book are fictitious. All names, places, events are of the authors imagination and any similarity to real persons, living or dead is coincidental and not intended by the author.

No part of this book may be reproduced or transmitted in any form or by any means, electronic, mechanical, photocopying, recording, or otherwise, without express written permission of the publisher.

Cover designed by: Aqsa on Fiverr

Editing, proofreading and formatting: Emberlust Press

Publisher: Anna Elle, New Zealand.

Print ISBN: 978-0-473-73200-4

Kindle ISBN: 978-0-473-73202-8

Ebook ISBN: 978-0-473-73201-1

For Becca and Angela — my ruthless beta readers, tireless champions, and the poor souls still trying to teach this stubborn creature how to live online. You saw the wreckage before it was pretty, believed in the story when I doubted it, and refused to let me quit. This book is stitched together with blood, teeth, and your faith. I hope it was worth it.

P.S. This book has the word fuck 303 times. For the readers who like their dialogue as filthy as their tension—you're welcome. To those who don't—oops.

Enjoy the werewolf fuckery!

NOTE FROM THE AUTHOR

Although this is a stand-alone novel, this is the second book based within the Blackfern Valley pack. The journey starts with *Enlightened by the Eclipse* and whether you want to start the journey at the beginning or join the werewolf fuckery in book two makes no difference, the pack is just happy to have you here. Happy howling!

TRIGGER WARNING

Although some of these instances may happen behind closed doors, I would like to caution that the following sensitive topics are covered in this book: mental health, suicide, and sexual assault.

CHAPTER 1
VINNY

Ring! Ring! Ring! My phone began to shrill out on the nightstand, my sister's name flashing angrily with the vibration on the cheap wood.

I was dreading this phone call. Not because I didn't love my sister; of course, I did. I was dreading this call because it was most likely a summons. Alpha Liam and Luna Clementine had been dropping hints over the last few months that it was time to end my sabbatical and come home to the pack. It was time to go home, meet my niece, and stay for a while.

The pack had raved about my niece every time I had talked to one of the members. Little Lacey! With her pitch-black hair and bright eyes. She was at least ten months old now, and other than the occasional video call, I hadn't officially met her.

I was training to be a pack warrior at eighteen, with the plan to be in my sister and Alpha Liam's personal protective circle. Shortly after my twentieth birthday, however, I raced to my sister and brother-in-law and requested for an out-of-province assignment as calmly as I could. I had asked Alpha Liam if I could be granted leave and become a pack ambassador instead. Clementine's dark eyebrow raised at me as she'd taken in my façade. I schooled my expression to be unreadable. I demanded my heart to slow down and stared back at her with what I hoped was an equal look of respect and indifference.

That was five years ago. Five years of hiding my half-breed scent so I wouldn't put an unnecessary target on my back. Five years of meeting other packs, representing Blackfern Valley and pretending to search for my true mate—or at least letting the pack believe I was trying. The truth? I had found my true mate on the first full moon after my twentieth birthday. I'd found her, and damn it, I hated her.

Her pitch-black wolf had looked at me curiously as I came out of the thicket of brush and followed my pounding heart. I watched as understanding crossed her dark brown and purple-ringed eyes, quickly followed by horror, disgust, and then anger. *Well, honey, the feeling is mutual.*

She shifted back instantly, and I tried not to look at her perfect, curvy little body that instantly made the blood run down to my shaft. She flicked her black hair over her shoulder, giving me a look of such malicious contempt that it made my wolf spirit, Vali, retreat and snarl before whimpering at the intense confusion he felt. The mate bond and his instincts told him this was his moon-given mate—his one true love. I was telling him this woman was vapid, this woman was horrid, this woman was unwanted and ultimately rejected.

As I opened my mouth to utter the words, her usual honeyed voice was raspy with anger. My dick spasmed, but I forced myself to focus on the words rather than the way her voice came out of her lusciously full mouth, the way her tongue flickered against her pearly white teeth as she spoke the words before I could.

Searing pain bit through my heart, cold and frosty, leaving me with severe burns. Icy and frigid, much like her. Vali snarled angrily as the frostbite set in. I could taste the freezing cold as Vali came forward, frothingly livid. My heart was still beating in my chest, which surprised me. It had to be negative thirty degrees within my ribcage now, but my heart was slamming against the ice, hard and fast. With every pump, it sent burning, ice-cold agony throughout my body.

I finally allowed myself to look at her face; her sun-kissed, bronze cheekbones, the warm brown hues of her eyes, her rounded nose and the light-russet colour of her skin. They were the last things I saw before she turned, shifting on the fly, howling as she ran. Had she felt the pain, too? No! There was no way that bitch felt anything. She was without emotion, as cold and rigid as the day I had first met her.

To everyone else, she was an angel. Charismatic, funny, always willing to help out the elderly or the kindergarten class with something. Always willing to help a friend in need. The glowing laughter would follow her wherever she was. But the moment her almond-shaped eyes met mine, they would lower into slits; the iridescent smile would flatten into a disapproving line, and her entire body would act like rigor mortis had set in.

I had spent the last five years trying to forget her. Moving from town to town, waiting to be invited into pack lands, meeting their officials, offering alliances, and sleeping with their she-wolves before I would boot out of town. Whenever Vali started to pine and lick his wounds, I would find the nearest bar and drown myself in a waitress or two. He disapproved of my methods, but the alternative was to sit with the constant icicles that inhabited my heart. At least if I kept moving, the icicles stayed still; they didn't shift or threaten to end my life. They were in stasis. Until I thought of her that is, and then the fragments would start to vibrate one shard at a time. She was the reason I hadn't returned to my home over the last five years.

Sighing, I answered my phone, "Johan's brothel, where we have two for one Wednesdays and all-you-can-eat Mondays."

"Cute." I could practically hear the eye roll through the phone.

"What's up, Clementine?" I probably should have called her by her title, but I forgot. I often forgot that my short, slightly chubby, previously four-eyed loser of a sister was now the most important she-wolf in my pack.

"I was just checking in. We haven't spoken for a while." I heard the squeal and coo in the background, and Clem's gentle shushing noise with "Mommy is on the phone" in a gentle but firm whisper.

"I really don't need to hear what you call Liam in the bedroom, Clem. You could have called me afterwards."

"Hardy-har-har. Your uncle is hilarious, Lacey," she said to her daughter before turning her attention back to me. "I was just checking in to see how you are doing—"

"And to tell me that I am needed back in Blackfern Valley," I interrupted her, knowing that it was inevitable that the conversation would be manipulated that way.

"Well, truth be told, I thought you would have been back by now—"

"I enjoy the road."

"Dad misses you. You haven't even met Lacey yet. You are a member of this pack, Vincent, and the pack hasn't seen you in five years!"

"Did you forget what I look like? I can remind you: tall, green eyes, blond hair, well-endowed, great in the sack," I quipped.

"Wrong audience, Vinny. Look, I know you enjoy being... What do you call it? Nomadic? But we could really use you home for now." She fumbled a little bit, which made Vali's ears twitch. Something wasn't right. There was something she wasn't telling me. Finally, she took a deep breath, her voice triangulating directly toward Vali. "Something happened."

"Have more rogues attacked?" my tone sharpened, instantly protective.

It was well known that the Blackfern Valley pack had a half-breed as a Luna, and although our pack had accepted her, there were still outsiders and purists who thought that my sister was an abomination and an easy target. That was often their first and last mistake. My sister was calm and collected when she was unprovoked, but when she was tested, she was a hellcat with delicate ferocity.

And then there was her true mate. Alpha Liam may have seemed a gentle, fair, and just ruler to the outside world, but there were also whispers about the darker side of his legacy. It was rumoured that a part of his uncle's cruel essence had embedded itself in him the day he killed his uncle's only living son. Liam was in his early twenties when he'd delivered that fatal blow and some claimed that act stitched fragments of his uncle's temperament into his own.

There was no way Alpha Liam was as sadistic as his uncle or cousin, but I had been on enough enforcement missions when rogues attacked to witness firsthand how ruthless he could be. If my sister hadn't been taken not just once but three times within five years, maybe Liam would have remained his passive self. But he'd been tested three times too many. His fury was terrifying, calculated, and unrelenting—a stark contrast to the gentle demeanour he showed in times of peace.

I knew how he felt. My first-ever shift was triggered when my sister was taken the first time. I was barely sixteen years old and hardly had time to register what was happening. I never even thought I liked my sister that much, but suddenly, quiet-minded Vali was sprouting forward, ready to kill anyone who would threaten her. She was not only his Luna but his kin, and she was in danger.

The next time she was taken, I was eighteen and had just started training as a pack warrior. A rogue had kidnapped her from a gas station. Unfortunately for the rogue, she was with her friend Sophie and Sophie's brother, our pack beta, Ryan. The rogue didn't get far, and when Ryan and Sophie caught up to him, the rogue didn't see the other side of the hour.

The last time was shortly after I left. Unfortunately for that rogue, my sister was over being abducted and sliced her claw through his eye socket, curling it and popping out his eyeball.

From what I was told, it had dangled comically before she pierced her claws through his soft underside and left him to bleed out. She had returned home before her bodyguard, Luca, had even realized she'd been taken.

"Not me," she said softly. "We had some information that some rogues have learned about Lacey." Vali growled in the back of my mind, his hackles high and his teeth glinting with saliva.

"I'm on my way." I abruptly ended the call, throwing my clothes into a rucksack before grabbing my toothbrush from the bathroom counter.

I dropped the key into the drop box of the motel before revving my engine, twisting the gas a few more times to hear the engine purr, its throaty rumble making me grin. After attaching my rucksack, I slung my leg over my steel-black Boulevard C50 and skidded out of the parking lot.

CHAPTER 2
ROMAN

I STRETCHED DEEPLY, groaning with appreciation as I felt each vertebra pop and click throughout my back. I removed my hairband from my hair and then flipped my head upside down to gather my hair into a messy top knot on my head. Nightshift was dragging on at Kempthorne Memorial Hospital. It was four in the morning, and not one person had come in to be triaged in the last few hours. And now I had two more hours before I could head home, collapse into the pillowy down of my bed, and sleep for eternity.

Home time couldn't come soon enough after pulling a double shift. People thought I was crazy for pulling doubles all the time, but the truth was I loved being a nurse. Scrap that. I loved being an emergency department nurse. Even being surrounded by werewolves, the emergency room could be chaotic with drunken students and their stupid decisions, which provided me with a great distraction from my life. Helping the doctors reset dislocated shoulders or pulling artifacts from places they shouldn't be was like a drug—addictive adrenaline that coursed through my veins.

I was used to distracting myself these days. When I wasn't at work, I was getting my ass kicked at pack training, and when

I wasn't training, I was having hot sex. Eventually, I would tire myself into a state that would sedate my wolf, and I would be able to sleep.

My wolf, Rue, was volatile, hence why I needed the constant supply of distraction. She had always been a little on the bitchy side, the complete opposite of my happy-go-lucky character. But over the last five or six years, she seemed to have gotten progressively worse, and now I was using any means necessary to keep her calm.

When I started to realize that Rue wasn't normal, I tried to keep my distance from my friends. At first, I just tried to avoid them completely, which resulted in them camping out in my living room, refusing to leave until I told them what was wrong.

Even after Rue attacked them at some point or another, they were warier but still wouldn't abandon me. Slowly, I saw fewer and fewer of them, often due to my strenuous efforts to keep Rue at bay. But I didn't feel isolated from them. We still kept in touch via a group chat, and even though all of them had merged with their wolf spirits and didn't need to attend the monthly pack run, one or two of them would usually participate in the pack run to keep me company.

I hadn't merged with Rue, and at twenty-six years old, I had long accepted that it would never happen. Merging only occurred when the two halves of our shared soul were completely in sync—that was unlikely to happen with Rue being so volatile. I even went to see Doctor Todd, the pack doctor, to discuss a theory that I couldn't sync with her because she was rabid. He chuckled lowly and told me my wolf was high-energy and dramatic but not rabid.

Dramatic. That was the biggest understatement of the century. For a while, I had woken up and found that I wasn't in my bed. Repeatedly. Not only was I not in my bed, but Rue had taken me halfway across the province while I slept. I didn't even know that she could do that! The first few times it happened, I panicked. The next few times, I was angry. And then I became resigned to the fact my wolf was untrustworthy.

We would argue heatedly every time this happened. Each of us fought for dominance when I tried to return to Blackfern Valley. It wasn't that she wanted to be rogue—that idea was abhorrent even to her—she just physically didn't want to be in Blackfern Valley. She wanted to be elsewhere. She needed to be anywhere but there.

I would have said it was the mate bond that was making her act this way, but I couldn't feel the mate bond. It froze and shattered into a million pieces the moment the words left my mouth, Rue's voice echoing through mine. I think that was the first time we had ever been on the same page: the moment we rejected our true mate.

No, there was definitely something else wrong with Rue.

"Nothing is wrong with me," she grumbled sleepily, her black ears twitching as she lay her head between her front paws. I rolled my eyes and walked toward the vending machine by the front door. Being a werewolf meant I had an enormous appetite, and most of my pay was transferred straight into the big black box of junk food.

Boredom also did not help in this situation. I scanned through the glass front, deciding between Reese's Peanut Butter Cups and a bag of all-dressed Lays potato chips. Both. I smashed the keypad and watched as the little springs released each item in turn.

I bent over, and a sterile scent wafted by my nose seconds before I heard the voice say, "Salty and sweet?"

I snapped upright and looked over my shoulder, flashing a megawatt smile at Simon, a ward nurse. Very sweet, very human, very breakable Simon. His eyes scanned my body before landing on my face as they often did when he saw me. I knew he was interested in me, but the feeling was definitely one-sided. It had nothing to do with the fact Simon was human and more to do with the fact that I could break him both physically and mentally. I used sex as a tool, a weapon, and an escape, but I also had a firm rule: No one from my workplace.

"Just something to tide me over for the next couple of hours."

"You should let me take you out for a proper meal. We both finish at six, and you know the new pancake house is now open." His eyes were full of suggestive intent, which made me certain that pancakes weren't the only thing on his mind.

"Excuse me, but this is a proper meal! It covers all the food groups: carbs, protein and chocolate."

"So I see." He smiled at me again, adjusting his gold-rimmed frames and nervously running his hand through his hair.

"How is the world of the surgical ward going?" I asked, directing us both out of the doorway and back toward the nurse's station. The TV screens were flickering between the ambulance bay, the public entrance and the foyer. No movement was seen on either. I suppressed the urge to sigh.

Due to being surrounded by werewolves, our hospital was more like an after-hours clinic than a regular hospital. There were three floors. The ground floor had an emergency department, a small surgical wing, radiology and a physio-gym. The middle floor was a mix of outpatient clinics, a few offices and a small cafeteria. The top floor was the in-patient ward. Some nights were chaotic and busy, but tonight wasn't one of them.

"About as quiet as down here, but you know, it's supposed to be quiet up there." I nodded but said nothing. One Mississippi. Two Mississippi. Three— "Extremely dead down here tonight, eh?"

Chirp. Chirp. Chirp. Crickets would have been better conversationalists. An eye-roll almost escaped.

"Yeah, it is a bit, hence the junk-food fix." Rue let out a big fake snore, and I suppressed the urge to grin and laugh at her.

"You know, maybe if we show him what's between your legs, he would come up with more interesting topics." I pretended to focus

on opening my bag of chips. It was a trick I learned to do around humans to hide the conversations with my wolf spirit. Thankfully, Rue was too exhausted most of the time to push forward and show her lilac aura, so at the most, my eyes just seemed unfocused and vacant.

"What are you on about?"

"Your pussy is the holy grail. He wants to worship at its altar. I say let him; that way, these dead-end conversations get better."

"My pussy isn't that special."

"Then even better, fuck him, and maybe he will leave us alone."

"Or cling harder."

"Shit. It's a lose-lose. We are never getting rid of this guy." She huffed and flicked her tail.

"He's a nice guy, Rue. Most girls would kill for the opportunity to date a nice guy. Just not me for obvious reasons." I gave her a pointed look. She smirked and shook her head.

"It's just because he's a bore, and you know it! I can always come out and play for a bit, you know, if you want me to." Her voice had taken on a sultry, playful quality, which made me instantly flash her a warning look, and she responded with a wolfy chuckle.

"Oh, it looks like duty calls," Simon said morosely, nodding toward the screens where a bus had just pulled into the ambulance bay. "Think about having a meal with me, okay?"

I scoffed my mouth full of chips instead of answering, and tossed the bag into the trash can, wiping my hands on my purple scrub pants. I sanitized them before I walked out the side door to see if they needed a hand. I was more than grateful for the interlude. If I had stayed talking to Simon any longer, I may have taken pity on him enough to actually go to the Pancake House with him. I may have given in and shown him my holy grail, too. I may have broken him in like a horse and then *broken* him just because the boredom was killing me so much. Thankfully, my action came in a different form—a gushing head wound. Yup, that will do.

I DROVE up the gravel road that led to my cabin. The sun penetrated through the canopy above me and twinkled through the leaves, creating a mottled effect on the road as I turned around the bend.

A large log cabin burst out of the woods, and I smiled as I parked my car and cut the engine. My bed was awaiting me. I closed the car door with a small bang and gently sniffed, appreciating the earthy smell after being surrounded by the harshly sterile scent of the hospital. The strong chemicals irritated my nasal passage and usually burned my nose so badly that it often took a while for Rue to heal it. Either that, or she was just being a bitch.

I sniffed the air again as I turned the door handle of my front door—was that lasagne? I followed my nose to the kitchen as my stomach rumbled at the smell. Sitting in the warm oven was a large pasta dish. Familial smells wafted toward me, and I knew that my eldest sister, Arizona, had been here. *Trust the scent of real food to make Rue heal my nose faster.* I sniffed again and detected the tones of my brothers, Israel and Jordan. I looked around and saw the telltale signs that my family had been here. The couch cushions were fluffed, the floor had been vacuumed, and my laundry had been washed and folded. I opened the hide-away garbage can and rolled my eyes at its sparkliness. I wasn't a slob; I just didn't have time to clean up with my busy schedule. Or shop. Or cook. Or eat proper food. Canned tuna or brown beans on toast was fine, as I constantly ran between the hospital and Blackfern Valley.

I didn't live in the Valley anymore. I lived alone in my log cabin in the middle of nowhere. Blackfern Valley and Kempthorne were in the middle of nowhere, too, but my house was even more secluded than theirs. This place was my first attempt to stop the erratic behaviour of my volatile wolf. It hadn't worked, but the independence and isolation had grown on me, so I had stayed. I stayed in the hope that one day I could bring my kid sister, Indiana, here to live with me.

But that hope was in vain; my baby sister was gone. And my so-called true mate was the reason I was never going to live with her again.

CHAPTER 3
VINNY

I opened the throttle and leaned forward, hollering out a whoop of delight, which was met with Vali's yippy howls of excitement—he loved this as much as I did. All I wanted to do was take my helmet off and feel the wind in my hair as I zoomed down the country. I wore a helmet not because it kept my brain inside my skull but because it really sucks when you get a mouthful of bugs.

I tried not to think of my destination too much and just enjoy the open road. I estimated that it would take four days to get back to Blackfern Valley. As I got closer to my dreaded destination, my thought process betrayed me. It kept bringing me back to my final few days in Blackfern Valley.

I tried to force my brain to think about my dad, my sister, my niece—God, even my mother, who died when I was fifteen. Each time my brain would start to behave, little snippets of unwanted memories and thoughts would intertwine themselves, popping forward and back like little poltergeists of doom.

Vali was no help, so I picked up speed in the hope that the adrenaline would keep my nightmares at bay. Faster. Faster.

Wait, what was that smell? Vali grumbled as the scent hit his nose. His ears flattened against his skull, and he let out a low, whiny snarl. My heart spasmed, and I felt the icicles threaten to take over.

I spun and slid as I hit the corner at full speed. I tilted my bike to try and counteract the pull of gravity and correct myself, but I was going too fast. *Shit!* The hot tar seal ripped my jeans as my body scraped against the rough road, and my bike catapulted in the opposite direction.

I rolled a couple of times, gave myself a couple of breaths and tried to reason with my galloping heart. There was a strong jasmine fragrance in the air. Jasmine was the smell I detested the most. But there was no way that it was her scent I was detecting. Not all the way out here. I groaned and lifted myself up, taking off my helmet and walked over to my bike.

"Are you okay?" a squeaky voice called.

I turned to witness a petite, busty blonde running toward me, and I tried to smile at her. It came out looking like a grimace I'm sure. I took a gentle sniff as she approached. She had big blue eyes, a heart-shaped face and a scent of pure human.

"Yeah, I'm okay." I raked my eyes down her body, taking in her tight jeans and a crop top that emphasized her rock-star body. *Damn.*

"You flew off your bike," she stated the obvious, but her eyes were large and full of concern, so I suppressed the urge to roll mine.

"Not the first time," I said with a nod as I pretended to heave my bike up. It wasn't heavy. Not at all. In fact, I could lift it above my head with little effort. Humans, however, do find motorcycles heavy.

"That was a gnarly crash! I don't think your bike is going to start." Her eyes ran over the motorcycle with interest.

I gave it a quick once over and concluded that she was correct. It wasn't going to start.

"Shit." I closed my eyes and knew I was going to have to

stash the bike and get the concerned citizen to leave before I shifted and ran the rest of the way.

"Come on, you can put it in the back." I blinked at her. *Put what in the back? Of where?!* My wolf grinned stupidly at me. She pointed back to the blood-red half-ton truck parked on the side of the road. *Oh.*

"It's okay—"

"You are one of those, aren't you?" Her blue eyes flashed with annoyance.

"One of what?"

"You never accept help from people. From women."

"Of course not—" I started to shake my head.

"Good," she said in a final tone, going back toward her truck. She looked back and gave me an expectant look. Defeated, I pushed the bike toward her.

I wondered how I was going to get it onto the bed of her truck without giving away my werewolf strength while she popped the tailgate down and shimmied up onto the tray. She pushed a few moving boxes to the side before sliding a ramp toward the back and gave me a grin.

"Connect the ramp and push your bike up. I have some straps here, too. We can secure it and then I'm taking you to the hospital." *Who is this girl?*

"I don't need a hospital," I said as I followed her directions.

"Just humour me. You flew off your bike at such a speed that your neck should be broken." I grimaced again. She was right; if I hadn't had my werewolf reflexes, I would never have been able to prepare myself for the catastrophe of that landing.

"What are you? A doctor?" I grunted at her as I pretended to struggle slightly, pushing my bike up the strange angle. A tinkly laugh echoed as she helped me direct the bike.

"No, I'm a history student." *Ah. A student.*

The nearest tertiary provider was Kempthorne University, nestled within the forest, about an hour from Blackfern Valley. Although the town was predominately werewolves, a few humans oddly gravitated toward it rather than staying clear as per usual. Their presence meant that the mixed packs in town had to be more careful and a little more secretive than we were on our own pack lands. She didn't seem like a local, though, and the semester had already started.

As if she was reading my mind, she said, "I'm transferring to Kempthorne. My name is Camille." A small hand reached around the bike, and I gripped it in mine, giving it a gentle shake.

"Vinny." She flicked her blonde hair over her shoulder, giving me an appraisal before shaking her head and handing me a strap.

I THOUGHT that I would be able to lose her once we made it to the hospital, but she was adamant about following me in. I was committed now, there was no way she was going to let me walk away. She walked straight up to the receptionist and beamed at her. "Hi, I just witnessed this idiot coming off his motorcycle at full speed."

"I'm fine." I rolled my eyes at the middle-aged receptionist.

"No," she snapped. "He should be dead. Can you check him for functioning brain cells? I swear!" She sounded exasperated, but when I darted my eyes toward her, I saw her lip twitch in humour. "Perhaps you will find them in his penis?"

Vali chuckled deeply, and I even cracked a grin, but before I could retort, my nose was invaded by the scent of jasmine petals. It wasn't an illusion this time as the jasmine merged with an undercurrent of canine. The gates of hell had swung open and spat the keeper of the hellmouth in my direction, causing my heart to stutter and stall. I instinctually spun and looked directly into Roman's warm brown eyes. The icicles in my heart expanded to the size of a glacier but with the speed of an unexpected snowstorm. Vali growled and whimpered, flashing his canines and lowering his head toward the worst demon known to man.

"V-Vinny," she stammered as she took me in.

I didn't answer; my tongue had shrivelled up and was so dry it was basically dust. The glacier kept growing, and Vali kept growling. I felt a slight breeze travel through my nerves, a wind-tangled snarl of pure hate, bitter and cold, as it fed into the icy pit in my chest. I knew the silver ring around my irises was most likely glowing with anger.

A warm hand touched my arm, but it did nothing to ease the cold. I just stared at Roman, frozen to the spot. It felt like an eternity, standing there staring at each other, but in reality, it was no more than a minute—a minute of twisted torture.

"Hi, I'm Camille!" The sassy blonde broke the tension. "My friend here flew off his bike, and I was hoping that he could be seen to."

Roman looked at Camille, and her big brown eyes flashed with an icy purple for a brief second before Roman regained her composure and offered Camille a megawatt smile. "Sure, come on through, Vincent."

CHAPTER 4
ROMAN

I smiled at Cybil, my regular elderly patient, as I offered her the discharge papers, reminding her to take her medication and directed her out through the emergency waiting area. The sudden aroma of peppermint followed by canine and human and a loud bantering conversation made me freeze in my spot. The girl's voice was loud and squeaky, and even though I hadn't heard her companion speak yet, I instantly knew who it was.

My heart spasmed and pounded erratically as I looked up and took in the stunning specimen standing before me. His hair was longer than I had seen it, sitting between his chin and shoulders, flicking at odd angles at the end. When he was a teenager, he always had a military-style conservative cut, which contradicted his bad-boy nature. But now, he was more synonymous with his rebellious nature, and I was doing everything in my power not to drool as I perused him. His broad shoulders fit snuggly into his leather jacket, and his jeans were ripped in a way that was not intentional. His green and silver eyes found mine, and I felt as though I had been hit with a blast of frosty air. The malice and contempt could not be mistaken for anything else. Rue stood in shock, gaping and unable to make a comment or a sound.

"Hi, I'm Camille." The voice broke through the rushing sound of water that was echoing through my ears.

Rue snarled menacingly at her, triangulating on the petite girl whose hand looked tiny against Vinny's enormous bicep. I forced Rue back and smiled at the girl, taking control and forcing the cold fires back into the depths so I could concentrate on the job I needed to do. The quicker I could do my assessment, the faster I could get him out of there.

I swiped my card against the little black box on the wall and walked toward the nurse's triage. Vincent was stiff and mechanical as he followed me into the room. I closed the door behind us. He still said nothing. The awkward hatred swirling between us. The tightness in his jaw was emphasized by the dark blond beard smothering it. As if I was addicted to hatred and pain, my eyes observed every inch of him. He looked fine. He looked more than fine. He looked goddamn edible. *Fuck.* Why did someone I hate so much have to be so goddamned fuckable?

Rue started to react to my thoughts and the cold tension that intensified with every moment we stood in silence.

"What happened?" I asked, trying to push Rue back again, unsure if she was going to kill him or rip his clothes off.

"Flew off my bike." His voice was gravelly and stirred something deep inside. I chose to ignore it. Rue's tail twitched as she watched Vinny with disdain.

"You flew off your bike," I repeated. I rolled my eyes dramatically. It was the only thing I could do as I tried to suppress my inner urges. I wanted to scream in frustration. He was a werewolf with the ability to heal without medical intervention unless it was severe. I saw no damage as I ran my eyes down him again, telling myself I was looking for any indication he needed a doctor before settling a moment too long at the spot between his legs. *Fuck! Why the hell is he here?* I closed my eyes and only opened them when he cleared his throat.

I knew my eyes were swirling with lilac. My tolerance level

was highly taut and agitated. I could feel the little bubbles grating against my nerves, making Rue pace and snarl. Vinny watched my eyes with interest, his own eyes illuminating in silver. After another moment of silence, he dropped his face into his hands, covering his eyes, frustrated.

"I flew off my bike at over one-hundred-and-twenty kilometres an hour. I was picked up by a human. How was I supposed to tell her that I didn't break my bones because of superhuman reflexes? That my road rash healed within minutes? That the only thing that got hurt was my fucking bike?" He took a deep breath and removed his hands. "I had to humour her."

"Who is she?" The words were out of my mouth quicker than I could rein them in. Vinny arched a single blond eyebrow at me, and I scolded myself.

"I just told you." There was a slightly curious tone to his voice that I ignored. *Shit. He did just tell me.*

"Right." I shook my head and tried to clear my thoughts. I was drowning in an icy peppermint scent, and it was like I had forgotten how to swim. "A-are you in pain anywhere?" I stammered. His eyes flashed bright silver again.

"No." His voice was harsh and cold.

"Any dizziness or nausea?"

"No."

"Any tender spots or cuts—"

"No. I told you I am fine."

"I know that!" I snarled. My mouth closed with an audible snap, and my jaw locked. The staring game commenced again. Burning hatred zipped through us, creating a foreboding tension in the air. I didn't want to yield first, but the alternative was unfathomable. "Give yourself a few more moments so it appears like I did a more thorough examination for your human *friend*. And then get the fuck out of my hospital."

I stalked out of the room and straight into the nurse's station, hyperventilating slightly as I tried to rein in my burning anger. With each deep breath, Rue paced agitatedly. *"I can't believe he came back! I thought he was gone for good."*

"Apparently not."

"You should have let me destroy him."

"What good was that going to do?"

"Well, for one, you wouldn't be having a panic attack and hiding right now!"

"I just wasn't expecting to see him. I'll be fine."

"You should have asked the fucker how long he planned on staying for."

"I don't own Blackfern Valley or Kempthorne. He has every right to be here, too."

"Does he really, though? That asshole hurt—"

"I know what he fucking did!" I snapped. *"But at the bare minimum, he is a member of our pack. Not to mention, his sister is our fucking luna. He probably has more right to be here than we do!"*

A MOVEMENT on the display monitors caught my eye. The triage room door opened, and Vinny's large frame invaded the screen. I watched as he turned and went back into the waiting room. The tiny blonde girl threw a magazine down onto the seat and ran over to him, her face full of concern. Rue grumbled as I watched. Their conversation was unheard, but I could imagine what was being said through the animation of her features. Her face scowled prettily in protest. He said something else, and she glared at him, watching him closely before sighing. He bent down toward her ear, and her face lit up a little before she schooled it into a controlled expression. She gave him a nod and turned toward the automatic doors of the emergency room. Vinny's hand landed on the small of her back as he walked out with her.

Rue's hackles rose menacingly and she thrashed violently against my mind. Shit! My skin started to hum, and I knew I needed to sedate her quickly. I raced down to the locker room and almost ripped the locker door off its hinges. I yanked my cashmere sweater on over my head quickly and dug around in my purse for my phone. I scrolled down the contacts as I made my way hastily toward the exit. I wasn't watching where I was going and smashed directly into Simon, causing him to wobble.

"Hey! Where's the fire?"

I looked up at him in piqued interest, my body churning with need. Thoughts of pushing him back into the locker room invaded my mind. His clothes would be shredded within seconds, and my need would be satiated. Hot, primal sex was what I longed for, and he could be just the man to give it to me.

No! Not Simon. Maybe Simon?

I felt the bones in my arms start to dislodge, and I suppressed a whimper against the burning pain. Hot acid was running through my bloodstream, and I knew I only had moments before Rue managed to rip through.

"I-I got to go!" I said, barrelling past him. Black fur was starting to pop out of my arms, hidden by the soft blue cashmere. Rue wasn't calming down, and the instinct to run was too much to handle. There was no stopping the shift now, and with her volatile nature, I needed to ensure she didn't kill anyone in wolf form. That she wouldn't follow her rejected mate and attack like a rabid animal. And after this run, I would have to use one of my many tools to keep her sedated. I knew just the person who could help me to tame the wild animal, both in the forest and in the bedroom. And if my rejected mate was sticking around, it was even more possible that I would have to increase the regime. I pounded the call button on my phone and sprinted toward the forest. He answered on the third ring.

Thank fuck!

CHAPTER 5
VINNY

As soon as I stepped away from the hospital, the aroma of jasmine started to dissipate, making it a little easier to breathe. Each breath in there had felt like razorblades to my throat, but the further we got from the hospital, the more my lungs opened to receive the oxygen they were so badly struggling for. There was an icy void in my chest, but I had convinced Camille to come to a bar with me, so it was only a matter of time before I filled the chasm.

I was starting my third glass of bourbon, smiling as Camille amicably told me about herself, like this was an actual date, as if I wasn't trying to ignore the gaping hole in my chest. I kept sniffing the air, high on alert, trying to detect the hints of jasmine before they arrived. I was convinced my bad luck had just started, that Roman would follow me into this bar if only to make my life a living hell.

"*I hate that she looks good,*" Vali grumbled, placing unwanted images of Roman in my mind. Even standing in lilac-coloured scrubs with her hair tied back messily, she was sensational. Her curves were hidden beneath her uniform, but I could still make out her womanly figure beneath. The slight bagginess of her uniform created an unwanted but alluring fantasy in my mind.

A kink I didn't know I possessed. Her light brown skin looked creamy and soft, and her heart-shaped mouth was dying to be kissed.

I took another large swig and growled at my wolf, *"Vali!"*

"Sorry," he mumbled sincerely. I could feel how sorry he was. His anguish was my anguish, and vice versa. We were both in immense amounts of pain the moment we smelled her. And as much as I wanted to react to the pain, all I could do was stand, frozen in horror, while she barely batted an eyelash. Her sweet voice, which should have soothed me, cut deep instead, leaving ugly scarring over my soul. I loathed her so fucking much. I slammed the rest of the bourbon back and threw my hand up for another. The bartender obliged immediately.

"Whoa! I know there must be a story about the nurse at the hospital, but don't you think you should slow down a little? I already saved your ass once. I don't exactly want to do it again."

"I'm fine," I muttered.

"Sure you are. The speed at which you're drinking hard liquor really convinces me of that." I huffed. "Look at it this way, if you keep drinking like that, I'll have to take you back to the hospital to get your stomach pumped, and you know, your ex-girlfriend would be the one to do it." I froze, lifting the glass of bourbon to my lips and looked into Camille's big blue eyes. She had a point. Or she would have if I was human and couldn't handle my alcohol.

"Sorry," I mumbled, lowering my glass and gazing at the table.

"Hey, toxic ex, I get it."

No, you really don't. "We never dated."

She tilted her head at me. "Well, she's obviously under your skin."

"Not in the way you're thinking," I said, then gave her a sheepish-apologetic look. "We've always hated each other. Actually, hate might be too soft of a word."

"Oh. So, there is no unrequited love story?"

I snorted. "Not in the slightest. She really isn't my type."

"Beautiful but vapid," Vali said in agreement.

"What is your type?" Camille sprung forward. I gave her a crooked smile, which she returned with a slight blush staining her cheeks. Easy—way too easy.

MY DAD WAS greyer than the last time I had seen him, the strands of silver weaving through the pitch black of his hair. His crows' feet had deepened, and the contrasting streaks in his groomed beard rivalled the amount on his head. I tried to swallow my guilt. Had it honestly been that long since I had video-called my father?

"Thanks for picking me up," I grunted my appreciation as I put my arms around my dad and patted him roughly on the back. Though he might have looked older, he remained as solid as ever, standing just half an inch shorter than my six foot three.

Releasing him, I picked up my feather-lite bike and hauled it roughly onto the back of his truck, securing it in place with some straps.

"Do I want to know what happened to your bike?"

"Just took a corner a little too fast."

"Do I want to know why you were in a halls of residence?"

"Oh, don't worry there, Pops; I definitely didn't take *that* too fast." I grinned at him, and he shook his head exasperatedly, his eyes twinkling with mischief.

"So, are you bringing her home for dinner?"

"Didn't I tell you? I proposed right on the spot. She could do this pretzel thing, and I decided that's the woman I want to mate with and bear my pups." I jumped off the back of the truck and pushed the tailgate back into its locked position.

"Your sister will be thrilled. Assuming, of course, that the girl said yes."

"Over and over again."

Dad chuckled deeply. "Get in the truck, Casanova."

The door whinnied a familiar sound as I climbed into the passenger side of the cab. "How has everything been?" Dad asked as he clambered into the driver's seat and started the engine.

"Good, up until I managed to total my bike."

"I'm sure it isn't totalled."

"Yeah, once we get back to Blackfern Valley, I'm going to see how much work it's going to take to repair it. Hopefully, it won't be too damaged, and I can get back on the road."

"Vinny. You are allowed to stay, you know," Dad said carefully.

No, I'm not. "There is nothing for me here, Dad. I can't exactly hustle pool or count cards around here." I shook my head. "Nope! As soon as I get a whiff of whoever is after my niece, I am out and hunting him down."

"You didn't want to be a warrior, Vinny. Leave it to the pack warriors and trackers.

"Dad, this is family."

"Yes, it is. And you decided you wanted to be free and travel." Dad reminded me unnecessarily.

"It was never about leaving my family, Dad," I grumbled. "My family is the most important thing to me. Why the fuck do you think I'm back?"

"If family were so important to you, you wouldn't be in such a hurry to leave!"

Touché. I audibly snapped my mouth closed and glared out the window as we drove the windy highway back toward the Valley. Refusing to answer and refusing to tell him the truth. The silence was bitter.

After a few moments, there was a gentle scratch in my mind as my father's voice travelled through it. It had been an age since I had communicated this way. The distance I had kept from my pack made it almost impossible. The further away I was, the harder and more painful it had become to try and mind-link. I was warned about this when I decided to leave, that my mental voice would have been dimmed to near nothing. I had tried it a couple of times when I was up with a pack near the border of Alaska, and all I got back was harsh white noise and a nosebleed. I could feel the connection to my pack, I just couldn't contact them. I was in true solitude—genuinely nomadic.

"The prodigal son has returned," my father's voice grunted to me and another. I felt my sister's amber and honeysuckle aura on the mind-link. *"Be home in an hour or so."*

"Try not to kill each other," she replied. I huffed, and my father chuckled.

The howling mountains greeted me as we entered the boundary. I felt the familiar pop and buzz as we crossed the threshold. The need to flee erupted over my skin like an itch I couldn't scratch. I ground my teeth. There was no turning back now.

DAD PULLED up to the ancient garage that looked out of place next to the more modernly designed house. Where the old house was a small bungalow that often felt cramped, the new house was architecturally designed with large windows that made it feel light and airy.

The fire was a blessing in many ways. After Mom died, it was very obvious that Dad needed to keep busy. He needed a project. The bungalow became his project. A project that would have taken years and years to complete. That would have taken years and years of my patience. The fire had gutted the structure down to its foundation and left Dad with a blank canvas.

But that was not his only project. There was a reason he had moved his family to Blackfern Valley after the love of his life died, and it wasn't just to overcompensate for a midlife crisis and fix up a house. His first project was trying to keep me from going off the deep end. His first project was telling me he had lied to me my entire life. And the omitted truth could have saved me a world of hurt. That was the first and only time I had ever punched my dad.

I'd been in more than my fair share of fights the moment my arrogant ass stepped into the Blackfern High school yard. I brought on some of them myself, thanks to my attitude. The rest? Well, I was targeted for being a half-breed, although at the time, I had no idea. I was going crazy with my body's changes, and blood-haters had targeted me. So yeah, I felt justified in punching my father straight in the mouth when the truth had finally come out.

"ARE YOU DONE?" he growled, his eyes flashing with the silver rings of his wolf.

A gash in his lip glistened with drops of crimson. I wasn't remotely done. I was furious. But after a few deep breaths, the epiphany hit me—I wasn't going crazy. The amplified sounds, the smells, the sweats, and the uncontrollable rage were all because my wolf spirit was waking up. It was as if everything suddenly clicked into place, and unsurmountable relief ricocheted around my body. I was a werewolf. But I wasn't just any kind of werewolf; I was half-human, and that alone could be a death sentence.

I THOUGHT the bullying would stop once I discovered my wolf, especially when my dad told me I came from some forgotten alpha lineage, and *that* information to an arrogant nearly sixteen-year-old boy was gold.

It became quickly apparent, however, that it wasn't an uncommon trait among my peers and meant nothing for social status or hierarchy. My attitude changed quickly—on that information, at least. Other stuff, I was definitely still a dick about. Slowly, over time, I won the respect of my peers, and the odd few remaining blood-haters were weeded out when Liam gained his title.

I was unsure of what lineage our wolf side belonged to. Dad never really knew, thanks to everyone on his side of the family tree being deceased. Alpha Jed's reign had a lot to do with that, of course—his leadership tore many families apart. But not all of it could be blamed on Jed.

The information had disappeared a lot earlier. A lot of my ancestors just died of natural causes. Old age, accidents—nothing glamorous—just life running its course. With each death, the truth died a little more, leaving fragments of a story no one could fully explain.

He had always told me, *"We come from a powerful lineage of alphas."* The family motto had been passed down to him. But when I asked him the name of the alpha bloodline, he just shook his head and admitted that it was mostly hearsay and that by the time my dad was born, all that remained were vague legends. He said that was how it had been for generations—our ancestors passing down the idea of our greatness without the proof to back it up.

We weren't even sure if the stories were real or just family folklore; the only thing that was evident, or had some truth in it was the fact we had small amounts of alpha power woven into the fabric of our makeup. I had a minuscule amount of alpha power, and my sister had a little more than I did, which made sense, seeing she was destined to be mated to our alpha. It wasn't only the moon pulling them together, but their alpha blood seeking each other out. I can't say that alpha blood always sought alpha blood, though; my dad mated to a human and I... I was mated to the queen of hell.

When I left Blackfern Valley, I wasn't stupid enough to announce my blood status to the world. My pack may have accepted me, but that didn't mean others would. While other packs were similar to mine in many ways, they were vastly different in others. There was the odd blood-hater, internal diabolical politics and smatterings of passive-aggressive cattiness that would make anyone snap. But anything out there was better than returning to my own pack lands.

I threw my bag onto my bed in the room I had once called mine. It was empty now—a dresser, a bed, and a desk was all that remained. I cleared out all my personal junk the day after the full moon, trashing it. I didn't need it anymore. I wasn't coming back. Even if Alpha Liam hadn't granted me permission, I would have left anyway. The difference would have been if I was just nomadic or whether I was living as a pack-less rogue. Thankfully, my sister came through for me. And neither she nor my dad ever asked any questions. I knew the questions were burning into their essence.

My phone buzzed, and I grinned as I placed it to my ear, but before I could get out any smartass comments, my best friend and Liam's brother, Sean, beat me to it.

"I thought I smelled your odour polluting the air around here. You've been here for like five minutes and you're already stinking up the joint."

"Come a little closer and I can make sure I trap you with my real odour." The braying laughter echoed down the phone.

"Fuck, man! It's been ages. I've just finished up with training and I'm about to meet Ryan for a drink. You should come along. Let people see that you haven't fallen off a cliff and died somewhere."

"No cliff. Did come off my bike, though."
"Ouch. Bad?"
"A sweet piece of ass made it all worthwhile."
Another braying laugh. "So... Beer?"
"Always!"

CHAPTER 6
ROMAN

My eyes pinged open, and I looked around the bedroom, which wasn't mine. The room looked like it belonged to a teenage boy, with clothes haphazardly tumbling out of semi-open drawers and more piles on the floor. The walls were covered in car and music posters, and an electric guitar sat on a stand in the corner. The owner of the room seemed like a teenage boy, but he was definitely older than that. I would never sleep with a teenage boy.

I heard the shower turn off, rolled off the bed, and started to dress myself quickly. I tugged on my black panties and scrub pants and had managed to clasp my bra before the bedroom door opened and in walked Murdoch, my saviour in my time of need.

"Morning, Rome."

"Hey," I muttered, pulling my camisole over my head and looking around for my scrub top.

"You want breakfast?" I froze. We didn't usually do breakfast. We both knew what this was, and canoodling over oatmeal was not part of the agreement. I schooled my face into a mundane expression and spun to look at him.

"Why?"

"No reason. Just thought you might need someone to talk to about yesterday."

"You've already helped me with that."

"Oh, I know I did. I would just like to understand how you suddenly lost control of Rue. It's been a long time since I've received a phone call like that."

"Thank you for coming to my aid," I said, trying to ignore the gentle prying.

I couldn't tell him that Vinny was back, even though I knew I should. It was only a matter of time before he found out. If I told him Vinny was back, he would understand why Rue reacted the way she did. He knew about the bad blood between us and had been witness to what happened to my sister. But there were other things I was determined to keep private, and there was a small chance that Murdoch would unravel the truth. And if the truth came out, where would my odd friendship with Murdoch be?

I had never told Murdoch that the moon had fated Vinny and me to be together. I hadn't ever told anyone. The backlash of my pack would have been justifiable and even tolerable, but the pity after the collective anger had worn off would have been unfathomable.

Murdoch was a year behind me in school. I was already friendly with everyone, but when Murdoch and Sean started talking to my friend group, we merged and became a part of what you would call the popular crowd. His best friend, Sean, was the son of the alpha, and Murdoch was the beta's son. He was incredibly sporty, a talented musician, and reasonably wealthy. He would often be caught flashing his money around whenever he could. All this shit should have made him an asshole, but he was actually a decent guy once you got to know him.

When Vinny came to town, an instant rivalry had

commenced between them. Vinny seemed to want to get into fights with anyone. He didn't even try to make friends. He had some issues, all stemming from losing his mother and not being told he was a werewolf until it was practically too late. But even after he was told, he was still a loose cannon—an adrenaline junky with no moral compass. He was often caught shoplifting or running illegal gambling rings, even repeated grand theft auto incidents. The majority of my friends, including Sean, Murdoch, and my sister, Indiana, were swept up in it. My distrust toward Vinny had grown, and he started to grate on my nerves, especially when he would flash his crooked smile and give an arrogant wink, like he was God's gift to women.

He was dangerous, and it was only a matter of time before someone got hurt. And as Murdoch witnessed, it was my sister who had been the first casualty. There was no remorse, no apology—just the pure arrogance of Vincent Stevens. My intolerable distrust and animosity had finally merged and solidified into unyielding loathing. And then, Fate thought it would be hilarious to make us mates.

"Is Indiana okay?" Murdoch asked cautiously. My stomach churned. "Is that what set off Rue?"

"She's fine." My voice was abrupt.

He released a heavy breath, and I understood the instant relief. Murdoch used to date my sister. He wasn't the only wolf she was seeing at the time, which didn't bother me. It was common for werewolves to date around, to share. But to my utmost disgust, she was also seeing Vinny.

That, I never could stomach. Even thinking about it now made my blood boil. Vinny, of all people. And then he hurt her like I always knew he would.

I shook my head, trying to push the memory away. Murdoch was one of the only ones who had stayed after the accident. The only one who had helped my family pick up the pieces. And he continued to help me—maybe out of some misplaced guilt, because he couldn't help her, I don't know.

Whatever his reasons, I was grateful. Just not thankful enough to have breakfast with him—or be fully honest.

I just needed to use him to keep Rue in check. Eventually, he would work out that Vinny was back, but I was hoping, as Murdoch lived in a condo in Kempthorne, that it would be a few days before he did. And when he did, I was hoping he would be smart enough not to ask any questions. I was also hoping Vinny would leave again soon. I didn't care that it was selfish, Vinny being back disrupted my life.

I DROVE through the borders of Blackfern Valley, feeling the gentle tingle against my skin as if tiny water droplets were dancing across it. I smiled as the scents of my hometown infused the air. There was the tangy smell of wet forest and the underlying scent of canine.

I pulled into the parking lot of Lupus' Bar and Grill and grinned as the scent of beer and poutine joined the aromas in the air. The bar hadn't changed much since I was a pup. It was your typical small-town bar with a stag head peering out from the wall above the bottles, pool tables in the back corner, leathered booth seats under the windows and basic wooden tables and chairs in the dining room. French patio doors led to a gorgeous outside seating area covered in fairy lights and an outdoor fireplace for when it started to get cold. And even though it wasn't the only bar in town, it was the town's favourite. It was my happy place in Blackfern Valley.

I bounded up the porch steps and into the building, smiling at my best friend, Liv, behind the bar. "You made it!" Her unruly auburn hair was knotted on top of her head, and you could see black inked flames licking her neck subtly from under her work shirt. Not many shifters had tattoos due to the effort it took to get them, but my bestie Olivia wasn't your standard she-wolf.

"Of course!" She poured me a pint of beer as I shuffled up onto a bar stool. She gently sniffed the air and grinned at me.

"Now I know why you're late. A little afternoon delight, eh?"

Damn. I sniffed myself and rolled my eyes. I smelled fine. Did I have other evidence of my rendezvous on me? I scanned myself quickly. Not a thread out of place. Damn, she was just too good.

"I don't know what you're talking about."

"That you and Murdoch are back at it?"

"That implies we stopped." I grinned at her cheekily, looking around the bar and noticing my brother, Israel, sitting with some friends in the back corner, staring at me. *Always so watchful.* I gave him a small wave.

"Sorry I'm late." My friend Caitlin said as she gave me a quick hug. "What gossip did I miss?" she asked, perching onto the bar stool next to me.

"Not much. Alpha has got us trackers working on something." Liv tapped her nose twice, indicating that she couldn't talk about it—or that she couldn't talk about it around so many people who were super-hearing in the room. "My sister is being...my sister. Oh, and..." Her voice took on a curious tone. "Vincent is back."

My heart stuttered, and I froze, lifting my beer glass to my mouth. I took a painful gulp, which I hoped was convincingly nonchalant. Two sets of blue eyes watched me expectantly.

"What is Cassie up to now?" I tried to redirect the subject.

"Really?" Liv asked. "That's what you want to talk about?" Her rust-coloured eyebrows shot so far up her forehead that I was afraid they would get stuck.

"I know he's back, I've already seen him."

"And how did *that* reunion go?" Caitlin enquired.

"Frosty," I replied honestly.

"How does he look?" I glared at Caitlin. "Oh, that good," she surmised.

"It doesn't matter how good he looks. He is still an asshole."

"Are you doing okay?" Liv asked softly.

"I'll be fine, Liv." She looked me over and gave a single nod, although I knew she would be watching me even closer now. I knew she suspected there was more to my nemesis than met the eye, but I never confided in her about our status. I let her believe that this was pure hate birthed from his personality and from what happened to my sister.

I was just about to ask what happened with Cassie again when the air suddenly changed and became frigid. If someone was to drop a pin, it would have vibrated and echoed around the bar. I did not need to turn to know who had come through the door—the aroma of peppermint made itself known. Coldness seeped into every cell, and my heart stammered in my chest. Liv looked over at the door, and her blue eyes were wide and alert. She flicked her eyes toward me again, watching, observing my reaction.

Ever so slowly, I flicked my gaze over my left shoulder. Green eyes bore into mine as if they were seeking me out like a short-range missile. Even though there was pure heat in his eyes, it could not ward off the deepening chill I felt. He looked away as quickly as he looked at me and stomped over to the booth in the corner. I let my eyes trace his movements as he sat down and pulled out a menu, blatantly ignoring me. I couldn't look away. It was as if I was possessed. I once again found myself checking out his rigid posture and admiring the smooth curves of his biceps. The tendons in his arms were taut and at attention. His fingers were gripping the menu with such ferocity I was amazed his claws hadn't punctured a hole in it.

I needed to give myself time to pull myself together before turning back to face Liv's inquisitive expression, so I gave myself a few moments to absorb him. Sean and Ryan came in, and there was a loud booming of laughter as bro hugs and back slaps were exchanged with my arch-nemesis. Vinny's face had lit up with so much boyish charm that my stalled heart suddenly revved back to life.

I turned back to Liv and Caitlin, trying for a convincing smile as I attempted to slow my galloping heartbeat. I went to take a mouthful of beer and noticed that my nails had minutely sharpened to a subtle point and were scraping against the glass.

Fine. Everything was going to be fine.

CHAPTER 7
VINNY

I ENTERED THE BAR, and my eyes instantly grazed over the flash of light brown skin on Roman's lower back as she leaned forward on a bar stool. It was like I had no control over the direction of my stare or the length of time I was staring. The skin was smooth and flawless as it disappeared into the hem of her top and her tight as fuck jeans that showed off her glorious ass. Now that she wasn't hidden under her uniform, I could really appreciate just how mesmerizing her curves were, even from behind, just for a moment.

When her eyes met mine, the flickering purple broke my trance. My legs, which were frozen to the spot, moved me away as if a sudden determination had overridden my body. The ice in my heart solidified as I sat on a leathered booth seat and picked up a menu. I could feel her gaze. It was as if every cell in my body was tuned to her—even the ones covered in ice. The smell of jasmine was irritating my nose as I tried in vain to keep my breathing shallow.

An icy burn was travelling around my bloodstream, sharp and jagged, making Vali itch in irritation. The door opened, and I looked up to see two large units coming through it. Sean's face broke into a grin as he saw me. I was enveloped in a bone-crushing hug and received a rough pat on the back. I turned to my old mentor, Ryan, and embraced him quickly, too.

Alright, enough hugging.

"So you're alive?" Ryan grunted.

"It appears so." Fingers whipped the edges of my hair as I ducked my head out of range. My wolf senses had felt the hand coming milliseconds before and reacted accordingly. I glared at Ryan, who pushed me playfully before sitting down in the booth I had selected.

THE BEERS WERE cold and frothy as we chatted, but I could barely enjoy the taste. Jasmine seemed to be coagulating against the hops and barley, slightly choking me. Vali paced my mind in agitation. I braved a look in her direction and even though her body was taut with tension, her smile was radiant as she chatted with Caitlin and Liv. There was a flash of her white teeth as her husky laughter echoed and vibrated straight to my crotch. I felt myself twitch.

Well, at least that wasn't frozen by the ice queen.

"Geeze, you're only back in town ten minutes, and you're already looking for some ass!" Sean laughed.

"What?" I snapped my eyes away.

"You're staring at either Caitlin or Liv and basically dry-humping the table."

"Doesn't Liv bat for the other team?" I asked distractedly. Before I left, Liv had been in a relationship with a she-wolf.

"She likes to play both sides. And she does play well." Sean grinned.

Ryan shook his head exasperatedly at the turn of the conversation. I often forgot that he was happily mated with a toddler at home. His irresponsible single days were far behind him, even though that's basically how he met his mate.

"What about this other chick who rescued you like a damsel in distress?"

"Rescued you?" Ryan enquired, his eyebrows high on his forehead. "That sounds like a story."

"I flew off my bike, and she happened across me... so I happened across her." I shrugged nonchalantly as I casually scanned the room. Roman was staring directly at me, all laughter in her face gone, her face stone cold. The purple of her eyes swirled like rapids hitting a rock in a wildly churning river. I blinked at her curiously. She turned her attention back to her friends, and the cold seeped through me once again. *What the fuck is her problem?*

I turned back to my companions and took a swig of my beer. "So, tell me about this fucker who's after Lacey. What do we know?"

"Shh!" Ryan growled, looking around. I raised a singular brow at him. *"Alpha is trying to keep it quiet."* He finished down the mind-link.

"Why doesn't he want people to know? Surely, a pack full of wolves protecting the pack-princess is better?"

"He's very protective of his daughter. He wants to make sure that no one in the pack is helping the rogue," Sean offered through the connection as he gave the waitress walking past a wink.

"So it is a rogue then?" I asked.

"Intel says that a band of rogues have been sniffing around," Ryan grunted through the mind-link.

"A band, as in more than one?" I raised my eyebrow again. It was almost unheard of for rogues to band together. Rogues were solitary wolves by nature—usually because they hated the idea of a pack structure and taking orders. Collaborating was rare.

"We are unsure whether it is related. But we are keeping an eye on them," Ryan said.

"How many?"

"Last count was about thirty."

"Thirty!" I choked on my beer, and Vali's hackles rose. *"What the fuck!"*

"Tell him the rest," Sean said, closing his eyes in an almost bored fashion. Ryan looked over at him and huffed. Vali mirrored the sentiment.

"One of our scouts has indicated that there is a rumour floating around that Lacey basically is the next messiah." This time, I spat my beer all over the table. Sean opened an eye and wiped the spittle off his arm in disgust.

"Where do people come up with this crap?" Sean grunted out loud.

I looked between them both and then asked through the mind-link, *"Why do they think that Lacey is the next messiah?"*

"I think you better talk to your sister."

I STROLLED INTO THE LARGE, cavernous kitchen of the pack house and smiled at the baby toys that cluttered every other surface. I could hear cooing coming from the upper level. It was impolite to head up the stairs to the alpha quarters, so I called out, "Clem!"

Within seconds, my short-statured, dark-haired sister bounded down the stairs with a baby on her hip. Even juggling a baby, she managed to pull me into a bone-crushing hug, her head barely reaching my shoulder.

"About time!" she growled. "Why am I the last person you have come to see? You've seen Ryan, Sean and Dad. But you chose to see me last?"

"Because you, my dear sister, are a pain in my ass," I said, looking at my niece affectionately. Dark brown hair and large eyes popped adorably from her pudgy face.

"Did you want to hold her?"

Ugh. Shit. Um.

Before I could refuse, my niece was thrust into my arms. I fumbled a little before I managed to get her into what I hoped was a comfortable position and followed Clem toward the kitchen.

"Tell me," I said as I watched Clem flitter around the kitchen, turning on the coffee machine and pulling out coffee mugs.

"Rogues have been trying to get in every month for almost a year, like clockwork. We assumed they were trying to find a weak entry point."

"They've been snooping for a year?" I snarled.

"We were handling it. We assumed that they were trying to infiltrate. It didn't become a concern until a scout came back with some harrowing information—that they were after Lacey." Vali's hackles rose.

"Ryan and Sean mentioned something about her being a messiah?" She nodded curtly as she handed me my cup of coffee. I put Lacey down in fear of burning her, and she instantly wiggled away.

"Apparently, there is a prophecy that the one true alpha would be born on a solar eclipse." I raised an eyebrow at her. Then she sighed before reciting it. *"Twice born under solar moonlight of alpha blood washes and wanes. Twice born under solar moonlight mounds and twists in the earth's grain. Twice born under solar moonlight bends nature and spirit at will. Twice born under solar moonlight bounds and ties until all is still."*

"What the hell does that even mean?" I asked as Vali tilted his head in confusion.

"Well, if you listen to these crazy rogues, the most powerful alpha in the history of alphas will be born under a solar eclipse. Lacey was born during a solar eclipse."

"Many wolves must be born under a solar eclipse," I reasoned diplomatically, my head buzzing with confusion.

"Yes, which is why we were not worried initially. But the threat kept coming. So, Ryan sent out a few scouts to gather more intel. Allegedly, it's the twice-born part of the prophecy that has them all agitated."

"Twice born?"

"I didn't have a wolf, Vinny. My wolf was born under the light of a solar eclipse. My direct descendent was born under the light of a solar eclipse. Twice born. It also doesn't help that her father is Alpha of one of the biggest packs in Canada, and her half-breed mother was also descended from some line of lost alpha lineage."

"So they put two and two together and got fifty?" I growled. *This is insane!*

"You don't believe in the prophecy then?" She smirked.

"That Lacey is the next alpha of alphas? One, wrong gender. And two, I mean, has she shown any phenomenal earth-moving powers?"

"No, of course not." Clem chuckled, then sobered. "But I guess at the end of the day, it doesn't matter if she is or isn't this prophetic alpha. Those behind the threat thinks she is, and *that* is all that matters."

CHAPTER 8
ROMAN

My skin itched and burned. My blood was boiling through my veins. The mechanical, fake and forced laughter died in my throat as piercing green eyes met mine. Then there was silence. The conversation that I was desperately trying to ignore and listen to at the same time muted. I looked over again and saw that the conversation had turned telepathic.

Rue was snarling and pacing, sending grotesque images through my mind—lots of bloody carnage. Sweaty muscular bodies slamming against each other, hard and dirty. Fingernails scraping, lips being painfully bitten and pulled. Teeth entering carotid arteries and ripping. Blood, then even more blood. Hands running over nipples and tweaking them painfully. The building sensation of an orgasm being ripped away before the climax. Pools and pools of blood. A neck snapping. Lifeless green eyes. It was like she couldn't decide if she wanted to rip him apart or fuck him senseless. Maybe fuck him, then rip him apart? I forced the thoughts back and tried to concentrate on my breathing, trying to focus on Caitlin's prattle through the pounding sound against my eardrums.

"Let's go!" Liv commanded.

"Go where?"

"Run. Rue needs out."

"I have her under control."

"Tell that to the bar." I looked down where Liv was indicating and noticed that my claws were out and gently piercing the wooden bar top. It was strange to see my smooth hands ending in black fur and thick dark nails. It was even stranger looking as it was only my ring finger, index finger and thumb that appeared to be changing on each hand. The other four fingers were still perfectly slender with clean, cut nail beds. The skin on my clean fingers was wriggling. It looked as though I had tiny worms underneath my skin. I breathed deeply, trying to bring my human skin to the surface. Nothing happened.

"Out the backdoor. Now," Liv said, coming around and pushing me toward the storeroom. Caitlin quickly slipped behind the bar.

The backdoor led into a small loading area, and beyond that was a thick and dense treeline. When I turned back to look at Liv, she was already naked and stashing her clothes behind a dumpster.

"Shift!" she ordered. Within seconds, a rust-coloured wolf was bursting out of her skin. No pain registered on her face—something Liv had done a billion times without thinking.

Most warriors were bulky, brutish beasts, and in comparison, Liv was considered a petite wolf. She was fast, zippy and deathly quiet and along with her keen sense of smell, it allowed her to be an excellent tracker. And she used these skills against me as she came stealthily out of the undergrowth and knocked me off my feet again. Rue snarled menacingly at her as I chuckled against the impact. This was precisely what I needed.

Vinny was all but forgotten about. All I could feel was the dirt beneath my paws as Liv told me the latest story of Cassie's attempts to win over the Alpha. I felt for Cassie, I really did. But honestly, at this stage, I felt like the she-wolf needed to go get some actual help.

Cassie had dated Alpha Liam in high school, and anyone who knows the story would tell you that he was never into a long-term thing. They broke it off repeatedly, and Liam wasn't exactly secretive about his body count during the years that followed. That all changed when he met sweet, shy Clementine, Vinny's elder sister. And she was the total opposite of Vinny, so even though it was obviously Fate that had brought them together, I could totally understand how anyone could fall for her—if they were smart enough to get past her heritage. Cassie, on the other hand, became obsessed with winning back Liam. Scarily obsessed. And after the deliberate burning of the Stevens' house, Liv and her parents disowned Cassie, and she had been banished.

Even after Cassie was welcomed back into the pack, Liv kept her emotional distance, waiting for the proverbial other shoe to drop. Nothing as drastic as the fire had ever happened again. But she never did move on from Liam and spent most of her time volunteering for every job he put out. Anything to be close to him, to prove to him she was the better match for him.

But this one took the cake—Cassie had offered to be Lacey's nanny.

After a couple of hours, Rue retreated back, with clear signs of exhaustion overtaking as she allowed me to take the lead and wander back toward the bar. Liv walked my flank, her blue and silver eyes twinkling with triumph. She needed this as much as I did. She needed to run and vent about her sister, and I needed to run and distract myself from the shitshow that was my life.

"THANK YOU," I muttered as I squeezed back into my jeans.

"You want to talk about it?"

Why did everyone want me to talk about it? "No," I said with a slight defensive snap. I looked over at Liv, who was trying to tame her auburn curls into a bun again. Her eyes were patient but expectant. I sighed. "It's just Rue. I always found her hard to control, and then, after what happened to Indiana, it was like she went completely rabid. The doctor says there is nothing wrong with her. But I'm telling you, Olivia, my wolf is demonic."

"She isn't demonic. She feels guilty that she couldn't protect your sister."

"It was years ago."

"You aren't exactly over it either," Liv pointed out as we meandered back into the storeroom. I perched myself against a box as she started rummaging around.

"Do you blame me? He's walking around the pack like he didn't hurt her. Like she doesn't even exist."

"He was acquitted on the charges—"

"His brother-in-law is the alpha; I'm pretty sure that there was some nepotism there."

"I recommend you keep that theory to yourself."

"No shit." I closed my eyes and ran my fingers over my face. "I barely have control of my wolf as it is, and seeing Vinny just riles her up. She never got to act out her justice."

"So, are you going to avoid the pack while he's here? What about the pack run?" The idea of hiding out was abhorrent to me. Besides, I really needed to join the pack runs. I wasn't merged, and running with members of my pack was a necessity —a deep and ingrained connection that I couldn't fight.

"No. But I am going to have to up the ante on my therapy," I said, opening the bottle of water Liv just offered me from a box. It was warm, but I didn't care.

"Therapy?"

"Murdoch is pretty good at keeping my mind calm. As is pack training." I grinned cheekily at her.

"Ah, tire yourself into sex oblivion so your wolf is dousing in endorphins. Great plan."

"Well, endorphins make you happy and relaxed, right? This way, I won't wake up and find my teeth around Vinny's throat."

"No, but you could still wake up and find your mouth around another part of his body." Liv winked.

I spluttered out my water. "W-what?"

"Come on! I've seen the chemistry between you two ever since we were at school. It's as volatile and explosive as your wolf's personality." I scrunched my face and watched Liv's eyes roll so far up into her head that I thought she was about to have a seizure. "Oh, my god! Yes, you hate him, I get that. Quite rightly so. But your issues stem from the fact that you are walking around with raging hard-ons for each other! Your wolf doesn't only react this way because she hates him, she reacts this way because you're denying your inner urges, and all she wants to do is rip his clothes off and run her claws over his muscular ass. She wants to punish him, sure. But she wants to be punished by him at the same time. Repeatedly."

My core momentarily fluttered at the thought, but I pushed the intrusive urge far back and shook my head. "No, I'm pretty sure any attraction you think you are witnessing died the minute he put Indiana into a coma."

CHAPTER 9
VINNY

I'D BEEN BACK in Blackfern Valley for two weeks. The sound of tools tinkering on the garage floor echoed into the quiet solitude of my father's empty garage. Usually, I would be blasting the terribly old FM stereo on the back wall as I fiddled around in the grease and grime of motorcycle mechanics, but this time, I wasn't feeling it. This time, I wanted to focus. I needed to focus.

My body had been taut with tension ever since I stepped foot in Blackfern Valley. I was like a wound-up spring, ready to react at a second's notice. Nothing felt right here. Even Vali was on high alert. I just couldn't decide why we were so on edge.

Maybe it was just because we hadn't been back here in a long time. Perhaps this was a natural thing to feel? Or maybe it's because my family was in danger, and I felt like I was sitting around doing nothing. I would've blamed Satan's favourite plaything, but the truth was, I hadn't seen her again since my first day back.

"Leave it to the trackers and the warriors," my sister had told me. I'd argued and demanded to know why she had brought me back if she didn't want my help.

"I do need your help, Vinny," she tried to tell me. "I need you here."

"I'm better out there," I growled.

"You can help when we have more information. But for now, I need you here," she had said with such gentle authority I felt a soft lick of power with it, and I was unable to react.

I needed to do something, but I was powerless, antsy and wound up. I had memorized the warrior rosters and asked them to keep me informed if they scented anything. They took pity on me, but their orders were firm. So, I staked out the trees, shifted and ran, joined pack training, and joined in on the family dinners and the friendly beers at Lupus', but the foreboding sensation never waivered. The anxiety bubbled through my blood, and I was almost out of ideas on how to calm it down. I thought about heading up to Kempthorne and surprising a tiny and surprisingly flexible, blonde human, and seeing if that would ease the tension, but then I remembered my bike was still in dire need of repair.

Tinkering took my focus, but it didn't take away my anxiety, and when Sean came out of the treeline, I almost hurled my wrench at him.

"Bro, you look like shit," he said as he casually leaned against the doorframe of the garage.

"Fuck off." I glared at him, not caring that I was being a grouchy asshole. I hadn't slept properly since I had arrived in Blackfern Valley.

"You up to much today?" he asked, ignoring my attitude. I waved my grease-covered hands toward the motorcycle I was obviously busy with.

"Want to go out?"

"Not really," I grunted, turning back to my bike.

"Come on, we can head to the watering hole?" The watering hole was halfway between here and Kempthorne but still within Blackfern Valley's territory. It was a large waterfall that ended in a deep crevice before meandering down the river. Of course, teenagers loved to frequent it during the summer and use it as a party zone.

"And spy on underage wolves getting their freak on? Hard pass."

Great, just great. Not only had Sean dragged me to a regular cesspool of teenage hormones, but he failed to mention the people who would be there.

Murdick.

Murdoch Evans was standing at the edge of the blue-green water, admiring something in the distance. I followed his gaze to the bubbling froth at the bottom of the fall and groaned inwardly as a dark head bobbed out of the rapid. Vali growled loudly as Roman swan-dived back under the fall, her ass perfectly rounded in the air for a brief second before it disappeared. I looked around, trying to find an escape.

Although I had seen many of our old group of friends over the last two weeks, hell's most charming torturer had been missing. I thought she may have actively been trying to avoid me; I was happy to think that she might be. I didn't want to see her or be near her. Yet, here she was, swimming around without a care in the world. She hadn't noticed me yet, so I knew I could disappear. I just needed to—

My eyes met with Murdoch as he sauntered over to me, his mouth in a thin, fake smile. Vali grumbled his displeasure.

"I heard you were back." He held out a hand, a handshake gesture that felt extremely out of place. I shook his hand quickly before letting it drop. I didn't say anything but gave him a nod. He looked out toward the swimming pool, watching Roman swim with almost a predatory glint in his eyes. Vali snarled low toward Murdoch. A few awkward seconds passed.

"Yeah, I'm back," I resigned, trying to ignore Vali's impromptu pacing in my head.

"It must be nice seeing everyone after so long."

"Weird would be a more accurate description." Silence. "But it's just a short trip. Then I'm back on the road."

"Sean told me how much you love being on the road," he grunted. I rolled my eyes. Anyone listening would have thought he was being genuine and that he was trying to make conversation. But, with Murdoch, his speech and his voice were always on two different levels. There was always an undercurrent that I had learned to listen for. He didn't give a shit. He wanted me to leave ASAP. And I knew why—his eyes hadn't moved from Roman's swim-model body the entire exchange. I let out a small, cold chuckle. He could have her.

"Right." I nodded. "Well, as fun as this has been..." I started to walk away.

"Still with the attitude." I stalled before looking back at him. His eyes had finally left the swimming hole and were staring at me with contempt.

"What?"

"You're still an asshole."

"Murdoch, trust me when I say this: I am here for my family. That's it. I have no interest in you whatsoever. I have very little interest in getting with the old crew and reminiscing about our teenage years." I looked over at Roman, who was now pulling herself up onto rocks to make her way out of the water. "And I definitely am not interested in fucking Roman. So, you can take your territorial bullshit and back the fuck off, pup." Murdoch snarled as I stepped away. His eyes flashed dangerously, and in the biggest insult I could muster, I turned my back on him.

Unfortunately, when I did this, I met Roman's gaze, and my irritation grew tenfold. The anxious bubbling in my blood had suddenly stopped then burned harder with an icy intensity. Murdoch was watching our interaction with piqued interest, as were Damian, Josh and Caitlin, who were gawking as they sat on nearby boulders. I willed myself to be indifferent.

Roman was standing a small distance away, wearing a simple one-piece that clung wetly to her curves, the tones of jasmine running off her body as she flicked water off herself. She was breathing deeply, the wolf in her eyes fighting for the surface. I needed to get out of here, my irritability was a pressurized volcano ready to blow. Therefore, the sudden idea of getting one up on Murdoch brought me a small amount of pleasure. I grinned crookedly at Roman before removing my shirt and pants, standing stark naked for a long moment, making sure her eyes raked every inch of my ripped body. Then, just as her eyes landed on my cock for a long second or two, I shifted into my cream-coloured wolf and ran into the trees.

My paws pounded over the leaf-littered floor, and I pushed each step harder. Usually, running would ease my racing mind and give structure to my thoughts, but with this run, each step made me more agitated. I was still wound up. Fixing my bike hadn't worked, going to the stupid watering hole hadn't either, and seeing Roman's soft skin glowing softly in the afternoon sun, the water droplets running down her shapely legs and the smell of jasmine infusing the afternoon breeze—really didn't help. Vali snarled at my thoughts and pressed harder as if he was trying to outrun them.

Slowly, the jasmine scent evaporated from my nose and my body started to warm again. I stretched out and leaped over a small creek, my foot sliding on the muddy bank as I cantered away. The forest was eerily quiet and echoed my mammoth steps. There was no bird life, no muskrats or beavers. There wasn't even a bunny rabbit or a frog. I had scared the forest with my noise, but I wasn't trying to be quiet; I was trying to unwind—to escape.

I felt the low buzz of the pack territory and wondered if I should just keep running. If I should just leave it all behind. My blood pounded in my ears as I stopped and sat on my haunches, trying to make the decision. But before I could step one paw over the line, the wind shifted, and my nose crinkled. My lips curled back in disgust as a dirty swamp smell choked me.

Within a second, I was flying through the bush again, yelling down the mind-link to the warriors on duty, *"Rogue."*

CHAPTER 10
ROMAN

THE BUSH WAS a blur as I sprinted through it. This time, it wasn't Rue that needed a release. It was me. *What a fucking shit show!* My life had turned into a well-choreographed disaster, and I was barely holding it together.

I wanted to take advantage of the last few warm days before the temperatures dropped into the dreaded fall and invited Murdoch to the swimming hole. It was an olive branch. We had been fucking non-stop for weeks to try and keep Rue satiated. However, my wolf was more volatile than ever, and even if she didn't want to burst out of my skin, she had made me irritable with uncontrollable mood swings. Each time he tried to talk to me about what was bothering me, I shut down and reminded him that I wasn't looking for a boyfriend. All I was after was a distraction. He was happy enough to provide said distraction, but when the mood swings hit, he always looked torn.

THE SWIMMING HOLE was supposed to be a non-confrontational day out. A day of relaxation. A day of bonding and hippy-like meditation. I should have known that word would get out and that Vinny would somehow be invited. That he'd come just to ruin my day. I felt his presence the moment he got there. The peppermint swerved and waved toward me like a beacon, and Rue growled low. So, I dove deeper, trying to get away from it.

Then I realized I was being a coward. If he was going to be around, I needed to face him. I needed him to know that his presence didn't bother me. So, I pulled myself out of the water and made my way toward him, breathing slowly, trying to calm the nerves that were zinging throughout my body on a low hum.

The moment he'd taken his clothes off had startled me. The sunlight bounced off his muscly physique, and I felt my eyes tracing every curve of smooth muscle, which was emphasized by his light golden tan and explosion of freckles over his shoulders. Rue whimpered in my head, confused at his sudden display. My brain had stalled, and warm tingles started to spark in my belly. By the time I had regained enough composure to tell him to cover himself up, a large cream wolf disappeared into the forest.

An hour later, my twitchiness hadn't subsided, so I had taken off into the forest myself. My friends had asked if I needed somebody to run with, but I shook my head, desperately seeking solitude, which was rare for me.

Murdoch had been watching me with such intense scrutiny during the whole Vinny exchange. One look at his face, and I knew he wanted to talk about it. To tuck me safely into his arms and blur that line between friend and boyfriend again—to protect me from the person who had hurt my sister. He wanted to, but he knew this wasn't the time or place. He didn't say a word as I stripped off my swimsuit and shifted into an ebony wolf. He saw my face and had read my emotions: I needed space, and I needed to run. Murdoch and his conversation would wait.

I bounded over logs and whipped past low brushes as I barrelled through the bush, not caring how much noise I was making or the erratic racing of my heart. I barely managed to dodge tree trunks as I picked up speed clumsily, each step as erratic as my heartbeat. I skidded to a stop at a shallow creek, but the momentum kept me going, and my lower legs ended up cold and wet. I succumbed into the water for a bit, letting the water lap at my underside as I tried to catch my breath.

I took a deep breath and released it. Then another. And another. Then— *Wait, what is that smell?* I had been running for a while and hadn't realized I was approaching the border of the Blackfern Valley territory, which was approximately fifteen kilometres from my house. I knew this area well. But everything smelled off, tainted and dirty.

I jolted upright and snapped my head left and right, trying to determine the direction of the odour. Rue let out a vicious growl and lowered her head between her shoulder blades. *Left.* Instinct took over, and we raced forward, snarling and salivating at the mouth.

In the brief second before I pounced, I took in a lot of information. A large mottled-brown wolf was standing there, one that wasn't supposed to be within our pack boundaries. He had no escort, and he was so deep within the woods that I was more than convinced he hadn't come through by way of the main road. He had snuck in through the trees. When I sniffed again, his scent registered as dirty and musty, as if he had been living in a swamp. I ran my eyes down him again, noting that his appearance complimented his smell. Every instinct in the world was screaming 'rogue,' and those same instincts told me to take him out. And then Rue took over completely.

I felt the freighter-like impact hit my side as I was midway through the air. The wind was knocked out of me and I rolled— a cream-coloured wolf was nipping at my neck, trying to exert his dominance over me. I growled and rolled, baring my teeth and tried to get the upper hand. Over and over, we rolled down a leaf-littered bankside, changing back to human as we spun and landed at the bottom with a loud and painful thump.

We were both stark naked, his arms wrapped protectively

around me, his eyes glittering with the prettiest shade of silver, and his breathing laboured. My breathing matched his as my wolfy instincts started to calm and recede.

I became aware of every warm inch of him. The smooth arms that encased me, the hard, bony hip that dug into my side, and his hairy legs that caused just enough friction that made me want to slide my smooth legs up and down them repeatedly. And, of course, I noticed the growing heat and hardness of his erection, and in the ultimate betrayal, my nipples responded—taut and sensitive against his solid chest. I moved slightly, and his eyes flashed dangerously. He was aware of me, just as I was aware of him. Usually, this realization would have given me a boost of confidence to take control and get what I needed. Looking into his brightly green and aroused eyes, watching his nostrils flare as he smelled the pooling sweetness that was tingling in my core, made it almost impossible to resist. *Fuck.*

"What the fuck was that?" I hissed. My gravelly voice gave away more of my arousal.

"What the fuck was what, Roman?" His voice was deceptively soft. Peppermint swirled around me, and I clenched my aching pussy in response. The sound of my name vibrating from somewhere deep in his throat was not the usual tone I received from him, and that alone made my instincts falter further.

No! No, no, no! I pushed against him, and he seemed momentarily reluctant to give me a fraction of space.

"Get the hell off me! Why did you attack me?" He tilted his head much like a confused wolf would, even though he was looking at me in human form.

"You were about to attack a rogue," he grumbled, backing away and propping himself up, nonchalantly against a large pine tree. I instantly felt the chill return between us, freezing me down to my core. I shivered as goosebumps covered my skin. If he noticed, he said nothing about it.

"Of course, I was about to attack a rogue. He was trespassing on my land," I shot back.

"You would have been hurt!" he snapped. "I was protecting you."

"I didn't ask for your protection."

"No, but you got it anyway. Do you think I would have stood by and watched him rip you to shreds?"

Sanctimonious prick. "Who says he would have won? I'm stro—"

"I'm not saying you're not strong, you stupid—" He raked his hands through his blond hair in agitation. "If you took a moment to assess him, that wolf was built like a fucking tanker. I wasn't even going to take him on. He was fucking sitting there, waiting for someone to attack. It was all calculated. He was waiting calmly and patiently, Rome!" I glared at him and opened my mouth to retort, but he charged forward like a steam engine. "I was watching for a full three minutes and mind-linking the fucking warriors to come up with a plan before you decided to come flying out of the bush like a bitch on crack!"

Silence rippled over us as the truth hit my ears. Then, in the distance, I heard the warriors taking down the rogue. The battle sounds were dangerously raw. Rue snarled at Vinny, then whimpered as she reassessed the situation. My own mind was hammering against the possibility that I could have been seriously injured. That the man I hated most in the world had come out of his stealthy hiding spot to save me. He had trained as a warrior, and all his instincts were different from mine, but even so, he had abandoned his post to keep me safe. The fact that I needed saving at all stung more than any of the other facts put together.

I glared at him and stood up to my full five-foot-seven height, annoyed that I only made it to his chin. I looked up at him indignantly. "Don't fucking touch me again."

CHAPTER 11
VINNY

I PACED the living area of the pack house as I waited. Back and forth. Back and forth. Each step ricocheted my anger off the floorboards. In my mind, Vali mimicked my pacing. We were both wound up and agitated. Ready to snap.

My sister watched me pace as she bounced Lacey on her lap. I looked up toward the office door every so often and grumbled softly when the door remained tightly shut.

"Would you stop pacing?" my sister murmured exasperatedly.

"This close, Clem!" I growled, pushing my thumb and finger millimetres apart. "We were this close to getting one up on these fuckers. Then she had to go and get in the fucking way. If I wasn't dealing with her, I could have helped the warriors—"

"There were three trained warriors, Vinny, three!" She held up three of her short fingers. "They should have had it handled. Even on the off-chance you were there to help. Honestly, what more could have been done?"

"He shouldn't have got away."

"No, he shouldn't have, which is why your alpha and beta are doing a debrief now."

"It's all her fucking fault," I mumbled.

"Roman?" Clem arched an eyebrow.

"Roman," I repeated with distaste. Vali grumbled deep within.

"Do you want to talk about it?"

"About the fact that she majorly fucked up? About the fact that she shouldn't have even been there, let alone tried to take on a rogue by herself, completely untrained? The fact that we have lost our latest intel lead? The fact that this could have been all over with the information I could have tortured out of this fucker? No, I don't want to fucking talk about it!" I raged, clenching my fist to try and control the fury that had mounted.

"Vinny," Clem said in a soft voice often used to calm children. "She is free to roam where she likes. These are her lands, too. And I'm pretty sure it wasn't her who tried to take on the rogue."

"Clementine! Have you not been fucking listening? I smelled her the minute she came upstream, and so did he! Here I am, hiding from the rogue, making sure that I am masking my scent as much as I can and staying downwind, and she fucking charges through the woods without even a moment's of thought. Without taking time to assess the situation beforehand. I had two fucking choices: let her get torn to shreds by the mutt or take her the fuck out and give away my hiding spot. The warriors were still a few minutes away. And unlike her, they tried to be quiet and take a sneaky approach! She was a fucking disgrace!" I spat.

Lacey made a grizzly noise. "Vinny," my sister's voice was reproachful as she jiggled Lacey again before putting her on the floor with a teething ring.

"I really hope Liam rips a strip out of her hide. Or Ryan! Or you!"

"Well, that's not going to happen."

"Why the fuck not?"

"It wasn't her," she snapped. "Roman has always had a level head—"

"She's always been an unpredictable bitch," I snarled.

"No, she hasn't. She's one of the nicest she-wolves around. I know you two have a feud, but this is stupid."

"Stupid? She could have been killed!"

"And I will talk to her, but I am not going to grill her for this. Not when it's not her fault."

I stared at her incredulously. "Not her fault?"

"Vincent!" Clem stood up to her full five-foot height, craning her neck at me as she stared me down. "It wasn't Roman, it was Rue."

"Rue?" I snapped.

"Her wolf. She has never had control of her wolf."

I scoffed. "Since when?"

"Since always."

Roman lacked control? I had no idea she lacked control. Most werewolves struggled to control their wolf spirits as pups, but this was remedied or at least subdued by the time they were adults. The lack of control usually resulted in minor disagreements between human and wolf, and the odd hormonal imbalance put werewolves in some compromising situations. But these things didn't make wolves attack a mutt like a rabid bitch. No, there was something more feral in the way Roman acted.

I looked at my sister, and her facial expression confirmed that Roman's lack of control wasn't just fighting for the need to shift and run or the need to fuck around. She had no control at all; her wolf had completely taken over. Her wolf was in control; it was out for the kill. That was fucking dangerous. Someone could get killed. *And my sister is letting it happen?*

"So, let me get this straight, you're letting a she-wolf run around who has no control—"

"Vincent Stevens, I dare you to finish that sentence. I dare you." The amber in her eyes flickered dangerously as her voice took on a more authoritative tone. She was no longer my sister, she was my luna. I took a deep breath to calm myself as Vali instantly submitted in my mind.

"She's dangerous," I whispered softly.

"Not usually, which is why I'm going to talk to her. Something has upset Rue, and Roman no longer has control of her. I need to help her through this, not punish her for it." I took another breath, then another, trying to calm my rage. Roman was not only a raging bitch, she was dangerous; and all my sister could do was pander to her. "Unless there is something you feel like telling me?"

My heart jumped into my throat at Clementine's perusal. "No."

"*No?*"

"No," I affirmed. She pressed her lips together and lowered her eyes into a small glare. I tried to school my face into something that resembled calm, but inside, my body was zinging with electricity—I needed to get out of there, but I also needed to stay and help protect my niece.

"You're tense, Vinny. You've been that way since you arrived."

"No shit! Someone is after my niece."

"No, it's more than that. You're like a live wire. Or a volcano — you're honestly about to explode, and I'm worried about who is going to be in your path when you do. I need you to try and calm down." I grunted in response. "The pack run is in a few days. Are you planning on joining in?"

"No."

"Why not? I think it will be good for you to do so. You haven't joined a pack run in five years. Maybe this is what you need. Maybe this will calm you." My sister was right, of course. There was a reason wolves lived and ran in packs, but there was no way I was going to subject myself to the pack run, especially after what happened last time. I shook my head slowly, trying to push the cold memories back.

"Someone needs to stay behind and look after the little poop monster," I deflected, looking down at Lacey, hoping my sister would buy it.

"Yeah, her grandparents are. You remember them, eh? The previous alpha and luna who live in the cottage behind the pack house?" Her voice dripped with sarcasm.

I was saved from answering when the office door swung open, and both Ryan and Liam came stalking out, followed by three massive wolves who made their way straight through the kitchen doors and down the steps before disappearing into the woods.

I wanted to march right up to them and demand answers, but the look on my alpha's face halted my movements. I had seen Alpha Liam angry; I had seen him murderous. But the look on his face at that moment was something I had never seen before, and I'm unashamed to admit that it terrified me.

"Well?" my sister asked, unperturbed by his demeanour. He shot her a tired look, gave her a kiss on her temple and lifted Lacey into his arms.

"It's evident that he came onto pack land to toy with us. The warriors have gone to scout the perimeter again, and the trackers are attempting to pick up any scent that could lead us to where he was staying. Enough of this defensive tactic, I'm ready to switch to the offence." Alpha Liam looked at me. "You want to get your hands dirty?"

"Fuck yes." I gave a curt nod.

"Good, get ready to move. As soon as we have wind of where they are, we move."

CHAPTER 12
ROMAN

I was mad at Rue. She had almost gotten me killed, and instead of being reproachful or candidly reprimanded, she was acting like it was no big deal. She had reverted into her delusional and obnoxious self and started acting like she could have taken on the rogue. Like she didn't need help, especially from Vincent Stevens. That idea was abhorrent to her. She was obsessed with replaying the scene repeatedly, trying to twist or invent a way that resulted in her being victorious over the rogue without having to be saved.

It didn't help that the upcoming full moon was making her even more agitated and neurotic, flavouring my tongue with her bitter obsession. I tried not to gag on the unpleasantness, and frowned at her for what felt like the millionth time while she ran through her scenarios. She didn't even notice my mood or seem to care that I was mad at her. Rue was incensed, rabid, and fixated on something that was unobtainable. She was never going to listen, and unfortunately, I couldn't block her out. I always thought that was unfair, the way that she could put up a wall between us whenever she wanted time alone, but I couldn't do the same to her. If I could, then maybe I could have tamed her a long time ago.

A loud crashing noise came from the living room, and I spun, startled. Rue snarled from within me, pushing forward as lilac swirled within the warm browns of my irises.

"We need to talk!" Jordan came charging through the house. "Calm your fucking wolf down and sit!" he barked.

"What the hell, Jor—"

"Sit!" he barked again. My brother towered over me by half a foot, but with his stocky build, he felt over twice my size. His imposing stature usually didn't work on me, but right now, with his tight, broad jaw and his bronzed skin flushed with anger, he looked beyond livid. So, I submitted.

Rue's hackles rose at the intrusion and she flicked her tail in annoyance when Israel came in only half as gentle as Jordan had been. Their faces were even more identical than usual, from their deep-set eyes to their high cheekbones that hinted at our shared Polynesian heritage, both wore the same disapproving look.

My eyes darted from one twin brother to the other and I sighed. They knew. The family knew. And the twins drew the short straw on who was going to perform the intervention on their fuck-up of a sister. It was rock-paper-scissors on who would clean up my mess this time.

Sweat pooled at the nape of my neck, a habitual reaction whenever my family decided to intervene. I bit my cheek hard enough to taste the metallic tang of blood against my tastebuds. This was going to be bad—car crash meets train derailment bad!

"What's up?" I asked as casually as I could. The blue rings of Jordan's eyes glowed, so I turned my attention to the slightly calmer twin. "Izzy?"

"I'm sure you know why we're here," he said softly. I blinked at him and tried to look as clueless as I could. "A situation involving a rogue on pack lands?" he elaborated further.

"Oh...that." I waved my hand. "It was nothing. I'm fine, but thanks for the concern, boys!"

"You're fine?" Jordan roared. Israel grimaced at his hot-headed twin and turned back toward me.

"Don't antagonize him, Ro! While we're glad to see you in one piece, it wasn't nice for us to receive the news that not only had you tried to take on a rogue by yourself, but you interfered in an official pack warrior operation."

"That wasn't my intention," I muttered sourly.

"Oh, really. What was your intention, then?" Jordan spat.

"Honestly? Not this."

Israel put his hand up toward Jordan, and his mouth opened to give me what I could imagine was a large reprimanding stream filled with angry adjectives and creative language. "Can you explain what happened?" Israel, always the voice of reason, asked me. Rue rolled her eyes at his diplomacy.

"I was just running along, minding my own business when I scented the rogue, and then it felt like something snapped inside me. Suddenly, I was flying through the air toward the rogue, and just as quickly, I was intercepted and crashed down the bank." I looked at both of them squarely. "Nothing happened."

Rue grumbled and lowered her head between her paws as she sulked.

"That's not entirely true, is it? Rue happened, didn't she?" Israel asked. Releasing an exasperated breath, I nodded.

"You need to get her under control, Roman!" Jordan spat. "Stop making excuses and just merge with her already!"

I instantly lost my composure, not Rue, who just flicked her tail in irritation. It was all me. "Don't you think I know that? I've been trying to control her for years! I've seen doctors, psychiatrists and the freaking Dalai Lama, and I'm telling you there is no help for her! Do you know how hard it is to lay on a psychiatrist's couch and try and explain that your wolf is out of control, that you hate her, and that the only way you can keep her under control is to fuck anything that moves and to work yourself to death? The shrink basically called me a self-obsessed nympho, reminding me unnecessarily that Rue is actually me! She basically told me that I was a sex-addicted-whore-attention-seeking-crazy-bitch. And then the feral woman charged me for the fucking session!" I fumed, flicking my eyes between them. "Well, I don't do this shit for attention. I would love to have a normal wolf spirit, merge with her, and attend functions without worrying about what the fuck she was going to do. There's always been something seriously wrong with Rue, and I cannot control her! I'm sorry that I can't be as perfect as you two. I'm sorry that no one in this fucking family seems to understand that my mind —my wolf—is broken. Yes, I get it, I'm an embarrassment. But you know what? That isn't going to change anytime soon, unless I get a fucking lobotomy or somehow lose my wolf like Indiana did!"

Rue rolled her eyes and snorted at my dramatic outburst. My brothers both looked a shade paler, but I was pretty sure it had nothing to do with my speech. Maybe it was the mention of Indiana. They often liked to pretend that Indiana hadn't lost Isis, that our sister was simply away at school or something. More often than not, they pretended Indiana didn't exist—and that made me furious.

"You could at least show some remorse for what happened!" Jordan snapped.

"I have a fuck tonne of remorse, you jackass." I glared back at Rue. "Rue also had a small amount when she realized she could have killed us." Rue rumbled her displeasure. "But now, the stupid bitch seems to have forgotten that we could have died and won't stop coming up with scenarios in case there's a next time."

"Way to rat me out, Roman!" Rue growled. I ignored her and focused on my brothers.

"Roman, there won't be a next time!" Jordan snapped.

Well, no shit! I thought, then said, "How did you find out about this anyway?"

"Blackfern Valley rumour mill, no doubt," Rue said in a huff at the same time Jordan confirmed it.

"So let me get this straight, you came barging in here on a fucking rumour?"

"The rumour turned out to be true! Any rumour about our sister flying off the handle shows the need for investigation," Jordan hissed.

"Do you even hear yourself? You're investigating your own sister! Like a fucking criminal no less. I didn't know you'd joined the warrior squad. Should I go to the stone cells and wait for my sentencing, Jordy? What sentence do you think should be executed for losing control of one's wolf?" I snarled angrily.

"You need to try to be in control here. Rue shouldn't hold this much power," Israel answered in an exhausted tone. I blinked in disbelief. They hadn't truly heard my explanation on how I couldn't control Rue. And suddenly, I had the depressing realization they probably never would.

"And you both need to leave." I pointed to the front door they'd crashed through minutes earlier. "It's been fun and all, but get the fuck out."

Jordan's blue rings flashed again, and he made to say something further, but once again, he was intercepted by Israel interrupting him.

"Ro," Israel said softly. I was about to be reamed out in the most horrendous way: softly, rationally. I would rather take on Jordan's brunt anger than Izzy's disappointment.

"No, Izzy. No! Look, I am sorry it happened, but I need to figure this out on my own. Please leave."

The door closed behind them with a loud click, and I locked it for good measure. On the other side, Jordan growled under his breath when the deadbolt slid into place. I never locked my door, so in doing so, the act now echoed my ugly sentiments toward them.

I could still hear my brothers grumbling as they walked toward their vehicle. And then it went eerily silent. I peeked out the peephole, and they were still there, having an unheard conversation through the mind-link—a conversation about me.

As much as it was rude, I had learned to accept that this happened a lot, especially with my family. I'm sure they would have tried to mind-link me religiously—because giving a lecture over our collective consciousness would just be a whole new level of torture—but there was something broken with Rue, and now I was the only wolf in Blackfern Valley that couldn't mind-link in human form. Not even with my family.

The only ones with whom I could mind-link were the alpha and luna, but that wasn't the gentle scratching within my mind; it was more like a thousand sharp needles piercing into the folds of my brain. After each pack announcement or conversation, my body would be soaked in sweat and shivering uncontrollably. The needle pricks would turn into a migraine, and I would spend the next few hours in the dark. If Rue hadn't been knocked out and had felt even a little generous, she may have healed us faster. But more often than not, she would struggle after the intrusion on our mind.

Vinny's signature crooked smile sneaked its way into my thoughts, and Rue grumbled again. I guess we hated intrusions of all kinds.

CHAPTER 13
VINNY

"Top Pocket," I called as the white ball tapped against a red-striped one. The number eleven bounced off the felt wall of the table, rolling along a perfect angle toward the top right pocket. There was a light *clunk* as it found its way down the chute back into the collection box underneath the table.

"Nice shot," Sean said, chalking his cue tip. I said nothing as I lined up another shot and another, each ball entering their pockets with ease. I missed the third shot by a millimetre, and the ball bounced off the corner and back into the middle of the table. Sean grinned and went to line up his move.

It was extremely busy at Lupus'. I had forgotten that the weekend before the full moon was the busiest of the month. There was a buzz in the air as the Blackfern Valley Pack started to feel the effects of the approaching full moon. Each month, as the moon crescents got closer and closer to its monthly peak, the werewolves began to react to the pull. Many got agitated, a lot got horny, and most just felt the bubbling need to run. And Tina, the proprietor of Lupus', gave the pack a much-needed outlet by putting on a large party prior to the pack run.

Large party? More like enormous. There was barely any room to move. The French doors were wide open to give an illusion of space. The cooling, fresh air circling in was a blessing among the stale heat inside. All bartenders and wait staff seemed to be on duty tonight, skillfully maneuvering between the patrons as they delivered food and drink. Music was blasting out on the sound system, but an underage patron appeared to be connecting his laptop into a DJ mixer, indicating that we were all going to get terribly remixed music at any moment.

Sean had been smart enough to score one of the three pool tables before I had arrived. He was even smarter by getting a tray full of shots and a couple of beers each so we didn't have to try to swim against the masses of people who were camped around the bar. I don't say it often about Sean, but sometimes, this guy can be an absolute genius.

"Jailbait." Sean laughed as he sunk another ball.

"Eh?" I shot him a puzzled look.

"That girl is barely seventeen."

"What, girl?"

"The one who is fucking you with her eyes." I looked around and noticed a young, pretty she-wolf who was staring at me. I caught her eyes, and she looked away, slightly bashful, before turning her gaze full frontal again and trying to allure me with her sudden portrayal of self-confidence.

"Hard pass." I laughed, turning back to the game and taking my turn.

"Yeah, stay away from that family. I shagged her sister for a bit—crazy, the lot of them!"

"Is there anyone in this town you haven't been with?" I remarked cheekily. He flipped me the bird and downed another shot of liquor.

It was well known that werewolves tended to be loose and free with their body count. Blurring the lines between friendship, experimenting and being placed back into the friend zone unperturbed was also common. It was a culturally accepted way of life; it had something to do with animal urges or whatever. This wasn't to say there weren't some werewolves who were in longterm committed relationships. Hell, even the odd few found their true mates, and that was considered the most sacred partnership of them all. The one that every werewolf dreamed of while dipping their appendages in the communal lust pool. That's if they wanted to be with their Fate-given mate.

Vali grumbled at my thoughts, and I gave him an apologetic grimace.

"We are better off," I reminded him, *"We were going to reject her first, remember?"*

He gave me a reproachful stare and didn't respond.

There was no rhyme or reason as to who met their true mate either. My dad found my mom, and my sister found Liam. And even though my true mating was an epic disaster, it doesn't statistically trend in family circles. It is statistically improbable to find a true mate. It is brutally rare, and many werewolves never find their mate. Beta Ryan is the only one in his family who has found his. All his sisters have remained mateless, along with the majority of wolves in this pack. And as far as I know, none of my school friends have found theirs either, even Sean, whose father and brother were both happily mated.

The idiotic, romanticized idea of true mates made everyone even more antsy around the full moon. Werewolves could only find their true mate at midnight on the first night of the full moon after they had turned twenty. There was a buzz of excitement in the air as fresh twenty-year-olds started looking up their prospects. A few more girls looked in Sean's and my direction, and I rolled my eyes as Sean lapped it up, flexing his muscles as he tapped his cue and managed to sink the black ball with ease. I had taught him well.

I grinned and put another loonie into the coin slot as a couple of brave she-wolves approached to ask to join our game. Sean was more than eager and had already said yes before I could coldly reject them. I looked up and noticed one of the girls was Laurel. Laurel was Ryan's youngest sister and had been a couple of years ahead of me at school. She was totally hot and had left Blackfern Valley in a vain attempt to become a model or a movie star or some other bullshit. I hadn't seen her in years, and she definitely had used the time well. She flicked her blonde hair over her shoulder and lowered her extremely long lashes over her grey eyes as she looked me over.

"When did you come back into town?" I grunted at her.

"I could ask you the same question. Are you back for long?" she asked, giving me a saucy look that would make Ryan pummel me into bedrock dust if he saw it.

"I've already been back too long," I said in a joking manner, "Sean here has been mooning over me for weeks. I'm expecting him to ask me to run with him tomorrow night." Laurel let out a tinkly little laugh.

"Well, I don't want you to leave again, man! It's boring around here when you are gone," Sean said with a dramatic flair.

"No shit, it is boring. Why do you think I left?" A brief, pained look passed over Sean's face so quickly that I must have imagined it. He let out a braying laugh and started to set up the pool table again without a word.

Laurel and her friend Bree were pretty decent at pool. I was under the assumption that they would be terrible, or at least pretend to be, so that they could be taught. Maybe it was years of being on the road that made me think that. Many of the she-wolves I met pretended to be horrible at pool just to get me to teach them and touch them. Not that I complained; teaching them pool often led to teaching them in the bedroom—a hustle at its finest. I would pretend to be bad at pool, hustling unsuspecting people for money. Chicks would pretend to be bad at pool and hustle for sex. Same thing. The only difference was, nine times out of ten, they didn't need to hustle me for sex. I would have given it anyway.

It became very apparent quite quickly that neither Laurel nor Bree was going to play the damsel in these scenarios. Bree was a viper with her cue tip, and Laurel wasn't half bad either. Sean was hanging on their every word as the balls *clinked* around the table, and the waitress served us more shots and beer chasers. The lighthearted banter was chasing away demons, making me forget about stupid, out-of-control she-wolves who put everyone in danger. It even dampened the gut-wrenching concern I had for my niece. The almost carefree feeling forced me to admit that even though I loved being nomadic, there was a need for me to be around my pack.

The alcohol was warming its way through my system. I was in no way drunk, but I was starting to feel relaxed for the first time in weeks. Vali rumbled contentedly within as I let loose. I had been wound up for weeks, and finally, I was starting to release some of that pent-up energy. That was until I heard Laurel open her mouth and utter the words I didn't want to hear.

"Hey, isn't that that girl Roman? Didn't you use to date her, Sean?" My eyes instantly snapped to where she was standing at the bar with our—*her*—group of friends. But my eyes targeted on who was leeched onto her. Murdoch. Her hand was on his bicep as she stretched up to whisper something in his ear. The warmth I had felt from the alcohol evaporated instantly, and Vali growled deep.

Sean gave me a sheepish look. "Yeah, like for a couple of months when I was sixteen. Nothing too serious."

"Man, she's smoking hot!" Laurel turned to Bree and continued, "We should introduce her to Natasha." Bree raised a perfectly manicured eyebrow and looked Roman over with arrogant contempt. Vali glowered toward Bree as she assessed Roman.

"Natasha?" Sean enquired, not noticing anything other than Laurel's round ass.

"My agent. She's always on the lookout for new blood," Laurel offered.

"I don't think Natasha would go for her," Bree stated coldly.

"And why is that?" The voice was cold and hard. I was shocked to realize the question had come from me. All eyes snapped toward me as they heard Vali rumble through my words. The protective warning that had been entirely from my wolf and not me. *Damn it, Vali!*

Laurel grabbed Bree by the hand and started to pull her away swiftly. "Come on, Bree. Come talk to Roman with me."

"Bro!" Sean thumped me on the arm hard. I turned to him and pushed Vali back.

"What?"

"Want to talk about it?"

"No," I snapped as I watched Roman, Murdoch, Laurel and Bree all laughing at the bar like they were the oldest friends. Murdoch's arm was looped proprietarily over Roman's shoulder, ignoring the girl talk and talking to some of the guys instead. Vali growled lowly. Roman's eyes met mine across the room, and I felt a slight pull in my stomach, the bubbling of my stomach acid. "Not at all."

CHAPTER 14
ROMAN

"Are you sure you don't want to come to the pack run?" I asked for what felt like the millionth time. I frowned at the anxious, whiny tone of my voice. I was beginning to sound desperate. Not a good look.

"Why? Are you asking me to run with you?" Murdoch's voice held a teasing lilt. I grimaced.

A long time ago, when I was a different person, I probably would have said yes. But that was before my wolf became toxic, and my needs changed. Asking someone to run with you as a hopeless romantic teenager was one thing. Asking someone to run with you at our age was a sign of commitment. And as Murdoch and I had established many, many times before, I was never going to commit. I couldn't. It wouldn't be fair to subject anyone else to Rue permanently. And if I was honest, I was already committed to Rue, to spending all my energy trying to keep her contained.

I made a scoffing noise in my throat. "You would be so lucky."

Murdoch let out a bark of a laugh and shook his head. "Sorry, Rome. Busy with work tonight."

"You know, most werewolves use the full moon as a time to take it easy. No one works on a full moon!"

"Ah, yes, but most werewolves don't have my boss. And you know, I've got to keep him happy. Otherwise, I won't make it as a sound tech."

"I keep telling you you need to leave your job."

"And do what?"

"I don't know...anything. It's not like you need the money." Rue cringed at me, and I instantly regretted what had slipped out of my mouth. "Sorry, that's not what I meant."

"No. I understand." I sighed a relieved breath. "Everyone else is allowed to follow their dream except me because I have a trust fund, eh?"

"That's not what I meant. You just don't seem happy in your job."

"How would you even know? Whenever we have conversations, it's always about you and Rue. I actually enjoy what I do. Sure, my boss is an asshole, but that's life. Sometimes you have to work with assholes. But you know, I don't have to socialize with assholes—have fun on the pack run."

I WAS STILL KICKING myself for the stupid argument I had with Murdoch. We had been arguing a lot lately, and usually, when the arguments started, we called quits on our arrangement. But I had to bite my tongue and bear the disgruntlement because I was barely in control of Rue, and the thought of her being completely out of control was terrifying.

"Even I'm getting bored of Murdoch now," Rue said, stretching out comfortably, enjoying the preening as I combed my long, straight hair in front of the mirror. I scoffed but didn't say anything. *"Sex with him is becoming predictable. Now, if we could find some new blood to sink our teeth into... How about Simon?"*

I stopped combing my stupidly long hair and glared at

her. She was just trying to get a rise out of me. She always became malevolently facetious when we got closer to the full moon. She would grin playfully at me as if she meant it jokingly, but it never felt like a joke. It felt like she would actually do half the things she said. And when she'd said, 'sink her teeth into Simon,' I didn't think she meant it metaphorically.

I was becoming jittery with anticipation and bouncing off the walls by the time the moon was rising in the sky. It was still light out, but I could feel the moon calling to me, pulling at Rue. Something tight churned in my chest, and kept pulling and pulling. I was a fish snared on a hook, the difference was that I knew not to fight it. Time to go!

I planted my foot on the gas and drove toward Blackfern Valley, winding through the old forestry roads toward the main highway. My car was growing claustrophobic. I wound down the window and took a deep breath of the damp and chilly air. I looked around at the few reds and oranges reflecting against the mottled greens and yellows. Fall was basically here. Summer was over. Winter was on its way, and that thought depressed me. I hated winter.

"How can you hate winter?" Rue asked me. *"Snow in the paws, frozen streams and rivers, icicles that glow."* She knew perfectly well why I hated winter. Where most wolf spirits were like little heaters keeping the chill out, my wolf heater was broken. I felt the cold just like any human would. This meant that while my pack members would dress in simple sweaters and maybe the odd light coats during the cold season, I would be bundled up to ridiculous lengths, and my teeth would still chatter. I hated winter.

Choosing to ignore her again, I kept my car to the right as I drove down a narrow road. When images of a glistening snowy winter didn't cheer me up, she decided to change tactics—brutally. Images of cars skidding on the ice, bloody wounds, and flashing ambulance lights popped into my head. It startled me enough that I slammed on the brakes, my car screeching to a halt.

"*Rue!*" I snarled. "*What the fuck?*"

"*Oh, come on! You love your work.*"

"*You sadistic fucking bitch. That is not even remotely close to what I love about my work.*"

"*Well, sorry for trying to lighten the mood.*" She turned her back in a sulk, her tail twitching. Once my breathing was back on track, and I was sure she wasn't going to send me any other unwanted images, I turned onto the main highway toward Blackfern Valley.

THERE WERE ABOUT three hundred wolves partying in the amphitheatre by the time I strolled across the grass. Most of them were unmerged like me, so they had no choice but to run on a full moon. That's who the pack run was really for: newly-shifted and unmerged wolves. But any pack wolf could join, and a lot did, as the feeling of pack inclusion brought blissful contentment—at least for a little while.

I scanned the crowd for a friendly face. I spotted Liv instantly, but she was in a deep silent conversation with another warrior, her brow etched into a profound frown. A few feet from Liv, stood my brother Izzy, also deep in conversation with one of his friends. I tried to suppress the smouldering anger that sparked again. I hadn't spoken to him since the twins burst into my home. Rue itched beneath my skin, snarling softly as I watched him. His blue-ringed eyes were on alert, darting around every pack member. No, that wasn't right. He was scrutinizing the warrior squad. A squad he and Jordan didn't want to be a part of even though they would've been stereotypically perfect for it.

I followed his gaze as it flicked away from Liv. The warriors were circling the grounds, almost with an agitated demeanour about them. They didn't look at anyone for too long, but casually scanned the crowd as if something was amiss. Guilt churned in my stomach.

This couldn't be about that rogue, could it?

I returned to my task of locating my friends before spotting Caitlin and Theo on the top of the grandstand together, laughing loudly. I headed in that direction, giving overly enthusiastic waves to people as I walked by. I smiled at Josiah and Sierra, our retired leaders, as they played with their granddaughter on the lawn. Laurel and her friend were standing next to Beta Ryan and Sean.

The sky was turning pink and orange as the sun was finally setting, and the tugging feeling got stronger. Alpha Liam took centre stage and gave a general announcement to the pack before stripping off his clothes and shifting quickly into a large tawny wolf, then giving a howl that vibrated into my soul. Luna Clementine shifted moments after he did, joining her howl into his third before they disappeared together into the trees.

Time to run!

The internal tug burst into a thousand different directions. Heat surged through my veins, and my skin prickled as if it were on fire. I kicked off my flip-flops and yanked off my tracksuit. I barely had time to remove every stitch of clothing before Rue burst forward with a loud snarl. To my left and right, three hundred wolves were shifting and running into the trees behind the amphitheatre.

Pack members were zigzagging through the bush, playfully jumping out of the undergrowth before turning their tails and playing chase.

The smells of the forest heightened and gave my eyesight a bioluminescent quality. I could scent the heat of the trees and marvelled at their glow as their heat started to dissolve into the night. The weak thermal radiation was making my nose twitch as I rounded each tree. My nose twitched again as I used the infrared as a GPS to locate where each of my pack members was in relation to myself—using the infrared to ensure that I didn't stumble across any foreign werewolves.

Caitlin burst out of the trees, landing on top of Theo, who snapped at her heels as she darted away. A challenge to conduct werewolf fuckery was initiated—followed quickly by a loud splash, which was instantly backed up by a girly high-pitched shriek down the mind-link. Theo was saturated; Caitlin's tail disappeared into the brush, her evil laughter echoing in my head.

This was pack land, and this was the pack run, a chance to bring out the most immature notions of us all. No one seemed to think they could possibly be in danger, that there could be rogues on our land. Rue scoffed at my caution and cantered down the middle of the stream, scaring frogs and fish back into their hiding holes. I knew I was being idiotic. There was very little chance that a rogue would be anywhere near Blackfern Valley, not with this many wolves thundering through the forest. It would be suicide.

There was a time when it didn't matter if it was a full moon or not. When word got out that our luna was a half-breed, it seemed that every other week there was someone trying to infiltrate the pack. It was bad enough that many pack members staged a coup when they found out who was rumoured to be our next pack matriarch, that their leader tried to kill our alpha-elect and very nearly succeeded.

I remember watching in awe as Sean, his parents, Vinny and his dad, along with a very small handful of pack members, created a protective barrier around Liam as Clementine and the pack doctor fought to save his life. She was my luna at that moment. She'd earned the title. Not because she saved Liam but because I knew she would have done the same thing for any member of the pack. Even the ones so dead set against her being welcomed into the pack. She would help anyone who asked for it.

She was always trying to help me with Rue. I was anxious

that she would lock me up at first, but instead, she worked with me to find distractions. I slammed myself into volunteer work, hard labour and an endless number of committees. When that stopped working, we reconvened and tried to up my exercise regime. She had always been one of my biggest supporters and was even the one who suggested I should study medicine, a dream she never followed through with.

That's how Clem eventually won over the pack—by showing every pack member that she could be trusted to nurture and defend them. It wasn't without effort though; Alpha Liam and Luna Clementine needed to prove their worth time and time again. I felt exhausted for them. Their true love was being doubted by bigots. His rule was being questioned. A few families left, to which I gave them the middle finger salute. But with every family who left, and with every breach in the border, not once did our new leaders let us down. After the teething period, a blissful time followed, and nothing happened. There were no internal coups, no outside packs sizing us up, and no packless rogues infiltrating our borders. Until the one rogue I had stumbled across in the forest recently...

Rue gave me a questioning look. *No, surely not! It wasn't starting again, was it?* Rue suddenly stopped running and released a low growl in my mind, baring her sharp teeth in the physical realm. I peered at where she was looking and realized that Vinny's cream wolf was up ahead across the river. The mate bond that had once lit up like a glowing furnace five years ago was completely gone. Now, there was a black shadow where the moon-glow once had been. He was creeping in the moonlight, the foreboding shadow slinking over his body.

Rue stopped in her tracks and observed his stealthy demeanour. He was up to something and I wanted to know what it was.

CHAPTER 15
VINNY

I wasn't to join the pack run.

Even after Clem had suggested it was a good idea, on the morning of the full moon, she had explicitly asked me not to. I raised an eyebrow at her change in attitude, wondering what could have changed her mind. Vali flicked an image forward of when I had asked her to leave the pack, and her face was almost a mirror image of her expression five years ago.

"There is no way she could know," I told him. *"There must be another reason she no longer wants me on the pack run."* But even as I said it, my gut told me that it indeed had something to do with Roman. Even if Clem didn't know about the extent of the degree of animosity between us. There was absolutely no way my sister knew that Roman was once my fated mate and that she'd rejected me. My brain buzzed as I tried to quickly decipher another reason for banning me from the pack run.

Maybe it was because Roman was unmerged and unhinged. If her wolf was still fizzing about our altercation, then it was very likely we could end up in round two. Vali shook his head in disagreement.

I was saved from asking her when Alpha Liam came into the kitchen. "Did you tell him he isn't going to the pack run?"

"I was just telling him," Clem affirmed. It seemed like Liam didn't hear her as he looked directly at me and launched into his orders.

"There was a reason that rogue came in so close to the full moon. We think it's because he was checking for weak spots, and we want to make sure that no one attacks on the full moon. My mom and dad are guarding Lacey tonight. Your dad is looking after the other pups and a few others who aren't joining. Sean, Ryan, Clem and I, along with a few other wolves, are running point within the pack to keep everyone safe and to keep up appearances. The rest of the warriors will be running the perimeter, so that leaves you." Vali's ears perked up as he stood to attention. "On the off-chance we find someone who is not supposed to be there, I need you to appear nomadic—vulnerable. I need you to be bait. And if it comes to it, I need you to be taken."

"What makes you think they would take me?" I asked, scratching my furry chin.

"Your blood status," Liam retorted with no apology.

I frowned slightly as the words bounced against my ear drum, and then slowly, my frown turned into a grin.

IT WAS ABOUT three hours before Liv's voice infiltrated my mind. *"Where are you dick-bait?"*

"Dick-bait?"

"Well, you are a dick and bait, so yeah, it fits."

"How old are you, ten?" I snorted. *"If we're calling each other juvenile names, what name am I calling you? I'd call you penis-breath, but you would actually have to suck dick for that to work."* Vali rolled his eyes, and Liv ignored my quip.

"Why do they think you would be good bait?" The question surprised me.

"Alpha Liam knows I will do anything for my niece. If these

wolves are purists, then a half-breed is the best lure. And the only other half-breed in our pack is my sister. For some reason, I don't think he would ever risk her life. Me, on the other hand, I've been risking my life for five years."

"What do you mean?"

I gave a harsh chuckle and then sobered. *"Being nomadic meant I couldn't rely on my pack, I didn't have safety in numbers, and unfortunately, I got myself into a few dangerous situations. I was prewarned that I would probably have to keep moving. I mean, most people were fine. Most. That was until I managed to screw them out of a large chunk of money. Then suddenly, it was racist slurs, heavy fists, and the occasional capture and torture."*

"Wait. Seriously?"

"What is that, Liv? Do I detect concern?" She snorted down the mind-link. *"I knew the risks, Liv. Alpha Liam knew about them, too."*

She didn't say anything for a few minutes, but I could still feel her scratching against my mind. I thought she may have been aghast, angry and processing that her benevolent leader would allow me to put myself in danger repeatedly. I was ready to remind her Alpha Liam wasn't about to start a pack war over me, that I made my decision when I left. Then her voice came over loud and clear, and I realized she didn't hold any such sentiments.

"I've found a rogue. Get ready dick-bait, it's time for you to play the half-breed damsel."

I skulked around the bend on the north side of the river, where Liv had told me the trail was leading to. I sniffed the air, trying to detect notes of the rogue. There was a very faint sliver of something, but it was hard to tell what it was or how old it was. In fact, it was almost impossible to detect as it blended into the natural smells of the forest. The only reason I was even following it was because Liv told me it was a rogue. Liv, with her powerful nose that could smell more than musty forest. Her nose was so good that if we could get cancer, I'm sure she'd have been able to sniff out the first mutating cells. Nope, I wasn't about to argue with the best nose in the pack.

I sniffed the air again, trying to pinpoint a direction. I was going to have to get her to guide me, hold my hand like a toddler and show me where to go. The idea was mortifying. I needed to find this rogue, and I needed to find him fast.

The odour hit me hard, causing Vali to growl low. The stench permeated my nostrils, and my hackles rose. It wasn't a dirty rogue smell, but that of jasmine. Disgusting, coiling jasmine crept up my nose. I spun and looked at a stunning black wolf with purple and brown eyes. Purple and brown eyes that were manic and feral. Was Roman in control or was it her wolf?

The scent infiltrated my every senses as Vali stretched out toward her purple pattern, the exact same shade as the iridescent rings around her eyes. My wolf pushed against the need to gag as sickly jasmine curled and weaved within the pattern before it stretched out toward my mind, making a clear bridge connection between us. Vali was tense, ready at any moment to fight off her feral wolf.

"What are you doing here?" I demanded the moment I felt the connection within her mind.

"I was about to ask you the same thing. Why are you sneaking around?" Her honeyed voice was raspy in my mind, but I didn't detect any sense that her wolf was calling the shots. Her wolf seemed to be taking a back seat—for now.

"Pack business," I said bluntly.

"What? Am I not pack?"

"Warrior business," I clarified, rolling my eyes. I needed to get rid of her quickly.

"You're not a warrior," she chaffed.

"Get lost, Roman." I turned my back on her and shouldered into the thick brush. Crap, now, I was going to have to scent the rogue again. Or worse, I was going to have to ask Liv to scent him again.

Teeth pierced my flank, and I let out a startled yelp. I kicked my leg while spinning to release the bite, half expecting to see the rogue on me. But I knew it wasn't the rogue. There was only one smell still in the air.

"What the fuck, Roman!" But when I looked into her eyes, Vali suddenly puffed out as big as he could and growled menacingly, showing the pinks of his gums as fresh saliva coated his canines. Roman was no longer in control. It was Rue. And I had committed the ultimate insult in our culture; I had turned my back on her.

Roman didn't submit to Vali's dominant stature. If anything, it made her wilder. Fur was flying, and teeth were snapping. Rue was holding her own against me. I wasn't going easy on her either. No, I didn't want to hurt her, but I also wasn't going to let her win. I needed to subdue her quickly.

I half-shifted and flipped over the top of her, giving myself over to instinct as I bent and moved, using the strength and agility of my wolf while keeping myself upright. Roman met each move with clumsy ferocity, and then she tried to mimic my advantageous half-shift. Vali growled, and cold fear slapped me right across the face.

"Roman. No!" I screeched.

It was incredibly dangerous to fight in both forms at once. While any werewolf could technically attempt it, it took years of training to master, and the pack only allowed those who had fully merged with their wolf spirit to practice the combined-fighting method. Doing it before merging was reckless—it could be deadly if you weren't completely in sync.

I pounced on her, forcing her to the ground. She bucked and snarled underneath me, but I held her down. *"Shift!"* I demanded through the mind-link. She bucked again. "Shift!" I yelled out loud, Vali's voice joining mine. Vali's voice was amplified with an infinitesimal amount of alpha power.

She bucked again, whimpering as her fur started to retreat into her skin. I allowed myself to become fully human again, my canines receding with a *pop*.

Roman was still thrashing violently beneath me. She was incensed. I didn't know what to do to calm her down, but it was increasingly dangerous to be out here. The rogue had to have heard us. Between a rogue and a lawless pack wolf—I was up shit creek.

I did the only thing I could think of and smashed my lips against her perfect, heart-shaped mouth and instantly, the thrashing stopped.

CHAPTER 16
ROMAN

His tongue found mine with desperate need. It dominated my mouth as his teeth gnashed against mine. I pulled away to get a breath and looked straight into startling green eyes. Eyes that looked horrified and apologetic.

He started to pull away, and I followed him into the kneeling position, pressing my mouth against his. I could taste the momentary shock before he opened his mouth and kissed me back. His mouth was less desperate this time, and his tongue was gentle as if he were hesitant. Tingles zapped around my body, and all I wanted was for his fingers to trace the sensations. But his arms were in rigor mortis against the side of his body. His fists were clenched tight.

He's not enjoying this. Cold awareness tormented me as I pulled away, my pride wounded. I pushed him off me and backed into a pine tree, breathing heavily as I tried to stop my racing heart and the hurt it was pumping throughout my body.

"I shouldn't have kissed you," he murmured as he leaned against another pine, eyeing me with caution.

"Yeah. No shit," I grumbled softly, then laced my voice with contempt. "Why were you violating my mouth like that?"

"I needed you back in control. Not your wolf."

"So, you thought putting your slimy tongue in my mouth was appropriate?"

His eyes narrowed into slits. "You stalked me, then you attacked me—"

"You turned your back on Rue. That was colossally stupid. But I shouldn't have expected anything else from you."

"Wait a damn second. You're blaming me? You're the one with an out-of-control wolf. Do you know how dangerous you are?" he grunted.

"Yeah, I'm deadly." My voice was waspish. Any embarrassment I had about our kiss had quickly morphed into disgust.

Rue kept replaying it, obsessing over every detail and growing more agitated by the second. I could no longer taste Vinny on my tongue. All I could taste was Rue's bitter fixation.

"I'm serious, Roman. You could get yourself killed. You *will* get yourself killed."

"Back off!" I growled, my eyes flashing dangerously purple. He watched me stonily.

"Get her under control!"

Rue snarled as I fought to maintain control. My skin vibrated with the need to shift. My mind was being flooded with Rue's need for blood. Vengeance.

"Roman!" His voice sounded like it was down a tunnel. "Roman! Breathe through it and push her back!" Garbled and distorted, I tried to concentrate on the tenor of his voice. Rue snarled menacingly. Her hackles were raised as she lowered her head between her shoulders, not giving me an ounce of leeway as she triangulated on her target.

A warm mouth met mine—again—as I was slammed hard against the tree, the bark scraping my back. There was an odd sweetness to his lips, a taste I couldn't place. The icy peppermint scent added an extra zing. Tingles started in my stomach as his tongue expertly caressed mine, and his hands shot into my war-torn hair. Peppermint swirled around me. I gave a soft moan into his mouth before logic and reasoning returned, followed by disgust.

"You fucking did it again!" I said, shoving him hard.

"Well, I needed to shock you, but I didn't exactly have an ice bucket to throw on you. Besides, you kissed me back."

Damn it! "No, I didn't!"

"Oh, it must have been someone else's tongue down my throat then." I glared at him. "Twice."

"It was a momentary lapse in judgment. I was under the influence and cannot be held responsible for my actions."

"Under the influence?" He arched an eyebrow. "I didn't know I was that much of an influence."

"Get your head out of your ass. You really aren't that special. It could have been anyone, and I would have reacted the same way. I was swept up in the moment. As soon as I get home, I'm going to sanitize my mouth!"

"You go around getting swept up in people's kisses often?" There was something primal in his voice.

"Well, as you witnessed, it's one way to tame the beast." Vinny's jaw clenched. The coating of thick blond facial hair stretched down and over his Adam's-apple, which bobbed as he swallowed.

My gaze travelled down his neck and over his body, quietly appreciating his naked form as the full moon reached its peak. I was expecting to see his body glow under the light of the full moon, but the fact his skin remained dull reinforced the reality that our bond was well and truly severed. The shadows that surrounded him were cold and foreboding.

I looked up at the full moon and grumbled deep. I could still feel the power from the moon, but it was corrupted, tainted and broken. It felt like I had taken an entire bottle of Novocain, and my body was numb to everything the full moon touched. Everything.

I glanced back at Vinny, who was still watching me cautiously. I made sure I focused on Vinny's eyes to ensure that mine didn't wander again.

My eyes wandered down to his lips, which were slightly parted. I could see the tiny calming breaths he was taking. I could still taste the subtle tones of peppermint mixed with the sweet... it was something I couldn't place. It was almost nutty in flavour. I hated that he was a good kisser. I hated that he managed to shock Rue into submission. Twice. My arch nemesis had kissed me, and my wolf reacted in a way that I had never seen before. I flushed, wondering if he could see into my head; if he knew the effect he had on me—on her.

The way he watched me made me feel exposed. Not because I was standing naked—werewolves were used to being nude in each other's presence—but because he had witnessed Rue taking over. Because he was watching me with a mixture of concern, wariness and egotistical hatred.

I needed to shift and get as far away from here as possible. I sidled away from the tree that I was leaning against and turned. Giving him one last glance over my shoulder, I shifted, turned off my mind-link, and sprinted in the opposite direction.

Rue, for once, was taking the backseat in my mind. She sat on her haunches, looking perplexed as I ran through the forest. This quiet reflection was unusual for her. Even after she had been tamed by my extracurricular activities, she would have a cheeky quip—satiated but still saucy. Now, she looked forlorn. Confused. She wasn't showing me images or trying to get me to talk things out. She just sat there shell-shocked and gobsmacked.

I kept running until the smell of icy peppermint had diffused out of my nostrils. And I kept going until I felt pain in my calves, and was almost out of breath. And even then, I kept on moving, not allowing the distraction of anything else. I ignored the sounds of wolves howling, playing and those of coupling. I ignored the bouquet of scents the forest provided, even the vile swampy, stagnant water stench that coiled up my nose. I kept running and running until I found myself morphing back into my human self and strolling through the front door of my cabin, dirty tears drying on my cheeks.

CHAPTER 17
VINNY

BLOOD RUSHED SOUTH. I needed to calm myself down. She couldn't know how much kissing her had affected me. I was on edge. Conflicting information was sending my synapses into a frenzy. I took meditative breaths through my mouth as the jasmine salting the air irritated my nose. But when I did so, it was as if my mouth had remembered the taste of hers, and the sweetness was being inhaled with every breath. I tried to keep my breathing shallow.

Her eyes were entirely brown now, her wolf non-apparent. But there was an untamed emotion swirling within her eyes. I wanted to reach out and talk to her. Apologize, and say anything to change that expression on her face. I wanted to say something, but my tongue had turned to dust, and the language centre of my brain was having a seizure. She edged further away, shifting and bolting before I could speak. Vali tilted his head in confusion as he watched the spot where she had just vanished.

"Dick-bait." Liv's voice travelled into my subconscious. I shook my head and concentrated on the mind-link. Her apple-cinnamon and blue pattern seemed duller as if she were trying to connect from a vast distance away.

"Liv," I grumbled back.

"Where the fuck are you?" she snarled angrily. *"Do you need me to draw you a fucking map?"*

I SAT in a small clearing which reeked of wet, mouldy forest. I pressed my nose into the ground, trying to give myself a reprieve from the putrid odour of rogue as I waited for him to find me. I had rubbed my fur against trees, scratching my skin and encouraging my scent to leech through my pores. Every werewolf had its own unique scent, but that wasn't the scent I wanted to spread. There was a distinctive aroma that only half-breeds had; it was the usual canine scent with an undertone of human. I could dampen and mask my scent when needed, but there was nothing I could do to amplify the individual notes within my scent. Rubbing myself against the tree trunks was the best I could do.

I heard the gentle paw pads against the mud and tried not to grin. He was trying to be quiet and sneak up on me. He didn't know he was walking right into a trap.

Vali stilled and waited.

The forest turned deathly quiet. My ears twitched, trying to determine where the rogue was. Anxiety started to bubble under my skin. *Come on!*

The bush to my right rustled. I turned my head toward the movement moments before I was nailed from behind. The decaying stench of the rogue's breath was overwhelming as his teeth went for my throat.

Alpha Liam had instructed to be bait and, if possible, to be captured. He hadn't instructed me to die. He hadn't instructed me not to fight back. I reacted. Dirty teeth latched onto thick amounts of my skin and fur. My muscles rolled under my skin as I forced myself out of the compromising position and into attack mode.

It was the same rogue as before, and I suddenly knew why three warriors had struggled to bring him down. The mutt was quick. He met each blow of mine with one of his own. He mirrored every move with a precise countermove. When I half-shifted, he didn't copy, but his enormous wolf seemed to grow in speed and size.

The mission had turned suicidal as soon as he had shown up in the clearing.

I yelled down the mind-link to the warriors. I wasn't going to be taken. That much was obvious. He was going to kill me. He was going to kill me on my own land.

Bark scraped my back as the sheer force of the mutt's hit sent me soaring into the trunk of a large tree. I barely had time to register what had happened before claws scraped the tissue of my belly as he gained the advantage over me. I growled in pain as blood trickled through my fur.

Vali snapped at the rogue, frothing and angry. The mutt clamped his sharp teeth down on my front leg. I howled in pain. He shook his head, left to right. It was slow to begin with, allowing me to feel every skin cell cleaved away from my muscles and tendons, ripping and tearing as he increased his tempo.

I panted with exertion as I tried to keep up with the wolf. I was bruised and bleeding badly from deep wounds across my abdomen, arms and leg. Shifting was almost impossible now, as Vali had been severely weakened. This wolf was stronger and more dominant, a true alpha. With one last shudder, I was lying naked on the ground, bleeding out into the clearing. It was over before it had even begun.

The rogue gave a wolfy chuckle as he towered over top of me. He had won. He was going to deliver the death blow any moment. I thought of my sister, my dad, and my pack. I even thought briefly of Roman.

I locked onto the frost-coloured eyes, and Vali started thrashing in my mind as he saw my plan unfold. It was suicidal if the warriors didn't arrive in time. But what did I have to lose? If I was going to die, I was going to die on my terms. As the old saying goes, *'If you're going to lose a fight, make sure the other person thinks twice before fighting you again.'* This way, I hoped he would think twice before going after my family.

I gave Vali an apologetic look as I pushed with all my might, throwing my weakened human self at the wolf, momentarily surprising him before sharp claws slashed at my head. My brain spun inside my skull, and Vali started to fall. I saw the thundering paws in my vision as I crashed to the ground. There was a warm, sticky trickle cascading down my temple and over my jaw. The last image I saw before I passed out was a straw-coloured wolf, the silver around her crystal blue eyes glowing as she let out a vicious snarl.

I HAD the world's worst hangover. Even worse than the time I had taken my first shot of aconite. My brain was pulsating, and my stomach churned. I reached out for Vali, hoping he would heal us, but just like when I took that aconite, he wasn't there. A large barrier sat between us, throbbing with my hangover. Damn it. It had been a long time since I had lost Vali. I hoped it wasn't going to be for long.

I tried to move and sucked in a pained breath. Hot agony cut across my abdominal muscles, seizing and making it impossible to move. I gasped and choked, determined not to move again.

What the hell?

"Careful!" a female voice said, a hand gently pressed against my shoulder. There was a gentle pear and honeysuckle fragrance, followed by a woodsy-pine scent. I opened my eyes, blinking at the invading light.

"What the hell happened?" I croaked.

"You got your ass kicked," my father said with an uncomfortable chuckle. His eyes were flush with emotion, the silver swirling against the wetness.

"You been crying, Dad?" I teased, trying to move again. I groaned in pain.

"Stop moving!" my dad ordered as my sister fussed about like a mother hen. "What do you remember?"

I pushed against the fog and tried to think. Everything came rushing in like a freight train. "Where is the fucking rogue?" I snarled, trying to sit again, and then I cried out in pain.

"For fuck sakes, Vinny! Don't move," my sister snapped as she pushed me back down again. "You're really fucking hurt. The doctor gave you ketamine. The more you move, the quicker it will wear off. So please stop straining yourself." I swallowed my pain with a sip of water Clem offered.

"Where is the rogue?" My voice was deathly quiet, but my father and my sister heard me.

"The warriors got him. Thanks to you, Vinny, they got him," my dad said, pride lacing his voice. "It took six warriors to take him down in the end, but they got him." Thank God for that. I reached for Vali again, frowning as I remembered he was hurt. My final move against the rogue had hurt him. I lifted my hand, frowning at the plastic tubing connected to it, before lifting my hand to my head. My fingertips grazed the soft bandage.

"I must look great. Worthy of a new photo for my Tinder profile."

"Wait, you're on Tinder?" Sean laughed, strolling into my bedroom and clapping me on the shoulder. I grimaced a little, and Clem gave Sean a reproachful look. "Are we sure the black and blue is the look you want to go for?"

"I think it makes me look dangerous."

"Dangerously stupid," Clementine muttered.

"He was just following orders," Sean reasoned.

"Stupid orders." Clementine's eyes flashed protectively. "I've already told your brother that it isn't to happen again."

"If it wasn't me, it would've been someone else," I said softly, her sisterly concern warming something within me.

She looked like she was about to retort with something when Dad piped up by saying, "Well, let's hope capturing this rogue will put an end to it all."

"What about Nola?" I asked, remembering the straw-coloured wolf.

"Nola!" Clementine startled. "What does Nola have to do with anything?"

"I saw her."

"No, you must be mistaken. She hasn't been here in years. She never returned after Lincoln's coup."

"I'm telling you, Clemmy, I saw Nola." I paused, puzzled for a moment. "At least I think it was Nola."

I scanned my bedside companions. Dad had a stony look on his face as Clem was mind-linking her mate to ascertain whether Nola was on pack land. A strange look passed over Sean's face, which turned into a cheery smile before he excused himself from the group, muttering about him being glad I wasn't dead, but he had to go back to work.

CHAPTER 18
ROMAN

My alarm blasted an annoying tune before I smashed it against the wall on the opposite side of the room. Plastic pieces flew in multiple directions. I groaned and rolled over, throwing my head under my comforter. Rue smiled sedately at me and gently nudged me awake again. This was the one day a month she was gentle and kind. On any other day, I would have been met with insults and aggression. I sighed and gave in, trudging my way to the bathroom to start my day.

After I showered, I stumbled into the kitchen and switched on the kettle before succumbing to the countertop of the breakfast bar. My face was resting in the nook of my arm as I replayed the events of the pack run in my head—every excruciating minute of the kissing incident, frame by frame. Rue was offering no help, and for once, she wasn't obsessing over the incident either. I was. *I* had kissed him. *I* hated him, yet that didn't stop my tongue from exploring his. The most confusing part of it all was that even though I still hated him, I think I wanted to kiss him again. *What the hell is wrong with me?* My stomach was churning with anxiety. Something had to be bothering me more than the kiss, more than the fact I wanted to do it again. Something was wrong, and I couldn't put my finger on it.

Liv walked through my front door, bright and happy, throwing my car keys into the bowl by the door, her nose twitching as she took in the new smells around her. She walked into the kitchen, where I was still propped up on the breakfast bar with my head in my arms in despair. I gave her a small acknowledgment as she approached.

"I wondered where you had got to last night. When I couldn't mind-link you, I'd assumed you had turned back. When you didn't answer my texts, I got a little worried, but then I saw your car parked at the pack house and figured you had run home." She handed me my cell phone. "And that was on the seat."

"Thanks. And thanks for bringing my car around."

"No problem. I know what day it is." Her voice was soft. She gave my shoulder a squeeze before going around the breakfast bar into my kitchen. She pulled out two coffee mugs and gazed at me. It was a look of tired concern. "What time are you leaving?"

I propped myself up properly and looked at the clock on the wall. "In about an hour. Where did you get to last night?"

"Pack business." I frowned at her as more unwanted memories of Vinny floated through my vision, and I shook my head sharply to remove them.

"What kind of pack business?"

She poured scalding hot water into two cups and started mixing the powdered coffee with a teaspoon. She added creamer to both cups before she looked at me and sighed. "I was hunting the rogue last night." Rue's ears stood at attention, but there was no other reaction. She barely moved from her comfortable position.

"What? You mean the one I tried to take out? Liv!" Terror washed over me as I remembered how big he had been and the rumours I had been hearing. "Liv, that rogue was massive. Three warriors failed at taking him down."

"I know."

"You could have been seriously hurt." Rue rolled her eyes at me, her head between her paws.

"It's part of the job, Rome." I shook my head in disbelief. "It's okay, though. We got him this time."

"Well, that's good." I sipped the boiling hot coffee and grimaced as the bitter liquid hit my tongue. It was disgusting, but a necessary evil for the day ahead. It was quiet for a moment; the only sounds were the gentle sipping of coffee. I gazed at Liv, who seemed to be overconcentrating on her cup and conversing with her wolf. She sighed again and looked at me, her face pensive. My stomach churned with anxiety again. "What's up?"

"I really shouldn't be telling you this, but you're going to hear it through the rumour mill eventually anyway, and I think it would be better coming from me." Her demeanour told me that this was something that was going to upset Rue. Something that could cause Rue to react.

"What?" I asked nervously. Rue's ears triangulated on Liv, twitching slightly.

"Capturing the rogue didn't exactly go as planned." She paused. I waited while she gathered her thoughts. "It took six of us to take him out, but a seventh wolf was severely injured." I instinctively knew who she was talking about without her having to say anything. My stomach churned in confirmation, a gut instinct I shouldn't have. My blood froze and then pumped loudly in my ears. With each *pump,* I heard his snide voice. With each *pump* echoed his arrogance. Pack business—*da dump.* Get lost—*da dump.* You're dangerous—*da dump.* Twice—d*a dump.*

"I see," I gritted out before taking a large gulp of burning coffee.

"He was set up as bait. The plan went south, and he took on the rogue solo while we all got into position. Another five rogues were spotted running through the forest in different directions, splitting our attention. It was a clusterfuck." She shook her head. "But he is stable. I checked in with Sean a little while ago, and he is being nursed back to health." My stomach churned with a small amount of concern. I peered at Rue, who gave me a slight smirk. She wasn't bothered by this harrowing information in the slightest, even with her vengeance thwarted.

"Well, I guess karma does eventually swing around," I muttered. "Thanks for telling me. Don't worry. If you were concerned about Rue losing the plot, she is still sedated."

Liv breathed a sigh of relief, visibly relaxing. Her nose twitched again, and she gave me a sly smile. "That wasn't the only reason I wanted to be the one to tell you."

"It wasn't?"

"No. Not entirely." There was a mischievous twinkle in her eye. "I just thought you would like to know... considering you reek like Vinny."

My face flamed, and my mouth opened like a gaping fish. *Damn her fucking nose.*

EVERY MONTH after the first night of the full moon, after Rue was calm and somewhat ordinary, I went to visit my sister. It was the only time I could see her without the risk of Rue tearing down the group home in anger. It took six hours of driving to see her. My parents couldn't have put her further away. I wanted her to stay with me at my house, and at first, she did, but seeing her daily in a catatonic state caused Rue to act out. That was when I accepted what my parents were saying. That she needed help from professionals. Unfortunately, there was nowhere suitable in Kempthorne to place her, and Blackfern Valley didn't have anything to help a werewolf in her state. In fact, there were no werewolf facilities to place her in because werewolves didn't go into comas and wake up without a wolf spirit and in a semi-vegetative state.

That was when my parents decided to hide her away with humans. Then, my brothers conveniently forgot she existed, as being in denial was easier than accepting what had happened to her. At first, Arizona and I visited her together. After a few false and devastatingly dangerous visits, Arizona suggested visiting Indiana after the full moon, when Rue was still riding the pack run endorphins. It was a nice bonding experience, driving six hours with my sister and spending twenty-four hours with our other sister before returning to Blackfern Valley. That was until Arizona started having pups of her own. Now, I made the drive solo.

"SHE SEEMS GOOD TODAY," I murmured as I stroked my sister's hair affectionately, taking in her features that were similar to mine. Her long, dark hair cascaded over her shoulders, and her full lips and high cheekbones gave her an effortless beauty that always made her seem so much prettier than me.

She was propped in a wheelchair by the window, looking out at the garden. I wondered if she was enjoying the leaves falling from the oak tree outside, but her eyes, which had once been full of life, were a sluggish brown and vacant.

"The doctor has changed her meds," her carer, Jane, replied.

I snapped my gaze over to the motherly woman. "Oh? Why is that?"

"She had an episode."

"An episode? When?"

"Last week."

"Why wasn't I informed?"

"Your parents were here."

"My parents were here?" I shook my head in disbelief. "Surprising." My voice was sharp.

"They didn't tell you?" Lines formed around Jane's face as her mouth dropped into a disapproving look.

"No." I barely spoke to my parents. "The episode was at them?"

"I believe so." That explained a lot. My sister may not be compos mentis, and she may not have a wolf, but even she must feel abandoned and outcasted by our parents. By everyone. Guilt flavoured my tastebuds as I stroked her hair again. Rue rumbled softly but didn't react. She was still happily anesthetized.

"Did you want to speak to Doctor Jones about it? I can see if he's able to come and answer your questions." I looked around the group home. The afternoon sun was streaming in from the large windows, creating an amber glow over the residents.

"No, don't disturb Travis. I know how busy he is," I murmured. "Thanks, Jane." I pulled up a chair and opened my bag, pulling out nail polish and gave my sister the biggest cheerful grin I could.

"Do you want that ghastly green again?" No answer. "Maybe a soft pink?" No answer. "Whatever you pick, don't pick black." Silence. I smiled at her and proceeded to buff and trim her nails, amicably filling the silence as I told her everything that had gone on in the last month.

"And then, of course, Vinny came back." I inwardly cursed. I had told myself I wasn't going to tell her that he was back, but of course, it just had to slip past the carefully crafted words as if the words had a mind of their own. Just to ruin my day. And hers.

I swallowed my guilt and looked straight into the murky browns of her almond-shaped eyes. Cold dripped down my back, and my arm hair stood up on end. I felt as though she was looking right at me, watching me and wanting to communicate.

"Rue..."

Rue shook her head sadly. *"Nope, still gone."*

I stared at my sister's eyes for another minute or two, willing for the blue rings to make an appearance. The blue rings of the wolf she was once merged with.

CHAPTER 19
VINNY

FIVE BROKEN RIBS, a cracked skull, severe muscle and tendon damage and a deep laceration to my abdomen—that thankfully missed any major organs—warranted a trip from the pack doctor and my would-be doctor sister fussing over me. I had been bed-bound for a few hours, and I was growing bored of the mothering.

"You remember I am a werewolf, right? I have enhanced healing abilities. You don't need to hover."

"I'm not hovering."

"No? This must be a new form of torture then," I grunted as she pressed buttons on the machine and fussed with the plastic tubing adhered to my hand. "Have you finished administering the truth serum? Am I going to tell you my dirty secrets now?"

"It's saline, you moron. And I don't think I *ever* want to know your dirty secrets." She rolled her eyes. "You were unconscious and dehydrated, and your injuries were bad enough for Doctor Todd to give you a very strong anesthetic." She gave me a sardonic smile. "Even with your enhanced healing abilities."

"Maybe he just likes pushing highly addictive substances. Sounds like a great marketing ploy. Give a werewolf a taste of the good stuff, just enough to get them to come back for more and *bam*, lucrative income revenue."

"Are you honestly accusing Doctor Todd of being a drug dealer?"

"Why not? He is in the perfect position for it. Small town doctor and a good-looking bachelor, friendly smile, great with the pups—no one would suspect a thing."

"I don't think I have ever heard of a werewolf having a substance abuse problem."

"Um... the town is full of borderline alcoholics," I deadpanned. She smirked. I had her there, and she knew it.

"Well, our healing ability lessens the effects of alcohol and narcotics. The heavy dosage that Doctor Todd prescribed is potent but wears off quickly. So don't worry, I don't think you are going to become addicted to it. Do you need some more?"

"Sorry, I stand corrected. *You* are the drug dealer."

TEN MINUTES after my sister finally left my bedside, I rolled off the mattress, unable to stand the sight of my four walls for another second. I gently padded down the hallway toward the bathroom. The carpet was plush under my toes, and each step felt like a triumphant call for freedom. The excruciating pain was gone, but my body still ached. It was a good ache, though. Similar to the ache after a decent workout when my legs turned to Jell-O; it was one that told me I was alive.

I looked at the blue-green bruises in the bathroom mirror and dark scabbing tissue on the side of my head, deep gashes in perfect symmetry. It had been several hours since I'd woken up, and even without Vali to accelerate my advanced healing, the werewolf gene was already doing its job—albeit slowly. When Vali woke, the dark scabbing would turn to a fresh pink scar tissue before disappearing almost entirely.

I reached back to try to stroke Vali again, but the barrier was still there, secluding a section of my mind. I frowned. As a merged wolf, I should have been able to touch him. It was a basic survival instinct which helped heal the soul of the injured wolf spirit.

It had been a while since I had lost Vali behind the wall. Unmerged wolf spirits were known to throw tantrums and push themselves into a pocket of the mind, erecting an impenetrable wall between the human and the wolf. Once the werewolf merged with its human, they were of one mind and soul, so it was almost impossible to lose a wolf spirit. It only happened when the merged wolf spirit sensed impending life-ending doom. Guilt washed over me as I reached back for the tenth time. I had seen him fall. I was the reason he was gone.

I splashed water over my face, knowing that there was no way he could stay behind that wall forever. I was alive and kicking, so eventually, he had to come out and grace me with his presence.

For now, all I could do was sit with my own thoughts. Thoughts of the six rogues infiltrating pack land made me feel sick. Especially when only one of them was captured; he was a decoy, and we had fallen for it. While I was trying to set up a trap for him, he was setting up a trap for me, knowing that our warriors would scent him – that was why he had been in the bush the other week. Laying his scent, enraging our warriors, and starting the foundations for his trap.

Now, all I wanted was revenge.

IT WAS another two days before I felt the gentle stirring in the back of my mind. I reached back and ran my fingers through Vali's creamy fur. The soft strands tickled. He let out a big snort in his sleep and proceeded to snore loudly. There were claw-shaped scrapes above his eye, and I knew that he would have the same breaks and bruises I had, even if they weren't visible. I frowned again. He was really hurt.

I was so far in my own head that I barely even registered that my lunch had arrived. I also hadn't registered that Sean wasn't talking, either. I looked around the patio of a small Kempthorne eatery and tried to find something to talk about. Anything that would stop us from looking like we were on the world's most depressingly awkward first date.

"Are you moping because Liam and Ryan are having all the fun with that mutt?" Sean grunted in response. "Look, man, I get it. I was expecting to be able to recreate the movie *Saw*, but Alpha benched me too." I put salt on my fries. "Although, I think that had more to do with my sister than your brother," I added dejectedly. No response. Not even a chuckle. "Seriously, Sean. What is up with you?"

"I found my true mate." Sean sounded depressed. I gaped at him. I was not expecting that to be the thing he blurted out.

"That is fantastic, man! Why aren't you over the moon?"

"She isn't exactly happy we mated," Sean muttered into the ketchup bottle as he poured an exuberant amount on his fries, then stared at them without even moving one toward his mouth.

Pain fissured through me as I empathized with his situation. Recollections of Roman's soft moans and tingle-ridden kisses twisted within the icy pain as memories of her rejection roared in my heart. I pushed the invasive feeling back and focused on Sean, asking the question that was going to feel like ten thousand barbed baseball bats whacking his soul.

"Did she reject you?" My voice was raw.

"No!" He shook his head; his eyes were wide with horror. "She just asked for time."

"That sounds...diplomatic," I offered, trying to lock down my own bullshit feelings and focus on Sean, which was proving an impossible task. Damn it, I needed Vali.

"It was...until she left."

"Huh? What do you mean?"

"She's gone. When I heard your emergency call down the mind-link, she took that distraction as an opportunity to get away." I gaped again.

"What the fuck! What are you going to do?"

"She asked for time. I'm going to give her a week, and then I'm going to go find her."

"Who was it? It was Laurel, wasn't it? I saw the way you were looking at her. Shit, bro, if you got with a model, slash actress, slash beauty queen, slash whatever else she does in Toronto, you are going to be the most envied wolf in the pack." I grinned at him.

He met my grin with a sad smile. God, she had really done a number on him. I knew firsthand how that felt. He had mated with someone as cold and awful as I had. Someone who could stomp all over his heart in her six-inch stilettos, do her catwalk turn and walk back over it without even blinking in his direction. I always thought Laurel was kind, but it was obviously just a mirage. Maybe all the she-wolves in our pack were the same —gorgeous girls who painted a pretty image and were phenomenal-earth-moving kissers but were toxic.

"Yeah, bro! Something like that. We will see when I talk to her next."

"I'm rooting for you!" I exclaimed enthusiastically if only to hide my discomfort. "Now, can we stop moping and come up with some awesome new torture ideas for when we are given the opportunity?"

I grinned, taking a bite out of my burger and barely tasting it before letting the lump fall into the pit of my empty stomach.

"My brother is naturally fuming. Your rogue was a decoy. We chased it and fell right into the rogue's trap. It's so fucking bizarre, man. Rogues don't act like this. They don't conduct military strategy. There is no structure, no order. They can't agree on anything and usually just fight amongst themselves—it's chaos. But that rogue was fucking with us since the beginning. Look at the left hand while the right hand is doing something else. Five fucking rogues were infiltrating the land in a different location, spreading us thin—" Sean ranted.

"But they didn't get close to Lacey," I reminded him. I had successfully distracted him from his woes when I asked him to tell me what had happened while I was taking on the rogue. I already knew, as my sister had given me the rundown, but Sean didn't know that. Sean was highly protective over our niece and loved to unravel plays and strategies, so it turned out to be the best distraction.

"No. They were intercepted."

"Wait. How many rogues are in the stone cells?"

Sean glowered. "Only the big brutish one you took on."

"None of the others. So, you're telling me that the other five rogues got away? How does that even happen?" My voice had gone dangerously low. Something was off. Way off. "It seems calculated. Like he wanted to get caught, like *I* had wanted to get caught."

"Exactly," Sean agreed.

I took a sip of my beer as my mind was buzzing. What the hell were these rogues up to? I lifted my head and looked out across the patio as if the answer would be on the horizon, and that's when I saw Roman. She was across the street talking to a tall, skinny guy with glasses. His face was lit up and animated, hers looked tired but friendly. She fidgeted a little, which, considering she had a neurotic wolf spirit, was unlike her. Roman always had a sense of calm poise and an infectious, bubbly personality. Was this guy bothering her? Why didn't she just tell him to fuck off? She was more than capable of doing so as she told me to fuck off repeatedly.

I stared at her for long enough that Sean looked over, too. "Oh, it's Roman," I said nothing but continued to stare, unable to look away as she chatted away to some guy who obviously wanted to bed her.

"Let's go say hi." I flicked my eyes briefly over to Sean and noticed he wasn't staring at her but watching me with interest. I shrugged my shoulders nonchalantly.

Sure, let's go escort this fucker away from her.

CHAPTER 20
ROMAN

I felt like a bit of a creep watching Vinny from across the street. I had just popped into the city centre to run some errands before my shift at work when I looked up and found myself staring at the bistro across the street. My feet were cemented down. At any moment, he was going to look up and catch me staring. Even though it would've been embarrassing if he caught me, I still couldn't move. Minutes ticked by, but he still hadn't looked up. I couldn't even pay attention to Sean or the cute-as-a-button waitress who was batting her long eyelashes at the both of them.

I told myself that I was just being a nurse and assessing the damage the rogue had caused. The scarring across his temple was dark red where it should have been baby pink. His bruises were green-blue where they should have been non-existent. There was a deep cut in his lip, lips that had kissed mine before I had fled—moments before he had been used as bait. Anger fizzled as questions swarmed my mind like angry bees. With each new question, my anger increased.

Why was he getting involved in warrior business? Why had he been used as bait? Why hadn't he healed yet? What the hell was his wolf playing at? Why the hell was I getting angry about this?

Rue rumbled questioningly as I sifted through my emotions. She tilted her head, taking her own assessment of his injuries. That's when I felt the world shift. Rue's sedation from the pack run was starting to wear off. My current anger would be nothing compared to Rue's. I needed to get out of here now.

I pivoted on my heel and smacked straight into Simon. "*Oomph*, sorry."

"Hey," he said, giving me a sweet smile, "I was calling you. Didn't you hear me?"

"Sorry, what?" I asked distractedly. Then, I tried to focus on what he was saying. "No, sorry, Simon. I must have been daydreaming."

"About food?" He smirked.

I crinkled my face at him in confusion. "Why would you think that?"

"You were staring at that restaurant over there," he said with a chuckle.

"I think he's flirting with you again. Or having a seizure," Rue grunted. I looked back toward the bistro to cover my conversation with Rue.

"I think it was meant to be a joke."

"Really?" She coughed in disbelief.

"Oh...right. Um, I saw my friends," I answered lamely, turning back to him. His eyes were twinkling with humour. *It's definitely meant to be a joke.*

"Did you want to pop in to say hi before we head to work?" he asked, instantly taking the unwanted role of chaperone. Rue bristled at his chauvinistic assumption. Her eyes narrowed.

"Oh, are you working today?" I asked innocently, trying to ignore Rue, who was looking at Simon with obvious displeasure.

"Yeah, and I noted you were, too." A dash of pink highlighted his cheekbones. "I'm walking back to work now. You're welcome to join me."

Rue rolled her eyes. *"Can you please just agree to go on a date with this pathetic virgin sacrifice so that he can stop stalking your roster, just to see if he will get the opportunity to speak to you? It's so pathetic it's heartbreaking."* Then I realized that Simon was still talking.

"Sorry Simon, I'm really not with it today. I'm functioning on little to no sleep. I spent all last night driving home from my sisters, and I haven't had any coffee yet." I gave him a warm smile.

"Oh, I forgot about your monthly sister visit. How is she?"

"She's fine," I said a little more brusquely than I intended. I gave him another small smile to soften the aggression in my voice. "What were you saying?" I asked, trying to redirect him from any personal questions. The less I had to lie about, the better.

"Oh, yeah, um. My friend's band is playing tonight, and I was wondering if you wanted to come and see them. Blow off a little steam."

"Hi, Roman," Sean's voice stopped the rejection on the edge of my tongue.

I spun to find Sean and Vinny had approached. Quiet and stealthy. *Man, I'm really off my game!* Rue grumbled, and her eyes narrowed as she assessed Vinny up close. His hair was long enough now that he could loop it at the back of his head, but all that did was emphasize the damage on his face. He looked like he had been through the meat grinder. Then her angry demeanour pivoted and became maniacal glee. I did my best to ignore him and Rue and gave Sean my attention.

Sean returned my smile with one that did not meet his eyes, and I instantly raised my brows at him in a silent question. If I could have mind-linked him, I would have, but this was the best I could do. He answered my brows with a gentle nod. He was okay.

"Oh, man, what happened to you?" Simon asked, directing his question at Vinny.

The words "he flew off his motorcycle" were tumbling out of my mouth at the exact moment Vinny answered.

"I flew off my bike." There was a spark of amusement in Vinny's eyes as they swiftly met mine. They darted back to the human, and the small spark I had seen turned blank as he slowly examined Simon. It was a look I didn't like, only emphasized by the bruising and cuts over his face. I instinctually turned my body so that it was subtly in between Simon and Vinny.

"Ouch," Simon said empathetically. "Is the bike okay?"

Vinny didn't answer. He just looked at Simon like he was something on the bottom of his shoe. Sean's eyes danced between the two and then toward me before he took pity on Simon and broke the awkward tension with a friendly tone.

"You must work at the hospital with Roman. I'm Sean, and this is Vinny. We're friends of Roman's." It took a special kind of person who could ease tension and make people feel relaxed. Sean had the talent in spades, and Vinny had the opposite effect.

"Simon." He shook Sean's extended hand.

"We saw you two across the street and decided to say hello." I raised my eyebrows at Sean. Vinny's expression was so sour I knew it wasn't his idea to come over in the first place. Sean met my gaze, and his lips twitched as if he was trying not to smirk. "What do you do, Simon?"

"I'm a nurse." There was a scoffing noise from Vinny.

I glared at him. "What's wrong with being a nurse?" I demanded.

"It's fine...for chicks," he grunted without looking at me.

"It's fine for guys, too. In fact, I think it's sexy that Simon is a nurse. He's a great nurse! Not many men can pull it off because not many have a sensitive and nurturing side." *What the hell?* I glared at Rue, who had spoken with my voice and whose tail was twitching mischievously. *Was she trying to start a fight with Vinny? Was she trying to create drama?*

Simon's smile was answer enough. Simon now thought he stood a chance. Vinny's expression was blank—he couldn't care less. But that didn't stop Rue from looking ecstatically pleased with herself.

"I invited Roman to come and see my friend's band tonight," Simon said. He looked at Sean and then reluctantly at Vinny. "You two are more than welcome to come too."

"Roman doesn't look like she wants to go," Vinny stated frostily.

"What?" I demanded, bristling at his unwanted commentary. "What makes you think that? Of course I want to go." And with that, Simon's smile widened. *Crap.*

I ENTERED the venue with Simon and his enormous smile. It was like the cat had finally caught the canary.

"Drink?" he asked.

"Many," I replied with a small smile of my own. I was going to need them. He grinned and led me toward the bar, where he proceeded to chat with the bartender on duty. I looked around the place and realized it was more of a nightclub than the tavern-like bars and Irish pubs I was used to. Even when I had gone to nursing school, I rarely frequented the clubbing scene. It may have been good for Rue, but I never wanted to risk it.

At one end of the nightclub, under stage lights of red, blue and green, there was a band belting out a song that had me tapping my foot in rhythm. I hadn't even realized that my head and hips had started joining in until Simon returned with my drink.

"They're good, eh?"

"They aren't half bad," I agreed as the guitarist gave Simon an acknowledgement nod from the stage. "Your friend, I presume?"

"Yeah, that's Rick," Simon said as the lead singer opened up her vocal cords and reached an impressive wailing note before another singer started the chorus again. Rue was bobbing her head along with me.

Okay, they were fucking good.

"Want to dance?" I looked at Simon, surprised. Rue nodded enthusiastically, and suddenly, all I wanted to do was let loose.

CHAPTER 21
VINNY

WHAT THE HELL was I doing here? I had repeatedly asked myself as Sean and I were blasted with rock music in a quickly filling nightclub. I couldn't even explain why I had come here. I had told Sean that I thought it was good for him to get out. To have some fun while he waited for Laurel. I told him I needed a distraction from a still-sleeping Vali and the rogue locked up in the cells. He agreed eagerly at the time, but now that we were in the thick of the crowd, we realized neither of us really wanted to be there. We were two moping guys listening to a band that I had never heard of and mostly ignoring the advances of gorgeous women.

We had finally made our way to the bar, and I tried not to be obvious as I looked around for her. My blood froze before it started to heat and simmer. Roman was dancing with what's-his-face. I watched as his arm extended, and she was spun around. The childlike laughter on her face as she dipped and spun churned something primal within me. I didn't know what it was, and I didn't even have Vali to help sift through it.

I needed a drink. Her laughter followed me across the noisy nightclub as if the band was drowned out, and my ears were just listening for her and that weasel. Even Murdoch had to be better than him!

"You want to do an aconite shot?" I asked Sean.

Sean looked like he was going to object, but instead, he nodded solemnly. "Fuck yeah!"

Aconite was a flower that grew sporadically across the country. It was also known as wolfsbane throughout different packs and was considered one of the most dangerous things in the werewolf community regardless of what it was called. Legend says the plant only grew in areas where masses of werewolf blood had been spilled, and some werewolves went out of their way to find these areas to collect the flower as part of their arsenal. Many packs also went out of their way to ensure it didn't grow close to their borders. It grew around Kempthorne, and taking aconite shots was one of Kempthorne's unique specialties due to Kempthorne's other unique nuance.

It was impossible to pick a fight with another werewolf in Kempthorne due to an ancient pack law that impregnated the land. This area was much like Switzerland—neutral. There was not one pack who owned this region and hadn't done so since the night the alpha of the Kempthorne Pack, upon the brutal murder of his daughter, sealed a command with her blood. Then, the entire Kempthorne Pack disappeared, and to this day, no one could claim Kempthorne nor fight within its boundaries.

Seeing that no werewolf with ill intent could harm another werewolf here, Kempthorne was known to be a place for experimenting with these shots. I fully took advantage of this as my side effects from the plant were more severe than your average wolf. The first time, I lost Vali for a couple of weeks to the void behind the mental block. He came back crankier than usual. My sister also lost her wolf for a couple of weeks thanks to her scumbag ex-boyfriend force-feeding her aconite. After this happy coincidence, we both realized that it was a weakness we couldn't afford to have. Especially seeing that we could always be targeted for our blood status. So, my sister and I self-medicated regularly with aconite to build tolerance to it.

But it wasn't just Clementine and I who went to the extremes with the plant. I had even heard of packs sending their members here to desensitize themselves to its effects. One warrior from the Northwest Territories told me that he had visited Kempthorne regularly until he was given permission to grow the flower in his own backyard. Understandably, the alpha of that pack was concerned the plant would be used against his own pack by a sleeper-agent. Unfortunately, a year or so later, I had heard a rumour that the warrior had used it against his own alpha. I never braved going back to see for myself.

THE BARTENDER LINED up four shot glasses: two each. A tiny gram scale was used to measure out the dried and ground purple flowers before he deposited them in each glass and added the golden liquor. The liquid glowed in their vessels; a thick layer of purple was floating near the bottom. The bartender used a swizzle stick to mix it slightly before giving us a wolfish grin.

I hastily picked up the first shot and downed it fast, trying not to taste the sickly-sweet liquor. I coughed as the aconite burned my throat. Sean had done the same. I grinned at him, clinked the second shot against his and downed it just as quickly as the first. The glasses were pushed back toward the bartender, with only a few crushed petals remaining in the bottom.

It took mere minutes before I started to feel the effects of the alcohol. A small amount of aconite slightly weakened the wolf gene without rendering the werewolf debilitated. Too much aconite and a werewolf would be poisoned, but thankfully, due to us being in Kempthorne, there was no chance of Sean or me being poisoned—at least not by another werewolf.

Therefore, I wasn't worried about Vali being further hurt by it, even if he was still unconscious.

Sean and I were finally enjoying ourselves, keeping our paces at the bar to ensure we could take full advantage of our weakened, blissfully drunk state. I could see the entire dancefloor from my bar stool, and soon, it started to fill up with more people—werewolves and humans alike. Whoever this band was, I had to admit they were good.

Sean was wrangled onto the dance floor by some eager shewolf. There was a brief look of panic before he visibly relaxed into the beat of the music. His voice travelled over to me, but I was too drunk to comprehend what he was telling me. Instead, I gave him a cheery wave as I downed another drink quickly, enjoying the fact the wolfsbane had lowered my tolerance and I could get drunk.

Eventually, I hobbled out onto the dancefloor, swaying my body to the music, knowing somewhere deep down that I must look extremely uncoordinated, but giving zero fucks about it. It was all tits and ass out here, and if my nose hadn't been affected by the aconite, I surely would have smelled sweat and libido.

The only thing I could smell now was Roman. However, she was nowhere to be seen. I twisted and turned, trying to catch a glimpse of her ebony tresses through the crowd. Nothing. Frowning, I went to look for her, drunkenly following her scent down the corridor toward the restrooms.

She came out of the ladies' room and was startled when she saw me, almost tripping over her killer stilettos. I raked over her tight jeans and those blood-red fuck-me shoes—Satan's enforcer in heels. I took a further moment to appreciate her beauty; her soft, light-brown skin glowed, her brown eyes were shadowed by large, thick lashes, and her perfect heart-shaped mouth was slightly parted in shock, reminding me of how she tasted. Then, in a moment of madness, I pushed her through the restroom door and slammed her against the stall wall. She smelled deliciously sweet and edible. The scent of jasmine was overwhelming but complimented the sudden arousal I could smell pooling between her legs. Suddenly, I wanted a taste. I wanted it all.

I pressed myself against her, sniffing down her neck and growling deeply. "I want to taste you," I slurred. "And bite you and devour you with my tongue." Her heat pooled deeper, causing my cock to stand at attention, or at least try to. The denim of my jeans was making it a little difficult.

"No."

"No?" I queried as I licked the column of her neck.

"N-no. I hate you." She whimpered and shifted against me, triggering an erotic friction as my jeans rubbed against the head of my cock. "Or did you forget?"

"I hate you too. But hate and sex don't have to be mutually exclusive." I nibbled at her jaw, and she gave a small sexy pant. "In fact, hate sex is the best kind. It's hard and without mercy." Her eyes collided with mine, purple flashing around the warm brown. I clapped my hand on her jeans-covered ass, pawing it through the denim. "Come on, Roman, even your wolf is intrigued."

"My wolf wants to kill you." Her honeyed voice didn't hide her intrigue; the sweet warmth of her breath seeped toward my mouth.

"Just one taste," I grovelled. My hand yanked at her hair, causing her face to angle upwards, giving me perfect access to her venetian-red lips. She moaned, wiggled and writhed as my lips brushed the corner of her mouth. "Say yes, Roman."

It seemed an age before she reluctantly agreed. "One kiss."

"One kiss?" I arched an eyebrow. "I better make it a good one then." I gave her a crooked smile and started to undo the button on her jeans.

CHAPTER 22
ROMAN

This was madness. I should tell him to stop. I didn't want him to touch me. *Oh, but it feels so good.* His hand was tugging my hair, on the cusp of being painful. If I moved, it would hurt, and the thought of that made this hotter somehow. My core started to tingle and heat, and I could scent my body betraying me. Mixed messages were zinging around my body. This was the man I hated. The man who I rejected. It shouldn't matter that he was a remarkable kisser, that I had been obsessing over our last kiss. It shouldn't matter that he was pure, walking sex. What should matter was my ability to be in control here. What should matter was my ability to say no. But my body didn't want to cooperate.

His teeth, gently scraped my jaw, flushing my entire body with heat. How was something so simple, so erotic? I squirmed slightly, feeling the painful tug in my hair, testing me. I stopped squirming and looked at him. His eyes were cloudy with alcohol. There was no way he would remember this. I could give into this desire, fuck him in this stall, and he wouldn't even remember. I could have disgusting, dirty, hate sex with my arch nemesis, and he would wake up with a killer hangover as further punishment. It was a win-win.

My body was humming for his, and I whimpered. I looked

back at Rue and saw that she, too, was enjoying this sensation a little too much. I went to her in the hope that she would be my voice of reason. Instead, she was a bitch in heat. The tone of his voice melted my last bit of resolve.

"One kiss." I breathed, trying my hardest to stay in control. If I could limit it to kissing, maybe I could still walk away with some dignity.

"One kiss." His voice was gravelly, and that crooked smile made my already thundering heart quiver and skip a beat. "I better make it a good one then." My breath caught as he started to undo the button on my jeans.

"What the—"

"Shh." He placed a drunken finger against my lips. I parted them softly, darting my tongue out to lick the pad of his finger before puckering and sucking gently on it. His eyes widened, and the silver flashed. "Those fucking lips," he whispered, giving me a wicked grin. "As much as those lips are my undoing, I don't want to waste my one kiss on them. I need to taste you and feel you squirm out of control."

He lowered himself to his knees, slipping off each of my stilettos with a soft thud. His hands moved to the waistband of my jeans, tugging them and my thong down in one fluid motion. After shucking them off my ankle, he gave me a predatory smirk and slid my shoes back on like I was some dark, depraved Cinderella. His fingers rubbed along my calf, lingering as his gaze roved upward with a hunger that made my breath hitch. Then, his hands followed, tracing the path his eyes had already claimed.

Tingles erupted in their wake. I bit my lip as he ran a hand on the inside of my thigh, smiling coyly. If he was expecting me to orgasm, he was in for a rude awakening. No one had ever made me come this way. I needed penetration. I needed deep, thick rubbing. I grinned wickedly, thinking about how he was wasting his one kiss. I grinned, knowing that this would reinforce that this was a terrible idea—

Wait, this is a terrible idea!

I had sobered in the thought and was about to call it off when his tongue ran the inside of my leg, following where his hand had just travelled. Sparks jolted, and I twitched.

"Stay still," he ordered huskily, groping my bare ass cheeks. His tongue flickered the inseam of my groin, and I jerked again. He chuckled softly, then made a tsking noise. "Stay still." He moved his teeth over the inseam, and I tried my hardest to do as he ordered. Teeth, tongue and lips were slowly inching closer to my clit. I shuddered and moved again. A harsh nip followed.

"Ouch!" But the feeling was soothed with a kiss and a lick.

"No moving," he reminded me. I frowned at him, but it was short-lived as his tongue proceeded to travel the wetness between my legs before circling up around my clit.

I shivered into him as he forced my legs open by placing one over his shoulder. His mouth sucked my folds, and his tongue curled my clit before his teeth came out once more. It made me jump again, but this time, he didn't bite down harder. Instead, he sucked, kissed and gently teased my clit over and over. His tongue mapped my folds as my pussy started to flutter in response. *Oh my...* I moaned and thrust myself toward him. A guttural sound came from Vinny as he dove his tongue inside, devouring me. His tongue flickered fast as he lapped at my tight entrance. I whimpered and mewed, the pressure building. My body hummed; sparks and tingles were racing everywhere. Lick, suck, lick, suck. I focused on the incredible pressure within my core as my fingers gripped his hair. I tugged hard. He grunted in pleasure and kept up his assault.

"I'm going to come." I gasped. "Keep going."

He kept grinding his mouth and tongue into my pussy, holding me tight as he listened to my breathless commands. I felt myself spiralling as his mouth sealed and sucked harder. The swells and waves of my climax came fast. I moaned loudly, not caring that we were in a public restroom and that, at any moment, someone could walk in and bear witness to this depravity. His hot lips captured my juices as he drank like a man parched. The final wave ensued, and he licked up the last remaining drop. His tongue curved the map he had made, and then he sealed it all with a gentle peck.

"Two-minute head start," I said softly, my brain still fogged. His head snapped up, and I noted his beard was glistening with my essence. Red stained my cheeks at the realization that he had done that. *Holy crap.* My pussy convulsed, and I wanted more. I wanted the bulge that was threatening to tear his pants in two. I wanted to be ripped apart and sewn back together. But I couldn't have more. This needed to end. Now. I picked up my jeans from the floor.

"Sorry?" He looked confused.

"Get up and get out." I waved toward the exit as I shuffled away from the stall wall and into the cubicle itself. I started to tidy myself up with the toilet paper, listening for the sounds of him leaving. I could hear his breathing, short and laboured, then long and deep, as if he was trying to calm himself. Seconds later, the restroom door closed with a soft thud.

After I pulled my jeans on, I headed to the sink and started washing my hands, trying to calm myself before I went back into the bar. I looked in the mirror; my face was flushed with a post-orgasm glow, my eyes were bright, and the lilac swirled the brown. I looked back at Rue, and she gave me a smarmy, satisfied grin in return.

After putting cold water on my cheeks, knowing that the moment I entered the bar, every werewolf in the bar would smell what I did. Thankfully, I didn't know any werewolves here, so none of them would care about my dirty little rendezvous in the toilet.

I returned to Simon on the dancefloor, glad that he was human and couldn't smell me or the sin I had just committed. I blushed again, trying to get the image out of my mind, trying to dampen the arousal that threatened each time I thought of how he had cornered me in the restroom.

My gladness was short-lived when I realized I had been cornered by a very drunk Sean. I waited for the nostril flare and the questioning look in his eyes, but Sean said nothing. Instead, he directed Simon and me to the bar and lined up the tequila. After the second shot, Sean and Simon acted like they were the best brothers in the whole world.

I slowly looked around the bar, trying to locate Vinny. He was nowhere to be seen. My heart lurched, and I frowned at Rue. Was I disappointed that I couldn't find him in the bar? Really? How pathetic. I chastised myself.

I shot my tequila back, barely feeling the burn before I snatched Simon's shot glass from his hand, seconds before it reached his mouth and downed the disgusting liquor within. I coughed and gave him a small smile.

"That a girl!" he cheered and gestured to the bartender for another refill, then told the bartender to leave the bottle and directed Sean and me to a booth on the edge of the dance floor.

The bottle was half empty thanks to two werewolves who were downing the shots. Simon was going to have a hell of a hangover in the morning but, thankfully, was too drunk to question the amount of liquor being consumed. Simon wasn't the only one who was going to have a hangover. I kept looking around the floor for Vinny. Surely, he hadn't left the bar and abandoned Sean in a drunken stupor. He wouldn't do that, would he? Actually, that sounded exactly like something he would do.

"You want to tell me why you smell like Vinny?" Sean whispered drunkenly in my ear.

"I don't know what you're talking about," I hissed back.

"My nose might be all screwy because of aconite, but I swear you smell like Vinny."

"Honestly, you're so drunk I wouldn't trust any of your senses right now." I laughed a bubbly laugh. "Where is Vinny anyway? I hope he didn't abandon you like this!"

"Nah, he's just getting his dick wet."

"What?" I asked. Rue's ears and tail twitched.

"Or at least he is trying to," Sean slurred as he pointed to a dark area of the room. "I think it's a swing and a miss." Sean's eyes clouded over slightly, and he chuckled. "Or maybe not."

Sean gave Vinny a cheery wave as Vinny wrapped his arms around a small blonde girl and directed her toward the exit. The petite blonde girl who I recognized as the human who brought him into the hospital. Hot green jealousy coated my tongue.

Asshole.

Rue snarled menacingly as I grabbed the tequila bottle and poured myself another shot, trying to subdue her before she went feral and chased them out of the club.

CHAPTER 23
VINNY

I was feasting on the most glorious pussy I had ever tasted against a toilet stall in a nightclub. One hot red heel over my shoulder only added to the kink. Hell and heaven collided at the sound of her orgasm, and the fantasy was sealed.

Anger riveted me as she had asked me to leave seconds after she had squirted her juices right onto my tongue, mouth, and chin. It was literally one fucking kiss! I was so sure once she experienced my *sex*pertise that, she was going to cave and allow me more than one fucking kiss.

I wanted more than one kiss the second her mouth grazed my finger. Her tongue sent zings throughout my body, straight down to my cock. When she gently encased my finger within her mouth, Vali's eyes snapped open, but I couldn't focus on that. All I could focus on was the electricity humming around my body, her red puckered lips, her glorious round tits beneath her tight t-shirt and that intoxicating scent that was emitting from between her legs. Her scent broke through my weakened nostrils as though it was for my nose only.

No, there was no way I was going to settle for one kiss. There was no way that would be all she wanted.

My heart thundered in my chest as she writhed under my

tongue, her scent and heady nectar making me crazy. My balls tightened at the sound of her orgasm. I hadn't pegged Roman for a screamer, but holy fuck, her notes almost made me ruin my pants.

Then, she dismissed me without even an offer to return the favour. The high I should have been riding was sluiced with her crisp words. Any warmth I had felt during our tryst instantly turned to ice. My mouth opened and shut a few times as she hid herself in the toilet stall. I clenched my hands tightly as I weighed my options. Part of me wanted to bust down the door and have it out with her. Shouting at her would make me feel so much better, especially if it led to hot, angry sex. My painfully hard cock twitched at the thought.

The other part of me knew that I should take the win and cut my losses. This was the Ice Queen herself, the reincarnated Caligula of Rome. She was never going to change. She was a bitch, and I hated her with every cell of my body, so I really shouldn't give a fuck. It shouldn't surprise me that she'd acted this way.

Vali grumbled in reluctant agreement. He was too injured to have it out with her, and we both knew that taking on her wolf right now would be suicide. As much as I wanted to have her sinful body riding my cock against the wall of the cubicle, it wasn't going to happen.

After a few deep breaths, I left the restroom and stomped over to the U-shaped bar, sitting as far away and out of sight as I could. I ordered a bourbon and downed the double before it had a chance to settle in the glass. I raised my hand to order another.

"I see your drink choice hasn't changed." I pivoted on my heel to find a tiny, busty blonde smiling up at me. I looked blankly at her, trying to decipher her meaning. "Camille," she reminded me as if I had forgotten her name.

"I know, I remember. How have you been?"

"Good. Surprised to see you here."

"Why's that?"

"Thought you said you weren't sticking around." I ordered another round, indicating to the bartender to get Camille one too. I had said that when she had asked me for my number.

"I'm not. The bike is just taking longer to fix than I anticipated." I handed her the glass of bourbon. "That's how I got these bruises. Didn't have my helmet on when I tried it out and smashed straight into a tree. Thankfully, I wasn't going fast," I lied. She tilted her head as if trying to find a hole in my story. If she did find a hole, she didn't say anything. I didn't know if I still looked like I had been through a garbage compactor or not, but Vali had already started trying to heal my face.

I sensed when Roman had re-entered the bar, but I refused to acknowledge her in any way, giving all my attention to Camille. Camille, who was the complete opposite of Roman. I found myself comparing the women as she excitedly told me about her classes and the fact that she was out clubbing with some friends. I let the stories wash over as she sipped on the bourbon, and I continued to note the differences between her and Roman.

Roman was far superior to Camille in every way, from the dark hair and heart-shaped mouth to her big brown eyes, that often looked at me in contempt. Camille, however, was eager and available, and I needed something to soothe the frosty feeling within my chest. The bourbon wasn't cutting it.

"You want to get out of here?" I asked Camille with a crooked smile. Her pink lips twitched, and she directed me toward the exit. On the way out, I allowed myself one glance at Roman and noticed she was sitting next to Sean, having a hushed conversation while her weasel of a friend was talking to one of the band members.

"Don't wait up, Sean," I chuckled down the mind-link. Then, I took Camille by the waist and made my way to her residence hall.

Her room was just as cramped as I remembered it. The desk was covered in textbooks and dirty coffee cups. Her laptop was thrown on top of the haphazard mess. Her bed was covered in several dresses strewn about, which told me that she hadn't been able to decide what to wear earlier.

Her lips brushed mine. I returned her kiss with drunken vigour, then pulled away just as fast. Her lips felt wrong beneath mine. I gave her a small smile and tried again. Her tongue entered my mouth, reminding me of a serpent. I pulled away again. I had kissed this girl before. Why was it suddenly such a disaster?

Images of heart-shaped lips and a bubbly laugh flashed forward from Vali. I returned to kissing Camille for a few more minutes. I encased her face with my hands and kissed her like my life depended on it. She moaned softly. And usually, the sound would arouse me, but my cock remained flaccid. Damn it, why did Roman have to ruin this for me too?

I kissed Camille harder and started to unbutton her dress, determined to see this through. I was kissing Camille but imagining Roman's lips. It was Roman's body curving into mine. I could feel Roman's heartbeat. It was Roman's scent, and I could smell it—but it was wrong—the scent was human. The scent wasn't Roman. These tits weren't Roman's, and these lips were flat and lifeless in comparison to hers. This kiss was mediocre. I pulled away again.

"I can't do this," I mumbled my apology.

"You can't do this?" she repeated in a voice that wasn't Roman's.

"Sorry, no." I paused awkwardly. "I'm going to go."

I made it to the edge of the forest and looked back at Vali, who seemed content with my decision to leave Camille. I wanted to run, but Vali was too injured to shift and run. I could go back to Sean, but then I would have to admit that I flaked out with Camille. I didn't know if my pride could take that hit. I entered the trees on foot, determined to walk back to Blackfern Valley. Walking eighty-odd kilometres through the bush, drunkenly and on human feet, seemed like a great idea.

I forgot how tiring it was walking in human form, and soon I started to sober. Vali assured me that I was heading in the right direction and just to keep moving. Hours passed as I roamed around trees and sloshed through small creeks, bending down and drinking occasionally.

"We are almost home," Vali said. I knew he was lying, but I allowed his words to give me encouragement. It was another hour before I came across a well-trodden path. I was exhausted. I was practically falling asleep on my feet, but I didn't stop. I followed the path for a while. It eventually led me to a house. It was a large log cabin in the middle of nowhere. And the porch was where I finally collapsed from exhaustion and closed my eyes, dreaming of a jasmine fragrance.

CHAPTER 24
VINNY

I woke up on a couch and instantly scanned my surroundings. The open-planned living area was minimalistic in décor with a few pieces of white Ikea furniture and a floor rug. There was a large pot plant by the front door, which looked as though it was on its last leg. There was no TV. In the space where a TV should go, there was a large bookshelf. The bookshelf was jam-packed with pristine novels, mostly thriller and fantasy, but that wasn't what caught my attention. Nursing textbooks were shoved in among the fiction.

Nursing books, and the place reeked of jasmine. Fuck. Somehow, I had managed to find my way to Roman's house. I groaned softly and then looked around the room again, curiosity getting the better of me. I was behind enemy lines.

I got a glass from the kitchen cupboard and downed some water before refilling it and watering her sorry excuse for a houseplant. The irony that this she-wolf's career was based on keeping people alive and healthy, yet she was killing her houseplant wasn't lost on me.

I spied around her living room again, noting how empty it was. Instead of being cozy, her home was rigid in appeal; her house was a show home, devoid of colour and personality.

Which was opposite to the bright and bubbly girl everyone knew and loved. Even the couch I had slept on was hard and unyielding. It was like she was never here. Was it because she was always frequenting beds that were not hers? The ghost of her orgasm ricocheted through my memory. Did she squirm and come like that for other wolves? Did their sheets stink of jasmine and her inner essence? Vali growled territorially, and I mirrored the sentiment.

I heard her stir in her bedroom. I knew that I should just walk out the door and avoid the awkward and hostile encounter that was about to happen. My feet started moving. Not toward her front door but down the hallway toward her.

She came out of her bedroom firm and rigid, with a hateful glare in her eyes. "What are you doing?"

Shit. What was I doing? "Um. Bathroom?"

"Oh." She flushed a gentle pink and pointed to a door I just walked past. I excused myself into the bathroom and breathed deeply, trying to ignore the fact that she was wearing tiny shorts and a camisole with no bra. She had to be wearing that to torture me.

The bathroom was just as empty as the rest of the house. I quickly peed and washed my hands. Curiosity got the better of me again. There was nothing personal in this bathroom. I wasn't expecting to see perfumes or body lotions covering her basin as heavy fragrances irritate werewolf noses, but I was expecting something. I opened the cabinet drawer, and inside was a toothbrush, toothpaste and a first aid kit. I opened her cupboard and found an extra toilet roll and spare soap. There was nothing else. No cosmetics, no silly eye masks or bottles of nail polish. No personality.

Vali shrugged in my head, and I flicked the light switch as I left the room.

"If you're after breakfast, I'm sorry to disappoint." Her voice was waspish as I walked down the hallway.

"Why? Are your cupboards as bare as the rest of your

house?" I retorted as I stalked into the kitchen. I tried to ignore the way her midriff stretched as she tied up her hair on top of her head.

"Been snooping?" She snorted as she opened a cupboard and pulled out a jar of instant coffee. It appeared to be the only thing in there.

"Behind enemy lines," I said with an uncaring shrug.

"My sister Arizona has just been here." I gave her an odd look. "Arizona pops in semi-regularly to ensure that I have at least one balanced meal and that I'm not living off tuna and ketchup, and she often does a quick clean while she's here. I blame her maternal instinct."

She made herself a coffee without offering me one. A clear dismissal—not an invitation to stay—so I sat down at one of the stools at her breakfast bar. She glowered, her eyes momentarily flashing purple. Vali chuckled, enjoying her quiet torment.

"What could she possibly have to clean? There's nothing here." She ignored me and changed the topic.

"So, you want to explain to me why you were on my porch in the middle of the night?"

"Went for a walk," I said indifferently. If she could change the subject, so could I. "You play that human weasel like a fucking harp, you know that, right?" Her head snapped up from the coffee cup she was focusing hard on. Rage flashed through her eyes.

Jackpot!

"I don't play anything with Simon. He's a work colleague, that's it."

"He seems a bit simple-minded."

"That's rich coming from you." She raised her perfectly sculpted eyebrows at me, refusing to take the bait.

"How long have you been fucking him? Does *Murdick* know?"

She chuckled sourly. "One, Murdoch is just great to have

around when I get an itch. He gets no say in my life. Two, as much as Rue would love to fuck around with Simon, she knows he's off limits."

"So, why do you lead him on?"

"How do I lead him on?"

"You know how. You bat your long eyelashes, flash your teeth, give him a smile—"

"What?" Her voice was stony, but all that did was encourage me.

"Then you feed him some bullshit about not dating or not being interested."

"Wow. You seem to have some experience in this. You sound like you've been burned. Did your night not end with your inch long in someone's garage-sized pussy. Sorry about that."

Vali chuckled a deep, wolfy chuckle. He was amused. I glared at him, still annoyed that I couldn't seal the deal with Camille, that Roman's orgasm had ruined it for me. My cock stirred, and I tried not to stare at her nipples that were poking through her camisole. I tried not to imagine slipping them into my mouth and rolling them between my teeth. I moved my eyes back to her face. My cock jerked as I watched her pouty mouth blowing gently on the steam swirling from her mug.

"You know," she continued, taunting me as she blew softly. "If I didn't know any better, I'd say that you were jealous. You're reaching great heights with your stereotypical moronic behaviour."

"What the fuck are you talking about?" I grunted, trying to clear my thoughts.

"Rue was bored, and you stepped into her game like an eager contestant. She wanted a reaction, and she got one. All she had to do was plant a seed and let your Neanderthal brain take over. That's the reason you cornered me in the toilet at the club. You couldn't stand the idea of Simon going home with me." Anger simmered.

I started this hostile banter, and now I was losing. *Simple*

Simon didn't go home with you." I scoffed. "I don't smell human here."

"No, and I don't smell cheap slut on you," she countered. Her eyes flashed again.

"You think I'm jealous? You're jealous!" I laughed.

"No, I'm really not."

"If you wanted me to take you home, you shouldn't have kicked me out of the restroom."

"Sure, because home is where we would have ended up. You would have fucked me against the cubicle, dirty and rough. No bedsheets needed." My cock saluted to attention at her speech, restricted only by my pants.

"Are you sure Rue was baiting me?" I asked as I continued to watch her lips like a horny fifteen-year-old. I needed to get a grip! Or I needed to fuck her out of my system. "It sounds like *your* Neanderthal brain has also taken over. She didn't just string up a helpless human into a web of werewolf fuckery. She didn't just get me. She got you, too. And I bet she's watching this play out like a soap opera." A purple flash. I leaned across the kitchen counter, my pants now painfully tight against my cock. "You know there are other ways to get through boredom, little wolf."

"Like what?" Roman's voice directed straight into my cock again.

"Lots of things. Riding motorcycles, getting into barfights." I smiled crookedly at her. "Fucking your arch nemesis repeatedly until you see stars."

Her eyes widened. "W-what?"

"Come on, Roman. Let me show you what this *inch* can do."

My phone vibrated in my pocket. "Hold that thought." I looked at the caller ID. "I've got to go. Think about it, Roman. No strings. Just dirty, untamed sex." I gave her a wink and answered my phone. "On my way. Be there soon."

Vali stretched in the back of my mind. I could feel how much better he felt. I stretched, too. I felt amazing, considering the fact my balls were turning a pitiful shade of blue. I was pissed drunk last night, and not to mention, I was beaten up within an inch of my life only a few days ago. It felt as though it had never happened. I removed my clothes, hoping she was watching but not daring to look back as I shifted and disappeared into the trees. I let out a cheeky howl as I turned in the direction of Blackfern Valley.

CHAPTER 25
ROMAN

I PADDED through the dark house toward the kitchen. I opened the fridge door, allowing the bright glow to illuminate the kitchen. I pulled out a bottle of milk and fumbled around for a glass in the cupboard. I had been home for hours, leaving shortly after Vinny did, dropping Sean back at his house in Blackfern Valley before driving myself back home. Nothing was out of the ordinary, but I was agitated and couldn't sleep. I had spent the last hour tossing and turning, and anytime my body would relax into slumber, I jolted myself awake. I blamed Rue the first half-dozen times, but she was happily snoring away without a care in the world.

I heated the milk, hoping it would help me fall into slumber and scrunched my nose as I gulped it down. I placed the glass in the dishwasher before making my way back to bed for another attempt to get some sleep when an icy peppermint wafted to my nose.

What the?

I followed the scent to find a man sleeping on my porch—a gorgeous blond man. Vinny. How the hell had he gotten here? Rue grumbled herself awake as I opened the door and made my way toward him. He was out cold. I checked his pulse and gave him a gentle shake.

"Vinny." There was no response.

"Stupid fucker has passed out drunk on our front doorstep," Rue muttered with a bored yawn.

"No, he doesn't smell drunk. I think he's just exhausted. By the looks of his clothes, I would say he was walking through the bush."

"What an idiot." I couldn't disagree with her. I gave him another shake. *"What are you doing? Just leave him there."*

"I'm going to put him on the couch. It will be a little more comfortable than the porch."

"Fuck him." I ignored her. I managed to rouse Vinny a tiny amount.

"Come on, Vincent, let's go inside."

"You've ruined me," he murmured sleepily as he linked his arm over my shoulder and stumbled inside. I deposited him unceremoniously on the couch, and a loud snore told me he had fallen asleep again.

I stared at him for a few moments, watching him breathe. His face contorted as he snored and then softened as he relaxed into a deep slumber. His face had healed with fine pink scar tissue, and the bruising had disappeared entirely. His wolf had finally healed him. A pressure eased in my chest. I reached out and gently stroked the pink lines, knowing that they would eventually disappear, too. My fingers trickled down into his full beard, which was surprisingly both soft and scratchy under my fingertips.

A small sigh escaped him, and the room was filled with a sweet aroma. A sweet aroma that made my mouth tingle. I stared at his mouth for the longest time, remembering his sweet kisses and what he had done to me in the restroom earlier. My core started to heat. Sharp pain erupted around my prickling gums, and I licked them to feel my teeth had retreated and sharp canines were now pressing against my tongue.

Then I remembered how he'd gone home with the blonde.

Brash, hot anger burst out of nowhere. I stomped off quickly and slammed my bedroom door. Rue nodded in agreement, growling in the back of her throat. I threw myself on the bed and chucked the pillow over my head. After many deep breaths, my body calmed enough that I finally felt the pull of slumber.

I WOKE WITH A START, hearing noises in my house—the sound of a cupboard door and the gentle trickle of water. I stared at my ceiling and waited for him to leave. A few more minutes passed, and I still hadn't heard the front door. Slowly, I made my way out of bed and to the bedroom door, opening it ajar and peered out. He was coming down the hallway. Visions of him throwing me on my bed had me exiting my room quickly. There was no way I was going to get cornered again.

I bristled as I met him in the hallway. This was my territory, and I was ready to defend it. He excused himself to the bathroom, and I breathed a sigh of relief. My entire body was wound up as I listened out for him. The toilet flushed, and then there were the soft sounds of drawers and cupboards opening and shutting. Was he snooping? Rue snarled softly.

I wanted him to leave as soon as he came out, but instead, he sat himself down at my breakfast bar. Rue grumbled at his behaviour, but as soon as the heated conversation started, she altered her position and was thoroughly entertained.

This had to be the longest conversation I had with Vinny since he had arrived. Actually, it was the longest conversation we have ever had. Our previous discussions had always ended in one of us walking away angrily. We could never be civil. Even with our mutual friends acting as a buffer, we always found a way to combust around each other.

I was sure I was going to burn under the looks he was giving me now. The look had changed from one of pure loathing to one of pure possessive wanting. I found myself enjoying the look and the banter, bouncing quips back and forth. Neither of us was willing to take the bait and lose the round. As quick as the banter started, it was over, and he was out of my hair again.

The house was quiet. Too quiet. Vinny's earlier proposition lingered in the air, echoing around me as I tried to find something to eat in hopes of distracting myself. But all I could think about was him. That panty-dropping crooked grin made my heart do somersaults, and the idea of hate-fucking him to oblivion made my stomach flutter. Could I really sleep with him? Did a five-minute, somewhat civil conversation change anything? He was still an arrogant asshole. He had no remorse for hurting my sister. He hadn't even asked after her. How could I lower myself to that level? How could I sleep with someone like that? What would Indiana say? Would she judge me?

It was three more days of self-inflicted torture before I saw Vinny again. My wolf, who was supposed to protect and guide me, was cackling with glee at my torment the entire time. I thought she might have at least tried to stop me as I made my intention known, but she was watching it unfold with morbid fascination, like a car crash she couldn't look away from.

I stalked him to his house, where he was polishing his motorcycle. I knew nothing about motorcycles, but the way he looked at them was almost endearing. The way his hands rubbed over the curves of the bike instantly made me want his hands to do something similar to my body. Nerves fluttered. But after three days of sex dreams, regardless of whether I was awake or asleep, I was feeling desperate. I could have called Murdoch, but I didn't want him. As ashamed as I was to admit it, I wanted Vinny.

He didn't even look at me as I walked up the driveway. I saw his nose twitch, so I knew he was aware of me, but he continued to look at his bike. I scanned my eyes over him again. His body was fully healed and almost glowing under the early morning sun. He looked more godlike than ever, and I was about to worship at his feet.

Prick.

"I was thinking about your offer." His eyebrow rose, interest piqued, and a smarmy smile twisted on his lips. He had won. He knew it. Asshole. I changed my mind at the last second. "Teach me to ride a motorbike."

His smarmy smile morphed into a surprisingly sexy grin before he disappeared into the house without saying a word. I stood there dumbfounded for a few seconds, wondering if I was meant to follow. I waited for a bit longer, and a bit longer, my building anxiety finally making Rue start to bristle.

He returned and thrust a helmet at me, his eyes twinkling. Instincts told me he was up to something.

"Let's go." He straddled the bike and flicked his head in a come gesture. A challenge if I ever saw one. I took a deep breath, clenching my fists and ultimately refusing to back down.

I climbed onto the back of his bike and wrapped my arms around him with the strength of a limpet. He drove us out of Blackfern Valley. He didn't turn toward Kempthorne but drove us the opposite way for about an hour before he turned off onto a dirt road. He slowed down a little as he approached a parking lot. I looked around the secluded lot and saw the blue and white sign of a hiking trail ahead. He killed the bike, and I quickly untangled myself from his solid body, hastily getting off the death trap. He kicked down the stand, got off and looked at me expectantly. Anxiety fizzed and bubbled through my bloodstream. Could I do this? I didn't even know how to ride a bicycle.

"I thought you wanted to learn how to do this?" he grumbled as I looked at the bike with apprehension.

"I do."

"Then what are you waiting for, get on the bike." I continued to stare at the motorcycle. "You're scared," he surmised.

"No," I denied quickly, shaking my head. "Well, maybe. But do you know how dangerous these things are? They're death traps. You could get seriously injured. There's nothing to stop you from breaking your neck. No airbags, not even a metal box to protect you—" I stopped rambling when I realized he was bending over and clutching his stomach in boyish laughter. "What's so funny?"

"You think you're going to get hurt? Roman, you're a werewolf. You have superhuman reflexes and enhanced healing abilities—"

"That doesn't make me invincible," I snapped as Rue was also laughing in my head. Vinny's eyes were sparking with mirth as he tried to contain his. I glared at him. "Fine. Let's do this!"

CHAPTER 26
ROMAN

"Kill switch." I flicked the switch. "Clutch in." I squeezed the clutch. "Find neutral." I kicked the small pedal upwards half a click.

Vinny was voicing random commands at me. The stand was still down, and the motorcycle was switched off as I practiced switching up and down gears, pressing my brake pedal, and gently twisting the throttle. I felt like a tiny idiot balancing on this monstrous hunk of metal.

"Okay, I think you're ready to take it around the parking lot." He nodded. "Throttle nice and easy, and remember—both brakes, but go light on the front."

I frowned, tapping the front brake lever. "What's the point of having a front brake if you don't use it?"

"I didn't say don't use it. I said don't yank it like you're trying to stop a runaway train." He gave me a wolfish grin. "You've got a six-hundred-pound bike under your sweet ass, and that brake's powerful. One wrong move, and you'll be flying over the handlebars."

"Werewolf healing, remember?" I shot back, smirking.

"Oh, I don't care about you. I care about my bike." I gaped at him, and he grinned maliciously. My eyes narrowed. *Asshole.*

"Alright make sure you're in neutral and then kick the stand." I pulled in the clutch and put the bike into neutral before kicking the stand away. The bike instantly felt heavier. I gave him a small smile as my finger pressed the starter button, and the motorcycle roared to life. Rue purred along with the vibrations. He said nothing. There were no further commands. He just waited.

I kicked the motorcycle into first gear and felt the pull. I released the clutch slowly. I rumbled down the parking lot, gently turning the motorcycle and trying not to tip it over. This was harder than it looked. I stomped on the brake pedal before placing one foot on the dirt. Shit. The bike sputtered and died—double shit.

I took a deep breath and placed the motorcycle back into neutral before hitting the switch. The bike rumbled again. I took each step carefully, and before long, I circled the parking lot like a professional—driving in third gear and only going thirty kilometres an hour.

"Alright, Evel Knievel," Vinny said as I came to a stop in front of him, grinning from ear to ear. I was proud that I hadn't toppled or stalled the motorcycle when I stopped. "Ready to open her up on the road?" Rue grinned and wagged her tail excitedly. She wanted to see what I could do.

I startled as Vinny slid onto the motorcycle behind me. He rested his hand softly above my hip and leaned into my ear. His breath tickled, and icy peppermint encased me. I tried to ignore the flip in my stomach. "Just listen to the bike. And remember, no front brake!"

I eased the motorcycle out of the parking lot and onto the road, travelling on the shoulder and at a snail's pace, constantly looking in my mirrors for someone coming. Rue started to make loud fake snoring noises in my head, and I was shocked when I heard it echoing in my ear. I craned my neck backward, then refocused on the road as the motorcycle wobbled.

"What?" I growled, squeezing the handles in irritation.

"Boring. Come on, Roman, give it a bit of gas. Jerk that throttle like you jerk Simon."

What the fuck? Rage simmered, and I twisted the throttle toward me. The motorcycle jerked, but somehow Vinny kept it upright and streamlined. His hands were hot on my hips as he leaned into me slightly. My body curved with the bike as we went around a slight bend in the road.

Rue grinned excitedly as the road became wider, and I ventured into the right-hand lane. I opened the throttle, and before I knew it, I was at top speed, zooming down the road. Rue howled in excitement in my head as trees whipped past. The motorcycle wobbled but stayed upright.

"Go faster!" Rue hollered. I laughed and accelerated. Vinny's arms tightened around my waist, but he didn't say anything. All I could hear was the rumble of the engine and the howling excitement in my head. No wonder he loved this so much.

My mind, which had been pinging around like a pinball machine for days, was finally at peace as I rode. All I could focus on was the warm body at my back, his scent wafting up my nose, the rumble of the bike and the fact that Rue seemed to be mellowing out after the initial excitement. The air was brisk and refreshing against my face. I was sure the open-faced helmet he had provided was done to mock me, but even if that had been the case, the reality was that I was enjoying the ice-cold air slapping me, and for the first time in a long time, I started to enjoy the fall colours in the trees and the fact winter was on its way.

THIRTY MINUTES LATER, he squeezed my side and pointed to a pull-over bay. I nodded and started to slow down. The bike wobbled as I pulled into the rest stop, and then the bike sputtered and died. I frowned. How had it stalled? Vinny got off and kicked the stand down in the process. He raised his visor, and his piercing green eyes were full of humour.

"How was that?" he asked as he helped me off the bike. My legs felt like Jell-O. I couldn't answer him, but I was sure my grin spoke volumes.

He removed his helmet and placed it on the bike seat, then with featherlight fingers, he removed the bucket from my head. Tingles resonated from where his fingers had brushed my skin. He smirked at my hair and gave it a quick swipe with his fingertips. I batted his hands away, scowling as I tried to fix my own hair.

"What did you think?" he pressed again, watching me with curiosity. I stopped fiddling with my hair and met his curious gaze head-on.

"Better than sex," I deadpanned.

His eyebrow quirked upwards. "Better than sex?" I nodded. "You must not be doing it right."

"I can guarantee you I am."

"Your sex comes with a money-back guarantee?"

Rue growled low. My fist reached out and thumped him hard on the arm. He didn't even flinch. "I am not a prostitute! I don't sell my body for sex."

"What's wrong with selling your body for sex?"

"Just because that's the only way you can get sex doesn't mean the rest of us have to stoop that low."

"Trust me, sweetheart, with you sleeping with *Murdick* and that weasel Simon, you have stooped that low. The bar is parallel." Purple flashed in my eyes as Rue's hackles rose. I pivoted on my heel and stomped away. "Where are you going?" I didn't answer. He called my name twice. I still didn't answer. I heard his footsteps catching up behind me. "Learn to take a joke, Roman. Fuck."

I turned and glared at him. "If we are going to do this, Simon is off limits," I snarled. My brows were furrowed, and my arms were crossed over my chest. Purple swirled with the added agitation of my wolf.

"Do what?" He looked momentarily confused, and then a light sparked in the silver of his eyes.

"Simon is off limits," I repeated to his comprehension.

"Simon is off limits." His voice was gravelly. "For you as well. Include Murdoch in that. I won't be sharing. For as long as this lasts—you're mine."

His possessive tone sparked something deep inside. Usually, a domineering fuck-buddy would be a turn-off, and I would instantly walk away. But this time, I walked toward him. This time, the dominance thrilled me. But even if it excited me, I wasn't about to be dominated by the likes of Vincent Stevens.

I pushed him squarely in the chest. He frowned, his jaw going rigid. I pushed him again, and his hands encased my wrists, pushing them down to my sides and making my cleavage push up. My breathing was laboured, creating a hypnotic rhythm within my bra. His eyes dipped low, and I grinned wickedly. His eyes met mine, and within seconds, our mouths were colliding.

CHAPTER 27
VINNY

ROMAN's hot mouth abused mine. Her hands were in my hair, her short fingernails scraped against my scalp. Her tongue tangled with mine, and when she mewled into my mouth, all I could think of was taking her right here out in the open.

I pulled away and stared at her in awe. Her lips were puffy from our fevered kissing, and her breaths were coming out in pants. I captured her bottom lip with my teeth gently, and the purple of her eyes brightened. Her sweet arousal flooded my nose, and my dick hardened in response. Her mouth crushed against mine, and her hands had moved toward my zipper. I jolted as her hand cupped my cock. I pulled away again and was caught in the mischievous twinkle in her eyes.

Game on!

There was a buzzing at my fingertips as I started to stroke the skin at the top of her jeans. She fidgeted, slightly, pressing herself further into me. Her mouth was in a large smile beneath mine, and I realized that she was trying to suppress a giggle. Was she ticklish? Vali grinned at the information and stored it away for arsenal to use against her later.

I moved my hands under her t-shirt and up the length of her spine. Suddenly, she erupted into musical laughter. My dick reacted to the sound. This woman kept surprising me with what turned me on about her. Her entire body was vibrating with uncontrollable, carefree laughter, which made her glow with happiness. And all it did was make me want her more. If that's what my fingers did, what would my tongue be able to do? My teeth? I wanted to push her into the privacy of the trees and experiment with it. See what other noises I could coax out of her. But at the same time, I wanted to prolong this for as long as I could. That way, when I finally got to sink my cock into her, she would be singing my name, and once I had fucked her out of my system, I would walk away knowing I got one up on her.

"Sorry." She took a breath as she tried to regain some control, her eyes dancing with beautiful youth.

"Well, I guess it's time to go," I said as bluntly as I could. My pulse was thumping hard in my neck, and I was praying that she couldn't hear it.

"What?"

"You killed the mood." Her face hardened; all signs of humour vanishing. My cock twitched again as if it was saying, 'are you sure you want to walk away right now'?

That's precisely what I did. I walked toward my bike, pretending not to care if she followed or not.

"You're such a fucking asshole." I heard her mutter, her simmering rage evident.

I pulled my helmet on and mounted my bike, counting slowly in my head to stop me from going back to her and grovelling, knowing I would lick her toes if I needed to. She might even be ticklish between her toes. The thought aroused me further. I took a deep breath and willed myself to think of something else.

By the time she approached the bike, I was minutely calmer and determined not to give in. Even with the tantalizing smell of her arousal lingering. It had been dampened, but it wasn't gone. Vali groaned at me, warning that I was playing a dangerous game, but I held my resolve and started my bike.

She said nothing as she buckled her ridiculous helmet and then climbed on behind me, moulding herself against my back. I felt her enraged breathing and smiled to myself, wondering if I could make her any angrier.

"Don't kick the hornet's nest. Quit while you're ahead," Vali advised. I grinned at him and nodded, curious as to why her psychotic wolf hadn't lashed out again. *"She's enjoying this too much to lash out. At this stage, she's happy to see how the game plays out,"* Vali informed me. I trusted Vali's assessment. Werewolves had an ethereal mystique when it came to other wolf spirits. The spirits could not communicate with each other directly, but they could sense things. Sometimes, they just knew what was going on, even if they couldn't fully explain it. I took it down to being part of a hive-mind, a pack.

"You let me know the moment that wolf is about to lose the plot."
"Don't worry about that. I'm all over her."

I grinned as I dropped her at her car, which was conveniently parked several blocks from my dad's house. An interesting move on her part. She hadn't parked in an area that would be frequented. She didn't park at her childhood home, at Liv's house, or at the pack house. She was hiding the fact she was coming to visit me and avoiding the rumour mill for as long as possible. I was intrigued as to what would happen when the pack rumour mill eventually found out we were fucking like bunnies. It was almost impossible to keep anything a secret for long in this town.

She climbed off the bike as I removed my helmet. The second I had it off, her lips were brushing mine. The kiss wasn't desperate or crushing like it had been earlier. It was soft, delicate and sent an electric current straight into my cock. I unconsciously reached my hand up to cup her cheek and prolong the kiss. I didn't get a chance as she pulled back, took off her stupid helmet, and then shoved it hard into my chest.

She bounced off to her car, opened her car door and brought her middle finger to her lips, kissing it and flicking it toward me as if she was blowing me a kiss—in reality, she was flipping me off. She drove away without looking back.

I was unsure who ended up winning that round, but one thing was crystal clear: this was exactly what I needed. I needed to play this game. I needed to fuck her out of my system. Then I could go back to hating her.

CHAPTER 28
ROMAN

"You killed the mood." Wait. What? The heat frosted over as quickly as it had begun. Then, it started to blaze again, but not with lust, with white-hot anger. The simmering rage was ready to bubble over. Rue sat on her haunches, slightly annoyed, but she offered me no guidance or support as I tried to keep my emotions in check. He walked away from me, and I felt the heat scorching my blood cells. Humiliation washed over me, and I fought every urge to run, every urge to cry and scream. My face heated with sheer embarrassment.

I stiffly got back onto his bike and grudgingly put my arms around him. I didn't even want to touch him, but I had no alternative unless I wanted to strip, shift, run back to Blackfern Valley and then drive my car naked all the way home. I didn't have a change of clothes in my car, so every time I tried to come up with an alternative, it was apparent I was still going to have to drive home naked.

I could have called Liv and asked her to come get me, but I didn't want to endure her interrogation. I knew it was going to happen at some point, but considering I had no idea what the fuck was even happening, I wanted to hold that off for as long as possible. She had a sixth sense about these things already. I didn't need to hand her any ammunition.

The motorcycle rumbled beneath me. I was enveloped in the warmth of his back, his peppermint scent and the pleasant vibrations of the bike. It eased the humiliation slightly and lulled me into a semi-meditative state, which allowed me to sort through my wayward thoughts.

His kisses had tasted sweet and tangy on my tongue, and his growing erection had rubbed against my stomach. My entire body reacted to his as his arousing tongue fought for dominance in my mouth. All I could think of was shredding his clothes off and riding him like I rode his fucking motorcycle. I didn't care that we were at a rest stop where anyone could come past at any time. The need for friction between my legs was too great.

Rue was purring at the thought, desperate for it. His possessive, dominating persona was making Rue temporarily submit. I knew he was equally as affected. His thick cock that had been twitching into my stomach had spoken volumes, as well as his hands which had been all over my skin, tormenting me as I tried not to giggle at the odd sensation.

His calloused fingers were gentle, while his mouth was rough. It was the perfect combination. I never considered myself a ticklish person, but when he touched me, tiny tickling sparks erupted and danced over my skin. I couldn't help but laugh.

Then, suddenly, he stopped. The kisses stopped, and so did the touching.

The prickling in my gums stopped, and my canines, which had started their descent, had retreated with a pop. His voice was cold and distant. Hot and cold. He retreated back to his bike. His cool arrogance humiliated me. The memory of mixed messages irritated me all over again. It haunted me as I replayed the kiss over and over. The memory of his erection made me sure that he wanted this, yet he had changed his mind at the click of a button. Asshole.

Rue started laughing at me. The laugh grated on my nerves more than his rejection had. I glared at her. *"You're supposed to be helping me through this, you know! Not laugh at me. Why are you not more enraged at this? He's hot and cold like a fucking tap—"*

"If you stop bitching for a minute, you'll figure it out." I stared at her, blinking stupidly.

Things clicked the moment we pulled up outside my car. *That fucker!*

The moment his helmet was off, I pounced. I smiled seductively at him, then gently caressed his mouth with mine. His lips were soft beneath mine, and there was an echo of his refreshingly tangy taste on them. A slight pull tugged in my belly as a thread of electricity buzzed between us.

His arm wrapped around my waist, supporting me as he balanced awkwardly on his bike. He was barely touching me, but his hand still seared my skin. The kiss was innocent and gentle yet full of unsaid promises. I felt a low, quiet rumble from him. His hand came up to caress my face, and he tried deepening our kiss. He wanted more.

Gotcha! I pulled away and scooted back to my car, flipping him off and blowing him a kiss at the same time. *Take that, asshole!*

Rue was rolling around, laughing uncontrollably at his expression. She replayed it over and over, trying to get me to join in her humour. I gave her an indulging smile and drove toward my house. The sweet kiss was still lingering on my lips. He had started this cat-and-mouse game. I just hoped he knew what he was getting into. I hoped *I* knew what I was getting into.

My phone beeped at me, letting me know that it was time for pack training. I knew instantly that I didn't want to go. Rue was satisfied and thoroughly enthralled with the day's events that her need to embarrass me at pack training was nullified.

Maybe it was because it was something new. The motorcycle had excited her. The cat and mouse game was amusing her.

I pulled out my cell phone as I drove and flicked Murdoch a quick text message, letting him know I wasn't going to training and that I would meet up with him later. Then, I threw my phone onto the passenger seat. Rue grumbled softly at the idea of meeting up with Murdoch. I frowned. If she were getting bored of Murdoch, that would only lead to disaster. She became dangerous when she got bored.

I needed to cut it off again. Vinny had given me the perfect excuse to do that—not that I would ever tell Murdoch my plans to sleep with the enemy. That was my dirty secret. No one was going to know. It was going to be a one-time thing, a night of mind-blowing hate sex and then I was going to move on and forget him.

I PULLED up in the driveway of my house and scooted inside. I walked straight to my bedroom and started pulling out clothes at random, throwing them into a backpack. I dug around in the bottom of my closet for a pair of shoes before zipping up the backpack. I darted back outside and opened the trunk, throwing the bag into the empty space.

I smirked at the new emergency supply of clothes in my car. In the likely event of the thing with Vinny blowing up in my face, I wouldn't have to drive home naked. I slammed the trunk lid shut and re-entered my very quiet and empty house.

It was going to be at least four hours before Murdoch got home, four hours before I turned up at his condo and broke off our agreement in person.

I had to find something to do to occupy my time. Rue grinned knowingly at me as I trotted back to my bedroom and opened the bottom drawer, pulling out a large pink vibrator and relaxing on my bed with it.

CHAPTER 29
VINNY

I walked into the pack house and straight down to the alpha's office. I wrapped my knuckles against the wood and waited.

"Come in." Alpha Liam's voice was distorted through the door. I entered and sat down on one of the armchairs.

"Alpha," I greeted him.

"Sean has gone," Alpha Liam said, cutting to the chase. "He said he had something personal to attend to and asked for permission to leave. I'm unsure of when he's going to be back, so I need you to take over Sean's duties."

Sean had left. I pulled out my phone and quickly looked at the date before shoving it back into my pocket. It had been eight days since the full moon. He had gone to talk to Laurel. I didn't want to say anything in case Sean hadn't given Alpha Liam the specifics of where he was going.

I nodded solemnly. "Sure thing, Alpha. I'll help out where I can."

"Ryan can send you the roster later, but his duties mostly consist of training and the odd perimeter guarding." He gave me a levelled look. "I know you've been out of the training schedule for a while, and you have been injured. The training is taken by two warriors as per normal. But I'm not expecting you to be at that level; just take it easy and play more of a supporting role. How are you feeling, by the way?"

"I'm perfect." I nodded again. "It's like it never happened."

"You don't need to put on a brave front for me, Vinny. You were in bad shape."

"It wasn't as bad as you think."

"I remember when Lincoln tried to take me out. I was sore for days. Even with the mate bond trying to repair me, fuck, I was sore—"

"You were a lot worse off than me, Alpha. You were in a coma."

"I know. I shouldn't have lived through it, and even if I did, I should have come back a lot worse off than I was. I'm pretty sure it was severe enough to lose Lucian, and the only reason both he and I came back was because of your sister. Being Alpha probably helped with the speed of my healing, too." He shook his head free of the memory. "I'm just trying to say that I empathize with how sore you must be. You don't have to play brave in front of me."

"Honestly, I'm not." He looked curiously at me. "How is the interrogation going with the rogue?" I asked, changing the subject.

"Ryan is down in the stone cells with him now, but how about you go and check it out yourself after the afternoon's training sessions? It's a mixed grade adult class first, then pups in wolf form after school is let out."

"Clementine benched me since I got hurt."

"But weren't you just saying that you were feeling better? Perfect even."

I grinned at him. "Are you going behind your luna's back? Brave man."

Alpha Liam chuckled and waved his hand in dismissal.

Luca beamed at me as I walked across the training grounds. Luca was a huge werewolf in his mid-thirties. He was extremely good-looking, with long chocolate brown hair and bright blue eyes. He should have been intimidating; however, he was a shameless flirt, a notorious ladies' man and a real class clown, which made any attempt to be intimidating a joke. It was all a ruse. Like anyone in the inner circle, Luca was dangerous. Lethal.

"Heard you get to visit our friend," he said in a way of greeting as he reached out his arm to grip mine in a Roman handshake. When Luca became Clem's bodyguard, he took me under his wing, and we started to hang out, and pretty soon, he became one of my closest friends.

"Word travels fast."

"It's Blackfern Valley." He winked. "Nah, Alpha told me that you would be helping with the session today but then to escort you to the cells."

"Escort me?" I bristled.

"Don't think anything of it. No one goes into those cells alone. That dude is a wolf on steroids." He laughed before changing the subject. "Do you want to go and get the balancing equipment? The next class should be arriving soon."

The warrior training grounds were an ample dusty open space situated to the side of the amphitheatre. There were a few grassy patches and the odd stubborn weed growing from small cracks in the ground, but other than that, it was barren. On the very edge of the training ground and next to the spectator grandstand sat an old building that housed training equipment and a few gym machines.

I trudged into the building, through the empty cavernous space that was used for winter training and straight toward the back where the training equipment was held. I pulled a cart and started loading it with foam mats and obstacle course equipment before taking the cart back outside.

I got to work quietly setting up the mats and equipment, reminiscing about the first time my dad brought me here as a teenager. Training was used as a safe outlet for the sudden increase of energy and hormones of a manifesting wolf spirit, and I definitely needed a safe outlet.

I opted for more training than my allocated classes during school, pushing myself to the extreme and acing every class. After I graduated high school, I continued with the compulsory training schedule until I had been signed off from being a pack warrior. It had merely been a formality to tell the pack I was competent and didn't need to attend training anymore. But like many werewolves, even though the training was no longer compulsory, I chose to keep training. I learned how to fight in both human and wolf form, and then when I merged with Vali, I pushed myself and learned how to use the combined fighting style. I needed to learn this to become a warrior. That was my goal. Sean and I were both to be a part of the alpha's inner circle—bodyguards to the elite.

My warrior novice was due to end at the age of twenty. I was still to be paired with another warrior, but my initial training would have been complete, and I would have been a fully-fledged pack warrior. But the week I turned twenty, everything turned to shit, and my whole life was uprooted.

I placed the large, weighted bag on the ground as werewolves came tramping across the would-be field. I quickly counted fifteen, and one of those wolves was Murdoch. I groaned.

"What the hell is he doing here?" I asked Vali.

Vali smirked. *"My guess would be training."*

"Fuck."

"Play nice."

"I always play nice." Vali snorted in response.

Luca called the class to attention, introducing me as a

trainer and giving everyone instruction on the routines planned for the next three hours. His smile was carefree as he told everyone to get into pairs and warm up with a quick spar. Murdoch paired himself with me. Vali gave him a lopsided grin. Big mistake on Murdoch's part.

"Where's Sean? I thought this was his training session," Murdoch demanded and gazed at me with a disgruntled look.

"I was asked to cover," I said.

"Where's Sean?" he repeated.

"I'm not at liberty to discuss warrior business."

"Is that because you're not a warrior, and they don't tell you their business?"

"Sure." I rolled my eyes and got myself into position.

"So, where is Sean?" Murdoch mirrored my movement.

"He didn't tell you? He's gone to get hookers and blow."

"Have you ever given anyone a straight answer?"

"Only when they deserve it." I started to move lightly on my feet, waiting for the first punch. Murdoch stayed stationary.

"You don't know where he is, do you?"

"Not his exact coordinates at this very minute. But I do know where he's going."

"Where is he going?"

"I told you; he's gone to get hookers and cocaine. Glad to see your listening skills have improved over the years."

"Stop being an asshole and tell me where he is."

"Look, I don't want to get in the middle of your lover's tiff. Why don't you take it up with him?"

"Right. He didn't tell you either."

"He told me. I'm not betraying his confidence."

"Since when do you care about anyone other than yourself?"

"I care about a lot of people, *Murdick*. You're just not one of them."

"It only counts if they care about you too, and trust me, no one cares about you. No one missed you while you were gone.

In fact, people are just waiting for you to fuck off again." The brown ring around his slate-grey eyes flashed with the sign of his agitated wolf.

"Don't worry, it'll happen soon." Then because I couldn't resist fucking with Murdoch, I decided to bait him. "I didn't realize Roman was so ticklish."

"What are you talking about? Roman isn't ticklish."

"Sure she is. Her skin is hypersensitive. I mean, obviously, she's ticklish in the usual spots, her midriff and her spine. She laughs so hard. But I was pleasantly surprised about her toes—you suck on her toes, and she squirms and giggles." I bluffed. "It's endearing, really."

"You're full of shit. One, she's not ticklish, and two, she wouldn't stoop that low to let you suck on her toes. She loathes you."

"Oh, but she is ticklish. And she let me suck on more than her toes."

"You're so full of shit." His eyes flashed dangerously.

"Really, tell that to the small mole on the inside seam of her groin. That very hidden mole that you would only see if you were up close and personal." I watched as comprehension crossed his eyes.

"Sure, Vinny. You can have my sloppy seconds."

"Why not?" I said with a shrug. "You've already had mine."

It wasn't true, of course. Indiana and I had never been like that. But the rumour had been whispered so often, it might as well have been pack-law. Murdoch's control wavered just enough to give me an opening. I tilted my head, my voice deceptively soft.

"Although..." I let the word draw out, savouring the moment. "I have to admit, you're right about one thing. Roman really is the better sister."

Murdoch's fist came for my jaw. His knuckles were featherlight against my skin as I dodged the blow. His next fist aimed for my stomach, and I bounced away, chuckling. It had been years since I had gotten into a dustup with Murdoch. When I lived here, it seemed to be a regular occurrence as Murdoch was easy to rile up, and I was always happy to put my training into practice.

His fists kept flying toward me as I feinted and blocked on the defensive. He raged and charged ahead. Vali chuckled as I out-maneuvered him again and again. Murdoch hadn't changed; he still charged ahead with rage instead of skill. Of the few strikes that met their target, only one of them hurt. But I refused to visibly react. I just kept up the defence, letting him tire himself out. Finally, Vali had enough entertainment and twitched his strength forward—time for a workout.

I quickly attacked, moving fluidly as I advanced on Murdoch. He stumbled as he tried to defend himself. His moves were sloppy, and I knew he hadn't kept up his training after being signed off. He was weak. What the hell did Roman see in him?

I heard the sickening crunch as I broke his nose for the seventh time. The bones turned to mush and moved sideways.

"Great warm up, team!" Luca's voice called out. "It's time to start training."

Murdoch glared at me and spat crimson on the dirt-covered ground.

CHAPTER 30
VINNY

LUCA and I left the training grounds and took the path behind the pack house, which led to the stone cellblock. Fifty feet from the werewolf jail, we ran into Liv's sister. Luca snarled at her. "What are you doing here, Cassie?"

"I was trying to get into the cells," she said simply.

"Well, that's honest, at least. Did you want me to open a cell and lock you up again?" Luca's voice deepened by the power of his wolf.

"I haven't done anything wrong, Luca." Her blue eyes were crystal clear with her conviction.

"Really? Then why were you trying to access the cells?"

"I was trying to help! I thought that maybe if I could get answers that—"

"Alpha Liam would forget his one true love and his daughter and run away into the sunset with you?" Luca suggested menacingly.

"No. I just want to protect Lacey."

"What do you think she needs protection from?" I asked.

"Oh, come off it," Cassie snapped. "Do you think I'm stupid? Alpha Liam and the warriors have been secretly covert for months. You're summoned home. It's obvious there is some threat you don't want the pack to know about. I don't know why, but these rogues are after Lacey."

"You don't know what you are talking about," Luca lied smoothly.

"Sure I don't," she scoffed, her blue eyes rolling upwards before meeting us with a stony determination. "I just want to protect Lacey."

"Alpha Liam already told you that he didn't think you were right to protect Lacey." I crossed my arms. "I have to say I agree with him."

"Why would you think that, Vincent? If you don't recall, I saved your ass once. And your sister's ass multiple times." She glared at us both and then retreated into the forest without a word.

Luca shrugged and rolled his eyes in her general direction before leading the way back down the path toward the jail block. I nodded at the guard at the door and walked straight down the stone corridor with Luca at my heel. We both said nothing as the dirty smell of blood, fecal matter and rogue leached through the stone. The door whinnied on its hinges as Luca unlocked and opened the silver-barred door. I grudgingly stepped into the mouldy cell, taking nothing but a bottle of water and a three-legged stool. Even chained, this guy was dangerous.

"I was wondering what happened to you half-breed." His voice was gritty. "I will give you this: you are tenacious."

I grinned at him. "I'm also surprised to see you're still alive. Considering the reputation of the alpha of this pack."

"You mean the one mated to a half-breed whore?" Vali growled. "Your sister, I'm guessing. Which would make that abomination your niece." Vali growled again, his hackles sky-high. I knew the intel said that these rogues were after Lacey, but hearing it straight from the enemy's mouth was completely different. It took all my willpower not to attack him.

"A big brutish wolf like you is scared of an infant." My laugh was hollow, and my gut churned and bubbled with angry anxiety. My protective wolf instinct was telling me to take him out. To disembowel him and be done with it. My human side reasoned that we needed information first.

I placed the stool as far from him as I could and sat, staring at his abused torso and splotchy face. Well, at least they had been torturing him at Hotel Blackfern. That was something.

"I'm not scared of anything. Your alpha is terrified, though." The rogue coughed and then rattled the chains that connected him to the wall. "I'm chained in silver, and I've been force-fed wolfsbane. I've been beaten and tortured to an inch of my life. Yet, he still sends his warriors in here in groups of two."

Luca's voice came down the mind-link. *"Keep him talking! It's been a week, and this is the most vocal he's been."*

"So, if you're not scared of my niece, then why are you crossing pack territory? Do you want to become alpha of the Blackfern Valley pack? You don't have to trespass the borders to do that. You can just enter through the main road and request an audience with the alpha. You could walk right up to the pack house and challenge him—"

"Don't give him ideas," Vali grumbled sourly at me.

"No! That's not it. You're a rogue, and you love the freedom of not having to answer to anyone. You love being by yourself. You don't want to take care of two thousand-odd werewolves."

I crossed my arms and leaned casually against the wall of the cell. "Nope, I don't see you as a leader. A follower, maybe. A deranged lunatic, definitely." The rogue said nothing but glared at me through swollen, puffy eyes. "You can't possibly believe in something so farfetched as this prophecy. Even a stinking rogue like you must see the flaws in it. You must have something more than Neanderthal intelligence rolling around in your skull. Life isn't a giant conspiracy. You must know this."

"I know that you must be getting desperate for answers."

"We are." I shrugged. There was no point denying it.

"I could give you those answers. For a price."

"What price?" I snarled. Vali's ears twitched.

"Your niece's head?" I launched off the stool, and my fist collided with his jaw. He laughed maniacally. "No? How about my freedom then?" Of course, he wanted his freedom, but he also wanted—

"You wanted to get caught."

"Yes."

"Why?" There was a moment of silence as if he was weighing his options. He had no options, and he realized it.

"I was waiting for your sister."

"What do you want from Clem?" Vali's voice blended with mine as his need to protect her surged forward. It was not only the need to defend his kin but also his luna.

The mutt didn't answer. Instead, he gave a saccharine smile that fed my anxiety. He closed his eyes, pursed his cracked lips, and let out a dry-sounding whistle, a tune that could barely sound between his lips.

I rested on the stool again, looking briefly at Luca, whose eyes were clouded over as he mind-linked back to the pack house. I tried to figure out what I was missing, what he could possibly need to tell the luna. What was I missing? I had heard the prophecy. Was there more to it? Something to do with the half-breed bloodline?

"What can you tell me about this prophecy?" I asked, rolling the bottle of water toward the rogue—a peace offering. If torture didn't work, maybe some humanity would.

"What can you offer me? Can you offer me my freedom? I was going to give this information to your sister, but she has failed to grace my presence. I will give the information to you. The price is my freedom," he said coolly.

"Sure. I can grant you your freedom," I lied.

He chuckled. "That was almost believable. But you have no power."

"Why are you willing to tell us now? I don't believe that you have finally broken after a week of torture. Nothing is that easy."

"No. I wouldn't break for your pack warriors, as brutal as they were." He coughed again, then reluctantly picked up the bottle and cracked the lid. He took a sniff before taking three large gulps and pouring the rest over his head. The wetness only amplified the stench.

"So, why?"

"Because I have done exactly what I needed to do," he said vaguely. He flicked dust off the rags he was given to wear, the silver chains jingling. "These four walls bore me." He added in a monotone.

Vali growled. *"I don't like the sound of this. He sounds way too cocky for someone who's been tortured for days."*

"Tell me, and I'll do my best to set you free," I stated coldly.

"No, you won't." He coughed and spat on the ground. "When I agreed to do this, I knew I might not get out alive. I accepted my fate half-breed. Have you accepted yours?"

"Fate is a crock of shit. You make your own fate," I snapped defensively.

The rogue gave a bloody smirk. "Sounds like you were burned by Fate."

"We aren't talking about me."

"Aren't we?" The frosty eyes twinkled at me from behind the puffy blue bruises.

"No. We were discussing what you were holding out to tell the luna. The information you were willing to give me." Cold fury washed through me as I heard the sentence out loud. It must have read on my face as the rogue laughed maniacally and gave me a wink. "You have been fucking with me, haven't you?" I growled.

"Oh, it was so easy! You were so willing to think that I was ready to tell you everything. I told you, I was getting bored of these four walls."

CHAPTER 31
ROMAN

I HAD MADE it to Kempthorne at the same time Murdoch did. Nerves battled within as it did each time I told him we needed to end it. As usual, the thought of ghosting him tempted me, but I wasn't that kind of person.

I gave myself a little pep talk and reminded myself he fully understood that things between us were never going anywhere. Each time one of us ended it, we had a mature discussion and parted as friends. Even so, it didn't make it any easier. Rue was bursting to tell him so we could get out of there and go torment Vinny some more. It had turned into her new favourite game.

The minute I saw him, I knew something was wrong. There was a fire in his step as he walked up the stairs to his condo. Any confidence my pep talk had given me diminished, and my prepared speech evaporated on my tongue.

"I'm going to fucking kill him!"

"Who?"

"Your chew toy."

"My... chew... Vinny?" I asked, startled.

There was no way he knew about Vinny's indecent proposal. I tried to calm my nerves. This wasn't about Vinny and me. Not that there was a Vinny and me. There never would be a Vinny and me. I tried to stop my runaway thoughts and focus on his venting.

"That guy has a serious screw loose. He hasn't changed. He's still that same angry kid who stole my car, ran gambling rings, and got us all into trouble. He's still the same kid who hurts people and then pretends it was nothing. You watch this space. I guarantee now that he's back, he'll find someone else to hurt, then he'll flee on that piece of shit bike of his." Indiana's face flashed briefly before my eyes, and I shook it back, trying to concentrate on what he was saying. "I swear I'm going to fucking kill him."

"What on earth happened?"

"He broke my nose." *Of course, he did.* Rue snorted her amusement as I grabbed his face and examined the healed break. He had managed to reset it, so it was somewhat straight. He pushed me away. "Totally unprovoked, too. Just like when we were pups. I don't understand why he's back. Is he staying for good? He doesn't seem to be in a hurry to move on. But I cannot get a straight answer out of the fucker. Instead, he says bad shit about you and then breaks my fucking nose. Then I had to spend the rest of training with the fucker. Dropping small delusional hints about you two fucking. Trying to bait me into another fight. He broke my fucking nose, Roman!"

"WHAT THE HELL are you playing at breaking Murdoch's nose?" I slammed through the back door of Vinny's house, glowing with anger. My hands clenched and unclenched at my sides, still enraged from the hours of stalking the streets near his house, waiting for him to show his cowardly face. He looked up from the bourbon he was nursing, arched his eyebrow and answered in a bored tone.

"We were at training. Accidents happen."

"Accidents tend to happen a lot around you, Vincent."

"He's a werewolf, Roman. He'll heal." He rolled his eyes.

"That's not the point!"

"No, you're right. The point is I shouldn't have been able to get his nose. He's sloppy and in serious need of training." Rue rumbled, but I couldn't tell whose side she was taking in this argument. "And instead of manning up and working harder, he runs to you and cries about it. Great boyfriend you have there, Ro!"

"Not my boyfriend," I said a little too quickly. I was always on the defensive about relationship statuses.

"Glad to hear it, especially since we agreed that I was going to be the only one fucking you."

"Well, considering we haven't fucked yet. I'm unsure why we need that rule."

"I don't share with Murdoch. Ever."

"No, you just get into ridiculous fights and break his nose. How many times is that now? Five?"

"Seven," he replied with a wicked grin.

"That's nothing to be proud of!" I snapped.

"Why not? You would think after the third broken nose, he would have learned to defend his face. Slow learner, that one. Is that why you were fucking him? Because he's dumb and easy?"

Rue's hackles rose and she let out a low warning growl through my teeth.

"Jealous much?"

"Why would I be jealous? He's easy. You're easy—"

Smack. My fist collided with his nose, Rue giving me a burst of power. His hand went straight up and cradled it. It wasn't broken, but it was red, and my knuckles hurt like a bitch.

"I guess Murdoch isn't the only one who needs to learn to protect his nose." Rue grinned proudly at my sass. I let my hand hang limply by my side, as I didn't want him to know he had almost broken my hand. The arrogant satisfaction on his face would have crippled me. Rue, still full of insurmountable pride, let me off the hook by sending her healing powers directly to my knuckles.

Vinny glared at me, and I spun on my heel to walk out the door. I barely made it to it before peppermint surrounded me, and I was smashed against the kitchen wall.

"Let me go!" I snarled. But even as I made my demand, I could feel the heat igniting and the low swirling in my stomach—the pretensive promises from our earlier encounter revving back into gear. My body started to hum for his, and from the way his nostrils flared, he knew it too.

"Are you sure you want me to let you go?" His teeth grazed my jaw, and I had to suppress a moan.

"Y-yes." He brushed his lips softly against my cheek and released me. Cold confusion ran through me. "What are you doing?"

"I'm letting you go." I stared at him, utterly bewildered. "You may hate me and think that I'm an asshole, Roman, but I have never forced myself on a woman. And I'm not going to start now. No means no." He gave me a crooked grin. I was in shock and had lost my ability to form words. My confusion was met with a smile that could only be classified as dangerously seductive. "Trust me, Roman. This will happen. You will beg me for it."

I ignored the somersaults and the gentle gravitational pull that was trying to lead me back to him. I was in charge. Not my body. I lowered my eyes and looked at him from underneath my lashes. "Or maybe you will be begging me."

I quickly escaped before I gave in and ended up on my knees. I pummelled the pavement with my footsteps, trying to get as much distance between Vinny and myself as I walked the ten blocks back to my car. Who knew that I could be so angry at someone yet so turned on at the same time? Was it all part of this cat-and-mouse game? How much of this could my mental health handle? My body ended up thrumming in anticipation every time I went near him. I needed to stop my sudden thirst for him. Rue didn't seem bothered by any of it, and that made it seem worse somehow.

When I got home, I stripped off my clothes and jumped into the scalding hot shower. I scrubbed my skin harshly until it felt raw. It didn't matter how hard I scrubbed. I still remembered. I remembered his touch and how it made me feel. I remembered losing control because of his kisses. And I certainly couldn't forget that the moment I started to paw at him, desperate for what was underneath, he'd stepped away. Instead of walking away with dignity, I'd found myself wanting more.

"Some wolf spirit you are!" I growled at Rue.

"What did I do?" she asked, affronted.

"Nothing. And that's the point. You're my wolf. You're supposed to protect me. Where are those survival instincts?" I whined.

"Dramatic much? You forget I helped you punch him in the nose." She rolled her eyes. *"And you call me neurotic."*

"You're the poster child for insanity. One moment, you're daydreaming about killing him. The next, you're allowing Vinny to kiss me and do dirty things to me. Allowing me to want more of those kisses and those dirty things!"

"Colour me intrigued." She gave a small shrug and then tilted her head, her purple eyes boring into me. *"You do realize we don't actually have to follow through with it? As he said, no means no."* I stopped scrubbing and blinked at her. She chuckled a wolfy laugh and winked. *"If we do follow through with it and the sex is bad, well, then we can kill him."* She seemed far too excited about that prospect.

"You're a real femme fatal," I deadpanned.

"Trust me. We would be doing it for all the females in the world. It would be a justifiable mercy killing. No one would have to have his bad cock ever again. They would make statues in our honour. A public holiday even."

I smirked at Rue and considered what she said. *"Are we really considering this? I mean, I know I almost broke it off with*

Murdoch today. But I really want you to understand that if Murdoch finds out the reason why, it would be the end to that permanently."

"Boo-fucking-hoo," she said with a dramatic eye roll.

I kept scrubbing as the icy peppermint started to wash down the drain. I rinsed off, then turned off the tap.

CHAPTER 32
VINNY

THE ROGUE HAD PLAYED ME. He had no intention of doing anything but entertain his boredom. I played right into it, thinking he was willing to part with the group of rogues' intentions. I was a fucking tool. I got no answers, and we were still no closer to stopping the rogues from coming after Lacey.

I needed a shower and a stiff drink. I managed the first one without any incidents, but when I went to take my first swig of neat bourbon, the scent of jasmine came wafting through the back door seconds before she did.

The bourbon was supposed to be my distraction from the rogue. Roman's fiery reaction turned out to be a better distraction. Her replaying of my fight scene with Murdoch cheered me up immensely. I had almost forgotten the feel of Murdoch's broken bones under my fist and the look on his face. How close he had come to losing control of his wolf and shifting right there at training. What a fucking disgrace.

Roman being irate over it entertained me even more. Her eyes were bright with anger as she scolded me for what I had done to Murdoch.

The punch surprised me. Pain radiated into my eyes, and my nose stung from where her knuckles had grazed it. The pain subsided as quickly as it arrived, and within seconds, I was pinning her against the wall, desperate for her to distract me further. I was ready to drown myself in her.

Her body moulded into mine, and Vali hummed in pleasure. My cock thickened at the little mewling noises she had made as I kissed and nibbled her jaw. The jasmine that I had once found so disgusting mixed with the sweet aroma of her arousal. This fragrance made my gums itch. I wouldn't bite her, though. That would be far too intimate. Instead, I would bend her over the kitchen table and take her hard and rough—

Instead, she'd made a hasty exit. I walked back into the bathroom, chuckling to myself. I turned the tap in the shower on before removing my pants, my shaft saluting skywards. I entered the shower and palmed my hot, thick cock, beating it hard and fast. Fuck me, I couldn't wait for her to give in. I just hoped it was soon.

After my second shower in an hour and beating all my tension down the drain, I felt more relaxed than I had in weeks. I walked back through the house in my towel, noting that Roman's scent barely lingered. Vali rumbled his displeasure.

I dropped onto the couch, bourbon in hand, and let the amber liquid burn its way down my throat. The dull warmth in my chest was a poor substitute for the fire Roman had stoked in me, but it was better than nothing. For a moment, I let myself drift, melting into the soft leather beneath me. But the peace didn't last long as a sharp knock on the door shattered the silence.

I groaned, setting the glass down on the walnut-coloured coffee table. I scrubbed a hand over my face and scratched into my beard. It was probably Roman, back to lecture me about something else—or maybe she was about to beg me to bend her over the counter as she deserved.

I opened the door to find Liv standing there naked, her expression curious as she ran her eyes over me. "Perimeter duty. Let's go, dick-bait."

"I'm not scheduled until tomorrow!" I grunted. "I've been training hormonal pups and terribly trained werewolves all day. Then I had to visit the mutt in the cell, and I only just got his stench off me. Now, my plan is to sit down with a bourbon and relax." My voice was heavy with irritation.

Liv's nose twitched as she scented the air. She tilted her head, and her eyes glittered with amusement. "Yeah, well, plans change. We've had sightings near the perimeter."

My jaw tightened. So much for a quiet night. "How many?"

"Just one so far, but it's enough. We're doubling shifts."

Vali stretched eagerly within my mind as I glanced over my shoulder at the couch, the promise of a few stolen hours of rest evaporating like smoke. I grudgingly followed Liv out the door as she shifted back into her rust-coloured wolf and bounded into my backyard. I shucked off my towel and shifted, bouncing down the front steps and circling the house to the treeline at the back of my section.

The perimeter stretched out before me, an invisible barrier that hummed as I approached. But that was the only motion out here. It was quiet—too quiet. The kind of silence that set my teeth on edge.

I moved through the forest with practiced ease, my paws crunching softly against the undergrowth. The scent of pine and damp earth filled my lungs, but I kept my focus on the faint, acrid smell that lingered just beneath it.

Rogue.

It wasn't fresh; I could barely scent it. I crouched near a cluster of bushes, examining the ground for any other sign that the wolf was scouting or infiltrating pack lands. Liv examined some old, dried paw prints with interest before scenting the air. She let out a yipping noise and took off. She'd found the rogue's trail, and I was supposed to be her backup, but she had taken off without me. I spun on my heel and followed her. Not nearly being as quiet as her stealthy wolf. She shot me a reproachful look as I caught up and ran her flank deeper into the territory.

Then she darted back over the river and started zigzagging through the trees, a wolf on a mission. She did this for an hour before she shot straight out of the perimeter and across a quiet road into the next section of trees. She followed the scent. I kept her flank as quietly as I could muster, but when she took off in another direction without warning, I had to scamper to keep up. She had turned off her mind-link, concentrating on her task. I wasn't in tune with her method; we weren't a fluid unit like we would have been if I had stayed and trained properly.

For another three hours, we stalked the scent that only she could smell. Then, she snarled softly as she stepped gingerly out of the treeline and onto the edge of the same highway where I had totalled my motorcycle on. One look at her posture and I instantly knew the scent had disappeared altogether—even for her.

She opened up a channel for the warriors on duty and for Alpha Liam—an impressive eight wolves. There were more wolves on duty, but she got enough wolves that the information would be shared.

"*I lost him,*" she grumbled as she let out a howl of frustration. "*He had to have been picked up in a vehicle. All I smell is gasoline everywhere: wolves, humans, forest, and countless vehicles that have passed through. It's a major highway. There's no way to pinpoint which car the rogue jumped into or in which direction it went. Fuck!*"

Vali snarled in my mind, his anger simmering just below the surface. We were bested again.

CHAPTER 33
ROMAN

When work proved to be a dead bore, it only took a few hours before Rue started to wind me up. It was my fault, really; even though she seemed calmer, I knew I still needed to dampen her crazy. She required my vigorous routine. I hadn't exercised or joined in pack training recently as I was avoiding my hound dog of a best friend. She would take one look at me and know something was different. Even if Vinny and I weren't actually having sex, I may as well have worn a neon sign on my forehead that read: Thirsty for Vinny.

If my brain became occupied with normal everyday thoughts, Rue would be flashing images of things I could do with Vinny instead—things that should be outright illegal if they weren't already. I think I preferred it when Rue was having uncontrollable outbursts. Her eerily calm demeanour made me uneasy. Rue seemed to be happy to play the game, though. She would wait and bide her time for now, but I knew, if I didn't do something about it soon, Rue would try to take charge and sort it out herself.

I had become so desperate that I had shoved my vibrator into the depths of my bag, ensuring it was with me so I could find a release. Yes, the simpler thing to do would have been to go and seek out Vinny, strip naked and beg him to make good on his promise. The problem with that was that I was a stubborn bitch. I wanted to fuck Vinny. But I wasn't going to give in first. I wasn't going to let him win.

So, instead of a roll between the sheets with the biggest douche-nozzle I knew, I was at work, putting in overtime and wishing my wolf would behave. It was my second double shift in two days, but instead of lulling her into a calm, sleepy state as per usual, it seemed to rouse her mischievousness. Her antics had reached a new level, and I couldn't block her out.

Now, I was paying the consequences. Her seductive images had agitated my hypothalamus, making me hornier than a teenager at their twelfth-grade formal. There were three issues with this:

One: I was at work and Rue was being totally unprofessional.

Two: Kempthorne residents were both werewolf and human.

Three: Adult werewolves never got sick and only needed medical care in extreme cases. This meant that the night shift could be incredibly quiet with only a few human patients. The humans weren't the problem; the werewolves were. A nose twitch and smarmy grin from the emergency room doctor told me as much. Rue scoffed and rolled her eyes. Then, I eyed him up again. Her interest was piqued, but not only for sexy locker room frolicking.

I knew she had appeared in my eyes when a doctor's eyes flashed with the interest of his wolf, a primal proposition that had me spinning on my heel and racing to my locker. I yanked my bag and hastily made my way to the toilet, snapping the lock as my sweetened scent infiltrated my nose. Rue chuckled as I dug around at the bottom of my bag and brought out my toy. I flicked the little switch, and nothing happened.

"You've got to be fucking kidding me!" I growled.

Rue laughed harder. *"Who forgets to charge their vibrator?"* she asked through her laughter. I glared at her. *"Now what?"*

I shoved the useless toy back into my bag and fled the toilets, power-walking past the horny doctors like I wasn't one flick away from climbing one—or more—of them like a depraved jungle gym. I didn't stop until I was at the staff gym, swiping my badge and pushing through the door like a woman on a mission.

It was my first time using the physio facilities at Kempthorne Memorial Hospital. The place had a wellness incentive that let staff use the gym equipment after outpatient hours, but I'd never needed it. Normally, my exercise involved running in the bush, pack training, or—well—sex.

I quickly figured out how to turn the treadmill on, cranked up the incline, and started picking up the pace—anything to control my inner urges and desire, to control the need to strip Vinny bare, scrape my claws over his torso, bite him, lick him and devour him—

My feet pounded harder. *Damn it! I don't want to be thinking of sex with Vinny right now.* If I thought of sex right now, I would spontaneously combust. It had also been a handful of days since Vinny's reiterated proposition, and I hadn't even received a single text message. I was sure the ghosting was part of the cat-and-mouse game, but I was winding up tighter than a spring and ready to snap.

The incline was painful on my calves, but it was a good pain. I pushed myself harder as Rue stretched and yawned. *"I think I preferred the vibrator in the bathroom idea."*

"I'm at work, you inappropriate sociopath!"

"What, are people not allowed to get horny at work?"

"I'm not even going to justify that with an answer," I said as I pulled my headphones out of my ears and stopped the machine. "Can I go back to work now, or will you pull something like that again?"

"I don't need to. You have the attention of every werewolf in the

hospital now. It doesn't matter that you're no longer horny, you've set the precedent. From now on, each shift will be met with a proposition to go into an empty ward, and that is entertaining enough."

She wasn't wrong. After I'd showered, grabbed something quick to eat from the little cafeteria, and returned to work, I noticed that regardless of the fact my arousal was no longer lighting up like a tiki torch, the male werewolves were a lot more attentive than their usual. Rue chuckled sleepily as I gently redirected their attention in the same manner I'd have redirected a toddler.

There was obvious interest and thus flirting, but no one had come outright and asked me if I needed help in the locker room or if I wanted to fuck in the supply closet like some terrible medical soap opera. Even if a couple of them may have been able to scratch my itch, I wasn't about to break my non-negotiable rule: no one from my workplace.

That didn't stop them from trying, however. My fake smile had been plastered to my face. My jaw ached from the artificial laughter coming from me. A few hours later, I excused myself toward the nurse's station and shut the door to get a break from the unwanted attention. I closed the door with a loud click, hoping it would emphasize my lack of interest in their offers. Collapsing into the chair, I groaned into my hands and closed my eyes for a moment.

Rue wasn't even enjoying the car wreck of the situation she had created. She was snoring softly in the back of my mind with her paws stretched out. I tried to reach back to stroke her fur but found it impossible. Only merged wolves could touch their wolf spirit. It was probably a good thing I couldn't. If I woke her, she would probably bite my hand off.

The screens flickered in hypnotic rotation as the security cameras peered into the quiet night. I yawned and stretched, trying to find something to keep me awake for the remainder of my shift. The day shift had left a small mountain of paperwork, and I was about to start sorting through it when movement caught my eye.

I stared in shock as a wolf boldly walked onto the screen into the darkened corner of the ambulance bay. Not a human, but an off-yellow coloured wolf. The humans around Kempthorne had no idea about the existence of werewolves. Humans didn't know about werewolves. Period. Most pack laws made it mandatory to keep it a secret unless there was an extreme circumstance. It was an easy rule to follow because humans avoided areas with large populations of werewolves. Kempthorne was an exception for some unknown reason. Therefore, the wolves in the area had a lot of opportunities to practice discretion. This one wasn't being discreet, though.

The wolf was gone as quickly as it had appeared. I blinked stupidly at the screen. Maybe I had imagined it? Was I tired enough that I had fallen asleep at my desk and dreamed it? Rue was fast asleep, so I couldn't ask her if she'd seen what I had. I waited to see if it would come back. Nothing.

I walked to the small kitchenette at the back of the nurse's station and poured myself a large cup of coffee from the pot. I took a sip—ugh! I really hated coffee, and this lot needed a dumpster-load of sugar. I hunted high and low through the cupboards, finding no sugar, only artificial sweetener. I dumped it in my coffee and turned back to the desk.

I sat down and pulled the first file toward me, opening it. There was another movement on the screen—a person this time. Simon was walking around the ambulance bay. He sat on the metal bench before standing up and moving again, looking into the dark as if he could see something coming. Seconds later, a big white ambulance drove into view before stopping. The paramedics lazily got out and walked toward the back, Simon on their heels.

I pumped the sanitizer onto my hands and exited the side door, walking to the ambulance to help. Simon was nowhere to be seen. I stretched my neck, looking for him, then shrugged

THE NOMADIC WOLF

and concentrated on my task when the doors of the bus opened fully.

I understood why the paramedics were unconcerned. It was Cybil, my geriatric frequent flyer, who was borderline senile and deep into conspiracy theories. She often forgot to take her medication and pressed her medical alert button when she was lonely. I suppressed the need to roll my eyes and helped her into a wheelchair.

I wheeled her over to a spare cubicle and placed a blood pressure cuff around her arm.

"Where did that other boy go?" she snapped at me.

"The paramedics have other jobs to attend to Cybil," I said as I tried to concentrate on the sounds coming through my stethoscope.

"No, not those silly boys. The blond one with the glasses."

"Simon?" I asked, taking off her cuff and writing down her blood pressure. It was a little low, but no cause for concern.

"I don't know his name. He looks like he could use a good meal. He's super skinny. A nurse, I think."

"Sounds like Simon."

"Well, where did he go? You should go look for him. He might be in trouble."

"Simon works in the wards. He's probably back there."

"Nonsense."

"What's nonsense?"

"He was right there." I frowned at her agitation. "Then he disappeared and followed that wolf." I stopped scribbling on the tablet and looked at her.

"Wait. What? What wolf?"

"The one the colour of straw. It was hovering by the emergency entrance of the hospital." My heart started beating quicker, and Rue stirred irritably at the sudden cortisol rise. "I'm telling you he went to investigate that wolf. He's going to get hurt." There was no way this lady saw Simon and a werewolf together. She was just batshit crazy, but—

"Cybil," I said carefully, "how did you see this? There were no windows in the ambulance."

"I watch out for that boy. I watch out for most people in this town. Every last ungrateful human. That boy was sweet on you and now he's mixing himself in werewolf business. I told him you were trouble and to stay away. He just thought I was crazy. They all think I'm crazy."

"Cybil, there's no such thing as werewolves." My tone was firm.

She scoffed. "Sure, like I haven't seen you race out of here and turn into a black wolf like your life depended on it. You don't think I hear the occasional howl coming from the forest? Most humans chalk it up to wild wolves. But I know better. You mark my word, missy, you lot are trouble. Always have been."

I quickly scanned the emergency room and then yanked back the curtain to give an illusion of privacy. With werewolf hearing in the vicinity, I knew it was pointless. I lowered my voice regardless. "How do you? I mean, how could you—"

"Know about werewolves?" She gave a small cackle but didn't answer my question. Instead, she stared at the patterns on the curtain as if they fascinated her.

"Cybil?" She didn't respond. I tried again, giving her age-spotted hand a gentle shake. No response. It was like she was in a trance.

"Sorry, dear." She shook her head and then patted my hand affectionately. "What were we talking about?"

CHAPTER 34
VINNY

I THOUGHT I would hear from Sean within a couple of days of him finding his mate. I was wrong. I hit a wall when I tried to mind-link him, which told me he had closed off his connection. I tried texting and calling, but he wasn't answering.

It was understandable that werewolves turned off the mind-link when they found their mate. Even with chosen mates, it was common. They were consumed with the insane need to fuck each other raw, and their entire rationality left as the mate bond took over. It was worse with true mates.

My father had described it as the most intense moment of his life. All his senses were overrun with the gravitational pull of two souls being forced together. He described the electric tingles and a pulsating humming as the mate bond thickened and solidified between my mom and him. He made it sound enticing and like something every werewolf would want. It wasn't. I only experienced three excruciating minutes of the mate bond's insidious attempt to pair me with Roman. I hoped, for Sean's sake, that his outcome was a lot better than mine.

Still, the longer I went without hearing from him, the more annoyed I became, knowing that he was getting his dick wet while I was performing his pack duties. Each time I tried to reach out, I was hit with a block. There was no white noise, which told me he hadn't travelled far. It was just radio silence.

I thought his warrior duties would have been light, considering he was brother to the alpha, but his roster proved the opposite. Warriors tended to do a thirty-hour work week, with a mixture of perimeter security, training, scouting and other odd jobs.

Sean, on the other hand, taught two three-hour training sessions five days a week, one in wolf form and one in human. He also taught one training session in the combined method every Wednesday for three hours, and he had twenty hours of perimeter security and ad hoc jobs across the week. I didn't know when he found time to eat or sleep or fuck with a roster as harsh as his.

Sean's roster is cockblocking me. I didn't know when I was going to find time to eat, sleep, or fuck with a roster as harsh as his. How was I going to manage this workload, interrogate the rogue, look after my family and fuck Roman until she blacked out?

It was the dead of the night as I killed my bike in the gravel driveway outside the pack house. Light glowed from the downstairs windows of the identical-looking house across the driveway. I stepped onto the front porch and raised my knuckles to rap on the door gently, then paused in fear of waking up the beta's toddler. I was about to mind-link him when Ryan opened the door, looking like death warmed up. A blood-curdling wail followed him out the door, indicating my attempt to be quiet had been in vain.

"You look like shit," I said politely.

"Declan has decided that he doesn't need to sleep at night."

"Right," I said with a nod. I knew nothing about kids. "I think I have some ketamine left if you guys need a good night's sleep?"

Ryan shook his head at my attempt at humour. "Ready for the horrendous night shift?"

"Are you sure you're up to it? Being Beta means you can order other people to do it, you know."

"Oh no. I need a break from *that*." He thumbed toward the house, where I could hear a toddler's high-pitched scream again.

"Nature's contraception," I muttered as I returned to my motorcycle and quickly stripped out of my clothes. If anything could make my balls shrivel up and die, it was that sound.

When I turned back, Ryan had already shifted into his large wolf and was trotting toward the bush. I quickly shifted and hurried to catch up. We raced to the edge of the perimeter, meeting some of the other wolves in the shift changeover. There was a playful scuffle before the two wolves turned tail and left us to it.

My paws were thundering the treeline at the border of the pack territory, feeling the power coming from the boundary. It was like there was an invisible fortress dome surrounding our pack lands, and anytime a wolf got close to the edge of it, the wolf got a gentle zap. The feeling happened at any location along the boundary line, but somehow, it felt more powerful in the forest. Maybe because I was in wolf form, and my senses were heightened. I ran down the side of the boundary line, sniffing the air, enjoying the bolt each time my paw crossed the line.

Ryan shook his wolfy head at me as I danced back and forth across the perimeter, edging closer to see when I would get zapped.

"How old are you?" Ryan's wolfy chuckle came to my mind.

"Hey, something has to keep me entertained on night shift. It's always so boring!" I said cheekily.

"Be careful what you wish for."

"You think I can make wishes on this power?" I grinned stupidly at him. *"I wish for hot, naked blondes serving beer."* I tilted

my head and waited. *"Sorry, Chief. I don't think the boundary has any power."*

"That's what you would wish for if the boundary had powers?"

"Pfft. Wouldn't you?" Ryan shook his head. Ah, right. He's another one who was *blessed* with a true mate. I instantly thought of Sean and wondered how he was getting on with Laurel. *"How's your sister?"*

"Which one?" He had three.

"Laurel."

"Fine." His voice came down the link cautiously and with a hint of warning. Then, a moment later, he added, *"She better not be one of the hot blondes you were wishing for."*

I blinked at him. *"What? Hell no. She's more Sean's type than mine,"* I hinted with humour. He didn't acknowledge it but let out a low grumble. Surely, he would know that they were true mates.

"I told him to stay away from her. He knows better. You, on the other hand, can't get what you want, so you will try to bang anyone that moves. So, I will say this once: my sisters—all of them—are off limits."

Vali tilted his head in confusion, but Ryan really didn't know! *"Even Sophie?"* I baited.

"Especially Sophie."

"What about Briar?"

"All of them!" he barked. I shot him a playful grin.

"Okay, I promise I'll stay away from your sisters."

"Thank you."

"But I can't guarantee the'ill stay away from me."

"Oh, I can guarantee they'll stay away from you."

"Have you seen me man?"

"Yes, but my sisters are smart. They've never gone for someone who's pining for someone else. Even if that someone is way out of your league."

"Wait. Who am I supposed to be pining for?" The wolf gave me a pointed look, and Ryan kept quiet. Roman's face flashed

before my eyes, and I grumbled low. I wasn't pining for her. I just wanted to fuck her. There was a difference. But I wasn't going to say this to Ryan. I wasn't going to give him the satisfaction of thinking he was right.

So, I remained quiet as we stalked and sauntered through the bush, continuing our perimeter sweep. We didn't say much more for the rest of the shift. Both enjoying the quiet. And it *was* quiet.

It felt as though everything had gone back to normal. The rogue's friends hadn't come back. It had been almost two weeks. There wasn't an attempt to even rescue him or negotiate his release with Alpha Liam. It made me think he was probably acting alone and true to rogue form. His friends were only thinking of themselves. There was no loyalty, no pack-like structure with these wolves. Vali blinked at my chain of thought.

Had we caught the threat that had been after Lacey? Even if there was a rogue sighting recently, it could have just been a coincidence. He could have just been passing through. What if it was just this one rogue? If we killed him, the threat could be over and done with.

"Yet, he wanted to be caught," Vali reminded me. Crap. I had forgotten that.

"Any insight on what you think he's up to then?"

"He's after Lacey."

"Well, no shit!" I rolled my eyes. *"I just want to go. Can you get a read on his wolf?"*

"No, I couldn't. Which is understandable since he isn't pack." Vali looked at me. *"Besides, you don't really want to go just yet."* Roman flashed before my eyes for the thousandth time this evening, and I grinned at my wolf.

"Alright, conquest first, rogue killing second, then we get the fuck out of here."

The sky was still dark as I returned to my bike. I opened my bag and removed my clothing, pulling them on with haste as the crisp air hit my naked ass. I pulled out my phone and pressed the unlock button, turning on the backlight—no messages from Sean or Roman. I looked back at my bike and grinned. Roman was apparently out of my league. Let's see how out of my league she really was.

Time to go wake her up.

CHAPTER 35
ROMAN

Once Cybil was hooked up to a saline drip, I casually walked through the automatic doors to the ambulance bay. Taking a gentle sniff, I tried to differentiate the scents that lingered in the air as a mixture of different aromas hit my nose—human, werewolf, something musty, even gasoline. But I couldn't smell anything definitive. *I wonder if I should call Liv.*

"You want to wake Liv up in the middle of the night and get her to drive the hour to Kempthorne because some old bat got you spooked?" Rue grumbled sleepily, then rolled over and let out a snore. Rue was right. There was no way Liv would come all the way out here without good reason. What was I was going to tell her, that I saw a wolf on the security feed in a town full of werewolves? That an old senile woman claimed to know about our kind, and she informed me that a friend had followed a wolf like some reverse Red Riding Hood?

I walked around the bend in the driveway and called Simon's name, all the while thinking this was stupid, that he was probably back inside in the ward. I called his name again, but I couldn't scent Simon out there. I kept walking, looking through the darkness with the help of my slightly enhanced vision. My eyes would be better in wolf form, but I obviously wasn't going to shift for this. Nothing was out of the ordinary. I called Simon's name once more, walking a little further before I heard someone call my name. I spun around.

"Roman?" Simon was getting out of a sedan in the staff parking lot. I headed toward him.

"Hey, Simon," I said as casually as I could.

"Were you looking for me?" He gave me a small smile. I took a delicate sniff through my hospital-damaged nose, but I couldn't smell any werewolf on him. His scent was sterile and human. This was further proof that I had let myself believe Cybil's deranged conspiracy theories. Even if she did know about werewolves, that didn't mean Simon did.

"Yeah, I thought I saw you coming out here. You know that old bat, Cybil? She's back. I think she's taken a liking to you and would like to see you." He chuckled. "Where were you?" I asked as casually as I could. *Have you met any werewolves lately?*

"I went into town on my break. There's this twenty-four-hour all-you-can-eat Chinese place that has the best kung-pow chicken."

"Right," I said, giving him a megawatt smile. "So, can you come visit Cybil? Let her see that you didn't get kidnapped?"

"She thought I was kidnapped?"

"I'm telling you, she's sweet on you."

"Ah, it's always the cougars!" he joked, giving me an exaggerated wink. I laughed and led him back into the hospital.

"Better than the wolves!" I teased.

I STAGGERED up onto my porch and opened my front door. I had barely made it inside when I heard the loud revving of an engine. I turned toward the sound and glared as the black bike came to a stop.

"What do you want?" I demanded.

"Want to go for a ride?" Vinny's voice was muffled by the sound of the engine.

"Not particularly. I just got off a shift."

"So did I." He grinned. "Come on, let's go chase the sunrise."

I looked back toward the house where my bed awaited me to crawl inside. I looked down at my scrubs that I hadn't bothered to change out of, then glanced back at Vinny, and he flashed me another grin as he revved the engine again.

Somehow, I found myself closing the door and straddling the back of the motorcycle. The silly little helmet was back on my head, and my arms stretched around Vinny's warm torso. He skidded slightly as he spun the bike around in the driveway before careening down the drive at top speed. I clutched him tighter and closed my eyes, leaning my forehead into his back.

My body hummed along with the bike as Vinny opened the throttle and sped up. I pressed my face into his back further to protect myself from the cold wind. I took a sniff, secretly enjoying the scent of his leather jacket, mixing with his natural peppermint.

I wasn't paying attention to where we were going, but slowly, the darkened sky became a soft purple-grey, and the sun started to move up on the horizon. He hooted and hollered toward the sun and leaned forward on his bike, chasing it. I clung on tighter and felt an electrical current run through me as if the sun was charging me. He crowed again as he sped up, turning and twisting with the road. The sun dipped behind the treeline, creating a dusky dark shadow, and then the bright purple-grey sky would open again. In and out, the shades changed fast as we kept whipping past the trees.

Rue let out a playful howl, and I chuckled. I mirrored her sentiment and let out my own excited howl. I was grinning from ear to ear as we chased the sun, the warm rays trying to breathe life back into my frozen face. It was a losing battle, as the cold fall wind continuously lashed past, chilling me to my bones.

I lost track of how long we rode. The sun had gone past the point where it was level with my eyes, causing a terrible sunstrike. It was still relatively low in the sky as Vinny slowed and pulled into the parking lot of a Tim Hortons. Where the hell were we? The nearest Tim Hortons was about six hours away and in the direction of Vancouver. But we hadn't been travelling that long or in that direction.

"Where are we?"

"Just outside of Craigs Creek." That was still about three hours away.

"What the hell, Vinny! Why the hell did we go so far?" I looked at my fob watch which still hung from my scrubs. It had been two hours since he'd picked me up. How fast had we been travelling? Rue chuckled and grinned at me.

"Well, I didn't want to take you anywhere where people would recognize us. The second someone saw us together, your friends would have been blowing up your phone, asking questions that you wouldn't want to answer." My eyes narrowed into slits. It sounded like a thoughtful thing to do, but his tone was extremely arrogant. "And I just heard that this Timmy's had just opened, so I had to come check it out." He shrugged, then pulled off his helmet. When he made for the entrance; I reluctantly followed. He opened the door for me. It was an odd gesture but one I couldn't help but smile at, especially when Rue puffed herself up importantly as I walked through the door.

"What would you like to drink?" the server asked.

"A double-double, please," I said instantly, thinking of the warm coffee that would defrost my body and recharge me.

"And you?" She smiled toward Vinny, who returned her smile with a crooked one of his own. Rue growled low.

"Black coffee, darling. Thanks—"

"Black like his soul." I interrupted with a fake smile. The way she fawned over him suddenly irritated me.

"And a dozen chocolate glazed doughnuts." He gave the server a wink before he smirked at me. I glowered, my irritation growing. When we were handed our order, Vinny led us to a some seating.

I looked at the tan-coloured table as I sipped at the disgusting liquid. I shuddered at the bitter taste, then took another deep slurp. I glanced up to see green eyes scrutinizing me.

"If you hate coffee so much, why do you drink it?" he asked.

"It's a necessity." I shrugged.

"There are other things that contain caffeine, you know. You don't have to drink it."

"Ah, you don't have a neurotic werewolf and have never been on a double shift finishing at four AM—"

"I did just finish at four AM—"

"Multiple days in a row." I shook my head at him, wondering why I was even bothering to explain. "Working keeps me sane, and coffee gives me the ability to get through it."

"Try something other than coffee. Like an energy drink or something." He took a bite out of his doughnut and pushed the open box toward me. I ignored it and took another swig of the swirly brown sludge.

"I should be tucked up in my bed right now, with the covers pulled up over my head and avoiding the light of day. Instead, I'm out here with you, chasing dawn three hours away from where I live."

One Mississippi. Two Mississippi. No response.

"You know that it's not normal to drive me all the way out here, eh?"

"What's that got to do with drinking an alternative coffee source?" He raised an eyebrow as he demolished his first doughnut, reaching for a second.

"It doesn't. I just wanted to know why we drove all the way out here."

Vinny rolled his eyes. "I don't care what people think,

Roman. I don't stick around long enough to take stock of their personal business or for gossip to affect me. *You,* on the other hand, do care." He looked pointedly at me.

"I don't care!"

"Yeah, you do. And that's okay, you're allowed to. Your life is based there, intertwined with everyone else's business. As for me, I'll be gone as soon as I can. Chasing wind, chasing tail." He took a sip of his coffee and eyeballed me. "So, for our first *date,*" he continued sarcastically, "I took you somewhere where you didn't have to look over your shoulder every thirty seconds." I didn't know how to respond. "Besides, don't underestimate how far I'm willing to go for doughnuts...*and* sex."

"You have to travel three hours for sex?" I asked innocently, baiting him.

"The 'far' I was referring to isn't measured in distance or time."

My laugh was hollow. "Ah, so you thought you would show up on my doorstep for some early morning booty. I told you that you would come begging me first."

He winked at me as he demolished his third then fourth doughnut. "Hey, at least I took you to breakfast first. I'm a true gentleman."

Despite my irritation, musical laughter burst out of me. "Uh-huh. 'Cause every woman wants to be wooed over cheap doughnuts and sewer-dredged coffee."

"Well, I was going to let you ride the bike home; give you another lesson, but if you're going to take your insane hate for coffee out on my favourite place in the world, I might just leave you here instead."

"But then you wouldn't get the dirty hate sex you spent all this energy planning for," I said cooly before reaching forward and taking a doughnut from the second box he'd just opened.

"I'm sure Timmy's have cubicles too."

"Wow, you really know how to treat your dates. Cheap

coffee and doughnuts *and* a quickie in the bathroom stall of a doughnut shop. Should I remove my panties under the table now or?" I slowly licked the chocolate off the pastry. Rue grinned at me as Vinny's eyes flashed, watching my tongue with blatant arousal.

CHAPTER 36
VINNY

Her mouth was all I could focus on. I knew she was being sarcastic and in no way dirty, but it didn't seem to matter what came out of her mouth. I enjoyed it. I loved watching the way her tongue flicked around her teeth and the honey tone of her voice. Her voice, which usually frosted my blood into icicles, warmed me instead. It warmed me quicker than the coffee did.

I wanted to keep her talking, but when her tongue darted out and licked the chocolate off her doughnut, I suddenly wanted to shut her up. I wanted to be that doughnut. She licked the frosting again, the purple flashed within her eyes. It confirmed she knew exactly what she was doing. The game had officially started for the day. Vali grinned his wolfy grin.

"You know, if you're going to remove your panties, you might want to do that in the restroom. That way, you can fix your hair first."

"What's wrong with my hair?" She looked into the terrible reflection of the glass window, touching her messy knots. She then pulled out her hairband, which caused her hair to fall messily over her shoulders. "Don't you like the 'just fucked' look?" She swooped her hair back up and fixed it into a messy top-knot, exposing her flawlessly long neck.

Her honeyed words made me want to jam my fingers in her messy hair, twisting and pulling as I forced her to her knees. The way she continued to lick her doughnut didn't help my fantasy. I shifted in my seat, pulling at the crotch of my pants.

"There's only one true way of getting that look."

"That's true," she replied casually. Lick. "I suppose." Lick. Most of the chocolate glaze was gone now. She continued to ignore me as she licked the doughnut casually. With each lick, my pants grew tighter.

"Do you know what's better than chocolate?" she asked.

"What's that?" My voice came out in a strange whisper. Lick. Lick. Lick.

"Nothing. Nothing is better than chocolate." She gave me a seductively sweet smile as she split her doughnut in two. "Especially when you're licking it off a large, hardened cock." She then shoved half the doughnut into her mouth lengthways and took a bite out of it, smiling slyly at me. "Too bad there're no large cocks around here, or I would have to demonstrate."

Vali growled low, and my eyes brightened. She smiled again, her eyes twinkling with mischief.

"I would be up for that demonstration."

"Why? Do you need to practice sucking cock?" she feigned innocence. Vali growled again. This time, the rumble sounded low from my chest.

"No, darling, I'm pretty sure, should I ever fancy going down on a dude, that I would be fine in that department."

"How do you figure?"

"Well, just think of how quickly I made you come." Colour brightened her cheeks, and I grinned. "I think our first bathroom kiss was one for the record books."

"Sure was," she murmured quietly.

"And your mouth is delicious, too."

"Are you looking for another kiss?"

"I'm always up for another kiss. Panty-dropping kisses are my specialty."

"That's because you physically pull them down."

"I didn't hear you complaining. Only moaning." She twitched in her seat, and her eyes flashed purple. Her delicate tones were subtle, but it wouldn't take much to amplify them. I adjusted my pants again. I needed to get her out of here before I threw her into the restroom and re-enacted our last interlude. And as much as I wanted to throw her against the nearest wall, I had higher standards than a Timmy's restroom—marginally.

"Time to go." I ate the remaining doughnuts and stood to leave.

"Where are we going?"

"Home." Confused emotions splashed over her face briefly before her face turned to stone. Roman stood up and pushed past me, going straight for the door without looking back. I stopped at the garbage can and deposited the disposable cups and doughnut boxes into the garbage, before tossing the receipt with the server's handwritten phone number on it with a small smile. Then I turned and followed her to my bike.

"Here," I thrust my leather jacket at her. She looked at it as if it would bite her. I rolled my eyes and threw it over her shoulders like a cape.

"Wha—"

"You got cold on the way up here. The least I can do is offer you my jacket."

"I don't need—"

"Yeah, you do. You were basically a corpse when we got here, and I'm not into necrophilia."

She shrugged her arms into the jacket sleeves and took a gentle sniff of the collar. I stared at her as her jasmine scent mixed with my own. My throat constricted, and my chest rumbled. Who knew she would look so hot in my jacket? I looked her over again, and the rumbling in my chest deepened.

"What?" she asked at my blatant staring. She looked down herself to see if anything was out of place.

"N-nothing." I shook my head. "You want to drive home?"

Her stony face broke, and she gave me a large, excited grin as she took the key out of my hand, straddling the bike with sweet determination. She looked like a goddess on my ride, gift-wrapped in my leather. I imagined her wearing only my leather jacket as she bent over the seat, how I'd run my fingers down her smooth, exposed skin before smacking her naked ass and sinking my cock deep inside her. I shook my head to try and clear the image. My throat had gone dry, and my boner was straining against my zipper again. I stifled a groan. I swear, this she-wolf was going to leave me with a permanent state of blue balls.

I stiffly climbed onto the bike behind her, carefully positioning myself so she couldn't feel how hard she made me. I wanted to ignore her messy hair which had been squished down by the ridiculous helmet I'd loaned her; hair that was now pushed into my face. But instead, I gave it a gentle sniff as I curved my bicep around her waist and spoke soft instructions into her ear again.

The bike roared to life, and within minutes, we were back on the road. This time, she didn't ride at a snail's pace but confidently opened the bike up and raced down the open road. She let out a crazy howl as she changed gears. The bike jutted, and I instinctively leaned into her protectively, helping her guide the bike. Her butt slid right into my cock, which was still hard. We rode like this for the longest time, her butt shifting against my shaft as she leaned and turned corners. The friction and vibration of the road, the scent of her, made me want to lean in, start kissing her neck and paw at her tits from behind. I wanted to tweak her nipples into perfect peaks and see what gaspy, sexy little sounds she would make. I wanted to see how wet I could make her. The only thing stopping me was my helmet and the desire to keep us alive. Distractions for a novice rider were deadly.

An eighteen-wheeler came off an on-ramp at breakneck speed, and my blood froze as Roman reached for the front brake. Fuck! Vali flicked his speedy reflexes as I fastened my hands over hers on the handlebars. One hand slammed on the horn while the other tried to stop her from jerking the front brake in panic. The bike careened out of control and skidded off the road.

We had stopped. Barely. I could feel the thundering of her heart against my chest before I whipped my helmet off. I jumped off, killed the power to the bike and checked her over for injuries. My pulse hammered out of control as I tried to swallow the lump in my throat. Vali looked over her anxiously.

"Roman! Are you okay?"

"He came out of nowhere." Her voice wobbled.

"I told you not to hit the front brake," I said softly, taking off her helmet and helping her off the bike. Her legs were wobbly, so I held her hips for a moment until she regained her balance. "Are you okay?"

Her breathing was laboured as she looked at me. She seemed okay, but I needed her to say it. It was the only thing that would calm Vali down as he pawed agitatedly at my mind. Her mouth parted, and she licked her lips. I followed the movement, momentarily snared, before looking back into her eyes. The purple collided with the brown in a chaotic swirl.

"I'm more than okay." Her mouth met mine in a crazy attack. Jasmine and the sweet smell of her arousal floated to my nose as her hand cupped my cock, before popping the button of my pants.

Holy shit!

I snaked my arm around her waist and up under my jacket and whatever top she was wearing under her scrub shirt. Her smooth skin was hot against my fingertips. Our kissing was fevered. Her soft moans were clouding my mind and my judgement. I felt the piercing in my gums before my canines tried to extend outwards as her body rocked against mine.

The only sounds were laboured breathing, moaning and the sound of my zipper. I jerked into her palm when I felt her rubbing my cock through my boxers. Her fingers stroked the head in fast, deliberate circles. I shuddered into her touch. I wanted more. Needed more. As if she heard my inner desire, her hand popped my cock out of my underwear.

Cool air blew up against my thickened cock, and her hand grazed against the skin of my shaft. I threw my head toward the sky and closed my eyes. I was about to get a hand job on the side of a main highway. My toes curled in anticipation as she stroked the head of my cock, swirling the precum over it and making me gasp.

Holy fuck!

CHAPTER 37
ROMAN

My adrenaline was pumping, causing Rue to spin out of control within my mind. The pure excitement of almost being flattened by the truck made her reach out and grab Vinny in a crushing kiss. I was giddy with arousal and adrenaline. I knew he was ready for me; his erection had been digging into my back for at least an hour. I didn't care that we were on the side of the road, that anyone could come up the highway at any moment and see my hand encasing his girth. The thrill was rampaging through me, and I needed him now.

When I pawed at his cock, I had to gulp back my surprise. I shouldn't have been stunned; I had seen Vinny naked loads of times, and the boy was hung. But seeing it and feeling it were two completely different things. It was enormously thick and solid. I was pretty sure he had to have a license to carry the damn thing.

His eyes were skyward in prayer as I started to pump his shaft with my hand. He dropped his head, and the silver of his eyes sparked, his beast within awakened, savage and ready to fuck. The pure carnal look in his eyes inflamed me further, my heat and desire soaking my panties.

Vinny snarled as my scent reached his nose and slammed

his mouth over mine. His tongue was dominating as he kissed me passionately. Each time he pulled his mouth away, I tried to catch my breath, only for his tongue to possess mine again. His hands had moved from the middle of my back; one was now tangled in my hair as the other one moved up and over my lacey bra, cupping and squeezing. My nipples perked to attention as sparks flew downwards. His thumb ran over my nipple, and I whimpered against his mouth and thrust into him. He stroked it again. My entire body was begging him for more. I squeezed his cock. He bucked into me and then pulled his mouth away from mine.

His eyes were swirling with silver, and his breathing became laboured as he rested his forehead against mine. "Fuck, Roman," he growled, the sound of his wolf etching his voice. Rue puffed herself out proudly. He was unravelling under my touch, and it was the hottest thing I had ever witnessed.

His breathing hitched before he let out a raw, beastly sounding grunt. He came hard and heavy. Hot, sticky juices seeped over my hand as I continued to pump him. He bucked forward with each wave of his climax, gasping and grunting before he rested his head against mine as he tried to catch his breath.

That's when I noticed the cars zooming past us on the highway and the treeline a mere five metres away from where we were standing. One hand was still wrapped around his cock as I slapped my other hand over my mouth and giggled hysterically. I wasn't usually such an exhibitionist. Vinny gently removed my hand from his junk and tucked himself back in as someone honked their horn excitedly at us.

I pulled out my scrub hem and wiped the sticky residue from my hand smiling softly to myself. I had upped the game. Now Vinny was definitely going to come begging me. His canary-cat grin had me smiling even more widely. Another horn sounded, and we both burst into laughter.

"Come on, Evel Knievel. I'll drive." He hooked his arm

back around my waist and placed me on the back of the bike before shoving his helmet on. Was that it? No comment. No sign of gratitude. No offer to get me off? His hot and cold attitude was getting old, fast. Fucking asshole. I looked back at Rue, who just shrugged as if to tell me, *well, what do you expect?*

"You know what?" I hissed. "Fuck you!" I got off his bike, removed his jacket and threw it at him. He looked confused as I stripped off my scrubs and threw them at him. I turned and ran naked for the trees before attempting to shift into a wolf.

Rue chuckled at me as she came forward and burst out of my skin. *"Way to make an exit! I'm sure the motorists really enjoyed the grand finale too."*

"Rue, do me a favour and shut the fuck up."

"Roman! What the fuck is your problem?" the prick's voice vibrated around me. I slammed the connection closed and ran. I didn't want to talk to him right now. I was shaking with fury, and I needed to run. The trees were less dense than I thought, and I had a feeling I was going to come out on the road momentarily. My ears swivelled at the sound of the bike. The purr of the engine hummed loudly, then started to quieten as it drove further away. He had gone. Good riddance.

I wasn't worried about being stranded; I knew my wolf had an internal compass to find home. I skipped in and out of the trees as I bounded up the highway. Even though wolves weren't a common sight on Canadian roads, it wasn't uncommon to see wildlife on the highways, so I wasn't too worried about being seen. Even so, I stuck mainly to the trees and was out of direct line of sight.

The idea was great until I skidded to the end of my coverage. I had to cross the highway to get to the next patch of trees. I sat at the edge of the trees, waiting for my moment. After a minute or so of waiting for the heavy traffic to die down, I made my move, darting between two large trucks. The air whipped around my fur as my paws landed safely on the other side of the road. Rue grinned at me as I turned and ran back into the trees without looking back.

I ran for hours, my paws hurting, and I was thirsty as I had only managed to drink out of small puddles along the way. The sparse trees started to thicken into a dense forest as I turned in what I hoped was the general direction of Blackfern Valley. I was tired, and I just wanted to sleep. Finally, a familiar scent wafted on the breeze and I knew I was close to home. Rue smiled with relief; exhaustion had taken her hours ago.

The sun was setting as I trotted through the forest toward the beaten path that would take me home. I had literally been out the entire day with no food and no sleep. Exhaustion overtook me as I clambered up my porch steps and shifted back into my human skin.

My front door opened aggressively. I looked up wearily at furious green eyes. Any exhaustion I felt was suddenly on the back burner as peppermint filled my nostrils.

"What the fuck, Roman!" Vinny bellowed. "Are you fucking insane? You suddenly take off without a warning. Then you turn off your mind-link! Why the fuck would you do that?" I blinked at him a few times, his anger palpable. His angry tirade continued, "Don't you have any regard for your fucking safety? Not only did you go radio silent and remain that way for the entire day, but you left your fucking front door unlocked? Do you have a fucking death wish? Anyone could be waiting in here, ready to murder you."

The irony that he was, in fact, standing in my house with a murderous look on his face wasn't lost on me, but I chose to ignore it.

"You didn't seem to mind leaving me behind," I said waspishly, redirecting his rant back to his first point. He glared at me and crossed his large-corded arms. I followed the veins right up into his neck, where they seemed to be throbbing below the coating of facial hair as he looked at me with uncontrollable rage.

"You fucking take off like a psycho. Of course, I was leaving your ass behind."

"Then what does it matter? Why are you here?" I pushed past him into the house and grabbed a thin house coat that was strewn across the laundry-covered couch. I wrapped myself and crossed my arms tightly. He ran his eyes down me as if he was taking an injury count.

"Because when your sulk went into the fourth hour, I started to think you might've been in trouble; that you were seriously hurt or that a bear had taken a bite out of your ass—then again, you're so fucking toxic it probably would've spit you back out again."

"Charming. Your mother really should have swallowed you."

"Just calling it as I see it, darling." His eyes flashed.

"Well, you can see that I made it home in one piece. So, you can fuck off now."

"No."

"No?"

"No."

"Get out of my house!" I demanded.

"Make me!"

"What are you, twelve? Get out of my house!"

"No." The guttural tone of his voice vibrated into my core, and I clenched my legs together. He stomped forward and towered over me. Rue started to rouse from her sleepy state. She growled at his proximity, but I couldn't tell if it was a defensive grumble or morbid sexual curiosity as my body reacted to his. I clenched my teeth and squeezed my fists in annoyance. I glared at him, and he returned the look, his nostrils flaring. I knew there was no way I could physically remove him from my house. He had to be almost twice my weight, and that was without adding the weight of his charming personality. I was sure that being this much of a pigheaded asshole added infinite pounds.

"Well, suit yourself then." I shrugged past him and walked toward my bedroom.

"Where do you think you're going?" he snapped following me.

"Bed. You can see yourself out."

I had almost made it to my bedroom door when a large hand reached around my waist and pivoted me against the wall. His forehead rested against mine, and the silver of his eyes glowed as he breathed in the same intimate breath as me.

Two more dizzying breaths made me close the small distance. His hand gripped my housecoat, and I folded myself into his hard body. The contact of his soft, warm lips made me open my mouth as I grazed his mouth with mine. His tongue dipped inside with a soft moan, and his arms encased me closer. His lips and tongue devoured mine with passion.

When he finally pulled away, the anger in his eyes had dissipated and was replaced with longing. He started toward my lips again. I smiled coyly at him and placed my finger against his mouth before he could make contact.

"Now get the fuck out of my house."

CHAPTER 38
VINNY

As soon as I smelled her coming up the path, my heart had spasmed with relief. She was okay. Then, anger seeped in. That stupid bitch had left me in a state of worry. When I opened the door, she looked exhausted; her lips were dry and cracked, her hair was in disarray, and her naked body seemed to fumble with each step.

Even the sight of her looking so worn out and vulnerable didn't calm my ire. It boiled over instantly. The hot anger coiling my tongue refused to dampen. All I wanted to do was grab her and bend her over my knee as I spanked some sense into her. My cock twitched at the thought as her soft expression locked into a resting bitch face, and she shrouded her sinful body with her housecoat. She'd become a formidable tyrant in a silk robe.

My heart thumped angrily in my throat as I tried to rein in my swirling emotions. I wanted to punish her as much as I wanted to pound into her. I wanted to run my hands over her body reverently as I trussed her up and chastised her repeatedly. And I had a feeling she wanted it, too.

The kiss proved as much. Even as exhausted as she was, she

wanted it as much as I did. She wanted to be a good girl and submit to me.

Then she went and kicked me out! I didn't want to leave, I was ready to fight and claim her the way we both wanted. I needed her out of my system—I was prepared to beg.

It was Vali who reminded me to keep my pride and ego intact. Even though he reminded me of this, it didn't stop him from snarling at her as I stormed out of her house. I swung my legs over my bike and skidded down the drive, turning back toward Blackfern Valley, giving the throttle as much gas as I could.

I stomped into my house, feeling the permanent brand of her lips seared onto mine. The feel of it only added to my irrefutable anger.

Dad had raised an eyebrow and smirked but said nothing as I stormed around the kitchen. I heard the his chuckle as I wrenched the kitchen cupboards open and slammed them shut, pulling out pots and pans. My dad was still chuckling as he left the kitchen, showing great restraint and survival smarts by not asking what or who had crawled up my ass. If he had stayed with that chipper demeanour of his, it wouldn't have ended well.

My thoughts were chaotic as I made my supper. I reached into the cupboard above the sink and pulled out a bottle of bourbon, hoping that the liquid would cool the anger and help me make sense of my thoughts. Two drinks later, I wasn't any closer to collecting my thoughts nor was I any calmer. All that was reiterated was that she needed her fucking head examined.

I slammed the third glass of bourbon back before I began eating my tasteless meal, taking my anger out on each bite.

After fifteen minutes of stabbing my food, the only thing I managed to conclude was that Roman was a crazy bitch and she wasn't any good for me. The smart thing to do would be to stay away from her from now on. I had to abandon any notion of bedding her—flashes of her hand on my junk made me fidget, courtesy of Vali. No, staying away would be the only way to get out of this alive.

Can I stay away from someone as wild as her? That had to be the best hand job of my life. And it was on the side of the road! I couldn't imagine how good fucking her would be. But did any amount of mind-blowing sex make up for her personality?

I pulled at my crotch before groaning into my hands. Why did I have to be attracted to the sadistic queen of the damned? I couldn't even work out why I suddenly had a change of heart. Everything about her used to chill my insides, but now, everything about her revved them up. She had become a dangerous obsession ever since I had cornered her at the nightclub. She had been a dangerous obsession leading up to my twentieth birthday, too. Prior to that, she was just an annoyance—a beautiful yet irritating presence in my life.

Suddenly, I had a terrifying thought. *No.* There was no way! The tie was severed. *But why else am I acting like this?* My heart pounded in my throat as I looked at Vali. He nodded in understanding and attempted to feel for a mate bond. I waited in anxious anticipation.

There was nothing. No tug. No fated cord between us. I sighed in relief before my heart twisted in pain for a moment. Vali whimpered, and I gave him a grimace. It was better this way. No mate bond meant my obsession was a momentary thing. It meant I could fuck her and get her out of my system. It meant I could give into my lapse in judgment and feel nothing. I could still leave and live my life how I wanted to. Her crazy didn't need to affect me in the slightest. If I could deal with her crazy for a short amount of time, then I could get my dick wet— maybe even more than once, and then be done.

With a full stomach and a new determination that I could give in to the madness that had plagued me since I'd returned home without consequence, I placed the dirty dishes in the dishwasher. Dad re-entered the kitchen and leaned against the granite counter.

"You're still here. Good. How badly are you brooding?"

"I'm not brooding." I snorted.

"Sure you aren't. You're like one of those characters out of the vampire romance books Clemmy used to read."

"Fuck off. No, I'm not. And how do you know the characters were brooding?"

"She left them lying around," Dad said with a shrug. His eyes sparked with mischief.

"Gross Dad." I shook my head.

"So if you've finished your sexy brooding, Alpha has requested a meeting. If you're not finished, I could talk to Clem and see if she has any tips from her books on how to get you out of your funk."

I rolled my eyes and started to make my way toward the back door. "I'm not brooding, and the alpha doesn't request anything. Let's go. You can ask Clem all about Alpha Liam's sexy brooding when we get there."

"Has the rogue said anything more?" Dad asked Alpha Liam as he frustratedly paced the living room.

"No. He was whistling a show tune when I went to see him," Clem replied in a clipped tone. I snapped my head toward my sister, impressed and upset with her at the same time. Vali grumbled his displeasure, but we both stayed silent. She outranked us and could do whatever she liked. By the look on my dad's face, it was evident he was biting his tongue, too.

"What do we know?" I asked Alpha Liam.

"Not enough," he grunted through gritted teeth, "No amount of torture will loosen his lips. I'm beginning to think he doesn't know anything."

"Then why is he here?" Dad muttered rhetorically.

"Distraction, obviously. The rogues are up to something. I'm ready to slit his throat and be done with it," Alpha Liam snarled, his angry pacing sending small pulses of energy throughout the room.

"And we're sure it's rogues leading this?" Dad asked.

"There's no indication that another pack is behind it," Alpha Liam replied, "But of course, at this stage, we can't rule anything out. I want some fucking answers. I want to be ahead of this. And I want it over."

"What are you going to do? Go hunting for rogues? Torture and kill every single werewolf you come across regardless of who they are?" Clemmy rolled her eyes, her tone frosty.

"If that's what it takes," Alpha Liam growled.

"That's stupid, and you know it." The room suffocated with stale animosity. *What the hell?*

"Sitting here is stupid. This is my daughter," he rumbled irritably.

"Yes, your daughter, who only turns one once. We should be living in the moment, not allowing this bullshit prophecy to take over our lives!"

"Having a party is putting her on display, making her an easier target. I'm not risking my daughter."

"So, are you going to cancel all the other events too? Enforce a curfew?" she argued. "No more parties at Lupus', no more Fall Festival—"

"Of course not!" he snapped impatiently.

"What's the difference?" she asked. He exasperatedly threw his face into his hands. "That's right! There is no difference!"

"What's going on?" Dad asked gently, his eyes darting between them, trying to comprehend how a strategy session suddenly turned into a domestic argument.

"We've decided to cancel Lacey's birthday party," Alpha said from behind his hands.

"You've decided," Clementine corrected.

"What?" I grumbled, a little perplexed at the turn of conversation.

"Lacey. She turns one soon." My sister rolled her eyes at me as if it was something I should've known. "Our scouts believe that it'll be a prime time for an attack." She looked back toward her mate. "But they will attack regardless of whether the pack celebrates Lacey's first birthday."

"The answer is no, Clementine."

The look on Clementine's face told me that the conversation was far from over, and true to form, Clem opened her mouth to argue.

"So, is there a new plan for the rogue?" I rushed out before Clem could continue their disagreement instead of talking about the pressing issue.

Alpha Liam took his face out of his hands and eyed his mate before turning back to Dad and me.

"The plan is exactly what your luna said," Alpha Liam said. "We go hunting. We move this bullshit away from the pack land. No more stealthy moves. No more information collecting. If a warrior comes across a rogue, then that warrior has my permission to use whatever means necessary."

"And what is that supposed to achieve?" Dad asked guardedly.

"I'm hoping after we rough up a few rogues, word will get around, and the leader of these rogues will come forward."

"You're banking a lot on the theory these rogues care enough about each other to step forward," Dad advised. "These are rogues, Alpha. They have no pack loyalty."

Alpha Liam shrugged. "Then there is one less rogue in the world. I don't see an issue with that."

Dad frowned deeply. "That's not the way." His voice was soft and careful. Dad had been best friends with Liam's father, and even though Alpha Liam said Dad could speak freely, he always had a cautious approach.

"Then tell me. What is the way?" he snapped. His canines grew in length, and a wave of alpha power rolled off him. My father fell down to his knees, mimicking my position, neck bared and whimpering in submission. "There are no conversations to be had. No one has come down the main road and asked for an audience. Instead, they have infiltrated and attacked. Repeatedly. I think a few dead rogues will send a message loud and clear. It will send the message that I'm done waiting for these fuckers to make a move. That if they dare attack, I will send them back in body bags."

I was suffocating under the weight of his power as Alpha Liam breathed heavily. Clementine, who was unaffected, placed her hand on Alpha Liam's shoulder. He closed his eyes and breathed out. The power lifted, and oxygen came rushing into my body. Vali shuddered and gave a cough.

"What about the prisoner?" I asked weakly. "Give the order, Alpha, and I will execute him for you."

"No way!" Clementine said, ignoring Liam's scowl. "Do you really want to kill him before we get answers? He was planted here for a reason. He will eventually crack, or someone will come for him. Either way, you will get answers." Liam's scowl deepened, his eyes flashing dangerously. She released a small, exasperated sigh. "And when you get your answers, you can kill the mutt and whoever helped him."

CHAPTER 39
VINNY

I NEEDED A DRINK. I picked up my phone to call Sean, frowning when I remembered that he was still radio silent. I scrolled up my contact list and hovered over Roman's name. After a moment of uncertain hesitation, I scrolled up to Luca's name and tapped the call button.

The bar was pumping when I arrived. Everyone in town appeared to be here, and there wasn't even a full moon. I grinned as I found Luca and his twin brother Milo, who were already starting the shots with some of the guys, which unfortunately, included Murdoch.

I didn't need to wonder if Roman had broken things off with him. It was evident she hadn't. She was occupying a booth with her mob of she-wolves and deep in conversation, unaware that Murdoch was furtively leering at her. Every time her laugh echoed above the rest, he looked over at her in a way that made my hackles rise.

I risked a glance over at the booth as she flicked her hair over her shoulder in a boisterous laugh. She wasn't paying attention to anyone in the bar except her friends, reminding me of the friendly, bubbly she-wolf she'd been during our school days. That honeyed laughter had caught Murdoch's eye again, but even he wasn't brave enough to encroach on her space or interrupt her fun without a signal.

I smirked to myself and tried to reach her through the mind-link, just to stir the pot and ask her if she needed me to tell him about our arrangement. I could help her let him down gently. I tried to find her mind-link pattern only to be hit with a blanket white noise, similar to the sound when a wolf was out of range.

It was confusing and slightly disorientating. I pressed against it again, and it got louder. It wasn't a typical mind block, but whatever she was doing, it was evident she was doing it to keep me out.

How long can this she-wolf hold a grudge for?

Her eyes caught mine from across the room, and the spark of purple was evident. She turned back to say something to Liv and her attention didn't waver back to me. As the night went on, she was steely in her determination not to look at me. There wasn't even a flicker of registration that I was attempting to access her mind-link. The bitch was stubborn. I was just happy she hadn't been paying any attention to Murdoch, who was now looking dismayed with every passing hour.

As time went on, her heavenly scent made me itch with need. Her mind was a wall of white noise, so I couldn't push my thoughts onto her even if I wanted to. I wanted to replay the public restroom scene or our side of the road interlude, even the sudden nurse fantasy that had crept into my mind since the first time I'd seen her in her uniform. I discreetly pulled at my crotch as I took the next shot, my awareness of her humming over my skin.

"Fancy seeing you here." Murdoch had approached Roman. Even though he was across the noisy bar, his voice travelled right to me. If I was closer, I was sure I would smell the stench of desperation.

"It's strange to see a pack member at the pack bar?" I could basically hear the eye roll and smirked into my drink.

"I haven't seen you in a while."

"Sorry, I've been really busy."

"Doing what?"

"Erm. Just stuff." Her voice had taken on a tone that I couldn't place. I sneaked a peek at her to assess her body language but instead, my eyes perused her body.

Fuck me, she doesn't just look good, she looks edible. A little flash of pink string peaking from the top of her leather pants made my heart pound.

"I thought that maybe you were mad at me for how we left things the last time I saw you. I've missed you." His hand reached over and hooked possessively around her hip. Vali growled.

"You've missed sex," she clarified with a laugh. Vali growled deeper.

"Let me buy you a drink."

"Since when do you buy me drinks?"

"Hey, I'm trying to be a gentleman here, but if you would rather we just get on with the fucking, I'm keen for that, too." Vali's growling had blocked out every other sound in the room. He was hyper-focused on the conversation, and the hum over my skin was transforming into a burning itch. I gripped the fresh shot that was placed in front of me, but I didn't hear the cheering and banter from the friend who placed it there. "So, am I taking you back to your place tonight?" I waited for her response, my blood thumped much too loudly in my ears. There was no response. I turned and watched as she smiled seductively at him before walking out of the bar.

I smashed the empty shot glass against the bar while attempting to control my burning rage. Tiny slivers of glass embedded into my palm, but I didn't feel them. All I could see was her seductive smile that was full of promise and his filthy paws all over her ass.

"Bro! What in the actual fuck!"

"I've gotta go!" I snarled as I shook the glass shards from my hand and stomped out of the bar.

I couldn't believe she would go home with him. I scanned the parking lot and couldn't see Murdoch's piece of shit sports car or Roman's sedan. It had only been minutes before I followed them out, yet it appeared they were so eager to get on with their fucking, that they'd raced out of there. I stomped down the street, regretting I had walked to the bar instead of riding my bike.

I circled the streets for twenty minutes before giving in to Vali's demands. His anger was my anger. It tasted awful on my tongue, hot and fiery like I had eaten a chilli pepper. I coughed a few times to get rid of the taste, but nothing was going to calm it. I needed to let my wolf free.

I barely got my jeans off before Vali ripped out of me. It was one of the most painful transformations of my life. I didn't have time for a rest. Vali was charging through the trees and leaping over logs and small shrubs. He growled loudly as his enormous paws thundered against the ground. It didn't take me long to work out where he was heading, and what was to come next. He was going to claim what was his.

He slowed to a trot as the trodden path to her cabin came into view and gently sniffed the air. I couldn't scent Murdoch, but that didn't mean he wasn't here.

I stepped with four paws up onto the front steps and took another sniff—definitely no Murdoch. I let out a quiet huff, and at the same time, the door flew open. Roman glared down at me with her arms crossed. She was pissed. But not as pissed as me.

My bones started to click and reposition as the fur retreated into my skin. I rolled my shoulders and towered over her. She hadn't budged at all. I took a predatory step forward. She still didn't move or say anything. I took another step closer. I was so close I could taste the nutty, candied flavour that lingered in the air as she let out a tiny breath. The scent made my gums tingle as I raised my hand to her throat, feeling her erratic pulse before

I aggressively pushed her backward, my mouth invading hers. When we were inside her house, I used my foot to kick the door closed. It rattled in the frame.

I kept moving her backward, devouring her mouth as I tugged at her clothes. I removed her top with a swift motion, her perfect tits popping out with a firm bounce. I grabbed at them, kneading them and tweaking her nipple hard. She pulled away from me to let out a sharp gasp, but it was soon followed by the scent of her drenching arousal.

Her teeth bit down hard on my bottom lip as she started to move backward, pulling me along like a well-trained puppy. It hurt, but my hard cock pulsed and thickened more, precum spilling out of me. We tumbled into her bedroom, her pulling me by my lip and me trying to undo the button on her leather pants. She released my lip and whacked my hands away, tugging at her pants, which peeled down her long brown legs.

I stood back just to marvel at her for a minute. Her hair was messy, her eyes bright, and she looked like a goddess standing in a little pink thong that left little to the imagination. She gave me a challenging smirk, and I pounced like a predator, wrapping my arms around her and throwing her on her bed. My teeth scraped her skin as I aimed for the thin piece of fabric that was taunting me.

Her body shivered in anticipation as I toyed with the flimsy material. Small goosebumps littered her flesh. Her scent drove me wild. I licked her inseam, which caused her to buck. I gave it another swipe, then gave a quick snap of my teeth, leaving a little mark. She had forgotten she was mine and I was more than happy to remind her. I bit her again before I pushed the flimsy material aside and inserted my digit into the arousing warmth, hooking it against the softness inside. Her groan caused my cock to twitch as she arched skywards, fucking my finger as I pumped it relentlessly.

I inserted a second digit, and her moans increased with the friction. Her deep pooling heat coated my fingers, and when she tightened, I knew she was close. I ran my teeth over her inseam again, memorizing her scent as she exploded all over my fingers. My cock spasmed, and I was desperate to feel her tight cunt strangling my cock. I ripped my fingers out of her heat and licked them. Her eyes found mine as she watched me suck. Her gaze was possessive and feral with need. Vali rumbled with pleasure.

"Fuck me," she grovelled, her voice barely a whisper.

I tilted my head at her, grabbing my dick and squeezing it as I continued to suck her juices from my fingers. "Sorry, what was that?"

She leaned forward and replaced her hand with mine. I jolted into her warm, soft hand. "I want you to take this cock and ram it so hard and fast into me that I see stars." She took her hand off my dick and removed her thong, revealing her bare, glistening pussy. "Well?" she questioned.

I gave her a crooked grin and angled my body over her. "Hard and fast, eh?" She gulped and nodded.

"You better hold on then." I flipped her onto her stomach and pulled her glorious ass high into the air. Her engorged, wet pussy was like a beacon, guiding me in as I slid in between her slick folds. She let out a mewling noise, and I stopped to give myself a second.

I was finally inside her glorious cunt, and there was no way I was going to be quick with it. I sent a silent prayer into the cosmos as I pulled myself out to the edge before plunging halfway in again. She backed her ass into me, trying to deepen it, to control it. I chuckled and pulled myself out again, teasing her. I pushed back in a little further this time; she moaned. Out to the edge again. I pushed an inch as slowly as I could, then pulled it out even slower.

"Vincent!" she snarled. And the sound of my name on her lips while I slid in and out of her slick wetness did primal things to me. I smacked her ass before thrusting into her hard, filling her completely to the hilt. She made a whimper as I started what I promised. Fast and hard, I pumped into her. Each slap made her pussy strangle my cock. Her tight, narrow channel rubbed over my head and shaft.

Instantly, my balls started to tighten. I groaned and started counting, trying to hold off my climax. I had barely begun. There was no way I was going to be a two-pump chump. I decreased the speed; each glide was torture as I felt her snug wet core smother my length. *Fuck.*

I rotated slightly to a different angle. A whimper escaped her. I rotated again. Another whimper. I gripped her ass as I increased my speed, her tits bouncing as the sexiest noises came out of her mouth. Her pussy pulsated around my cock, choking it. Warm. Tight.

I moved one hand to her nipple and played with it as her murmurs told me to keep going. She was close. I tweaked at her nipples mercilessly hard, and she shuddered around me, crying out as her climax rolled relentlessly through her body.

That sound was my downfall. My balls and shaft tightened, and suddenly, I was unloading with a guttural-sounding orgasm of my own. Ropes of cum shot out like fireworks. My scent swirled with hers, and Vali rumbled with pleasure. *Mine.*

I collapsed on top of her, trying to catch my breath. I pulled out of her pussy and rolled onto my side on the bed. She stayed on her stomach in a post-fuck glow. Fingermarks were embedded on her ass cheeks, but they would be gone soon. Damn, she was beautiful. I pushed a strand of hair off her face so I could study her a bit better. Her eyes snapped open and found mine instantly.

"I can stay," I murmured quietly, a man possessed.

"You're not invited to."

"Ouch, now I feel used." She raised her eyebrows at me and slid out of her bed, finding her silk housecoat, and covering her delicious body from view. I started to chuckle. "Okay. So, no to snuggling and pillow talk?"

"Hard pass."

"How about a kiss goodnight?"

"How about get the fuck out of my house?"

"Call me?" I batted my eyelashes comically at her. She started to push me toward the door. "Okay, Okay." I couldn't stop grinning as I moved toward the door.

"Hey, Vinny." I turned back toward the roughed-up sex goddess and raised an eyebrow. "I won."

"Are you sure? You begged me to fuck you."

"But you forfeited the game. You came to fuck me. Don't deny it."

"Of course, I came to fuck you!" *Have you seen you?*

"Then I won."

"Yes. Yes, you did," I agreed.

CHAPTER 40
ROMAN

I watched from the window as Vinny's wolf disappeared into the trees. When he was out of view, I stretched and clicked my back before looking into the hollow of my mind and grinning at Rue. She was practically purring as she rolled around happily.

"*We are going to have to do that again,*" she whispered to me. "*And again.*"

"How about we go to sleep instead?"

"*I didn't mean right now, but holy fuck, Rome! I think we are going to need to up our cardio if he continues to fuck like that.*"

"Okay, so it was good sex —"

"*That sex was mind-blowing! I mean, for years, we've seen him waving around his long, thick weapon. But to actually have it almost rip us apart? He has ruined me, you know. We now cannot kill him for the sake of other she-wolves. In fact, we should raise a statue in his honour.*"

"I think that's a bit dramatic."

"*It's not dramatic.*"

"The only reason he showed up here was because he felt threatened when I left with Murdoch," I reminded her as I stepped into the shower to wash his scent away. "*He hates Murdoch more than* he hates me. If Murdoch hadn't approached me, he'd still be playing his little games—"

"Did you expect anything less? I grunted, and then she gave a knowing smirk. "*His jealousy felt good, didn't it?*"

"*I hate him so much,*" I mumbled instead of answering her.

"*That's what made it so good. He's right, a hate fuck is so much better than a normal fuck. I never want to go back to normal sex ever again.*" She rolled over and gave me a wolfy grin. "*I mean, I knew his mouth was good; it had the right amount of teeth and tongue. But fuck —*"

"*You know it's not going to happen again, right?*" I cut her off desperately.

Rue pouted at me. "*Why not?*"

"*It was a one-time thing. We just needed to get it out of our system so we could move on.*"

"*And is it out of your system?*"

I replayed the primal look in his eyes when I opened the door. His pure jealousy-induced rage sparked the heat between my legs. His large muscles filled my entire doorframe, and it took all of my resolve not to move my eyes away from him; to keep looking at him with disdain rather than the lust I could feel simmering between us. It didn't matter that the last time he was here, I had kicked him out. It didn't matter that we were in a cat and mouse game, driving the other crazy; the ember combusted the second his hand wrapped around my throat as he greedily kissed me. All rational thought had left me as he pushed me further into the house. I clawed at him, scratching his huge, smooth muscles as we retreated backward. His rough hands pawing at me just as desperate, making quick work of my clothes.

I traced my hand down the water stream over my nipple, tweaking it as I remembered the feel of his cock filling and stretching me as he took charge. His unyielding speed and power, mixed with the sensual rotations rubbing directly against my G-spot. And just as I thought I was going to be ripped apart, the biggest orgasm I have ever experienced was torn out of me. I shuddered as my hand made a path toward my bud and groaned as I pleasured myself, thinking of Vinny and the fact that all I wanted was another one of those mind-shattering orgasms.

"I guess not," I whispered. Rue gave me a wicked smile.

After I thoroughly masturbated, I washed myself, allowing Vinny's scent to wash down the drain. I went back to my bedroom and sniffed the air. It smelled strongly of sex and Vinny. I opened the windows. The cool fall air swirled with Vinny's aroma. I stripped my bedding, walked down to the laundry and deposited the soiled sheets into the washing machine.

I gently sniffed the air as I returned to my room. That was worth dumping Murdoch for. Vinny's scent had been teasing me from across the bar. He laughed and joked with his friends, pretending that my presence wasn't affecting him. I knew it was. My body was attuned to his, almost to a premonition level. Each movement made was felt; every subtle glance scorched me with intimacy. The fire started low in my belly, and it took all my effort not to approach him and drag him away with me. Vinny was never going to approach me in public. He knew better than that, and he was far more in control of himself than I was.

Murdoch had approached me instead and escorted me out. By the time I had stepped into the crisp air, I knew one hundred and ten per cent that it was time to break it off with him. I knew I had disappointed him when I told him I couldn't see him anymore. He shrugged it off with a grin, but it didn't meet his eyes. He told me he understood and got into his sports car without a glance back. I knew he was expecting me to come back over time—I always did—and as long as he didn't find out what I was planning to do with Vinny, that door would remain open.

I shook my head as I slipped between the fresh sheets, the

cool air lulling me to sleep as I listened to the sounds of the forest.

I STARTLED at the sounds of crashing pots and pans. Groggy from sleep, I had a flash of Vinny making me breakfast in bed and a small smile crept across my face. Followed by a frown.

For the last four nights, Vinny had shown up after my shifts with the same predatory demeanour, stomping onto my porch before igniting every corner of my house with such ferocity that it had left me breathlessly tangled in mixed emotions, and Rue crumpled in an exhausted heap. He would give me that crooked smile and a wink before disappearing and leaving me to get whatever sleep I could before my next shift. It was evident that whatever had started that night at the bar had unleashed something primal, raw and unrelenting—in both of us.

Last night, however, our schedules clashed, meaning I didn't see him, so I definitely wasn't expecting him to be in my kitchen making me fuel for another round—especially since I never had food in the house.

I threw my legs over the side of the bed, getting tangled in the sheets and almost tripped as I raced out of my bedroom and down the hallway. A fiery mane of red hair erupted from the pot cupboard. Shit. I sniffed the air delicately. I couldn't smell Vinny, but seeing as she was in my kitchen if his scent lingered, it was too late anyway.

"Dude, it's the crack of dawn," I complained, hoping she couldn't hear the nervous tenor in my voice.

"Good morning!" she sang as she proceeded to fill a pot with boiling water from the kettle. I waited for a few seconds for the tenth degree, but she only hummed.

"What are you doing?"

"Making eggs."

"I have eggs?"

She snorted. "Don't be stupid."

There were grocery bags on the counter that seemed to be overflowing with food. I stared at them while I willed my brain to catch up. "Why are you here making eggs?"

"Because I told you if you were dragging me to volunteer, you had better give me a decent breakfast." Comprehension came crashing down around me. It was the Fall Festival, the annual fundraiser for the elementary school. Months of planning, arm twisting and fluttering of eyelashes as I badgered people with my clipboard. But as Vinny had rolled into town, it had completely slipped my mind, along with my sanity. Liv raised her delicate eyebrows. "You forgot? You forgot about your baby?" She asked in disbelief, and then her eyes sparked with mischief. "The sex must be good if little miss clipboard forgot her duties."

"W-what?" I croaked. "What sex?" I anxiously sniffed the air while her back was turned. There was no sex scent.

"Oh, come on! Your house is as cold as an icebox and smells like fresh forest. The only reason for you to sleep with a window open is if you're trying to get rid of the scent of sex or who you're having sex with."

"Maybe I just like the fresh air," I mumbled, and she snorted again. "I broke it off with Murdoch."

She pivoted from the stovetop to give me a toothy grin. "But that doesn't mean you've been going to bed alone." I glared at her. My best friend. My annoying, meddling bloodhound of a best friend. I needed to get her off the topic of my sex life and fast.

"And who did you go home with last night?" I asked, pointing to the large purple fingermarks glowing against the flames on her back. Her camisole, which was designed to display her fire, didn't hide any of the bruises or sex marks. She looked over her shoulders at the marks I was referring to and shrugged nonchalantly.

"What if I told you it was Vinny?" she asked as she started

loading my fridge with grocery items. Rue snarled possessively, but I laughed. She was trying to bait me back into the conversation on who she thought I was sleeping with. I wasn't going to confirm or deny.

"Oh, really? How was it?"

"Mind. Blowing," she said with emphasis, swirling a carrot in the air like a baton. Rue's hackles rose and she coughed in disgust, but I simply chuckled.

"I can see that. Those fingermarks must have been really deep. Or is there some other reason Orisha isn't healing you?"

She shrugged. "She likes their marks on me."

She adjusted the strap of her camisole and placed soft-boiled eggs in front of me. I took another sniff of the air, trying to determine who was marking my best friend without actually giving her a territorial mate mark. That was the werewolf's equivalent of going steady. The mark usually faded after a few days, but if things got more serious, it was either regularly re-bitten or replaced by the permanent mate mark—the one that bound chosen or fated mates at midnight on a full moon. Whoever had been marking Liv hadn't claimed the soft tissue between her collarbone and neck with any proper mark. Instead, they'd left bruises scattered all over her body.

Liv raised her brows questioningly, and I returned it with a sheepish smile. Then, I started digging into the eggs with a newfound purpose.

"Their? As in more than one?"

She grinned suspiciously. "Let's just say I'm one step closer to crossing 'being sandwiched between twins' off my bucket list."

"Not my brothers!" I choked aghast. We had both suspected that my brothers had liked her in the past. She had toyed with them both while we were in school, but it never amounted to anything, not even a kiss. Had they finally made their move? It seemed unlikely they would agree to share her though, and considering they both were still talking to each other, it was even more unlikely. Her eyes danced playfully.

"Milo and Luca," she clarified. I choked again, spluttering egg onto my plate.

"Now, I can see Luca doing a threesome, but Milo?" I took a sip of water to try and ease the tickle in my throat.

"Hence why I said *almost*. I tried to convince Milo, even telling him as long as his balls didn't touch his brothers, they would be fine." I gaped. "But it was a hard no. So, instead, I managed to convince Milo to ravage me first while Luca watched. Baby steps." I shook my head in disbelief. She was deep in thought. "Too bad they aren't identical; otherwise, I might have been able to convince Milo that he was just fucking himself."

"The last I heard, Milo had asked Sophie to mate with him." I was confused. If the rumour mill was accurate, this was a huge deal, and it was almost unheard of for mated wolves—chosen or fated—to partake in extra-marital activities.

"I heard that too."

"Then why—"

"Beats me. But she was pretty keen for him to try. I originally thought it might have been a test, but she was actually really into it. She was full-on finger-fucking herself as she watched. I think I might be able to convince her to join next time." Her eyes twinkled mischievously, her mouth twitching as she tried to keep a straight face.

"Next time!" I laughed as I threw my fork at her. "You fucking bitch. You had me going!" Her laughter echoed mine as we both bent over, clutching our stomachs. "You're being careful, though, right?" I asked. I didn't know how much of what she told me was true or if any of it was. It wasn't my business, but at the end of the day, I needed her to be safe.

"Yes, Mom. I'm using protection." She rolled her eyes as she shovelled food into her mouth.

"You know that's not what I mean!"

"You need to stop worrying about me. You're far too young for wrinkles." She grinned. "Though, I'm sure Vinny will have ways of ironing them out."

After we finished eating, I ran into my bedroom to quickly dress before opening the storage shed I called a garage and loaded up her trunk with supplies. Thank God for her station wagon, or I would have had to make multiple trips. Flicking a pigtail over my shoulder, I slammed the trunk and clambered into her passenger seat, delicately sniffing, trying to subtly determine if her mystery wolf had been in her shaggin'-wagon. All I could smell was the paints in the back. Her mystery wolf was still a mystery.

CHAPTER 41
VINNY

I LANDED in the dirt with a hard thump as Ryan and Luca laughed. This is what I got for demanding to join them on an outside-of-boundary mission. We were somewhere deep in the woods in the general direction of Vancouver, miles away from civilization. Alpha Liam's extra missions were coming up blank. I was beginning to think that the rogue wolves were being a lot stealthier than we gave them credit for. I was starting to believe that they were trying to bait Liam into making a bad decision. Like him leaving the comfort of Blackfern Valley. They were playing him. When the scouts came back with no news, Ryan volunteered to lead and, in the grand scheme of things, use himself as a lure. What better bait than the beta of the Blackfern Valley pack?

Luca had tagged along for Ryan's protection—not that he needed it—and I joined because my head had been in a jasmine-scented cloud that made me desperately return to the sinful succubus the minute I finished my shiftwork. I needed something to distract my mind and my cock from intrusive yet tantalizing thoughts, so when the opportunity came up to get away from the Valley, I rode shotgun.

I growled and tousled with Luca a bit more. I punched him

in his gut—it was a cheap shot—earning a grunt as I winded him. Unfortunately, he bounced back quickly and caught my face with a right hook. Ryan grinned as I spat blood on the ground. He had called to fight the winner when one of us finally conceded. *If* one of us conceded. There was only one rule to our little fight club: we were only allowed to fight in human form. A rogue was more likely to attack if they smelled a werewolf in its weakened form. Especially one that smelled injured.

We circled again. He crouched, ready to tackle. I lowered my body, prepared to counter his weight and use it against him. *Boom!* I landed in the dirt, but this time, I rolled with Luca and smashed my hand into his face, claws extending slightly.

"Cheater." He coughed as blood puckered against pinprick holes.

"Have you met me?"

Ryan gave a chuckle instead of a reprimand.

A dirty, mottled werewolf jumped out of the thicket. Finally!

We had smelled him what felt like ages ago, but he seemed to be taking his sweet time taking our bait. Ryan smirked as the skinny thing started to approach. We were supposed to be sending messages to the rest of them: hurt them, then dispatch them; let them know they weren't welcome in the area. That there was nowhere they could hide, even in a neutral place like Kempthorne, where they would be safe—because everyone had to leave their safety at some point.

Ryan started to descend on his prey when I realized how gangly the wolf looked. It wasn't only that he was unkempt and dirty, with matted patches of fur. He was small, but his feet were enormous, and his attitude was even bigger. He lunged for Ryan.

"Pup!" I warned. Even Alpha Liam wouldn't want us to kill a freshly turned teenager. Ryan let out an annoyed noise and bounced his fist off the pup's snout. The pup growled and attacked again. Same sequence. Ryan smashed his fist down in the same spot, harder this time, and let out a low warning tone.

The pup shook his head and lunged again.

"Enough!" Ryan roared as he grabbed the wolf by the scruff and pushed him down into the dirt. The pup snapped, scratched and snarled. "Trust me, pup, you don't want to take us on untrained. Shift."

The pup looked up at him defiantly, a battle raging in his eyes as Ryan patiently held him down.

"Shift," Ryan said in a paternal tone. The pup snorted, then kicked and scratched again. Ryan smacked him on the nose again. "Shift," Ryan repeated icily.

Ryan moved suddenly, giving the pup some room. A popping noise echoed as the gangly kid's bones dislocated and reversed into their human setting. A small boy, who looked barely old enough to get an erection, stared lethally at us, his sandy matted hair falling into his face. He pushed it back in annoyance.

"What's your name?" Luca asked. He glared at Luca. "Dude, I just want to know the name of the pup who had big enough testicles to take on the beta of the Blackfern Valley Pack." The pup's mouth cemented into a hard line. "Right, if you don't give me a name, I'm going to call you Balls. Is that good with you, Balls?"

I snorted. The pup remained defiantly silent. Ryan crossed his arms and glared back at the pup. They were at an impasse. Four werewolves had just entered the world's longest staring contest. It would have been the world's longest quiet contest, too, if Luca would just shut the fuck up, but no, as usual, the clown was trying to antagonize him to talk.

I gave it to Balls. It took another half hour of Luca being Luca before he reacted. Instead of reacting with words, however, he attempted to escape. He made it look like he was about to attack when he feinted and shifted on the fly, disappearing into the trees.

A communal fuck resounded as the four of us stripped and took off after him. I had to give it to the pup, he did have balls.

Unfortunately for him, he was young, stupid and untrained. I tackled him within minutes, chuckling to myself as Vali took his leg between his teeth and gave it a gentle reprimanding shake. The pup tried to push me off, snapping like an angry turtle. I chuckled inwardly some more.

After a few more minutes of all four of us being highly amused and Balls getting angrier, Ryan finally shifted back and looked down at the pup.

"Well, Balls. It looks like you are at another impasse. You tried to take me on, but you lost. You tried to make a run for it. You lost. This makes me think one thing: you knew who we were. You're a part of this threat on my pack. So, I tell you what, you shift and tell me what I want to know, and I will let you go unharmed." The pup's eyes read disbelief. To show him we meant it, I released my jaws from his leg. He looked at me, and I gave a gentle nod of my head. He leaped for an opening between the trees, crashing into Luca's wolf that materialized there.

Letting out a sound of defeat, the pup shifted back. "Just fucking kill me and get it over with."

"I was being sincere when I said we'll let you go."

"What's the point? I'm living on borrowed time anyway." Balls registered Ryan's confused expression, and crossed his arms over his scrawny chest arrogantly. "It's only a matter of time before I'm killed. Some dickwad rogue is recruiting other rogues. Acting like he's the alpha to all of us. It's literally sign up or die. He's fucking insane, enormous, and the strongest wolf in Canada. I didn't want my head on a spike, so I fucking bolted when he came around. I tried to go as far as I could, but a pack of his rogues found me, and joining him was better than dying."

"Did you get the alpha's name? His agenda?"

"Bro, what the fuck do you think? I'm lowball. I don't know shit."

"Then why did you attack?" Ryan smirked, not believing Balls one bit. His jaw audibly snapped as he shut it and glared at Ryan. There was a moment of silence before he groaned with attitude.

"Because I'm trying to escape, and you're in my way. I don't know anything about his agenda, or his dick size, or if he likes to beat one out while watching his grandmother blow his grandfather. I don't know shit!"

Vali huffed in annoyance. I looked the kid over, and as much as he was a menace, I found that I kind of believed him. Which meant we were back to square one.

It was dusk by the time we pulled back into the Valley. It had been an exhausting day, and we were due at the pack house to tell Alpha Liam what we had learned—or hadn't learned as it was. Up ahead, I could see flashing lights and heard laughter and music.

"What's going on?" I asked from the back of the cab.

"Annual elementary school fundraiser." Luca grinned, looking toward the mini carnival as he drove.

"Annual. Since when?"

"Oh right, you haven't been to one yet. What's it...about four years now?" Luca asked Ryan, who nodded in affirmation. "Yeah, four years. It's only a two-day event. But every year, people sign up to help out."

"You mean each year she twists arms and breaks kneecaps getting people to sign up for it." Ryan snorted.

"More like bats those pretty brown eyes. No one says no to her." Luca chuckled.

"Who?" But I already knew.

"Roman Andrews. This is her pet project. I'm surprised it has permission to go ahead this year, to be honest, but she really has mastered the power of persuasion, and it helps that the smaller pups absolutely love it."

"And the teenagers?" I asked, looking around and noticing very few high schoolers.

"They may turn up for an hour or two, then disappear to get into other mischief," Luca chuckled conspiratorially.

"Let's check it out."

"Really? Dude, I don't think this is your sort of fundraiser," Ryan said.

"What do you mean?"

"He means there's no poker tables here."

I scoffed. "Trust me, if I'm playing poker, the money isn't going to some fundraiser."

Luca pulled the truck over and looked at Ryan and me for confirmation that we really were going to go into a silly little carnival fundraiser. Even Ryan, who had a young pup, wouldn't be seen dead in a place like this normally. I was already out of the truck by the time Luca gave a shrug and opened his car door. Ryan grudgingly mimicked our behaviour.

I looked around the small carnival with a smirk. The local pizza place was serving pizza and corndogs out of a trailer. There was a bouncy castle with a bunch of squealing pups having a blast. It looked like there was a table with raffle prizes and a few arcade games thrown around for good measure. Live music was playing somewhere deeper on the school field as a miniature Ferris wheel took people skywards.

Luca returned with three and a half corndogs smothered in ketchup. "Oh, sorry? Did you want something?" He asked, his mouth full of hot batter. I snorted as he continued to stuff his face with the other corndogs.

A magnitudal tug made me look across the field. Roman sat at a face painting station, sitting in denim overalls and her long dark hair in twin braids. Her face and hands were covered in glitter, and there was a cheerful sparkle in her eye that told me she was enjoying every minute of it. This was the Roman that everybody else saw. And even though I saw it now, I also knew even the nicest plant could be toxic. Her sparkly, contagious personality always evaporated around me.

A small pup around the age of five bolted from the chair the second Roman was finished. Roman's carefree laughter beckoned me, and when those eyes found mine, my breath caught. Glitter-covered overalls and pigtails were another kink I didn't know I possessed. If I was honest, *she* was my kink. I gazed over her body once more, pausing where the sparkly denim smoothed over her plump tits and the clasp of her suspenders threatened to burst. My cock hardened instantly. I was acting like a pubescent pup, barely controlling my urges. I tried to bring myself under control, taking deep breaths as I willed my junk to soften, but with each breath, her scent infused my nose and coated my tongue, which only served to further drive me crazy.

My mouth dried, and I wondered if seeing me instantly made her think the same things I was. A graphic replay of my cock smashing into her tight wet pussy assaulted me. Her eyes gave nothing away, but her lip twitched into the world's smallest smile before her face morphed into the resting bitch expression I knew so well. She was a seasoned actress.

She flicked a braid over her shoulder, her eyes conveying challenge. Was I brave enough to approach her? Was I brave enough to take her behind one of these carnival rides, pulling and twisting those braids as I drove into her?

"I think you need art lessons," I said as I stepped away from my friends.

"I don't need lessons to know how to draw a dick on your face." She waved a fine paintbrush. "Or maybe write douchebag across your forehead?"

"After the mess you made on that kid's face, it's a hard pass." I lowered my voice to quieter than a whisper as my eyes roved her desperately. "I do like it when you make a mess on my face, but I prefer it to come from your pussy."

A purple flash graced her eyes. Where the colouring was

once a sign that her wolf was becoming agitated, I was now recognizing it as a sign of her wolf becoming horny—agitated and horny. I was beginning to like this side of her crazy wolf.

"Do you want to play again, little wolf?" I gave her a crooked smile.

"What happened to it being once to get it out of your system?" Her voice came out breathy, a direct link to my cock. Her words were saying one thing, but her body wanted more. She hadn't got me out of her system yet, either. As was clear by what had transpired on the last few nights I'd showed up at her place. Instead of answering her redundant question, I teased her with my own.

"Are you saying you don't want me to take you behind one of these rides and make you come? Are you saying you're done?" Another purple flash.

She parted her mouth and licked her lips. "I'm saying I don't think you could handle me again."

"Oh honey, I think I have proven I can handle you fine. Before was child's play. We're just getting started."

"Are you lot back yet? I thought you were coming to debrief me."

Cockblocked by the Alpha. Fuck me!

CHAPTER 42
ROMAN

Liv tooted her horn as she turned and drove back down my driveway after dropping me off. My paint supplies rattled in her trunk. There was no point in unloading them as there was a second day of carnival fun ahead of us. The rattling mirrored my nerves, which had been on edge ever since Vinny had sauntered across the field, looking like a sex god, his muscular arms bursting out the sleeves of his t-shirt, his golden hair messy, and his green eyes dangerously flirtatious. The second my eyes met his, I felt a warm tug from deep within, coiling and buzzing throughout my body, making me itch with need.

I opened my front door, ready to ease my jitters with my showerhead, when I scented something that poured ice water all over my frisky mood. My brothers had been here. I hadn't seen them since I had kicked them out. I thought I would've seen them at the carnival, but they had collaborated with the hired company and set up the entertainment before I had gotten there. I was convinced they were avoiding me. And rightly so.

I should have called them to check in, apologized for kicking them out, and thanked them for their part in setting up the carnival—extend that olive branch. I knew they were always looking out for me and that, no matter what, they would be there for me. I just wish they would extend that to Indiana. I wish that my family wouldn't treat her like a leper.

A piece of paper was sitting on the breakfast bar, and I instantly recognized the untidy scrawl in black ink as one of my brothers and then an additional scrawl in blue ink. I didn't know which one wrote which part as their handwriting was eerily similar, but the tone told me that Israel had started the note and Jordan had finished it.

They had done some much-needed maintenance around my cabin and told me that they had eaten the food in my fridge for their payment and then reminded me, as always, to stay out of trouble. I rolled my eyes as my lips tugged upwards. Then my smirk descended into a frown when I opened the door to my fridge and saw how deserted the shelves had become. All the fresh food that Liv had left in my refrigerator was gone. *Ugh, brothers!*

The only thing left was wilted celery. Depressing, wilted celery. I opened the cupboard to find my jar of peanut butter when my body tugged in a strange sensation. Before I could investigate the feeling, my feet were moving. Seconds later, I was standing at the bottom of my porch steps with my arms crossed. Waiting as an aroma weaved through the trees.

"What are you doing here?" I asked into the darkness.

His voice dropped into a deep, delicious treble which resonated low in my stomach. "Our conversation was interrupted."

Fuck, when did his voice get so sexy? "So you thought you would just come over here to talk?"

"Roman, we both know there are better things you can do with your mouth than talk."

Rue came forward instantly. I mimicked her coy smile and turned on my heel. I made it to the front door before I flicked my hair over my shoulder. "Coming?"

"Not yet." He coughed, his eyes on my ass, following me inside.

A deep sound vibrated the room, and the silver of his eyes flashed dangerously. He didn't approach. Instead, he stood back, his eyes drinking in my body as if he was committing it to memory. Yet, he had seen me a million times in various states of undress. There was no need to look at me like that. I tilted my head curiously. He followed the movement.

"Those fucking braids." His voice held a tremor. "Those fucking overalls." He stalked forward, large hands covering my hips and holding tightly. Warm tingles echoed where he touched.

"What about them?" I murmured.

"Don't you know how sexy you look?" I gave a snort, not a cute musical or sexy laughter but a full embarrassing pig snort. His lips twitched into his crooked grin.

"You find this sexy?" I asked, trying to ignore my faux pas.

"Incredibly." He nodded, his hand going to a braid. "But you would look good in a garbage bag." I snorted for the second time, unable to stop myself.

"Garbage bag. Are you planning on killing me and disposing of the body?"

His crooked smile deepened into a genuine grin, as he refused to answer. His fingers gently tugged at my braids as his mouth hovered over mine, our breaths becoming one. He didn't close the gap. Instead, he waited, testing me, playing his cat and mouse game.

One Mississippi. Two Mississippi.

I closed the gap. The instant our mouths connected, all rational thought escaped, and pure primal instinct took over, my teeth elongating as Rue got excited.

His mouth devoured mine before he pushed me into the bedroom, pulling roughly at the suspenders, which popped with a loud snap, pushing my overalls over my hips and allowing them to pool at my feet until I was standing in a bright pink, long-sleeved thermal and a pair of black panties. It didn't last long, though. He made quick work of the rest of my clothing, pulling my panties down before rushing my thermal over my head so I was standing in only a bra before him.

There was only one issue with this picture: his clothes were still on. He took a moment to watch me. When he didn't continue with his prowess, I tilted my head in confusion. He smiled crookedly when I huffed but didn't make a move. Another few seconds passed, and I almost stamped my foot in agitation. Was this another game for him? One where he got me mostly naked, then just stared at me?

"Getting good enough images for your spank bank?" I asked, crossing my arms. I felt a little foolish standing there in only a bra, but I wasn't going to give him the satisfaction of knowing that. His smile widened. Fine! Two could play at this game.

I reached behind my back and unclasped my bra, removing it slowly and placing it between my forefinger and thumb before stretching out my arm and dropping it softly to the floor. His face revealed nothing, and he made no move to remove his clothing, so I walked backward toward the bed, where I lay down and proceeded to run my hands over my breasts, tweaking my nipples. My fingertips travelled down my smooth, bare skin and onto the bundle of nerves at its apex.

A soft grumbling noise filled the room. A satisfied smile graced my face as I trickled my wetness over my clit. Sliding my finger through my folds back and forward and knowing he was watching me added fuel to my heat. The growling intensified as my arousal clotted the air. I closed my eyes as I pleasured myself. As I felt the pressure build, I let out soft pants. I needed more. Then, a large hand encircled my wrist as I made to insert my fingers.

"That is mine," he growled, yanking his shirt over his head, dropping it onto the floor before he reached for the fly of his jeans.

"Really?" I panted. "I thought it was mine."

"No, Roman. While we have this arrangement, your pussy and pleasure belong to me."

"Well, you didn't seem interested in taking it, so I thought I had better do it myself." My hand started toward my pussy again, purely to see what he would do.

One second he was shucking his demin and boxers in one fell swoop, and the next, he was pushing me roughly onto the bed. "Mine!" He snarled, grabbing both my hands and pinning them above my head. I gave him a defiant look, though my pussy clenched at his dominating tone. His eyes had a dark yet playful look to them. "Mine." He repeated in authority against my unmentioned challenge before smashing his lips against my mouth.

My fangs pierced his bottom lip in response to his cock slamming into me, causing my G-spot to shiver and my channel to clasp around him. He pulled his mouth away, the silver of his eyes shimmering as he licked the crimson droplet. By the time his tongue had swept his lip, the puncture was gone. A small amount of disappointment infiltrated my thoughts, but the emotion was quickly overturned as Vinny started to rotate and move within me, the hilt of his cock dragging hard against my clit, creating a delicious friction. It was a messy collection of teeth gnashing, hair pulling, and fingernail scratches as we desperately pawed at each other. All thoughts were abandoned as his mouth found my nipple, licking and scraping his teeth across the sensitive bud. My nipple was a straight connection to my clit, and I erupted around him.

I squeezed his ass cheeks as the first orgasm rolled through me, holding on for dear life. He didn't relent in his speed as I rode the orgasm, my fingers gripping at his flesh until my screams stopped.

He gave a small chuckle, running his nose down the length of mine. "Does the little wolf want to play?" I must have given him a confused expression as his hand went to mine and lifted it into my vision. My fingernails were claws, and I had used his ass as a sharpening tool. *Oops.* Vinny didn't seem disturbed in the slightest. In fact, his wolf seemed to have brightened, and if possible, his cock filled me more. "Let's see if we can do that again," he murmured as he pulled me upwards onto his knees. I straddled him as he wound his arms around me tightly. I was pinned, my arms wrapped under his as he pounded upwards. The tip of his cock was stretching and hitting my cervix at an excruciatingly pleasurable angle. My body ached around him as the pressure built. There was no way I was going to come this quickly. Surely not?

"Come for me!" he commanded. My body tightened at his words. I moaned and tried to grasp the feeling deep within my core. "You're so fucking tight." His assault continued, each pump making me clench. "This pussy is mine." He grumbled into my hair as his fingers played with my braids. His words added to the building pleasure. My orgasm was within reach; I just needed one more—

I shattered around him, screaming his name before my teeth punctured the hard, muscly curve of his freckly shoulder in pleasure. His eyes danced with humour as he took in my post-orgasm face, his grin tipped upwards as he continued to thrust into me. He lessened his hold so he could run his tongue over my shoulder and down onto my breasts, laving up the glistening sweat as if it was sweet nectar. I wrapped my arms around him and leaned backward, allowing his tongue to work over my nipples and at the same time, he hit *that* spot deep within again. When he started to pound faster, I returned toward him, and his tongue released its assault. His salacious smile widened with each desperate moan I made, his eyes never leaving my face as I was so fucking close. I rocked hard against him, chasing my need.

"Such a good girl," he growled. "Use my cock."

He repeated himself a few more times, his voice building along with the pressure within my core. I let out a startled cry as bliss hit me again. He let out a grunty yell as he bucked into me, joining me in my high.

His panting was laboured, and he just held me on his lap in a somewhat comforting embrace, his fingers playing with the ends of my braids. I could still feel him deep inside and tried not to moan as he twitched before he slid his cock out of me with a low grumble. He continued to hold me in silence for a few more minutes. An afterglow hum emanated, and I let out a strangled noise that was halfway between a choke and a laugh.

His breathing stopped for a second, and he gently pulled back to look at me—a question in his eyes. I took the time to examine his face. His eyes were bright green, framed by pale but full lashes. His nose was long and straight, and his mouth was twisted into his signature crooked grin. His cheeks were covered in light freckles that travelled into his warm honey-coloured beard. I wanted to trace my fingers over each freckle and massage my fingers into his facial hair. Instead, I just shook my head and gave him a small smile.

"Are you done?" I was so caught up in the warm hum emitting between us and watching the way his mouth moved that it took me a moment to register the question. Oh right. He wanted to go.

Awkward.

"Sure. You can go," I croaked as I slid off him and gracelessly placed myself on the mattress. His eyes raked my body, and he flashed me a cheeky smile.

"What if I'm not ready to go?"

"Huh?"

"What if I want to stay and fuck you all night?" My synapses were firing slowly. It was as if he'd fucked every decent brain cell to oblivion. And then spoke gently as he encroached on my space again. "If I leave, what am I going to do with this?" He pointed to his cock, which was saluting me from its half-mast state.

Oh. He wasn't asking if I was done. He was asking if I

wanted to go again. Rue grinned expectantly, nodding and drooling at the mouth. My stomach flipped. His cock began to harden under my scrutiny. My eyes met his and I knew that he was ready to go again. *Is he just as insatiable as I am?* I flashed him a dangerous smile. I liked that idea.

"I think I can help you with that." I reached out and ran the wetness over his tip, causing him to shudder and thrust into my hand. I continued to roll my fingers over his enormous, thick shaft, and as I pumped, my own pussy started to dampen further. I ran my hand down my body to my clit. His eyes followed the movement with an unquenchable thirst.

With a loud growl, he grabbed my hips, and I yelped in surprise as he flipped my body over and smacked me hard on the ass. A warm tingle erupted from my core. "Mine," he growled as he lined himself up. "This glorious pussy." I felt his head run through my folds, and I shivered, leaning back into him. Desperate. Needy. "Is mine." When I arched my ass into the air, he thrust hard inside, and I let out a loud moan.

He pistoned himself inside me. I ached. I was fucked raw, but I ignored the discomfort and focused on the pleasure that was building around the pain. Each pump made me push my ass further into him; I wanted him deeper and harder. He grunted and obliged, twisting my braids around his hands and giving them a gentle tug.

His movements were feral and dominating as one hand was wrapped in my braid, and the other was kneading my ass. I slanted forward, half collapsing onto the bed under the force of his attack. He groaned into the new angle, and I felt teeth scrape my back as he slouched over me. His tongue followed his teeth, licking the sweat from my back. He sat back up, and his fingers ran down my front, over my breasts and across my stomach. Setting every inch of skin on fire and claiming every cell. His enormous cock stretched me as it slammed into me repeatedly.

"Mine," he growled softly. I made a small sound which he

responded to by stroking a digit over my clit. "Are you ready to come again, beautiful?"

WE LAY ENTWINED in each other, nothing was said as the sound of our laboured breathing filled the silence. It was evident that fucking each other once didn't get it out of our system. Nor twice, or even three times. I had lost count of how many times we'd been together; all I knew was I wasn't ready for it to stop.

Vinny had collapsed onto the bed with a large smile and tucked me into him, and I cringed inwardly at the fact we were cuddling. My horror deepened as the warmth of his cuddle sent tingles around my body. The aroma of sweat and sex filled the air, and when I looked back at Rue, she was dozing with a satisfied look on her face.

His breathing, which had been laboured and harsh a while ago, had softened and relaxed as he dozed. I peered over at him curiously. Sleepovers were definitely not part of this arrangement. I should wake him and kick him out. I reached out and traced his bottom lip with my finger. He stirred and embraced me tighter. Warmth flooded me further.

Just a bit longer.

I snuggled into his embrace, feeling safe and warm with my arch nemesis, as a gentle hum lulled me to sleep.

CHAPTER 43
VINNY

Dead weight had my arm pinned. I opened my eyes slowly and peered at my surroundings. I had inadvertently stayed the night, and because my arm was pinned, I would say we had been cuddling while we slept. I gazed down at the beauty who had my arm trapped.

There was one thing I could say about Roman: she wasn't a beautiful sleeper. Her hair was a tangled mess, and her mouth was open with a small amount of drool trickling out. She was also super heavy on my arm. But somehow, I didn't want to move. I would rather die than wake her. Her unattractive sleep appearance was somewhat endearing and I couldn't help but smile.

A small, distasteful snort escaped her as she rolled and roused from her sleep. I tried to suppress my smirk but failed.

"What's funny?" she asked, her eyes narrowing into slits as she untangled herself from my arms. I felt her protective armour snap into place, and the bitchy attitude came to the forefront. Instinctively, I grabbed her fingers and brought them to my mouth, kissing each one gently, watching her face with interest as I did. The edges around her mouth softened minutely.

"Nothing is funny. I'm just enjoying the fact I've woken next to you."

"Does that line work?" she deadpanned.

"Usually," I admitted. She frowned ever so slightly. I pressed my finger to the corner of her mouth. "Jealous?" I asked. She made a scoffing noise and rolled further away from me.

"And where are you going?" I teased, grabbing her and pulling her back on the bed. Her naked, warm body fell into place beneath mine, and the hunger in her eyes told me that thrice last night wasn't nearly enough. I had to agree with that. I lowered my mouth to hers, waiting for her to close the gap, testing her desire and somewhat playing our game. Within seconds, she slammed her mouth into mine with such force I grunted in surprise.

Blood ran south as her tongue tangled with mine, and her hips thrust her hot pussy against my cock. I roamed my hand down her silky skin toward the heat between her legs as I dominated her mouth, nipping her puffy lips and kissing her without mercy. Her body jolted as I wet my finger between her folds and circled her clit with the moisture. Her body started to move with my finger instantly, trying to get more, and my chest puffed with pride and desire at the knowledge that I was making her squirm.

She was wet, warm and sexy as hell, and in this moment, the little vixen was mine. I was the one who woke up next to her; I was the one making her come. A warm, possessive growl rumbled through me as Roman came all over my fingers.

Mine.

The musical notes of her orgasm turned into panting breaths, but I was in no way done with her. I had a desperate desire to be buried inside her warm, tight pussy again, but first, I wanted to make her come with my mouth—I needed to taste her.

I inched kisses over her breasts and rolled her nipple between my teeth, flicking my tongue over it, making her gasp and mewl. Her legs tried to clench together, but my hand rested between them, preventing her from clenching them shut all the way. She squirmed and trembled under the assault of my tongue, her ass lifting slightly as her legs repeated their clenching motion. Her arousal was heavy. Interesting. Could I make her come with just my teeth and tongue on her nipples? Thoughts of feasting on her gloriously sweet pussy were abandoned.

I released the first breast with a pop and moved to her other, repeating the gentle but torturous grazing assault on the other peak. She bucked and clenched with the sexiest moan. I grinned and continued my assault as she tried to thrust her pussy into my hand. As tempted as I was to grind my fingers into her hot den of dreams, I refrained. Instead, I moved my hand down her leg, teasing slightly. My cock pulsed precum with every whimper and sound—desperate to bury into her.

She started rocking and arching into me; tiny baby snarls coming from her sexy mouth as she was desperate for the friction to get her release. I groaned as her dripping wet pussy rubbed against my cock. With surprising strength, she rolled and flipped me, pinning my arms to the side of my head, her eyes sparking with an unbridled lust as she claimed my mouth with hers again. I grumbled as I ceded control—for now.

An alarm shrieked from her phone, which seemed to ice her sexual prowess instantly.

"You have to go," she announced, stretching over toward the bedside table and switching the phone alarm off. I raised an eyebrow at her and bumped my cock against her leg, reminding her gently that we weren't even close to being done. She smirked knowingly. "It's the second day of the Fall Festival, and Liv will be here soon to pick me up. Raincheck?" she asked, leaning down toward me to give me a chaste kiss.

"What about breakfast?" I grunted. "I think we are both going to need food after last night." I pulled her mouth back onto mine for a longer kiss and felt her lips twist into a smile before she pulled away.

"Food was not part of our arrangement. Besides, I never have food in my house. So, you best get up and fend for yourself. You do know how to do that, right?"

"I suppose." I groaned into her neck before she shimmied herself away and threw herself into the shower. If it weren't for the second day of the stupid carnival, I would have kept Roman trussed up and indisposed. But there's no way she would let me. I was pretty sure I had outstayed my welcome.

"You can see yourself out!" she called over the sound of running water, a tinkle of humour in her voice.

Hot and irrational instincts exploded around my cells. She was actively scrubbing my scent off, and the idea of that angered me. It suddenly took all my willpower not to join her in the shower. Vali snarled rabidly as wave after wave of possessiveness came through me. My canines elongated in frustration. All I wanted to do was march in there, fuck her against the wall and mark her all over, letting every wolf know that she was mine—albeit temporarily. Vali snarled menacingly at the added thought, making it even harder for me to control the animal instinct.

After a few more moments of inhaling our mixed scent and committing it to memory, and at the same time reining in my destructively possessive instinct, I reluctantly got up, dressed and left the house. Fighting all my instincts to go back and mark my territory by biting the soft, erogenous spot between her neck and collarbone.

Mine.

I AVOIDED THE CARNIVAL. My overreactive instincts from earlier had dissipated, but even then, I wasn't stupid enough to agitate my wolf. It would have been too easy to stalk her and convince her to find a secluded place to fuck around in. Too easy to get wrapped up in her again. Instead, I made myself go to the watering hole that was blissfully empty. It was still too early in the day for teenagers to be around, which was a blessing. I was left to my own thoughts and Vali's loud suggestions about what we should be doing instead of swimming. It took all of my willpower not to give in to his—my—demands. Surely, I could spend a day away from her. It wasn't healthy to want to be with someone twenty-four-seven. The sex was phenomenal, but even with mind-blowing sex, people had lives they needed to return to. They didn't replay and obsess over every inch of their latest fuck. They didn't have to physically stop themselves from seeking out their fuck buddy and driving into them until they saw stars. I dove into the water and allowed the icy, cool stream to wash over me. *What the hell is wrong with me?* I was acting like an addict. *Or like a newly mated wolf?*

I frowned at Vali, who instinctively searched for the mate bond. He did this each time my mind started to spiral, which seemed to be happening a lot lately. But every time, we were met with the same results—the bond was severed. I would react differently each time: relief, anger, annoyance, depression. If the bond was there, then there was something I could blame my obsession on, but there was no connection.

So, why the hell was I standing outside her door again? I had absentmindedly dried off and walked through the forest toward the nearest grocery store to pick up something for lunch. I had no intention of buying so much, but sure enough, I suddenly had an excuse to see her again. My bike rumbled beneath me as the log cabin came into view. I felt a bit stalkerish.

It's better than showing up at the carnival, I suppose.

I sniffed the air, rumbling at the jasmine scent that surrounded me. It was a smell I had grown obsessed with, although, in a different way.

I snarled softly as I turned the doorknob. Unlocked again. I pushed open the door with an internal reprimand at her disregard for her safety, ready to have a frank discussion with her about it. A cool cross breeze met me and caught the front door, slamming it shut. I looked around the house and noticed that every window was open, which had created a wind tunnel effect. It didn't matter that her door was unlocked after all.

I quickly placed items in her fridge and found a pen and paper. Laughing to myself, I scribbled a note and placed it in the fridge, on top of the groceries.

There was a low rumbling noise disrupting the serenity of the house, which piqued my curiosity. My feet moved away from the kitchen toward the sound. I paused when I noticed another open door down the hall. My heart lurched as I nervously stepped across the threshold. The window was open in here, too, and it was probably the only time Roman had entered in a long time. The room was plain to the untrained eye, but as I looked around, I noticed small things that made it obvious who lived there. Or would have. Easels and canvases were stacked in the corner, and the front one was half finished. There was a bookshelf of smutty novels, and on top of the writing desk was a box containing way too many bottles of nail polish. Vali grumbled as I took in the room, I stepped gracefully away, suddenly feeling as though I was intruding in a place I definitely shouldn't be. I continued toward the rumbling noise.

A small laundry was located next to the bathroom, and I grimaced as I saw the pale green sheets that were once on Roman's bed, circling the front loader. As if the open windows weren't enough of a clue, the bubbling suds sloshing up the small circular window made it crystal clear. She was getting rid of my scent. I clenched my fist at the flash of unnecessary anger that simmered through me. Of course, she was getting rid of my scent. This arrangement was a secret—it was temporary. She wasn't the one acting like an obsessed idiot. She knew what this was. *I* knew what this was. My stomach churned at the reminder, and Vali gave me a low snarl.

It was better this way. I turned on my heel and stamped out the house and down the steps toward my bike. I closed my eyes and took a couple of deep forest-scented breaths before giving her house one last sad look.

It's better this way.

CHAPTER 44
ROMAN

I RETURNED to my bed in the early hours of the morning after packing up an entire carnival. Carnival rides were dismantled and placed on the back of large trailers before being driven away. The ground was trampled and littered with paper cups, plates and corndog sticks, but after a couple of hours of scouring the ground with large garbage bags, it was like the carnival had never taken place.

It had been a success, even if the warriors had found themselves scouting the perimeter of the festivities. Liv was working the Ferris wheel which had kept her nose twitching the entire time. I scowled at her repeatedly. Nothing was going to happen at *my* carnival. She wasn't going to suddenly rush off in an emergency and leave pups in the air—I didn't care if it wasn't very high. Knowing my luck, a pup would have jumped, broken their leg and been in a cast for weeks. Some Blackfern Valley pups tended to forget that they weren't invincible until they got their wolf at sixteen. Some Blackfern Valley parents tended to remember...for a very long time.

Between scowling at my best friend, painting whimsical creatures on children, and watching the warriors casually—but not so casually—guard the carnival, I kept an eye out for a certain blond thorn in my side. There was no sight of him, and I tried not to feel too disappointed that he didn't show up. It was a kid's carnival, and even though the thought of him taking me behind a ride and fucking me until I saw stars was highly appealing, it was also wildly inappropriate. Each time I saw a flash of blond on a larger bulking frame, Rue would chirp, only to grumble disappointedly. It was silly because I knew I would have sensed him before I saw him.

As much as I hated to admit it, my body has always been tuned to the frequency of his. I initially blamed Rue. Her instant dislike for him put her on edge and made her hyper-aware of his presence. From the moment he moved to the pack, an arrogant fifteen-year-old pup with a chip on his shoulder, Rue's hackles had gone sky high when we were around him. Every rumbly laugh, every snide comment, and every crooked smirk would irritate me to a breaking point and cause Rue to react. Then, when the mate bond revealed itself, the pieces clicked together, and suddenly, I understood. All warmth left my body with cold understanding before burning heat seared my cheeks. My body was in a war with itself, the mate bond zinging around, trying to pull us together versus the animosity I felt toward him.

Yes, I understood that the initial reactions to him were the ribbons of the unseen mate bond twisting and linking us. Logic told me this. But by then, the untamed hate I had for Vinny was too powerful. My hurt and anger had solidified when Indi had gotten hurt. I thought that with the bond severed, I would no longer feel this magnetic force, that I wouldn't be so hyper-aware of him, and that his scent would no longer simultaneously calm me and rev me. However, that wasn't the case. He apparently still got under my skin.

My phone blared too early, and I palmed around next to me until my hand connected with the plastic square. I hit the tiny stop button and dropped it haphazardly as I released a sigh and tried to snuggle into my pillow more. I reached out and patted the bed next to me. It was cold and empty. My stomach churned as I peered at the empty space.

I hadn't seen Vinny since I'd kicked him out the second morning of the festival. Work had resumed, and I had been busy avoiding the doctors, glancing at my phone periodically, and waiting for him to contact me. I knew he had taken over Sean's shifts, and he was evidently too busy to send me a quick booty-call text message. Or maybe he'd had enough, and I was officially out of his system. Perhaps he was ghosting me, like the festering boil he was.

Rue let out an angry grunt, but it was hard to tell if it was me or him she was irritated at. I was afraid to ask. The fresh forest aroma was thick in the air as I took a deep breath. Rue grumbled louder, and a prickly feeling went down my spine. My skin bubbled and itched as Rue paced, snarling and frothing at the mouth. Rue's calm was teeter-tottering. I rolled off the bed and stretched before padding over to my dresser.

I traded my pyjamas for yoga pants, a tank top, and a hoodie before braiding my hair and covering it in a toque. I rummaged in the back of the pantry, praying for a box of protein bars. Finding a box hidden in the depths of the cupboard, I walked out of the house, letting the door swing closed behind me, and then directed my car toward Blackfern Valley's pack training grounds.

Unfortunately, even though it was getting colder, training would be outside. Other werewolves didn't feel the cold like I did. A normal werewolf could withstand excruciatingly low temperatures, meaning that pack training was almost always outside unless the grounds were unusable.

Anxiety bubbled off me as I inched closer to Blackfern Valley. Rue was almost bursting out of my skin by the time I saw the twin wolves howling in the mountains, a road sign that told me I had reached the pack borders.

I smiled at Liv as she gave instructions and paired us all off for warm-up. I should have been at the warrior level based on the amount of training I've actually attended, but thanks to my broken wolf, my skill level was pretty atrocious. I never seemed to improve either; I just got worn out. Rue eyed up my partner with glee, joining the training members for a warm-up lap with a mischievous look on her face.

My partner, a young, quiet she-wolf who looked like she would rather be anywhere else, examined her nailbed as I studied her. She was no older than eighteen, tall and willowy, with short, cropped, blonde hair. Rue was going to eat her alive.

We circled twice before, out of nowhere, she lunged. She was a twig, but she was quick and lithe with a powerful right hook. *Snap, crack, punch!*

Did she just break my tooth? I ran my tongue over it, and it felt okay. But before I could brace myself, she was on me again.

WE HAD BEEN GOING HARD for over an hour now, and not only had I not gained a single advantage on my partner, but the young she-wolf was relentless, beating me with every move. My face felt bruised, and I was pretty sure my lower rib was cracked.

"*A little help, Rue?*" Rue was laughing from the depths of my mind. My wolf, which should have possessed the instinct to protect me, as usual, was letting my ass get kicked. "*Rue!*"

My legs were swept from under me, and I landed in the dirt with a thump as the young girl stood above me with the smallest of satisfied smirks. My breath was coming out in strangled puffs as I held my side and tried to gulp air. Great, this couldn't get any worse, right?

Wrong.

"Did you just get your ass handed to you by a pup?" My heart started thumping uncomfortably against my chest as his peppermint aroma surrounded me. I pushed myself off the dirty ground and glared at him as I dusted myself off. His green eyes roamed my body, and I felt Rue purr in my mind. Her maniacal laughter turned to quiet delight as she fluffed herself out importantly.

The communal scent of sweat and arousal was high in the air as werewolves kept training around me. It was often the case when werewolves were practicing together. The close proximity, the grabbing and rubbing of body parts, and the general primal, domineering nature made both male and female werewolves a little frisky. A three-hour training session could easily end up being three hours of foreplay, which resulted in pack members hitting the showers, the forest, or however far they could get before their war games turned into orgasmic cries.

I tried not to think of the sexual tension zinging in the air. I didn't need the smell of sex revving me up while Vinny stood there in all his sexy, muscular, arrogant glory. I couldn't help myself, so I gave Vinny a once-over, devouring his hard, muscular, bare chest, his strong arms and hands that knew how to hold my throat just so as he pounded me from behind, down to the tops of his athletic shorts sitting loosely on his hips. My eyes darted to his face as he pulled a hairband off his wrist and looped his hair into a lazy knot at the back of his head. It only made him that much more mouthwatering. I was tempted to walk over, shake it all loose again, and run my fingers through his wavy golden tresses. My heart leaped into my throat, pumping erratically as I looked at Vinny's impassive expression.

A zinging sensation erupted over my body as it started to heal. But that wasn't the only reaction Rue was suddenly inciting. Gentle tones of my sweetened arousal licked over me, my eyes swirling with purple lust. But Vinny's eyes remained stoic, his expression unaltered.

Rue grumbled a low, annoyed sound. I realized after a second that she wasn't projecting this toward Vinny's impassiveness. Instead, she was glaring at the young she-wolf who had just humbly served my ass to me. The she-wolf was devouring Vinny with her eyes, a thirsty look enveloping her quiet appearance. Rue let out a low growl from between my teeth.

The she-wolf's eyes snapped back to me, and she gave me a small smirk. Her demure was replaced with cockiness. I knew she would never submit to me; she just bested me multiple times, instantly putting me lower on the hierarchy. Rue vibrated with anger. It looked like she was finally ready to fight. Before I could edge into an attack position and take back my dominance, Vinny's voice broke my concentration.

"Nice work. Do you mind if I have a turn?" Vinny asked, looking over the pup before flicking me a subtle but amused look. I was sure the jealous rage was evident underneath the healing purple and blue bruises on my face.

"Not at all." Her voice whispered seductively as she took a step toward him.

"Thanks. Come on, Ro, show me what you've got," he said, taking me by the elbow and directing me ten steps away. I glanced back at the she-wolf and watched her face morph from sensual, to shock, to disbelief before her emotions were veiled over. Rue puffed herself out arrogantly, her focus directly on Vinny, watching his every twitch with increased interest.

Vinny lunged, and I reacted, boosted by Rue's instincts. His fingers grazed my belly as I dodged past him, leaving a tickling hum in their wake. He tried again, this time managing to brush my braid and give it a quick tug, reminding me of the last time he'd done that. Heat pooled instantly, and the tickling hum erupted into low-flying butterflies. His scent filled my lungs as I spun and attempted to land a blow. He deflected each one with ease, his hand always managing to graze a part of my body playfully; my ribcage, the underside of my boob, the top of my hip bone. Something that would ignite my body, reminding me of how our bodies could connect. Not that I needed the reminder.

I tried to ignore the amusement in his eyes as I tried to land punch after punch. He gracefully danced out of the way with each strike. The heel of my palm gravitated toward his nose, and as he pirouetted, he twisted his body and managed to grab a handful of my ass, giving it a squeeze and then a loud smack before he pushed me away.

I swear there was a handprint on my ass, and the tingly, bruised feeling ricocheted right into my tightened core, making me suppress a groan. I peered over at him, noticing the subtle flicker of his nostril and the brightening of his silver rings. Except for a tight twist of his lips, that may have been a smirk, his face remained blank.

Rue growled low, and before I could gain control, I lunged for him. No skill or plan, just pure aggression. He caught me as I attempted to tackle him to the ground, large arms cementing around me as we tousled, his budding erection rubbing the inside of my thigh. His breathing was not nearly as laboured as mine.

He dropped me to the ground, his hand encasing my throat, and his pelvis slammed against mine. He was using his weight to hold me down, and even though he was heavy, he felt perfect. I knew that if I twitched ever so slightly, the head of his cock would rub against my clit. I wanted to dry hump him right here in front of everyone. My arousal coiled around his nostrils, and I finally saw the kink in his warrior-level control. He rumbled low, the sound vibrating right into my core. I let out a breathy gasp, Rue pushing forward. My gums tingled as my canines threatened to descend.

His eyes flashed dangerously before he adjusted himself, making it look as if he was showing me a way to get out of his hold. Instead, his hardened cock ground into my heat, and I let out a moan.

He smirked at me and did it again, his hand purposely grazing over my hardened nipple under the pretense of encouraging me to break his hold. His eyes bore into mine, and I knew that if I didn't break eye contact, I would fall.

I *couldn't* fall.

I twisted my head away.

"Who's that?" I asked, pointing toward the edge of the training ground where a scrawny teenager was under the watchful scrutiny of Luca. Vinny's head snapped to the side, his eyes narrowing. Luca looked directly at our intimate position, and I felt my face warm. He was evidently mind-linking Vinny before he grabbed the pup's wrist and gave him a deadly look. I heard Vinny curse under his breath before he glanced back at me.

"Duty calls." I thought he was going to give me a small kiss. Or did I hope he would? Instead, he untangled himself from my limbs and gave me his signature smile. "You did okay." What? That's it? I was a heated mess. My arousal was lit up like a tiki torch, and my embarrassment burned even brighter. There was a gentle scuffing noise as he walked away.

CHAPTER 45
VINNY

I ADJUSTED myself as I made my way across the training grounds, Roman's thick arousal still swarming my brain and what I could have done as I saw her through to the end of training. How I would have teased her and edged her to the breaking point, and then I would have stolen her back to my house and taken her against the shower wall, but only after she'd begged me. God's name and my name would have been the only words coming from her mouth as I bent her over and showed her who she belonged to.

I really needed to stop thinking about that. I adjusted myself again, my cock throbbing against my shorts. I glared at Balls as it was his cockblock that had destined my testicles to turn an ugly shade of blue. I glanced back at Roman, whose mouth was open in a pant, and the purple of her eyes was bright enough for me to see from across the grounds.

It was like I was reading a book. I knew which move she was going to make milliseconds before she did. I thought she would have done a better job covering up her planned attacks and, most definitely, her arousal. Her expressions shouldn't have shocked me. I knew how responsive she was. But for the amount she claimed to hate me, she almost allowed me to debase her in public. I adjusted myself again. The thought of claiming her in front of other pack members nearly had me coming in my shorts. My gums were itching in an unpleasant way, and Vali was jittery under my skin. I was still in control—barely—I just needed to find something to douse my arousal.

I stomped over to Luca and Balls, who adjusted his ill-fitting borrowed shorts. A low growl emitted between my teeth when I noticed Balls was staring at my cock. It was a common rule around male werewolves that you never send your eyes south of the border, especially when one was sporting a raging boner. Balls not only didn't get that memo, but he voiced his amusement.

"Fuck, bro! I don't want to see your chubby. If you need to go beat the shit out of your stick, I can wait." His eyes were directly to my cock.

Luca smacked him across the back of his head before I got a chance to punch him in the throat.

"Hey!" Balls snarled, rubbing his head before he turned back toward me, this time trying to avoid looking at my raging hard-on. "Think of something else—grandma's saggy left nipple."

I raised a singular eyebrow at him and crossed my arms, flicking my gaze to Luca. "What's going on?"

"Balls here decided to come for a visit."

"Uh-huh."

"He was found coming through the forest."

He was caught trespassing. Interesting.

"He claims that he wants an audience with Alpha Liam."

"Most wolves head up the main road for that."

"He was informed."

"Most wolves lose their heads for trespassing," I deadpanned. Luca met my expression with a humoured glint in his eye.

"Only on the third strike. The cost of the first strike is a finger. The second is a testicle."

I made a show of looking at Balls' fingers. "Did you go straight for strike two?"

Balls rolled his eyes. He either was so cocky he didn't give a shit if he trespassed, or he knew that Luca and I were joking—mostly.

"Alright, let's go see my dear brother-in-law." I grinned as Luca gripped Balls' neck in a painful-looking pinch.

We marched into the pack house and headed straight for the open door of the office. An inner circle meet was due to convene, and I could hear Alpha Liam talking to Milo and Ryan in low tones about the rogue in captivity. I could also hear my sister dealing with a fussing baby in the alpha quarters and my hackles rose when I realized I was bringing a potential threat into Lacey's haven.

"Alpha Liam," Luca said, bowing in respect. I followed suit. Balls didn't. Luca growled and forcibly pushed his neck downwards into a submitting position.

"Who is this?" Alpha asked.

"Balls," Luca said triumphantly. "He has requested an audience with you, Alpha." Alpha Liam's eyes showed a small amount of curiosity, glancing at his pack members in turn before schooling his features and looking at the pup.

"I've heard about you." No answer. "I'm not going to call you Balls. What's your name?"

"Thomas," he said reluctantly before his eyes shot upwards to the baby sounds above us. Alpha Liam followed his gaze and cleared his throat. When the pup looked back, he showed no interest in what he'd just heard. Then again, he knew all of us were watching him closely.

"What's your real name?" Alpha asked.

"That is my real name."

"Don't insult my intelligence. You have a number of aliases that you use. All rogues do. But you sought me out. You asked for my audience. I have granted it and haven't locked you up or killed you on arrival. The least you could do is give me the common decency of being honest. Let's try again. What is your real name?" Balls looked at Alpha Liam, and an ice age passed before he answered.

"Jensen."

Alpha looked at him a moment before he gave a singular nod. "How can I help you, Jensen?"

"You're the alpha mated to the half-breed, eh?"

"My luna is a half-breed." Alpha Liam's voice grumbled with his wolf's voice.

Balls ignored the subtle sound of warning and continued brashly. "Yeah, I thought as much. There's been talk of a half-breed, a solar eclipse and an alpha of alphas." He took a deep breath. "I know information about the rogue alpha. I can help you." There was silence. The only sound was the final grizzle of my niece and the soft sigh of my sister, who had managed to get her down for a nap. Alpha looked at his beta, who looked at Luca, who crossed his arms and looked at me. All of us were weary.

"What's in it for you?" Alpha Liam asked him.

"I want sanctuary."

"You want to join our pack?" Alpha Liam asked.

"Fuck no. I just want a place to lie low for a while." Alpha Liam didn't even blink at the blatant disrespect coming from the irascible pup.

"You want to stay here?" Ryan asked. "Why?"

"Seems like I might be marginally less likely to die here. At least until the rogue alpha comes calling, but if I'm here, I should see him coming and be able to make my escape."

"Again, the question is why? There's an abundance of rogues around. I wouldn't think your alpha cares one way or another what happens to them. So why would he or anyone care about a little turd like you?" Ryan pressed.

Balls glared at each of us in turn, and then, as if someone had sprayed aerosol around the room, a scent hit my nose.

"You're a half-breed?" I asked in shock as the underlying scent of human unmasked itself.

"Apparently." He rolled his eyes. "I'm surprised you don't mask your scent. You almost wear yours like a beacon."

"Why would I mask my scent within my own pack?" I shrugged and glared at Balls. He was right, though. Being a half-breed came with challenges. Many unsavoury characters have attempted to end me over the years. My ambassador rank only protected me so much. And most alphas weren't going to risk going to war for me, my own alpha included, but there were always the odd one or two wolves who would try to take matters into their own hands.

"Who was human?" Clem asked from the doorway of the office. He turned and looked curiously at her. His eyes raked over her in assessment. Vali rumbled low, but Balls just let out an unimpressed huff before answering.

"Does it matter?" She said nothing but gave him a levelling look. After a few more minutes of a silent battle, he grunted his answer, "I never met my sperm donor. As far as I know, my mother was human. She died when I was twelve, so it's not like I can ask her." My heart gave an empathetic twinge that I pushed back. I could empathize with the kid, but he was still being a dick.

"How did she die? She could have still been a wolf." Doctor Clem's soft bedside manner was in full force—a strange contradiction to the building tension in the room.

"She never said she was a wolf." Another grunted answer.

"Neither did our dad," Clem informed him. "Vinny didn't know until he was basically sprouting a tail. And I found out at the same time he did. Parents sometimes have valid reasons for not telling their kids." She added, giving me a measured look. I returned her look with a raised eyebrow. This was neither the time nor the place to bring up old shit. Shit that we were both okay about, so what was with the look? When Balls said nothing, Clementine continued. "We know that sickness won't kill a werewolf, so if your mother died from cancer or something degenerative, then we'll know that your father—"

"Sperm donor."

"Sperm donor," she amended kindly, "would carry the wolf gene you inherited."

"Mother-dearest didn't die of natural causes," Balls said venomously. "She OD'ed."

"Oh," my sister said, her eyes soft. "I'm sorry."

"Don't be. She was an addict. We were constantly moving from trailer park to trailer park because she would rather spend her cash on angel dust than rent or, you know, on food and clothes." Vali gave a soft whimper, pitying the pup.

"I think we can rule out the wolf gene coming from your mother," Luca said matter-of-factly. He had surprisingly remained quiet this entire time, so all faces turned toward him expectantly. "If your mother were a werewolf, her metabolism would have burned through the drugs before she had a chance to get high or addicted. I mean, she could have weakened herself with aconite, but that's unlikely. Also, it's unlikely that she wouldn't have told you about your wolf heritage." His voice offered little pity, and when I flicked my eyes back to Balls, I could tell he appreciated it. Luca continued looking directly at Clem. "Your dad had a reason not to tell you about your heritage. What would be his mother's reason for not telling him? If she were a wolf, she would want him to be prepared, especially if she was a rogue. He would have needed to know how to survive. If she wasn't a wolf, it's most likely she didn't know who—or what—had knocked her up."

"How *did* you survive your first shift? Being alone?" Alpha Liam asked Balls, curiously.

"I don't know, I just did."

"You learned to cover your scent. Nobody taught you?"

He scoffed, "You get a few near-death beatings, you quickly learn to hide everything about you."

Alpha Liam sniffed again, his eyes flashing, then narrowing with scrutiny. "So, what else are you hiding?"

CHAPTER 46
VINNY

BALLS WAS COCKY. There was no doubt about it. But he was also smart. Living on the streets must have helped in that aspect. He wasn't saying anything until he had been given the royal treatment. He sat his dirty ass down in an expensive armchair and threw an ankle casually over his knee as he stared at my sister again. She raised an eyebrow at him in question.

"Are you going to be here for this?"

"Why wouldn't I be?" There was what seemed like a silent battle as he evidently communicated with his wolf.

"I came to see the alpha," he said flatly.

She tilted her head as she appraised him. She pointed at her mate. "And there he is. Kind of hard to miss him, to be honest." Alpha Liam smirked at her in a disgustingly loving way. She met his gaze lustfully, and it was suddenly as if all the air had left the room.

"Can I get some water?" Balls demanded of Clem, breaking through the connection and diminishing the powerful alpha-level emotions that had coagulated the air.

All wolves snapped their eyes toward him. His tone was off, almost disrespectful. His jaw jutted out arrogantly as he picked at his cuticle in a bored manner. He was virtually treating her like she was an ordinary housewife and not the luna of this pack. But even he wouldn't be that stupid...

Her eyes flashed amber before she smiled sweetly at him. "Sure. Would you like sparkling or flat?" I suppressed a grin, knowing she was baiting him.

He looked at her unabashed, "Tap water is fine." She stared him down—a total *mom*erism waiting for him to say please. "Hurry along now. The quicker you get out of here, the quicker you can get back to your motherly duties, and the quicker I can talk to Alpha Liam."

Oh, this pup was asking for it.

Alpha Liam's eyes flashed at the disrespect he had shown Clem, but she turned and gave her mate a small smile and a wink before leaving the room.

Moments later, she returned with the glass, and as he reached out for it, I half-expected her to tip it slowly over his head. As a matter of fact, I was wishing for it—just to see the expression on his face as the cold water washed over his dirty, matted hair.

Clem dropped down to her knees and handed Balls the glass in an overdramatic fashion. She then shuffled back and folded herself into an extended child pose at her mate's feet. "If that will be all my alpha, I better get back to the kitchen and start cooking." Alpha Liam's eyebrows were sky-high as she kissed his bare foot before shuffling backward again. When she made it to the office door, she slowly stood, bowed again, and pivoted on her foot. She couldn't keep up the charade though, and she snorted into laughter, chortling hard as she skipped out of the room.

Alpha Liam made himself comfortable in his chair, staring at Balls, who was still lounging in the armchair but now twitching ever so slightly. To the untrained eye, he looked calm and arrogant as the other inner circle pack members entered the alpha's office for their meeting. The room instantly became stifling hot with five inner circle members, myself and a rogue included. I was suddenly thankful that Sean was still AWOL and that Clem had excused herself from the meet. The inner circle looked on curiously at the interruption to their meet. Dad stepped up next to me and gave me a questioning look, but before I could explain Balls, Alpha spoke.

"First, we need to discuss accommodations for our visitor."

"Cell?" Milo asked.

Balls rolled his eyes. "I'm happy just sleeping in the woods."

"You can't just sleep in the woods around here." Luca smacked his hand over his face and dragged it down slowly.

"Why not? I'm fine sleeping there."

Luca rolled his eyes at Balls. "There are innocent pack members *and* warriors all over this forest. One wrong move, and you'll be dead."

"That's not a very hospitable sanctuary," he grunted. Alpha Liam chuckled lowly.

"You think sanctuary gives you free rein on my land? That's hilarious." He shook his head at Balls. "This is how it works. I give you a place to stay. You are escorted if you need to run. As a matter of fact, you are escorted if you need to go anywhere within my lands. Even if you're taking a shit, you'll have a shadow. I want you so close, I can feel you breathe. Usually, *guests* would have a room here, but I'm not offering you space at the pack house. I'm not stupid enough to put you within reach of my daughter." There was a zing in the air as Balls' eyes flashed with his wolf before narrowing toward Alpha Liam.

"Mom will take him," Ryan said, breaking the tension. Alpha Liam looked over at him. "She likes pet projects." He shrugged. "Although, I will suggest locking him up in the cells for the pack run." Balls' head snapped to Ryan as if he had only just realized the full moon was quickly approaching.

My mind started to wander through the negotiations. I didn't want to be here for this. I wasn't inner circle, and there was no way the dipshit would try anything on Lacey with the amount of werewolves in the house. The problem was, even if I wanted to, I couldn't sneak away unnoticed—and I wanted to. I itched to go back to the training grounds and play with Roman some more. Looking at the wall clock, I grumbled irritably. Training was finished. I had no idea what she was doing now, or who she was doing it with, and that thought angered me further. There was no way Roman had gotten that aroused without having to seek a release.

I started to rock on my feet as bubbles of anxiety pinged around my body, tightening the back of my neck and making me roll and stretch it to find relief. It wasn't working, and my fidgeting worsened. Dad looked at me curiously, but I shook my head at him before trying to drag my attention back to the meet, refocusing on the conversation.

"So far, you haven't really offered much," Ryan pointed out, his arms crossing over his massive build—a move that made him seem more threatening.

Balls ran a dirt-covered hand over his face before answering. "I think that the prophecy has been twisted and mutilated over the years, and honestly, it's probably just some story parents pass down to spook their kids into eating their vegetables." He paused, looking at the confused expression on our collective faces. "It was a common story among the rogue camps I *visited,* at least."

"Camps?" Milo asked.

"Groups of rogues," he clarified. "Banded together, almost like a pack."

Luca scoffed. "Rogues don't pack."

"No shit, dude." He rolled his eyes again. "But if something spooks them enough, they can pack together long enough to take out the threat." A low growl emitted from my left. Dad's eyes flashed, but he stayed where he stood.

"So our intel is right. There is a pack of rogues," Milo mumbled to Ryan. A few disdained nods from the other members followed. Was that a win for us? Or a loss?

"Not just a pack, multiple packs. All with a common goal," Balls clarified again

"That's impressive," Alpha Liam said. "Banding all those rogues together so quickly is a feat. Lacey isn't even one yet."

"The rogues haven't just banded together in the last year. They've been banding together for the last decade." A surprised look mirrored throughout the warriors' expressions fleetingly. He shrugged. "It takes time to build an army, especially since rogues have the habit of killing each other."

"Go on." Alpha Liam nodded.

"Bear in mind, these are just rumours from the camp," he reminded Alpha as if he was afraid bad intel would turn him out or put him underground. "The prophecy allegedly states that a descendent of human lineage and a powerful alpha will meet under a moon, and from its birth, a tyrant would purify the blood."

"For blood-haters, that sounds like a good thing."

"That's where it gets a bit murky in the camps. They don't believe the prophecy is about half-breeds or humans. They believe it's talking about werewolves." A pin dropping could have echoed loudly in the silence that followed.

"You're going to have to explain that," Alpha Liam grunted.

"The alpha of alphas is supposed to declare some miraculous alpha command that would move mountains toward the seas, cause world-ending natural disasters, and end all genetic mutations. They'd purify the land."

"And the werewolf gene is a genetic mutation." Surprise crossed Alpha Liam's face. "I'm a little surprised that the rogues are smart enough to piece that together."

"Not too smart if they believe in a conspiracy," I muttered. Dad grinned at me.

"But really, it's not smart," Balls growled simultaneously with me. "They're basing this off a twisted bedtime story. Genetic mutations cause evolutionary changes, in which some have made life better. Life always finds a way. So even if this so-called alpha of alphas manages to bring godlike destruction on the earth, evolution will find its way back. Just like it has over every other mass extinction event." He looked around at surprised faces all around, and his ears flushed pink. "I'm a history and natural sciences nerd," he mumbled.

Alpha Liam shook his head. "Okay, so do you know how they're planning to attack? Where and when?"

"I was a lowball. I wasn't even really a part of it. I was captured and to save myself, I joined their cause. I escaped three times, only to be caught again. But they don't really care. It was always a different camp that found me. They had no idea who I was. And then, as soon as I could, I escaped again."

"You must have heard something," Alpha Liam pressed. "Even a small tidbit could help. A time limit for the prophecy, perhaps. Anything down our channels?" Alpha asked the rest of the circle.

Ryan shook his head. "No, no time limit was specified in the prophecy that I heard. But the alpha of alphas wouldn't even get a wolf until he turned sixteen, and then it would take time to build skill and power. And nothing we've come across has specified an age in which to...uh...counteract the prophecy."

Alpha Liam gave Ryan a singular nod before running his hands over his face in frustration.

"Rumour has it, the rogue alpha has humans involved," Balls piped up again.

"As in, he's killing them?" Ryan asked indifferently.

"As in, they work for him." Another bout of deafening silence dominated the room.

"But he's a purist," Luca spluttered. "Isn't that why you're scared and asking for sanctuary?"

"I didn't say it made sense. I'm just telling you what I know." Balls rolled his eyes. "The guy is taking an urban myth and has convinced not only himself but everyone around him that it's real. And not only have the rogues all drunk the Kool-Aid, but a few zealot humans have joined ranks. We all know those humans won't see the end of this war. They'll be cannon fodder, tortured for fun. This war will be the death to us all, but it's not going to end in a catastrophic natural disaster. Everyone is going to kill each other. And I'm telling you I'm scared because any sane werewolf, human or non-existent mythical creature should be terrified. The guy is unhinged."

"Have you seen him? Can you at least give us a description of what he looks like?"

"No, I haven't. Like I told you, I'm lowball."

Alpha Liam nodded. "We need to continue our meet now, but I'm sure Steph will give you a shower, food and bed to sleep in. I'll call for you if I need you again. Thanks, Jensen."

"I'll go drop off the mutt, then I'll be right back," Ryan said, directing Balls out of the room.

The French doors closed, and heavy footsteps down the porch sounded before Dad spoke, "Is anyone else thinking it can't be a coincidence that Clem got her wolf ten years ago?"

CHAPTER 47
ROMAN

THE LAST HALF hour of training was the longest half hour of my life. After Vinny left, I stood, short of breath, the smell of my obvious arousal potent in the air. I looked over to Liv, who seemed to be busying herself with setting up the last section of our training, apparently oblivious that Vinny had even come here. Even when she caught my eye during instruction, there was no smirk or knowing twinkle in her eyes. Thankfully, she was keeping mum—for now.

My denials were futile at this point, considering anyone who had witnessed our training would have picked up on the tones of desire. It was futile, but that didn't mean I wouldn't try my hardest to keep the rumour mill from churning. I would still deny it if anyone asked me, simplifying it down to the usual animalistic instinct that came with training, the one that would lead people into lustful positions when it was over. I would reassure anyone brave enough to ask that I still detested Vinny with the power of a thousand suns. I would rather gouge my eyes out with a rusty fork than debase myself like that. It would be easy to lie to everyone else, but with Liv, the cat was out of the bag. There was no more deflecting. Nope, the next time I saw Liv, it would be a conversation worthy of a catholic confessional.

As she was pretending to be blatantly obtuse about the situation, I had a blessed time gathering my thoughts on what I would tell her first. My next work rotation had put me on the afternoon shift. Thankfully, they were eleven hours long. Eleven hours of emergencies, scut and terrible waiting room television, but more importantly, eleven blessed hours of avoiding Liv. I scurried out of training and jumped in my car, slamming it into reverse before punching the gas. My car made a horrible sound as it whipped back before I changed gears, shifting into drive and skidded down the driveway. Rue cackled loudly the entire ride home.

When I got home, I ran into the house, ripping my clothes off on the way and forced the shower to ice cold. Once I had successfully showered the smell of Vinny and my arousal down the drain, I got out, dressed and braided my annoyingly long hair back before looping it up into a bun. I put a little makeup on my face and tried to find my work sneakers in a pile of mess that had spontaneously erupted in my room.

I found them squeezed under the living room couch and shoved my feet unceremoniously into each. I grabbed a bunch of bananas from the fruit bowl and clutched my keys as I dove headfirst into my car. I wasn't going to be late for work, but I needed to get the fuck out of Dodge. Rue smirked at me as I threw all my weight on the accelerator, zooming down the driveway and directing myself toward Kempthorne.

The road twisted and turned as I took the corners a little sharply, trying to get as much distance from my house as I could. I'd slowed down marginally by the time I reached the crossroad, glancing quickly in the direction of Blackfern Valley before pounding my foot on the gas and gunning it in the opposite direction.

My stomach growled loudly. I shoved an entire banana in my mouth while I peeled the next. Multitasking as I directed my car further away from my problems. I looked back at Rue to see if she could offer me any advice as I chipmunked my food. As usual, she flicked her tail and looked mildly amused. She just shrugged as if everyone was beneath her and maliciously added fuel to the fire by replaying Vinny's greatest hits on repeat.

My phone buzzed as I made it to the outskirts of Kempthorne, and I glanced at Rue. That took longer than I anticipated. Grudgingly, I palmed my phone and swiped the screen.

> LIV
>
> You chicken shit! Where the hell did you go?

The little moving dots told me she wasn't finished.

> I went to the store to get junk food and 6 bottles of wine to ensure we had enough as you filled me in on what the hell is going on. And you aren't even here.

More moving dots.

> I will wait until you get your pussy-ass back here.

More dots. Then the boxes started exploding over my screen.

> Bitch, I can see that you've seen my messages.
>
> Where have you gone?
>
> Why are you hiding from me?
>
> Come on, Roman!
>
> Stop ignoring my messages!

> You know, if you're too scared to come give me the gossip, I could always go talk to Vinny instead.

I parked my car in the staff parking lot before punching the circle with her initials at the top of my screen. Then, I hit the phone symbol. It rang twice.

"Where the hell did you go?" she asked.

"Work."

"Sure, that's convenient." Disbelief was evident in her tone. I rolled my eyes and flicked the video button on. An unattractive view of my face entered the screen before she turned her camera on—red hair filling most of the screen. I smiled at her briefly before switching the camera to show her the hospital from the parking lot. "Oh. Okay, so you have work. But you know we need to talk about this, right?"

I flicked the camera back onto myself, but the image was still not the most flattering as I walked across the lot. "I'm aware."

"I want the full story."

"I know." A few moments of quiet.

"Are you okay?" she asked. I snapped my eyes back to the phone in surprise.

"Why wouldn't I be?"

"Your secret love affair is no longer a secret."

"It's still a secret," I prayed.

She made a scoffing noise. "Not after today, it's not. Before I left, there were already whispers starting."

"It's not what everyone thinks it is."

"Sure, it isn't." Liv mocked. There was the sound of cupboard doors opening as Liv moved around my kitchen. Her eyes scanned something before her face split with glee. "Did you make food before you went to work? Go into your fridge at all?"

"Um, I grabbed a bunch of bananas?"

"Really? That's all you were going to eat after training?" she growled.

"Of course not. I really don't even know why I own a fridge. I never have any food, you know that. I'm heading to the café right now," I interrupted her lecture with a roll of my eyes.

"Oh, so you haven't seen... This is too good. Hang on." She flipped her camera, so now I was seeing the inside of my usually bare fridge. Yet, it wasn't so empty right then. Inside were cans of god-knows-what, bottles of protein shakes and some other food items that I hadn't purchased. I tried to think of the last time I looked in my fridge and couldn't even recall when that was. I knew instantly that it wasn't any of my family who'd done this. They tended to leave pre-cooked meals to ensure I ate, not ingredients to ensure I cooked.

"What the hell is all that?" I demanded. She pushed her phone closer to the note attached to the food inside. It was so illegible on my screen that I couldn't make it out. "Can't read it, Liv."

"Oh, allow me to read it to you then." She cleared her throat, and her face came back on screen. "Dearest Roman, shall I compare you to a summer's day—"

"Cut the crap, Liv." Another playful laugh.

"*Roman, these energy drinks are for you. Hopefully, you can find a replacement for your ridiculous coffee aversion.*" Liv's smile was positively evil. "This is where it gets good," she continued. "*But more importantly, there is food in your fridge now. You don't have to feed me, but at least be aware that being cock-deep in your tight pussy makes me ravenous! And as much as eating your pussy is a delicious meal, I need actual food! Touch my food in your fridge and I will not only punish you, but I will enjoy it.* Then there is a little winky face. He's such a romantic!" She wiped tears out of her eyes as she chuckled.

"He's totally Shakespearean," I deadpanned. With a note like that, the cat was definitely out of the bag. Shit.

"Oh, I have so many questions."

"I know you do. I promise we will talk. But I have to get to work now."

"Oh, the torture of waiting!"

"Bye, Liv." I ended the call and quickly filled my plate from the café's smorgasbord. I only had twenty minutes until the shift change.

If I had thought Liv would have left me to do my job, I would have been sorely mistaken. My phone buzzed in my pocket as I helped patient after patient. I ignored the buzzing as I tried to entertain a small child whose arm was most definitely broken. I just needed the doctor to confirm the results and give instructions. The poor pup had overestimated his climbing abilities and fell from a tremendous height, his frazzled mother shaking her head as she relayed the story.

The pup was in agony, his wrist bent as he was raced through triage. Thankfully, it was quiet enough to do so, as I hated seeing the pain on his face. But after some painkillers, the tears stopped, and soon, the pup was distracted with the box of Halloween decorations I brought in, letting him know in a loud conspiratorial whisper that I had been told I wasn't allowed to decorate this year. Tear stains etched into his freckled face and a broken arm was resting on a pillow as he gave me a confused expression.

"Want to help me?" I asked with a wink.

"I can't wait to get my wolf," he murmured.

"And why is that?" I whispered back as he started sorting through small plastic bats, and I untangled a fake spider web.

"Then it won't hurt anymore. I'll just heal."

"Oh, honey. We can still get hurt," his mother said softly, her face imprinted with worry. He looked deflated at this new piece of information.

"But advanced healing is a pretty cool super-power," I soothed. "If you could pick any other super-power, what would you pick?" Before the pup could answer, the doctor was back.

He frowned at the cartoon pumpkin I had just stuck to the wall, and I made a dramatized show of hiding the box before I winked at the pup.

The doctor turned his tablet over and pulled up the pup's x-ray images. I knew the second I saw it that the bone needed to be reset, which required sedation. I excused myself to go get the Hulk-green plaster cast he requested and quickly looked at my phone. Thirty notifications. All from Liv. I rolled my eyes and put my phone away without reading the messages.

Turning around, with the bandages in hand, I bumped into Simon. "Oh, hey, Simon."

"Hey. How have you been? I haven't seen you in a while."

"Good, you know—busy." I indicated at the box of plaster I was carrying.

"Oh right, well, I won't keep you. I just wanted you to know Cybil is back up in the wards." Her visits were usually isolated to the emergency room. She wasn't usually admitted.

"Oh? Why is she here?"

"She had a fall."

"Oh no."

"Yeah, she's got a fractured hip, but she's okay. The doctor is just worried about her mental state."

"Is she depressed?"

"Depressed, no. Cranky? Definitely. She keeps smacking people with her cane and shouting about fleas and rabies and something about the moon. She's muttering what seems like conspiracy theories and telling everyone death omens. And if she's feeling particularly pleasant, she's screeching at everyone to stay away from her. Total delight. She only wants me to attend her at the moment, and each time I check on her, she gives me a watchful glare that reminds me of when my grandma found out I flunked French in high school."

I laughed. "She's always been a bit kooky. And that glare is lust. She's always had a crush on you."

"I keep telling you, these cougars can't get enough." There

was a twinkle of amusement in his eyes. "If you want to attempt to visit the old bat, I recommend taking a bedpan for a shield, she's got a wicked throwing arm."

CHAPTER 48
ROMAN

A FEW HOURS LATER, I made my way up to the wards and knocked on Cybil's door before entering. "Hi, Cybil. I hear you've been giving everyone a hard time." She looked up from her book and stared at me. Her face was sunken, so much older and worn since the last time I saw her. "How did you fall this time?" I asked, trying to gloss over the concern I had for this crazy old lady who knew about werewolves.

She huffed. "Bloody wolves are moving in."

"Well, you do live in Kempthorne." I shrugged, giving up on trying to convince her that werewolves don't exist. She eyed me.

"No. They're building an army. They're going to wipe everything off the map."

"Have you ever seen a fight in Kempthorne?" I asked. Her eyes narrowed. "This land is sacred—"

"Don't lecture me on this land!" she snapped. "Her blood and tears will release the Kempthorne Pack. When a worthy alpha comes, the command that sweeps the land will be broken." I gave her a speculative look. I shouldn't have been surprised she knew about the legend, seeing how she knew about werewolves.

"Yes, it's a good town legend, isn't it? The blood and tears of the alpha's daughter released the Kempthorne line, which died out—"

"Oh, you sweet, daft idiot. The Kempthorne Pack didn't die out. They're biding their time, waiting for their alpha. Waiting to sweep the world and get rid of the filth." I shook my head at her warping of the legend.

"The Kempthorne Pack was benevolent. They wanted no part in the war."

"*That* war, maybe. But they're the catalyst for the war that's to come. They've been blood-thirsty for centuries, and when their alpha rises, we're all doomed."

I suppressed the urge to roll my eyes at her as my phone started to ring. *Asshole* flashed on the screen. "Sorry, Cybil, I have to take this, but I'll try to pop in and see you a bit later."

He spoke as soon as I connected the call. "You disappeared in a hurry." The tenor of his voice sent shivers through me and made Rue rumble happily.

"Miss me?"

"Hardly. Although, I had a raging boner for the rest of the day." I could hear the smile in his voice, and I found myself grinning in return.

"I would say sorry, but you walked away from me, remember?"

"Didn't think you would appreciate letting the entire pack be voyeurs to our brutal coupling." My legs clenched as his words washed over me. "But if that's not the case, next time, I'll strip you bare and fuck you right into the ground." Rue's ears perked in untamed interest.

"No thanks. 'Specially since we are supposed to be keeping this a secret."

"You ashamed of me?" There was a smile in his voice.

"One hundred per cent."

"Ouch." He laughed.

"Just calling it like I see it. We hate each other, remember?" Silence. I pulled the phone away from my ear to ensure I hadn't lost the call.

"What time do you finish work tonight?" His voice sounded from far away.

"Midnight," I said, placing the phone over my ear. I didn't ask how he knew I was at work.

"Come over."

"Is that a request or an order?"

"When I give you an order, you'll know it."

"Then nope." *Yes! Yes!*

"Why not?"

"Your memory is short. You're an asshole, and I hate you."

"You hate that you love fucking me."

"That too. Don't you have work to do or something?"

"Are you trying to find any excuse to avoid coming over?"

Yes. "I don't need an excuse; I just won't come."

"Oh, you will come. I promise." The grit of his voice almost made me combust on the spot.

"We'll see," I said as I ended the call.

IT WAS a little after one by the time I drove up to Vinny's house. I parked my car ten blocks away, zipping my coat over my woollen sweater before covering my ears with a toque. Clutching my keys in my fist tightly, I dashed to his house but paused at the bottom of his driveway, debating whether I should just turn around and go back home. My house was secluded, and we were less likely to be discovered there.

"Playing chicken?" his voice whispered over to me through the dark. It didn't surprise me that he knew I was out here, deliberating. My body hummed as he walked toward me.

"Just wondering if you were still up," I lied.

"Well, as you can see, I'm still up," he said as he reached me.

He was close enough now that I could easily tuck my head under his chin and embrace him, but I didn't. I just stared at him through the dark, trying to make out as many of his features as I could.

"Waiting for me?" My voice came out breathy as his hand reached out and tucked a stray strand of hair into my toque behind my ear.

"I've been waiting for you all afternoon," he growled into my ear. "Could barely focus on any of my duties."

"Didn't think you were important enough to have duties," I quipped.

"I'm more important than you know."

"Not to me."

"Really? You sure about that?" he taunted, as his hand found the curve of my ass seconds before his teeth grazed my throat. A gentle prickle moved down my neck and intensified as it coiled around my body, settling warm and low. I hated and loved how this man made me react. Tiny whimpers escaped my mouth before he claimed it ravenously with his own, ruining me.

THE SOUND of a door closing woke me up, and it took me a moment to realize I wasn't in my room. I was enveloped in a warm peppermint scent and encased in large, muscular arms. Vinny grunted and pressed his lips to my temple, sparking a sequence of electricity to tremble around my body. I shivered, but instead of making my exit now that his house was empty of witnesses, I magnetized against him.

He grunted in his sleep and held me tightly. We were cuddling, his fingers lazily drawing circles against my skin, leaving goosebumps in its wake. My hand mirrored his as I ran my fingers over his hard hair-mottled chest and down his midriff, where my hand accidentally grazed the top of his morning wood. I travelled my hand back up to the safe zone before tauntingly moving it back toward his cock, playing with the crown of curly hair before moving it back into the safe zone, never touching him but feeling him twitch when I got close. His lazy circles had stopped as his breathing became uneven with each voyage south. His grip on me loosened as I teased him some more. I put my head under the covers and kissed down his stomach before sucking his entire thick cock into my mouth. He gasped and thrust, the blankets getting thrown off me as he marvelled and watched my naked body curved over his.

"Hungry?" he asked as he watched my mouth suck his heavy girth back into my mouth. I nodded and hummed my agreement. He made a noise that was halfway between a grunt and a gasp as I deep-throated him. He groaned again, thrusting deep and hard. "Me too!" he rasped.

Vinny grabbed my ankle and tugged. I came off his cock with a pop and a soft squeal as he grabbed my other ankle and hoisted me up toward his face, his beard tickling the inside of my legs, making me gasp. "Sit on my face," he ordered. "Let's eat."

I moaned as his tongue slipped its way into my folds and flicked at my entrance. I was briefly distracted from my task as I backed my pussy right onto his wicked tongue, wanting more. Gasping as the flat of his tongue did something I couldn't even describe before curling and heading dangerously close to my asshole. I started to pant as his he rimmed and teased the sensitive area, then cried out as his hand snapped hard against my ass cheek. I groaned as the assaulting tongue suddenly stopped.

"I told you to eat," his voice vibrated against my pussy. "Be a good girl. Take my cock in that pretty little mouth and then sit on my face." His fingers held my hips firmly as he licked my inner thigh and blew on my wetness, teasing me. I bit my lip and tried to edge myself backward, but his hands held me firmly in place as his deep voice rumbled, "And if I wasn't clear, that is an order, not a request." His hand met my ass cheek as his teeth bit down aggressively on the inside of my leg before he plunged his tongue deep within my pussy. I groaned when he removed it but gasped when his tongue started doing the same punishing sequence it had done earlier as his fingers gripped and kneaded my ass. I was close and moaned as I tried to rut against his face, enjoying the friction of his beard. He pulled away again, and I whimpered in disappointment. "Do you want to come, Roman?" I nodded and tried to arch into his mouth again. "Then take my cock into your mouth and blow me."

I groaned and did as he ordered, sucking him as he thrust upwards. His mouth descended on me like a man starved, his grunts and moans adding to the swirling vortex inside me. I sucked harder and fingered his balls before pulling off in a cry as he slapped my ass again. My teeth grazed his head in retaliation before my tongue traced his slit. His leg kicked as he grunted. I grinned evilly as I gently grazed my teeth and tongue over the sensitive head multiple times, then gave it a hard nip and sucked him entirely into my mouth to soothe the sting. His entire lower body shook as he tried to stay in control of his climax. His tongue worked me over in response, bringing me closer and closer. We were both on the precipice of world-shattering orgasms, and I knew neither of us wanted to concede first. The game had met a whole new level of torture as I held off for as long as I could, edging him and controlling him with my tongue.

When my own pressure was delightfully unbearable, I shivered and moaned deeply, my teeth deliberately scraping his shaft like the sadist I was. I rocked against his face as the orgasm burst out of me. Wave after wave rolled over me, coating Vinny's slippery tongue before he suddenly stopped. A muffled guttural noise came from underneath my pussy. Fingers gripped my hips as hot, sticky streams shot down the back of my throat. I instinctively swallowed, then gave his cock a final lick as if it was my favourite lollipop before I not-so-gracefully lifted myself from his face and lay next to him.

Rue rumbled within my mind, wholly satiated and submissive. She looked over at him possessively, and her emotions were suddenly my emotions.

Mine.

CHAPTER 49
VINNY

VALI RUMBLED PRIMITIVELY as I gazed at the long legs disappearing under my threadbare t-shirt while she filled a glass of water from the tap. I knew she was naked under there, and even though I had just come harder than ever before in my entire life, I was yearning for more.

Her well-fucked hair tickled the edge of her elbows as she moved the glass to her mouth. I tried to stop the urge to run my fingers through it, over her arms and underneath my shirt, to feel her glorious naked body underneath. She was wearing my shirt, owning it like she was beginning to own me. Fuck. She seriously looked good, barefoot in my kitchen with only my t-shirt on.

Mine.

As if she could sense my thoughts, she gazed at me from over her shoulder and gave me a small smile before spinning and crossing her arms across her bouncy breasts. "Nuh-uh," she said, shaking her head. "We've been going at it all night, and I don't know about you, but I could use a break, maybe some sleep before my shift starts."

"What time do you work at?" I asked, not taking my eyes off the hem of the shirt, knowing if she stretched her arms over her head just enough, her snatch would be winking at me.

"One o'clock. I'm on an eleven-hour rotation."

"We still have lots of time." I grinned at her, licking my lips ravenously.

"No, we don't. Like I said, I have to go home, take a shower, and get to work."

"You can do that all from here."

"Not a good idea." She shook her head again.

I raised an arrogant eyebrow. "Why not?"

She sighed, and I felt it move into my chest, tingly and warm. "Because, if I stay, there's no way you'll let me shower or get ready for work in peace."

"You can have a shower."

"Alone?"

"Of course not. I want to own you on every surface of this house."

Her mouth curved into a small flirtatious smile, and she gently shook her head. "Don't you think that's a little inappropriate? It's your dad's house. You can't just mark your territory all over it."

"So?" He's not claiming it." I released a panty-dropping grin. "And it's not the house I want to claim. It's you. No matter where you are, whenever I see you, I want to claim you." I took a predatory step toward her as her eyes flashed in unconcealed interest. Her lips and legs parted in anticipation. "I want to bend you over whatever I can and fuck you raw. Whether we're in a bar, at a pack meet, or at each other's throats, know this: all I'll be thinking about is ripping your panties off and stealing your sanity."

Her eyes flashed purple, and was followed by a delicious scent filling the air around us as her voice came out in a low rasp that tickled my balls. "So, I'm not out of your system yet?"

I gave her a crooked smile. *I don't think you'll ever be out of my system.*

She shook her head before I could verbally respond. "All you're doing is proving my point. We can't be in the same room without getting naked anymore."

"We could never be in the same room," I pointed out. She rolled her eyes at me, and it took all my willpower not to swat her behind, to playfully reprimand her for the act. Vali was eager for me to play on those instincts and remind her who she belonged to, but with whatever strength I had left, I resisted. "Fine. Challenge accepted."

"What challenge?" Her brows furrowed adorably.

"I'll prove to you that we can be in the same room and keep our hands off each other. You sit there, and I'll make us breakfast." I pointed to the breakfast bar.

"You're going to cook for me?" she asked as she leaned against the bar but refused to take a seat.

"Unlike someone, I *actually* have food in my house." I grinned, remembering the note I had left her after filling her fridge.

"About that, care to explain the food and note in my fridge?" she asked, obviously on the same wavelength.

"Well, you said that you could never feed me because of your lack of supplies—"

"Pretty sure I said I wasn't going to because it wasn't a part of our agreement." She rolled her eyes again as Vali made a rumbling noise.

"Well, now you don't have the excuse," I continued, as if she didn't interrupt.

"Presumptuous much?" she muttered. I met her scowl with a grin as I started beating eggs in a bowl. "I think I should tell you that I didn't actually find the note."

I barked out a single laugh. "Who did?"

"Liv." She shrugged. I broke into a full-hearted chuckle, imagining her embarrassment. "She helps herself to my house. You should know that for the next time you want to leave me poetry."

"That will teach you to lock your door." Her scowl deepened, and all I wanted to do was kiss her. Shit, how had I never noticed how cute she was? "Hey, it could've been worse. Could have been one of your brothers."

I watched as the colour drained from her face before flushing brightly again. She ran her hands over her face, laughing and groaning in embarrassment. Vali wagged his tail as he watched her adoringly. Yes, she was super cute. I dipped the bread into the egg mix as she started to walk away.

"Where are you going?" I asked.

"To find some panties. I suppose, if we are going to do this domesticated thing, then I probably shouldn't sit on your furniture with my bare ass."

My resolve was tested instantly as she returned to the kitchen wearing a pair of my boxers then sat on the bar stool with a wicked glint in her eyes. My primal urges surfaced as I gripped the pan handle with much more force than necessary.

I managed to make it through breakfast with amazing control. We had a pleasant breakfast, chatting about trivial crap like a normal couple. There was still flirting and playful banter, but we proved in the half-hour it took for us to eat breakfast that we could be civil *and* keep our hands off each other. We were positively domesticated.

When she asked me for a shower, I saw the challenge in her eyes, and it split my instincts into two. I really wanted to soap her all over and fuck her against the shower tile, but the other part of me knew this was a test. I had survived breakfast, barely.

She slipped my t-shirt up and over her head, her black hair swishing to the middle of her naked back before she fingered the waistband of my boxers. I fumbled out of the door in desperation. Vali surged possessively, snarling at me as the door closed with a click before resting my head against it. It took even more power to walk down the hall to my bedroom, squeezing myself to try and release some discomfort.

· · ·

I was still lying on my bed when her clean jasmine scent wafted down the hall and into my open bedroom, followed shortly by her, wrapped in a towel. She threw my t-shirt and boxers into the laundry basket and proceeded to pat her hair dry with a smaller towel. Vali rumbled happily. I watched every water droplet on her shoulders and gripped the mattress to stop myself from going over and licking them.

I can do this! I can do this! She removed her towel. *Fuck!*

"I still can't believe Alpha Liam doesn't want to do a pack celebration for Lacey's first birthday!" She scrunched the leg of her skinny jeans and popped it over her ankle before rolling it up her calf. My eyes trailed the hypnotic movement. I had mentioned that Lacey wasn't getting a birthday party before, but I hadn't told her about the constant threat to Lacey's life. All she knew was a rogue wolf had attacked, and the warriors were increasing security. If she had connected the dots, she never mentioned anything.

"His reasoning is that she won't even remember it." I barely registered that I'd answered her.

"But *he* will. And it will haunt him for the rest of his existence."

"That's a little dramatic."

"He let us have the Fall Festival," she pointed out.

I winked playfully at her. "I think he was scared of taking you on." She sent me a dazzling grin at my playful suggestion that Alpha Liam was afraid of her. Her smiles were definitely contagious. I would do pretty much anything for her to smile at me like that.

"The pack will be disappointed," she continued as she shimmied the jeans over her ass and buttoned them before looking around for the rest of her clothes. I shifted on the bed as I watched her, my eyes roaming her body, trailing from her legs and ass to her boobs which were threatening to slip out from the top of a black lacey bra she'd just put on. I fidgeted again.

"The pack will be partying hard anyway. In fact, they'll be

having much more fun getting plastered then playing pin the tail on the beaver or whatever," I mumbled distractedly. She was now standing in front of a floor-length mirror and looking back at me through the reflection. Just what I needed, two of her. She snorted into a carefree laughter, and I graced her with an indulgent smile.

"Pin the tail on the what?"

"You know, it's one of those kid's games." I couldn't take it anymore. I slinked off the bed and adjusted myself as a magnetic force moved me behind her.

"No, that's pin the tail on the donkey."

"Wonder what I'm thinking of then?" I asked, kissing her collarbone gently, feeling my canines burning within my gums. I moved my hands around her waist before unbuttoning her jeans again. "It's something related to a beaver." My finger edged down into her panties and circled her clit. She gasped and curved into me, her ass rubbing against my already throbbing cock. I needed to stop. I needed to let her go to work. When I met her eyes in the mirror, the hunger in her eyes told a different story. She was just as insatiable in her want for me, as I was with my need for her.

"I-I need to get going." She breathed as my other hand found her nipple through the sexy lace. It puckered to attention as I played. She threw her head back, relaxing into me. We both watched our reflection as I continued to torture her seductively.

"I know," I whispered with a small cheeky smile.

"Y-you need to s-stop." I circled her clit again and hummed a non-committal noise.

She opened her legs a little wider, the heat and scent of her arousal making my canines erupt painfully. Vali's instincts were flooding through my body, telling me to bite the soft flesh between her neck and shoulder. *Not a good idea. But oh, so fucking tempting.*

"Okay," I murmured in agreement, trying to force my canines to recede as I kept circling her clit lazily. Little whimpering noises were making it harder to resist marking her. But as much as Vali wanted to mark her, he knew she would never be ours. As soon as the thought entered my mind, his instinct wavered, and the need to mark her passed. I breathed in a sigh of relief before burying my nose deep in her wet hair. God, she was exquisite. I licked and nibbled at her earlobe, making her gasp and jolt back into me.

"You were supposed to be proving we could be in the same room without being naked." Her voice wobbled.

"Give me some credit. I lasted an hour. Besides, clothes are overrated," I grunted. I stopped playing with her tit and yanked her hair back, giving myself access to her heart-shaped mouth. I kissed her deeply, claiming her. My other finger slid from her clit and buried straight into her drenched pussy, making her moan. My cock ached to be free and inside her. I needed her now! I started to direct her backward, pausing briefly between my demanding kisses but simply long enough to make sure we didn't trip because I didn't want to give up the addictive taste of her mouth for more than I had to.

"Well, I guess I can call in sick," she said breathlessly as I braced her against the wall, then started stripping her gloriously tight jeans off.

CHAPTER 50
ROMAN

When I eventually got home, I was surprised to see Liv's car in my driveway. My stomach sank with weighted dread. Shit. Had she stayed here this entire time? Double shit! Before I had even cut the engine, I saw her figure looming on the porch, her arms crossed against her chest. Her expression was that of a parent waiting to catch their teenager sneaking back after breaking curfew—stern, a bit too knowing, but with undeniable underlying amusement. This was going to be painful.

"I was going to ask if you had pulled a double," she called as I climbed out of the car. "But from the smell of you, that's not the double I need to ask about."

Heat flooded my cheeks, but I had no clever retort. "Hi," I said defeatedly as I trudged up my porch steps. She pointed to my open front door, directing my walk of shame.

I skulked into the house and collapsed onto the couch, closing my eyes as she shut the door and walked toward the kitchen. I threw my arm over my eyes as if the simple act of hiding my face would shield me from what was coming. There was the unmistakable sound of gentle clinking followed by that of liquid courage being poured. A moment later, the scent of merlot filled my senses as Liv shoved a glass under my nose.

I opened my eyes, took the glass and downed it. She filled it again, but the wine barely touched the sides of the glass before I skulled it back. She obligingly refilled it three more times before I finally let the wine sit on the coffee table with a pause. I stared at the bottles she had lined up—a battlefield of wine between us. One bottle empty, the others about to meet the same fate.

Liv, on the other hand, sipped hers delicately like it was a casual Friday evening and not an impending inquisition. A pregnant silence hung between us. My pulse quickened as I finally broke it.

"Did you stay here? All this time?" I bravely asked.

"Yeah," she replied without missing a beat. "Cassie's been crashing at mine. I needed a break." Her tone was deceptively casual, but I clung to it, hoping for a reprieve, a detour. Anything.

"Cassie, what's she doing now?" I jumped on her thread of a topic change and yanked.

"Oh no, you don't!" Liv snarled softly. "Vinny. Spill."

"It's not what you think."

"So, you aren't fucking him?" Her voice dripped with sarcasm, the question like a blade, cutting through any pitiful defences and lies I could think of on the fly.

"Okay, it's exactly what you think." I groaned, closing my eyes and threw my head against the back of the couch. The smell of wine wafted directly under my nose again, and I peeked out of one eye to see Liv holding my glass near my face as if encouraging me to drown my shame. Her face stretched with a smug smile.

With a sigh, I took it in my hand and swallowed another sip, slower this time, gathering courage for the inevitable.

"We just needed to get it out of our system," I said in a small, embarrassed voice. *What will she think of me?* "This is all your fault."

"How is you opening your legs to his dick, my fault? I don't control your legs," she replied with humorous sass, her eyebrows sky-high and her eyes twinkling at my expense. She was enjoying this far too much.

"You're the one who said that we had explosive chemistry and just needed to release the pressure. That as much as Rue wanted to kill him, she also wanted to be owned by him. It planted the seed, and suddenly, Vinny is this thirst trap I can't avoid." I take another sip of my wine—the liquid was loosening my tongue now, and before I could stop myself, the rest tumbled out. "I think Vinny drank the same crazy juice as you 'cause suddenly, he's propositioning me out of nowhere, and it's all I can think about. Sex with Murdoch was safe and easy but quickly became a bore, which led me to wonder about Vinny Stevens. And I—" I paused, staring into the dark red of my wine as if it held answers. "For the first time, I thought, what if he could scratch that itch Murdoch wasn't reaching?"

"And did he? Scratch that deep itch?"

"Repeatedly." I smiled softly, embarrassment adding to my wine-flushed cheeks.

"So, he knows how to use that weapon between his legs." She grinned as she raised his glass in a salute before taking a large sip.

"You've noticed his dick?" I asked.

"Everyone notices everyone's dicks around here." She laughed. "But yeah, even flaccid, that thing can poke out an eye."

I snorted into girlish laughter with her. "Murdoch is a grower, not a shower."

"I noticed that too."

"I'm glad Vinny's *sex*pertise was up to par. I would have hated to hear that that beautiful specimen had gone to waste." She gave me a cheeky grin. "Although, even if he was bad at sex, I'm sure you would have fun teaching him."

"It was a one-time thing."

"How many times is one time?" she asked coyly. I gulped my wine down instead of answering, and she cackled with delight.

The sound was bright and full of mischief as she topped off my glass. "Not a one-time thing, then."

I snarled defensively. "I'm just *using* him. He's also using me, so it's a win-win."

"As long as you're being safe."

"Yes, Mom, I'm using protection," I mimicked her earlier speech to me.

"That's not what I mean, and you know it. Rue is a sensitive wolf. I hope you know what you're doing."

I flinched, her words hitting a nerve. "Rue's neurotic, yes. Why do you think I keep breaking it off with Murdoch every time he brings up being exclusive? Why do you think I haven't had a boyfriend since high school? I don't date, period. I know what this is. I'm not falling for Vinny." I snorted at the absurdity of that thought. "That's never going to happen. Years of rivalry and utter hatred don't just disappear because of a few mind-blowing orgasms. And that's all this is—pure, unadulterated hate sex."

"Sure," Liv said a little skeptically.

"I haven't forgotten what he did to Indiana," I snarled angrily. "I'm just using him, and when he gets on that crappy bike of his and blows out of town, I won't mourn, I won't weep. I'll just move on like it never happened."

She didn't answer me for a minute as she conversed with her wolf. "So, at the training ground yesterday, that was what, the world's hottest foreplay?"

"Pretty much. Rue was doing a bang-up job of not allowing me an advantage with that she-wolf. Then, Vinny came along, and suddenly, training wasn't on her mind at all. I thought I was going to combust on the spot. It was fucking embarrassing."

"Yeah, I got that when you sprinted out of there with your tail between your legs."

"I did have to work," I said defensively.

"Yes, very convenient that!" she smirked.

"I did," I protested. "Mind you, it's probably a good thing that our work shifts interfere; otherwise, we may not come up for air." I grinned cheekily at her as Rue rumbled her agreement.

"You seem to manage working around your shift work just fine considering you smell like a brothel."

"I turned up to his place after work to finish what he had started."

"I gathered. You have chunks of drywall in your hair, by the way." She plucked some white chips out of a few tendrils. I reached forward and poured another glass of wine for the both of us, thinking back to the training ground and how badly I'd slipped up in keeping my secret. I bit my lip in worry.

"Liv, you can't tell anyone about this. Not any of our friends. And definitely not Murdoch."

"I'm not stupid. But Ro, he's going to find out. Especially if you can't keep it in your pants in public."

"It was one mishap. It's not going to happen again. And I can deny anything the rumour mill throws out. I'm good at doing that."

Liv rolled her eyes and took a sip of her wine. "But the hate sex will continue?"

I looked back at Rue, who was nodding enthusiastically at the thought.

"As long as it keeps being a no-strings-attached fuck-a-thon I don't see why it wouldn't. You know Rue, eventually she'll get bored of him, and when she gets bored, she gets dangerous."

Rue grinned mischievously at me and gave me a cheeky wink.

CHAPTER 51
VINNY

IT WAS OFFICIAL. I was a man obsessed. It had barely been forty-eight hours since I'd seen Roman. She had called her work and requested leave from her shifts for the next few days. Sick leave was automatically granted with employment law, but werewolves never utilized it. Still, her boss didn't question her as she called in sick, chortling as he told her to feel better soon. Before she had even managed to hang up the phone, I was licking down her torso, bracing into a kneeling position. I gave her a sexy grin, letting her know that I was determined to make her feel better, as I lifted her leg over one shoulder and feasted on her pussy like a man starved.

Even though she was free of responsibility, it wasn't the same for me. As much as the thought of her trussed up and whimpering to my every debauched thought was a glorious reason for locking myself away with her, at the back of my mind, I knew the threat on my niece was still out there, which I was reminded about as I plowed her roughly on the carpeted floor. Carpet burns were a nice touch to her flawless skin.

Alpha Liam summoned me for a meet before I resumed my duties of agonizingly long training stints and perimeter monitoring. I kept hoping that she would show up to a training session, and found myself daydreaming about her silky skin or how she felt when I tackled her to the ground the last time we trained together instead. Vali was no help in reining in my thoughts but did provide dick-shrinking images when my fantasies became visible wet patches at the front of my shorts.

By the end of the second day, I was irritable, snapping at anyone who stepped too close and almost clocking Luca in the face more than once. I had resigned myself to only texting her once or twice a day if I wanted to keep up appearances that I wasn't obsessing over her. My fingers constantly hovered over her text window, wishing she would start the conversation so I had an excuse to break my less-than-five-messages-a-day rule.

Pop music assaulted my ears as I made my way up Roman's driveway. After my shift had ended, Vali directed me to her place to finally get my fix like the junkie I was. Knowing her door would be unlocked, I cursed at her lack of security and let myself in. After being nomadic for so long and experiencing the dangers out there, locked doors were a simple thing that gave a much-needed sense of security, and she was acting rashly by not locking them. Every time she didn't lock her door, I wanted to spank her ass pink.

That thought escaped as I watched my gorgeous she-wolf bouncing around the living room, belting out a song off-key as she shimmied in her leather pants. My eyes roamed her ass, and I felt myself instantly thicken. Suddenly, I didn't care that her door was unlocked, and if I could come home to her like this all of the time, I would never care again.

Within a second, I was pinning her against the wall, her cheek hugging the drywall as I held her arms above her head with one hand. She gasped as she felt my erection rub up against her ass.

"What are you doing here?" I gave her a non-committal hum as I ran my hand over her exposed midriff, enjoying her soft skin. She let out a slight purring sound before she pushed backward into my cock and managed to get herself off the wall.

I took a step back and marvelled at her outfit—form-hugging leather pants and a bronze-coloured camisole left little to the imagination. Her ordinarily straight hair had been curled and left floating around her shoulders.

"Going somewhere?"

"Yeah, I am. What are you doing here?"

"Where are you going?" I asked, ignoring her question again.

"And who with?" Vali growled possessively in my head.

"Girl's night," she replied, turning away from me and turning down the ear-piercing music. "Liv and the other girls will be here soon." She tried to usher me back toward the door.

"So?"

"So you need to go."

"Why?"

"The girls will be here soon. I don't want them seeing us together."

"Liv already knows about us, Roman!" I laughed, a mix of amusement and disbelief. "And after our display at training, I'm pretty sure the entire pack knows about us, too, including the other girls."

Roman grimaced and looked away from me, a nervous twitch apparent. "It'll be forgotten about soon. Some other gossip will take their attention, but that won't happen if people see us together."

"Is it really a problem if people know?"

"That was the deal," she replied matter-of-factly.

"Yeah, when we both hated each other, and you needed to save face," I snarled. "I thought we were past that?" She said nothing. "Do you still hate me?" I demanded as Vali grumbled.

"Not exactly." Her voice was a squeak. "But that doesn't mean I'm ready for the rest of Blackfern Valley to know about my sex life."

"It's none of their business who you decide to date, Roman."

"Exactly," she snapped, frustration evident in her voice. "And we aren't dating."

"We aren't?" I challenged, annoyance taking hold.

"No. We're fucking. Secretly. And need I remind you that it was only supposed to be the once?"

"It was," I agreed. "But I'm not ashamed to admit I've missed you—"

"Don't do this, Vinny."

"Don't do what?"

She ran her hand over her face exasperatedly before her hard gaze locked on me. "Try to become my boyfriend." I felt like I had been smacked in the face. "That won't ever happen."

"I wasn't."

Where the hell did that come from? I looked back at Vali, who looked toward Roman longingly. I shook my head, my throat suddenly dry. I just wanted to see her. That's all. I hadn't seen her for a couple of days, and I had missed that taste of her skin and the feel of her quivering around me. Surely, she was as desperate for me as I was for her. It was just sex, nothing more.

"When I saw you last, we were putting holes in my dad's drywall, which, by the way, he made me fix, plaster, sand and paint. I had to redo the plaster three times because it wasn't up to his standard. I swear, that man just likes to see me squirm, making cracks about how my plastering was like my sex life—all over the place." I chuckled before sobering quickly at her expression. "Don't worry, he didn't ask who I was with."

"I wasn't worried."

"Then why are you suddenly so tense? Why are you not allowing me to lick you up and down?"

"I'm going out."

"Cancel."

"I'm not going to cancel!" She glared at me incredulously, her eyes flashing with purple agitation. Vali rumbled deep within. She was as wound up as I was. I just needed to push a little harder.

"Tell me, Ro, do you like fucking me?" I took a predatory step forward, gently running my nose through her hair.

"Yes."

"Do you want to keep fucking me?" I grazed her earlobe with my teeth.

"Yes." She moaned, the sweet scent of her submissive arousal floating into my nostrils.

"Then stop arguing with yourself. Stop trying to put up walls. This is sex. It's all it is. So let me ease some of your tension before you head out." I ran my hand under her camisole, grasping her firm tit and rolling her nipple between my fingers. "Come on, beautiful, text Liv and tell her to give you an extra hour."

"An hour?"

"Right, better make it two." I squeezed her nipple harshly, and I was rewarded with a sexy moan. I licked at her marking spot, making her pant and squirm. My gums tingled, and I moved down her body, forcing myself away from the temptation of marking her. I bit at her hip bone as I fingered the edge of her leather pants, the thought of her dewy heat moments away from my mouth making me salivate.

"Say yes, baby. Consent is sexy."

A low moan sounded in her throat. "Yes."

She yanked and twisted my hair around her fist, causing precum to wet the tip of my cock. "But Vinny, if you fuck up my hair or make me smell like a cheap brothel, I will end your life. And you have to be gone within an hour."

"Two."

"One."

"An hour and a half?" I pouted in what I hoped was an adorable fashion.

"Deal." She laughed before she helped me remove the tightest, sexiest pair of leather pants I had ever seen.

THE NOMADIC WOLF

I JUMPED on my bike and rode down her drive as I left. Vali snarled and whimpered in my mind, furious at me for leaving her behind and letting her go without an escort. I gently reminded him that she wasn't our mate, no matter what he thought, and considering how skittish she was when I'd first arrived, how she'd tried to friendzone me and convince me that we weren't dating, following her right now was a death sentence to our agreement.

Although the idea of dating her and marking her as mine surprisingly didn't make me cower in fear. She obviously wasn't ready for titles, let alone letting the pack know we were together. I gave the gas a little more and leaned forward on my bike.

In the beginning, I wanted to own her, possess her, and torture her. I wanted to make her beg for more and be cruel in my dismissal. I needed revenge on her more than I needed air in my lungs. But at some point, I stopped hating Roman. At some point, I had actually started to like her.

Oh fuck! I skidded around a corner when I realized the truth —I actually did want to date her!

I wanted to hold her hand in public and take her dancing. I wanted to wake up next to her every morning and have hot shower sex before kissing her goodbye and seeing her off to work. Rinse and repeat every day for the rest of our lives.

My gums tingled uncomfortably as I throttled the gas. With my latest realization, Vali wanted to return to her house and mark his territory; tell the world who she belonged to. But in reality, we both knew it would be a long day in hell before Roman allowed that to happen. If she'd balked at the idea of a relationship, she would never let me mark her.

Vali rumbled in salty agreement.

Then, there was still the issue of her unpredictable wolf. Although Rue hadn't shown any crazy behaviour as of late, I didn't want to assume she had been tamed by me. I wasn't that conceited. Her wolf swirled haphazardly within her eyes, always hovering beneath the surface. Rue was unpredictable, and any pressure from me could cause Roman's control to shatter. I couldn't be the cause of that. I loved her.

Vali's ears perked up. My heart thundered in my chest, loud and uncomfortable. *Love.* Shit. Did I love her? Vali howled excitedly in my head, amplifying my own confusion. How could I? Sure, I didn't downright hate her anymore, but that was it—wasn't it? I didn't feel any different about her than I did when we were teenagers.

A sickening epiphany hit me. *Fuck, have I loved her all this time?* My throat tightened, and I tried to push the thought away. That couldn't be right. But deep down, I knew it was the truth. The mate who'd rejected me, my arch nemesis, the queen of bitch and the splinter under my thumbnail—I'd loved her all along.

A brief elation bubbled up in my chest, but it vanished almost instantly as a soul-crushing reality crashed over me for the second time in mere seconds.

She doesn't want me like that. She never will.

The best thing we had was right now, and it had to be enough.

CHAPTER 52
VINNY

"You smell like sex." The rogue spat as I entered the cells. He looked like absolute shit—skinnier and gaunt.

"You smell like shit," I responded.

He gave me a toothy grin. "I see they're allowing you to visit me alone now."

"They decided you weren't worth the effort of two wolves. You've been here for almost a month, and you're showing no sign of risk."

"Yet the *luna* visits with at least two others." The way he said luna made Vali's hackles rise. "She's the only one smart enough to show fear."

"You don't scare her," I scoffed, ignoring Vali's low snarls.

"Don't I?"

"Not at all." I shrugged as nonchalantly as I could, pulling up a three-legged wooden stool and perching on it as close as I could bear while breathing in his decaying scent. I opened my mouth to try and limit the stench, praying that I would not taste it.

"We'll see," he muttered, looking through the small window in his cell.

"How's the torture going?" I quipped.

"A total turn-on, thanks for asking." The rogue sniffed the air. "Speaking of turn on's, who's the bitch that's been sucking your cock? She smells fun—a little crazy, maybe. These four walls need a bit of entertainment. Maybe you could send her my way, and I can show these walls some *other* kind of bodily fluids." Vali growled, his ears flattening against his skull. The rogue's eyes flashed to mine. I knew I had warrior-level control over my emotions. However, that didn't stop him from giving me a dirty knowing smile. "Have you marked her, or is she free meat?" I crossed my arms and stared him down, refusing to react even though bile sat in the back of my throat. Instinct told me to take him out for speaking ill of my Roman, but logic told me he was baiting me.

He smirked before he sniffed again, his eyes glowing brightly against his inebriated state. "Her wolf is untameable. She'll be fun to break in. The feral ones fight so hard, but in the end, it's yield or die." He gave me a toothy grin. I gave him a solid stare, determined not to take the bait.

"Let me guess, she was Little Miss Ray of Sunshine, the class president and a pure saint." I steeled myself as Vali paced my mind, listening intently but grumbling his displeasure. "I've never met a feral wolf who wasn't the most annoying, chipper thing... Well, at least they were until the wolf went feral. Then they go crazy trying to wrangle them. Sex, exercise, overworking or studying. Anything to tame the beast. Their emotions go from happy to clinically depressed within years. Sometimes months. It depends on the wolf." He cleared his phlegm from his throat and spat it onto the floor. "But most of the time, their efforts are in vain. The feral wolf always wins." The rogue smiled viciously. Vali snarled and then whined as images of Roman shuttered through my mind. But I still refused to take the bait. I wasn't even sure he could smell Roman on me. As much as I hated it, our situation was still secret, and it wasn't like I was going to walk into the pack house with her scent all over me, let alone into the cells. His nose was also affected by the amount of aconite swirling in his bloodstream. Vali listened to my reasoning and rumbled in agreement, relaxing minutely as I scoffed at the rogue.

"You don't know shit," I snarled. "There is no feral wolf in this pack." He met my firmness with a malicious grin.

"Sure there is." He sniffed again. "Pure crazy. Well, maybe not yet, but soon." I said nothing but my face tightened momentarily, which must have spoken volumes. "You pack wolves are so sheltered." He laughed before spluttering into a coughing fit. He closed his eyes briefly as if he was in pain, then opened them again. His frosty eyes found mine. "Do you want to know how to tame her wolf?"

I felt Vali's instant curiosity swallow my resolve. *Her wolf can be tamed?*

"What I want to know is why you wanted to be caught," I said through gritted teeth, "Why you are after my niece, and how the fuck to stop the conspiracy madness that is plaguing the rogues."

"She can't be tamed. Well, not in the way you're hoping," he continued as if I hadn't tried to deter the conversation. "Her wolf needs to take over fully. She needs to allow her wolf the freedom to kill. To give up her humanity and give into her bloodlust. Beating her bloody, then fucking her into submission is a delightful, super fun way to try. Bringing her to the brink of death and sliding your cock into her ass—" My fist collided with his face, but all he did was laugh maniacally. "Protective over her, I see." He grinned. I wasn't out of control with protective instinct, I just wanted him to shut up. "The bloodlust will kill her, you know. Your choices are simple, really. Allow her wolf free, or fuck her senseless, and when you grow bored, slit her throat."

"Yeah, that's not going to happen." I rolled my eyes at him as I reperched on the stool.

The small jabs to Roman no longer irritated Vali. Instead, he listened closely, as if the rogue was the answer to everything.

"Tell me, is she your true mate?" I said nothing. He coughed a laugh. "She is, isn't she? Oh, this is perfect. Everything is aligning so well."

"We aren't here to talk about her," I snapped, accidentally admitting there was a she-wolf to talk about.

"Are you sure? The prophecy states a feral wolf's bloodlust will kill the alpha of alphas before he reaches of age." He grinned at me again. "You have a feral wolf in your pack, one who is mated into the family of the prophecy. How clever is Fate? Put an uncontrollable wolf in the pack house of the alpha of alphas."

"You're delusional."

"Am I?"

I stared at him, perching on my stool. "So, the prophecy doesn't just talk about an alpha of alpha, but who is supposed to kill him?" I asked casually.

"I told your luna all of this already."

"What do you mean?"

"What I was taunting you about the first time you visited me in this fine establishment. See, I wasn't just being an asshole. I had something to tell her. So, when she recently came to me, I told her."

"You told her what?"

"Prophecies are read in parts. The first is the birth of the alpha of alphas under the solar eclipse. The second speaks of the rise of an army, and the third speaks of the feral wolf." He grinned at me. "But then again, we can't guarantee that your feral wolf will give into the bloodlust."

My mind was racing.

"Let me get this straight, because you can't guarantee the feral wolf won't take out my niece, you plan to keep coming after her regardless of whether she's one, or two, or twenty?"

"She won't make it to two."

Crunch. His nose broke under my fist before I pivoted on my heel and stalked out of the cell.

As soon as I was down the path, I raced to the pack house, slamming open the door and, without pausing for a breath, spilled word-vomit at a thousand miles an hour to my sister and brother-in-law. I barely registered that they were scantily dressed and feeding each other ice cream with disgustingly lustful expressions. My brain didn't comprehend what was going on within their home; they only needed to know what the rogue had just told me—minus any information that Roman was once my mate or was thought to have access due to this.

"We know." My sister said softly, putting the ice cream down next to her.

"He mentioned as much. What the fuck is going on, and why am I just hearing about it now?" I snapped. "You brought me home to protect Lacey, and now you're keeping shit from me?"

"That's the reason he wanted my audience," she muttered, then gave me a steely stare. "And he didn't tell me straight away. He taunted me for weeks first. He only just told me the reason he got caught, and only after he was convinced we had a feral wolf in our pack. In his mind, everything aligns with the prophecy within this pack. He is here because he believes everything is set to happen here. According to the prophecy, he is to mate with the feral wolf, and between them, they will destroy the alpha of alphas." She looked at me sadly, deliberating her next words. "He's here for Roman."

I blinked stupidly at her, hoping my expression was neutral.

"Then there's the whole part about her mate," Alpha Liam added delicately, nudging Clem to tell me more. My ears felt as though they were on fire, and my cheeks too, as Alpha Liam side-eyed me.

"What?" I asked.

"The third part of the prophecy. Something about losing a mate and her bloodlust desire." Alpha Liam grimaced.

"I'll go get it. I wrote it down." Clem got off Alpha Liam's lap and walked into the alpha's office, returning moments later with a piece of lined paper, her meticulous print graffitiing the page.

Clementine gave me a pained look before she recited, *"Twice born under solar moonlight of alpha blood washes and wanes. Twice born under solar moonlight mounds and twists in the earth's grain. Twice born under solar moonlight bends nature and spirit at will. Twice born under solar moonlight bounds and ties until all is still."*

"Moonlight army raises the dead. Twice born leads them through dread. Moonlight army plunders and pulls until the ground is razed, mountains are shifted, and pure blood is spilled."

"Twice born meets bloodlust under moonlit stars, dancing greens and purple clouds. Cold, crisp white and still moon night, twice born may meet their demise, before their coming-of-age rise."

"Wild wolf with bloodlust dire, prowls the woods with savage grace. Her killing spree, a burning fire, in moonlit shadows, she finds her place. Her mate, forgotten in the mist, as she seeks another's scent, bound to one with fervent twist. Saviour of pure blood kind, a bond of hunger, wild and meant, moonlight army forever spent."

I blinked a few times, trying to make sense of the riddle. Vali snarled unhappily in my mind as parts echoed around my brain. My eyes scanned the page but didn't truly see any of the words.

"The only reason he wanted to tell me directly was to goad me. It was pure blood-hate dick-waving. No different than any of the other blood-hater over the years. He wanted me to confirm that there was a feral wolf in this pack. When I refused to tell him, he proceeded to tell me exactly how he was going to watch his mate peel the skin from my daughter's flesh." Her eyes flashed amber. "He can't find out about Roman. The rogues are already delusional about Lacey being the alpha of alphas. What happens if he convinces them she's the blood-lusting wild wolf? Belief is a powerful and dangerous thing."

"He already knows about Roman," I croaked guiltily. "I all but told him her name."

Silence. I scanned the paragraphs again, ignoring the

apparent mind-link conversation that was happening between my luna and alpha. I desperately searched for any indication that the words could be about Roman.

"*It's a poem.*" Vali rumbled within my brain.

"*Poem. Prophecy. Whatever it is, it doesn't make a lot of sense. How can anyone make heads or tails of this?*"

"Is this the full prophecy?" I asked out loud.

"As far as I know." Clementine nodded.

"But there could be more?"

"What more are you looking for?" Alpha Liam asked.

"Well, mention of the alpha of alphas for one. Balls was adamant that it was about the alpha of alphas and an alpha command that would move the earth, yet there is no mention of it." *And two, I need to know if there's a possibility it was referring to Roman. The slightest inkling that it could be true. I need to know if she's also in danger.*

A mind-link opened to me and a few others as Alpha Liam's tone flooded into my mind, *"Bring Jensen to the pack house."*

CHAPTER 53
ROMAN

I LAUGHED as I stuck the last crepe spider to the front of the reception desk in the waiting area of the hospital. It was a leg race between me and the surly doctors who were ripping them down.

I started putting decorations around the hospital, then they would be taken down, only for me to put them back up in odder, more difficult spots. I knew I was being childish, but I didn't want to back down from the challenge.

I even went as far as to put a witch's hat on Cybil's head and a decal of a cauldron on her hospital room door. While she met it with a laugh, the werewolves were definitely on the cranky side as I tittered around decorating their spaces.

"You know the full moon can make werewolves twitchy," Rue said, rolling her eyes as a doctor ripped a hanging bat from his face with unnecessary anger and then threw it in the garbage. I paused, filling a plastic pumpkin on the reception desk with sugar-free lollipops, fake tattoos and stickers, and gave her a confused look. *"The next full moon is on Halloween."*

This was something I should have realized; should have felt coming. She shrugged and stretched before lowering her head onto her paws.

THE NOMADIC WOLF

"How come I haven't felt the pull of the moon? How come you haven't?" She shrugged again as if it wasn't important. I took an exasperated breath. *"Rue, all wolves feel the pull of the moon. It doesn't matter if they're sixteen or sixty, merged or unmerged. Every wolf feels the pull."*

"I feel it. It's just not making me itch as much as it usually does," she said in a bored tone.

"But we haven't merged, so we still have to shift and run."

"Duh." She rolled her eyes impatiently.

I wobbled on my next question, something that had been bothering me ever since Vinny showed up at my house the other night, when I thought he was trying to redefine our situationship. *"Does it have something to do with Vinny?"*

She stared at me, blinking dumbly. *"Why would you think that?"*

"Well, he was our mate."

"And?"

"Well, it's known that mate bonds heal, etcetera—"

"There is no mate bond," she interrupted coldly. I frowned slightly as the temperature of her words settled in my heart. I rubbed my chest as if I could rub the uncomfortable feeling away.

BY THE TIME my double shift had ended, I was exhausted both physically and mentally. Rue seemed to be more bitchy than usual, which made me wonder if the approaching full moon was affecting her more than she was letting on. Or maybe it was my constant thoughts of Vinny and our severed mate bond that kept her on edge.

I yawned and waved goodbye to Simon as I left the hospital. I couldn't understand why I was so tired. Each break, I'd snuck away for a power nap. It helped me through the sixteen-hour shift, but it wasn't a full rest, which is what I obviously needed.

I put a toque over my ears as I stepped out into the cold. Sleet had been coming in soft drifts. But it wasn't cold enough for a thick, white blanket of snow yet. I yawned deeply and stumbled as I walked down the path toward the parking lot. I shouldn't drive home in this state, but I really had no choice.

As I approached the parking lot, I noticed a black bike blocking my car in. Smiling in spite of myself, I looked around for its owner. I heard a sharp whistle and spun to find him walking toward me. My heart beat erratically in my chest as he approached, and by the way, he watched me, I knew he was aware of what his presence did to me.

He tipped his head down and gave me an odd look before he slowly closed the distance, his mouth soft against mine in a gentle, almost romantic brush of his lips. A soft sigh and a warm rumbling emitted from him, and I thought I could feel a gentle connection coming from me in response.

"What are you doing here?" I asked, taking a gentle sniff of his scent as his hands rested on my hips. His eyes searched mine strangely, almost like he was searching for Rue.

"I thought I could take you on a date?" he murmured before giving me a crooked smile.

"I thought we had this conversation." I pushed his hands off my hips, irritation burning into cold anger. *Why did he have to go and ruin a good thing?*

"We did." He nodded arrogantly. "But I decided to ignore you."

"You know dating wasn't part of this agreement," I snapped, taking another step backward.

"I know. But neither were sleepovers, breakfast, or multiple orgasms over multiple occasions. But you gave into those more than once. So, what's the issue of going on one little date with me?" He flashed me a cheeky smile. "Or are you scared?"

Rue snarled softly. "No, I'm not scared."

"Prove it."

"What are you, twelve? I don't have to prove anything to you."

"Are you really going to turn down a challenge, just to save face?" I glared at him. "You're scared someone will see us together. I guarantee you no one will see you with me."

I rolled my eyes at his tactic. "It's one in the morning, Vincent. Even if I rose to your bait, very few places will be open." I gave him a fake smile. "And I'm not riding with you to Timmy's again. Sorry."

I went to move away from him and looked down to find he'd linked his fingers with mine. Pulling me toward his bike, he gave me a sheepish grin as he opened the satchel. Through the ambient glow of the parking lot overhead light, I could see a tartan blanket and what looked like Chinese food.

"I thought we could go for a ride, find a secluded spot, eat food and watch the stars." I snapped my eyes to his, ready to scold him for his audacity, but when my gaze met his, I saw a soft vulnerability that I didn't know he possessed, and my anger stuttered into nothing. His mouth curved into a sheepish smile, and pink tinged his cheekbones. A tingly warmth invaded my body.

"Watch the stars, really?" I asked, shaking myself out of the daze.

"Well, fuck under the stars," he clarified with a saucy wink. A wink that transformed the tingly warmth into pooling heat.

I SHIVERED as the crisp air settled in around our makeshift picnic. I kept my gaze on the stars above as I shovelled noodles into my mouth like a starving raccoon. There were light shimmers of reds that I could barely make out.

"Is that the auroras?" I asked around a mouthful of food as I pointed to the sky with my fork.

"Yeah, I believe it is." I didn't look at him, but I could feel a content smile settle across his face. "When I was travelling up North, they were some of the most amazing things I had seen. They were so bright and powerful in the sky that I didn't even need to shift to appreciate the magic. You could understand why first nations believe them to be their ancestors dancing across the sky, connecting the spirit world with the physical one."

"Did you enjoy travelling?" I asked a little awkwardly. I was the reason he'd taken off in the first place.

"Yeah, I do." I frowned, noticing he hadn't changed his tense. For some reason, that bothered me. I was trying to find a way to voice it when he continued. "Being on the road, meeting other packs, seeing amazing areas... I don't think I ever want to stop being nomadic." My heart lurched, and I felt his eyes leave the sky and fall on me. I refused to look at him, knowing he either heard or felt the skip in the beat of my heart.

He reached toward me and, instead of touching me like I thought he was going to, he picked up another container of Chinese and opened it. The smell of garlic prawn swirled in the air, and my stomach grumbled loudly.

"Hungry?" he laughed.

"This is good Chinese," I said unapologetically, snatching a juicy prawn out of the top. I shivered as another cold breeze twirled around us. An odd feeling of confusion washed over me seconds before a thick leather jacket rested over my shoulders. I was already wrapped in more layers than he was.

"Oh, you didn't need to—"

"I told you, I'm not into necrophilia." I rolled my eyes. Another strange feeling engulfed me, almost like pride and arousal. This time, my eyes did snap to Vinny's. His green and silver eyes were intense and glowing.

"You know, I have a fantasy of fucking you in nothing but my jacket while you're bent over my bike."

"What?" I coughed around a prawn.

"I want to fuck you while you wear nothing but my jacket,"

he repeated roughly. His arms had wrapped around my waist, and his nose was in my hair, distracting me.

"On your bike?" I asked dumbly.

"Yeah. On my bike." His signature crooked smile hooked low in my belly. Rue, who had been pleasantly quiet, looked over at the bike, intrigued.

"Have you ever had sex on your bike?"

"Never." He answered automatically. "Never done anything bad on my bike." His grin morphed into something sinisterly sexy. "But I really want to do bad things with you on it."

One Mississippi. Two Mississippi. The Chinese food was soon forgotten as his mouth found mine, pushing me back onto the blanket with a hunger that I mirrored. My hands roamed down his muscular sweatshirt-covered stomach for his belt. His hardness strained to be released. A low rumble vibrated from Vinny as he removed the leather jacket, followed by each item of clothing in quick succession.

His teeth traced each removal of clothing, causing me to moan at the sensation. He grabbed my hands in a power play, holding them above my head for a minute as his tongue travelled from my earlobe down my jaw. I was trussed up and naked beneath him, bucking, moaning and occasionally giggling when his teeth and tongue reached a sensitive spot. Each time I giggled, I was met with a low growl, another nip and a tickling kiss. Another moan, another giggle, another desperate thrust toward his covered cock that was now sticking out of the open button of his pants, dewy and wet from both his arousal and mine.

My body erupted into goosebumps before he finally lifted me into a sitting position and released me with a smouldering look, as he then slipped his jacket back onto my arms but left it undone. At this stage, I was unsure if the goosebumps were from the tickling sensation or the bitter, icy air. As I looked into Vinny's eyes, I didn't notice the cold as much. All I could focus on was the heat and lust warming us. My arousal was thick in the air. My inner thighs were damp with need.

His smouldering look ignited. Vinny scooped me up and laid my body across his bike with my back on the seat. "Grip the handlebars," he commanded.

I squirmed at his tone. His tongue was circling my ankle and making its way up my calf as I placed my fingers around each handgrip, my body down the length of the bike. "Good girl," he purred, running his fingers over my skin under his jacket and over my tits, tweaking my nipples. His tongue was darting up the inside of my thigh.

"Do you really think this bike is going to hold up our weight?" I whispered, arching myself as his tongue got closer to its goal. He left my pussy desperate for touch as he hovered over top of me, lining himself up with my entrance

"Sounds like a challenge." His green eyes twinkled mischievously. "And if it works this way, I'm going to have to flip you over and try it with your ass in the air."

"If your bike gets damaged in the process, that's on you." I groaned as he slammed himself inside me, filling me to the hilt. The bike groaned and wobbled at the same time.

We momentarily stopped, and glanced down at the bike. He started to retreat before filling and stretching me again. The bike stayed up, and our eyes met as he let out a bark of a laugh, his lips twisting into a triumphant smile that momentarily bubbled overwhelming emotions through me.

There was a strange, strangling warmth in my chest. But before I could determine the emotion, he reached between us and pinched my clit as he rotated deep within, eliciting an inhuman sound from me. He thrust harder, making the bike sway precariously underneath me. *Holy crap, I hope this bike remains standing!* But I couldn't focus on whether the kickstand would stay erect as the head of his cock, bruised my cervix with every passionate thrust. Another few minutes of this and I was liable to combust.

I lifted a leg and he grunted as he somehow sank deeper. The bike wobbled as I chased my toe-curling orgasm, screaming his name as my pussy strangled his cock in a vice-like grip. He grinned down at me before covering my mouth with a kiss as he thrust and rotated his hips, building up to the next crescendo. I moaned as he grunted with pleasure, his mouth and teeth claiming my nipple, branding me as much as his cock was.

CHAPTER 54
VINNY

I KISSED Roman one final time in our secluded spot on the edge of the parking lot, not wanting to let her go even for a second. Those lips and soft moans would be the death of me. *Okay, just one more.* I kissed her again, pulling at her braid and coaxing her to deepen it. She melded against me as if she was made to fit. My body buzzed with electricity at the contact.

"I need to go," she laughed when I finally let her have air.

"I know," I grunted, still not moving. She laughed again, wiggling away from me. I reluctantly gave her an inch of space. A draft came between us and cooled the warmth that had been shrouding our bodies. It felt unnatural, and all I wanted to do was close the gap again, but instead, I nodded to her and gave her a crooked smile as she took another step and then another. She gave me a cheeky grin over her shoulder and disappeared toward the parking lot.

I shook my head in disbelief at the fact not only had I managed to convince her to go on a date, we had fulfilled my depraved fantasy and fucked on my bike. I ran my hand reverently over the smooth edges of my Boulevard C50. I was never going to be able to ride it without getting hard ever again. Fuck.

With that thought, I crunched on my gas and skidded

away. About ten minutes down the road, a foreboding feeling washed over me. Vali snarled in my mind as my hair stood up on end.

"*Roman,*" was all he said before I did a dangerous U-turn and zoomed back toward her.

Within moments, I was back in the parking lot, watching as she walked away from her car, her cute toque-covered head lowered into the scarf peeking out of the collar of her jacket, her hands wrapped in adorable, bright red mittens. She was safe. Relief flooded me. I had no idea what had caused me to react that way, but now that I was here, intuition told me to keep her safe.

I skidded up next to her and took off my helmet, my hair catching on the cold breeze. I gave Roman a once over, the flakes of snow wisping around her toque-covered head like a halo and checking her out while I subtly checked her for injury. Vali rumbled in my head. She was safe.

"Did you forget something?" she asked, and I shook my head.

"I decided to follow you home."

"Why?"

"I don't know," I mumbled, shaking my head. "Just a feeling." Vali watched the treeline in the distance with interest. I sniffed the air subtly, but all I could smell was the perfume of jasmine mixing with my own scent. Vali's anxiety melted as our mixed scents calmed him. *Mine.*

"A feeling?" she queried.

I grunted a non-committal answer and pointed to her car. "Just humour me and let me follow you home. It's going to be colder than a witch's tit out here."

"Um, I can't," she whispered. I frowned and opened my mouth to launch into a lecture when she cut my speech off with two simple words. "Car's dead."

"Your car's dead?" She nodded, glancing back at the car before looking up to the sky and giving another little shiver.

"Yeah, I think it's the battery. I was just going inside to get jumper cables and hope it would start."

"Get on," I ordered. She glanced back at me. "I'll take you home."

"But my car?"

I rolled my eyes. "I'm sure it'll be safe here in the parking lot."

"I can just run into the hospital and get a jumper lead." I stared at her ludicrously, unable to fathom why she was being so pigheaded. It wasn't a mating proposal, it was just a ride home. There was no way I could leave her alone. Vali wouldn't let me, and even though I couldn't sense a threat, it was his ingrained need to protect her that had me turning off my bike. I straddled it casually as my eyes raked over her again—waiting.

"What are you doing?" she asked dumbly.

"Obviously, I'm sticking around to ensure you get your car started."

My mouth curved as my nose twitched in the swirling, icy breeze. Our mixed scents activated something primal in me. It was intoxicating as much as it was comforting. I let out a low rumble as she edged closer to me. I wrapped my arms around her waist and naturally protected her from the cold wind. I don't think she had realized she was moving closer, but Vali was super glad she did. My warm breath was heavy against her cold cheek. "But I have to say," I continued, whispering with gritty pride into her ear. "You're a brave girl going into the hospital smelling like me." She glared playfully at me, so I tapped her nose with my finger, giving her a smirk.

She rolled her eyes before bringing her lip between her teeth as she looked at the bike with apprehension.

"Is it even safe to ride in the snow?" she asked.

"It's not really snowing yet. If we leave now, we should be fine," I said as I gently ran my nose up and down the length of her soft cheek, taking in her intoxicating scent. Vali rumbled happily.

"Fine. You can take me home," she whispered, "But let's hurry. I don't want to be a popsicle."

I released my hold on her and instantly hated the distance. After pulling out her helmet from the saddlebag, I placed it gently on over her toque before brushing her cold lips softly with mine.

"Get on and keep yourself tucked into me for protection from the wind."

It was almost dawn by the time I had pulled up outside Roman's house. The drive was blustering cold, but the snow had stayed away until the last ten clicks. I killed the engine and waited for Roman to dismount. After a few more moments, I took her mitten-covered hands to help guide her off the bike. I scowled when I saw her pretty face, flushed red with blue lips, and she was shivering so hard I thought she was seizing.

"Come on, let's get you inside and warm you up," I said, leading Roman into her house. She was cold. Colder than she should be, so for once, her door being unlocked was a good thing. The quicker I could get her out of the elements, the better.

"Why are you so cold?" I demanded, rubbing her arms up and down vigorously. She knew why I was asking. A little snow flurry shouldn't render her useless. Her werewolf side should be keeping the majority of the cold away.

"B-broken w-wolf," she chattered. The cold seeped into my gut, freezing into a heavy dread in my stomach, followed by guilty frustration. I had given her hypothermia, all because she hadn't told me the extent of the issues with her wolf. If I had known, I would have found a way to keep her warm. I would have got her car started or a hotel room or something. She shivered some more, and instantly, my frustration dissipated. I needed to get her warm fast.

"You should have told me!" I said, pushing her toward the bathroom. "You should have said you were beyond cold. Damn it, Roman! I thought you were just being cute earlier with your toque and mittens. I thought it was a fashion statement! Rue should be providing you the warmth. It's basic survival instinct." My eyes widened as further truth was uncovered. "We were naked on my motorcycle in the freezing cold, and your wolf doesn't keep you warm! Why didn't you say something?"

"Because I didn't feel the cold with you." Her brown eyes searched mine desperately as if she could find answers there. "It was there, but it was bearable. The cold crept back in when I couldn't start my car."

I turned on the shower before I started to remove her clothes. There was nothing sexy about this. For once, I wasn't thinking about her bouncy tits or biteable ass. I only thought about the fact she was a human popsicle. The way she watched me with a curious expression, I knew pure worry was etched onto my face as I removed her clothing, dumping them outside the glass door before pushing her fully under the hot stream of the showerhead. There was no point trying to steel my emotions right then, so I let her see the man behind the asshole —the one who cared deeply for her.

I removed my clothes quickly and joined her, closing the glass door with a snap. The blistering heat washed over Roman, but I didn't move her from the fiery water. I encased her in my arms and allowed the lava to wash over me, too. Vali whimpered as he tried to find some connection to heal her. There was nothing there. I ignored the jolt of agony to my heart and focused on her.

I held Roman under the shower for a long time, pensively quiet as I rubbed her arms, trying to help warm her as I couldn't heal her. When she finally stopped shivering, I clambered out of her shower, water pooling on the floor. I grabbed a towel and dried quickly before wrapping it around my waist. I grabbed another sizeable fluffy towel, motioning Roman to climb into it.

We both entered Roman's bedroom, where she had quickly tucked into a pair of flannel pyjamas before towelling her wet hair to dry it off. Happy that she was now back to a normal colour, I quickly dressed myself. I watched her closely as she used the hairdryer on her hair, the wet tresses drying into the silky softness I loved to tug. Warmth flooded my chest. It didn't matter if she was dolled up for a night out or whether she was in fuzzy pyjamas. Either way, she was breathtaking,

As if she heard my thoughts, she gave me a soft, reassuring smile and then turned off the hairdryer. She toed toward me as the snow fluttered against the window, mimicking the beat of my heart.

"Oh, it's really coming down out there now." Her voice was surprisingly soft. Vulnerable. "You really shouldn't go out in that."

"You inviting me to stay?" I croaked playfully, trying to ease the vulnerability in the room and get back on a normal level.

She gave me another soft smile and linked my fingers with hers. She tugged me toward her bed. "Come on."

I landed with a thump, instantly tucking Roman safely into my chest, stroking her arm softly. I was content just to hold her, her body gently humming next to mine. Vali yawned and placed his head on his front paws, enjoying the closeness of the she-wolf that should have been his mate. I breathed in her scent, and my body hummed in response. A scent that used to cause me immense amounts of pain was now an aroma that was burned so far into my nostrils that it had become a part of my very essence. I thought I felt small threads of her emotions as she snuggled in deeper.

The sound of her heartbeat was soothing as she lulled into a sleepy comfort.

"I'm going to be gone for a few days," I regrettably whispered.

Her eyes snapped open. "Oh?"

"Yeah."

"How long?"

"Not sure. Less than a week, I hope." I planted a kiss on the top of her head.

"So, you won't be here for the full moon," she asked casually. *Was she going to ask me to run with her?* Vali perked up, instantly hopeful at the thought.

"No. I have pack business out of town," I muttered, really regretting Alpha Liam's direction now.

"Oh, okay." Her entire body deflated with those two words.

"I'll be back," I murmured my assurance against her head.

"Okay." She nodded awkwardly.

"Are you okay?" I pushed her up to get a good look at her face. She looked scared and vulnerable.

"Yeah, sure. Why wouldn't I be?" She was lying. Her heart was pounding loudly.

My eyes locked onto the pulse in her neck. Somehow, I could feel her kaleidoscope of emotions as I traced my fingers over the thumping vein before I started giving her gentle, reassuring kisses. "It's okay to miss me, you know," I mumbled.

She made an undignified scoffing sound. "I won't miss you. Did you forget that I have a vibrator?"

"And what are you planning on doing with that?" I asked playfully, easing back out of the vulnerable moment.

"Take back what is mine, I suppose." The gentleness that was in her eyes was now replaced with something more provocative. A teasing smile graced her perfect mouth. "You did tell me that my pleasure belonged to you, right?"

"I did," I agreed roughly. My hands started to roam more dangerously now as the mood changed and charged between us. "However, I suppose I will allow it this once. But before I do, I think I need some memories to take away with me."

My mouth stretched into a wicked smile before I claimed hers, my tongue dancing inside her mouth eagerly as one arm slinked under her flannel pyjama top and the other reached toward the drawer on the bedside table.

CHAPTER 55
ROMAN

Last night was a disaster. My car had picked a terrible night to break down. I could taste the snow in the air, and I pulled out my phone and weighed my options. Liv would have been the obvious choice, but she was at work. This meant that whoever I called would know about my arrangement with Vinny. I looked back at Rue for some advice, but she was snoring happily and totally oblivious to my predicament. My next call was to my brothers, knowing neither of them would ever leave me stranded. I tried Izzy first, thinking I was less likely to get the third degree from him, but he didn't answer and neither did Jordan. I didn't want to risk calling my friends on the chance it would get back to Murdoch, and of course, Murdoch was a definite no.

I was trying to determine whether Vinny could answer his phone on a motorcycle when the first soft flakes of snow hit my windshield. *Great. Just great.* I sighed and climbed out of my car, adjusting my coat and toque before putting on mittens, and then I staggered across the parking lot. Cold trickled down my back that had nothing to do with the sleet. I stopped. Rue pounced to her feet, her hackles raised as I looked around. I felt as though someone was watching me. Rue heightened my vision as much as she could while I was in human form, but I still couldn't see anything out of the ordinary. Then, I heard the rumble of a motorcycle, and my knight in shining leather had arrived.

I instantly regretted my choice as the bike roared along the road. There was a reason I wanted to get my car started and blast out the heat at a ridiculous temperature. It was far too cold as it was, let alone for riding motorcycles at this speed. I couldn't fathom why anyone, including werewolves, would ride these things outside of summer.

Vinny's expressive eyes were full of concern. They danced over me as he tried to thaw me out. A sensitivity I had never witnessed made me pause, and even though there was no desperate, hungry heat in those large green orbs of his, I felt my heart jolt all the same. As the frost melted off the tip of my nose, my contempt for Vinny melted a little bit too.

I didn't need to open my eyes the next morning to know that he was gone. My bed was cold and empty. Rue flicked her tail in agitation as I begrudgingly rolled into a sitting position before stiffly moving off the bed. My skin and muscles burned and itched with an uncomfortable ferocity. I hobbled down to the bathroom, ignoring the quiet emptiness of my house.

I turned on the shower, letting the shower warm up before sliding my sore muscles into the glorious heat. I felt drained, achy and downright miserable. It reminded me of the time I'd caught the flu as a pup. I felt like I was dying, my mother bringing me soup, her cool hands running over my fevered body. This was back when she acted like a mother. Before everything with Indiana happened. And before I got my wolf spirit, which ultimately had gone crazy.

Rue was the only reason I knew I didn't have the flu. I hadn't been sick since before my sixteenth birthday, indicating that werewolf trait still functioned.

The aches and pain were indicative of the full moon. Nothing was going to distract me from it now. It was coming in fast, and I still didn't have my car to get me to the pack run. My body felt as though it was getting pulled in multiple directions. I needed to get to the pack. Being around my pack would ease some of the discomfort until the moon ultimately ripped Rue from my skin.

I let the warmth unknot my muscles. Rue was pacing, but there would be hours before we had to shift. I could shift now and run with her, but I had learned, as a newly turned werewolf, that this didn't help any. It was actually worse being in wolf form. The uncomfortable sensations of the unraised full moon were heightened.

So, instead, I usually busied myself, trying to distract myself from the bubbling, nervous and sometimes painful sensation of the approaching full moon. I scrubbed shampoo into my hair before washing the suds down the drain, then reluctantly turned off the water and dried myself off roughly with a towel.

I still couldn't believe it had taken this long to start to feel the pull of the moon. It usually was a week of discomfort. Vinny had been a good distraction, but now with him gone and the moon almost large enough to force the shift, I was very aware of every niggle, itch and burn.

Usually, Rue would be an annoying gnat in my head, driving me insane with her persistent, eager chatter, but for now, Rue was silent, barely making a move. Every now and again, she would twitch as she focused on the atmospheric pressures, but she mostly sat quietly. And the quiet was a nice change.

I dressed myself in a tracksuit and tried to focus on the tasks ahead. Distractions were the key to keeping the full moon jitters away. My car was stuck at the hospital, and Vinny had gone before I woke without even saying goodbye. I was hoping he would have driven me back to my car, and I could try to sort out a jump. However, it was probably a blessing that he hadn't because the ground was slick with black ice, and I didn't feel like freezing or sliding to my untimely death.

Thankfully, after a three-minute conversation that

confirmed to my brothers that I was still alive, my faithful siblings agreed to do their overprotective and slightly chauvinistic thing and checked out my car for me. I wasn't complaining; it was better them out there in the cold than me. I was hoping for a cheap and easy solution as I needed the car for my monthly trips to see Indiana. I frowned slightly, feeling guilty that she had been absent from my thoughts lately.

I pressed the end button on my phone and made my way to the kitchen, my stomach churning as the wolf's ravenous, full-moon hunger broke free. Understandably, it was midday, and I had slept through breakfast, and my middle-of-the-night feast of Chinese food was dust in my stomach. I shoved bread into the toaster slot before finding a few cans of tuna to spread on it. Opening the fridge, I unapologetically pulled out Vinny's food, anything high in calories. The Cheez Whiz was so good! His protein shakes and peanut butter cups were even better.

Pulling out one of the coffee alternatives that Vinny had left for me, I cracked the top and slurped at the fizz. The tangy, sour taste hit my tongue, and I shuddered. This might be worse than coffee. It took another four sips to confirm it. *Gross!*

After tipping the rest down the sink and filling a glass with water to wash my tastebuds, I wolfed down my tuna on toast—all twelve pieces, before slinking onto my couch with a jar of crunchy peanut butter and a spoon. The light coming from the window was crisp and white as sleet had started coming down again. I shivered, even though it was warm in my house. I really wasn't looking forward to running tonight. I just wanted to go back to bed and hibernate for the winter. However, Rue had started pacing anxiously within my head, glancing skywards every once in a while.

I looked at my phone, wondering how my brothers were getting on. I hadn't heard from them in a couple of hours. Surely, if something were wrong with my car, they would ring and tell me the bad news? I flicked a text off to Israel and stretched in my itchy boredom. Even my friend group chat wasn't keeping me entertained while I waited for either brother to arrive.

Rue twitched again before settling on her hunches in a pensive way. She tilted her head before letting out a huff and laying down on her front paws, flooding my body with a melancholic emotion.

Tears sprang to my eyes, but I had no idea why. She refused to answer when I questioned her about the overwhelming emotion. Anger I was used to, delusional and schizophrenic behaviour—absolutely. *This*, however, was all very new.

I tried to breathe through the wave of her emotions, focusing on the light sleet outside. It was now three o'clock in the afternoon, and I knew I needed to leave soon. There would be the pack run gathering starting. The barbecues and patio heaters would be lit, and people would be socializing quietly with each other until the alpha addressed with monthly announcements, pack additions and essential information before the pressure of the moon would finally take over, and Alpha Liam would announce the start of the pack run. Then, the hundred-odd wolves that usually turned up, shifted, and ran into the woods, frolicking and being free under the glow of the moon.

A glow of headlights broke me out of my thoughts. My skin was raw from where I had been absentmindedly scratching it—damn jitters. I opened my door and shivered against the cold air. Israel bounded up the porch, smiling at me before noticing my jittery state.

"You okay?" I nodded quietly, glancing skywards and itching my hand again. "The moon?" He glanced at the raw skin on my hands and gripped my hand within his.

I sighed. "And the cold." *And the fact that Vinny is gone.* My heart lurched at the sudden thought.

"Want me to run with you?" His brown eyes searched mine as I tried not to roll mine.

"You don't need to worry about Rue. The second I get there, I'll be submerged in my friends."

"I'm not worried about Rue." My eyebrows shot skyward. "Okay, I'm not entirely worried about Rue. You just seem more out of sorts than normal."

"It's just the full moon making Rue jittery. Once the pack run starts, Rue will behave." His eyes searched mine again. I needed to change the topic quickly. "Are you going to the pack run?"

I knew what the answer would be. He was merged and very rarely attended the pack runs.

He gave a noncommittal shrug and said, "Sure, why not?"

Suspicion reared its head. Was I really that much of a nutcase right now that I needed a chaperone?

"Let's get going then," I muttered as I pushed us both back outside, letting the door snap closed behind me and shuffled across the ice toward my car. I looked down at the deep black tires on my car, contrasting against the slate-grey, snow-sprinkled gravel. My head snapped back toward my brother, who was shuffling behind me.

"Winter tires?" I asked.

"Yeah. Jordan was pissed when he saw you were still driving the other ones. So, while I tinkered with your battery, he went to purchase your new tires." My brothers' familial instincts had no competition. Tears welled behind my eyes. Izzy snapped his head up at the salty scent. Great, now he was probably forced into chaperoning me, as I was obviously unhinged.

"Don't worry, he left the bill in the car."

I barked a laugh of surprise, the tears subsiding.

We arrived at the amphitheatre at dusk and automatically, I was swept into a sea of my friends. Caitlin, Josh, Damian, Rachel, Tommy, Georgie, Theo, Krista. I ticked them off my fingers as each pulled me into a dizzying hug and chattered excitedly. Murdoch pulled me into a hug next, squeezing tight and holding on a little longer than the two-second platonic rule. Thankfully, I was saved by Liv's turn, her arm linking with mine. I looked around and asked about Sean. Murdoch shook his head, a worried frown etched onto his face.

"And *he* isn't here either," Liv whispered conspiratorially into my ear. I put a brave smile on my face and shook my head playfully at her.

Izzy hovered nearby, watching me carefully as he engaged in conversation with his own friends. He wasn't even being subtle about it either, darting his eyes back and forth in pretense. Instead, he openly stared at where Liv and I were cuddled together, but before I could shoo him away, Alpha Liam took the stage. While most of the pups were at the school hall for a Halloween party, Alpha Liam initiated four pups who had met their wolf spirits. A paternal warmth spread across as he made his announcements before reminding us to stay safe and announcing the start of the pack run with an ear-splitting howl.

I felt the heat surge through my skin, my palms burning hot against the crisp ground. I gripped into the earth as the bones in my legs dislocated and repositioned, and my once-clear skin burst out in dark, woolly fur. My snout popped forward, the freezing air making its way into my nostrils. I twitched and sneezed before standing and shaking out my fur.

Instantly, I was tackled by Damian's enormous tank of a wolf, and I chuckled as he sprinted away.

"Oh, it's on!"

CHAPTER 56
VINNY

My father laughed as I tucked my baby in tightly for the winter, giving the bike a gentle caress as I tucked the final bit of cloth down. "Very domestic of you."

"Fuck off, Dad."

"Most people take care of a loved one like that."

"My bike is my loved one," I retorted.

He gave me an odd look before looking back down the driveway. "Are you heading out?"

I nodded, following Dad through the open garage door. "Luca should be here soon."

I turned back to look at my bike that had been put away in the garage, under a blanket, with no plans to take it out until the end of spring. It was apparent, as I'd left Roman's place, that the early seasonal ice was already causing the roads to be too slick to ride my mode of transport. Early snow wasn't uncommon in this part of the province, but I was hoping it would hold off for a few more weeks.

I had initially dreaded the thought of being stranded here when the snow started, hoping that I could have come in, dispatched the threat and been gone in the blink of an eye. The idea of having to borrow or rent a more appropriate form of transport annoyed me, but for the first time, the idea of being stranded in Blackfern Valley didn't scare me.

I had spent the night with the girl I loved, taking care of her because she needed me. And even though I was desperate to tell her how I felt—how I had always felt—I was happy just holding her while she slept. Her gentle breaths vibrated over Vali, making him lovesick as he watched over her.

For the first time in a long time, aside the fact some assholes were still after my niece and attacking my pack, my life was looking up.

I closed the garage door, grasped my dad's shoulder affectionately and sauntered down the driveway. As if on cue, a large SUV rolled up onto the curb. Balls was sitting in the front passenger seat but quickly clambered into the back as I approached the door.

"Hey fuckers," I greeted as I climbed into the passenger seat next to Luca. "Where to?"

"We're off to see Balls' grammy."

"Grammy?" I asked. "I thought you didn't have family."

"She's not my real grandmother, you tool. She's human, and I'm trying to keep her out of all this bullshit, but you've left me no choice. If anyone knows anything more about the prophecy, it's Grammy."

"A human? Luca, this doesn't seem smart."

"It's a potential lead."

"Where is she?"

"She's at Kempthorne Hospital," Balls said. "And uh, I should warn you. She's a little senile."

I couldn't help the smile that spread across my face. Kempthorne wasn't far. Maybe I would be back in time to run with my girl after all.

"WHAT ARE YOU DOING HERE, JENSEN?" The sunken, skinny, grey woman snapped before Balls even sat down. "I told you to move east. Go all the way to Nova Scotia if you must. The rogues are gathering west. Their camp moves, but— Oh, you brought company. Hello."

"Grammy, this is Luca and Vinny." I nodded toward the old lady as Luca swiped up her hand, kissing it like he was some Victorian-era douche.

"You brought me some handsome wolves, Jensen. Why?"

"They want to know everything you know about the prophecy, Grammy."

"Which prophecy? There are many."

"You know which prophecy, Grammy." Balls rolled his eyes before slouching into the armchair next to the bed.

"Oh, you're telling me you believe in the prophecy now?" She glared at him.

"No, I don't, but the rogues do, and it's not safe out there for me or him," he said, looking directly at me.

"Fine. What do you want to know?" she asked me directly. I handed her the recited paper which she scanned.

"Is this the full prophecy?"

"Not exactly."

"What do you mean not exactly?"

She handed me the paper back. "Did you ever study history in school?" I shook my head. "Classics?" I shook my head again, and she let out an exasperated sigh. "Have you ever heard of the Iliad or the Odyssey?" I shook my head again, feeling dumber by the second. "Surely, you've heard about the Trojan horse?"

Finally, something I did know. "Sure. The Greeks built a giant wooden horse, hid inside, and went behind the gates of Troy, snuck out and killed all the Trojans."

"You saw the movie, didn't you?" Luca laughed at me down the mind-link.

"Shut up!" I hissed back.

"Right." Cybil nodded.

"Wait. Are the rogues planning to trojan horse us?" I asked, wondering why we were suddenly talking about war tactics.

"What? No, you idiot! Shut up and let me talk. The story of Troy was written by a poet called Homer. Homer wasn't one man, but many who told the story over and over. Eventually, the story found its way into written form, and because no one knew the original writer, or more likely, they didn't care, they just called the authors by the pen name Homer. Your prophecy is the same. The version you have is one of many. A poem twisted and rewritten to suit the narrator."

I blinked at her a few times, thinking hard when Luca spoke up. "But how do we know which one is real?"

"They are all real, son, depending on who you talk to."

"Do any of the versions mention the alpha of alphas? Or have any more information on the feral wolf?" I asked desperately.

"They all mention the alpha of alphas, boy. Did you read the poem?" she snapped, then softened her tone. "Twice born *is* the alpha of alphas, but that term for twice born is relatively new. As for more information on the feral wolf. What exactly were you looking for?"

"What causes her to become feral, a timeline, a name. Perhaps a cure? Anything."

"Nothing specific, I'm afraid. It would never be that easy!" She laughed until she started coughing. "The timeline has been set in motion since before you were an itch in your daddy's pants. Before your great, great grandparents had itches. The Kempthorne Pack will have its reckoning."

"What do you mean? What's the Kempthorne Pack got to do with this prophecy, they aren't even mentioned in this poem?" Luca asked, perplexed.

"She thinks this prophecy is related to the story of the Kempthorne Pack and that the Kempthorne Pack magically appearing from a void when all the things align," Jensen said, rolling his eyes. "She's not convinced they died out eons ago."

"Where is the evidence of that, boy?" she argued.

"Where is the evidence of the contrary?" he snapped back.

Before she could answer, a blond male nurse with glasses stepped into the ward. I instantly recognized him as the turd that invited Roman out the night I finally got to taste her. Vali growled his dislike.

"Cybil, it's nice to see you having visitors," Simon said cheerily.

"Oh, these are friends of my grandson's. They were just leaving." She smiled sweetly at Simon. A smile that didn't meet her eyes.

"Don't make them leave on my account. Your doctor is going to be in shortly to talk to you about being discharged. Isn't that great?" He handed her a small paper cup with a couple of pills, which she put in her mouth and took a swig of her water to swallow. He smiled down at her indulgently before leaving the room.

Cybil craned her neck to see past me, then spit the pills into her hand.

"Here, pretty boy," she said, holding the wet pills out to Luca. "Flush these down the toilet."

"Uh." Luca reluctantly held out his hand and stalked to the small bathroom attached to the ward.

"Grammy, why aren't you taking your pills?"

"I told you, Jensen, I don't trust them here. They are trying to kill me for knowing too much."

"Grammy, no." Jensen said with exasperation. He looked at Luca and me, his face red with embarrassment. "Last time, she was convinced the drugs were some kind of tracking system."

"They were, which is why I told you to go east, Jensen. If they find you—" She shook her head. "Just stay safe. Promise me." She then eyed Luca, who came out of the bathroom. "What you are really looking for is about a day's drive northwest. You won't make it before the moon rises so it can wait for now. Just remember that when the time comes, you need to be northwest of here. In the meantime, keep driving south-west. The camp was last spotted west and moving in. If you go south-west, you may find them and be able to stop this war before it starts."

Balls groaned as Luca and I exchanged an eager look. "Please don't tell me you want me to come west with you. I would rather go back to your pack."

"You shouldn't even be there in the first place, boy! It's not safe around here for you. I told you to go east! Find the rest of the Kempthorne Pack!" The old woman seemed to become more distressed as she spoke. I raised an eyebrow at Balls, who just furrowed his brows in apprehension. He caught my eye and shook his head.

"Cybil, there is no Kempthorne Pack," Balls said softly for the second time.

"Don't get smart, boy!"

"Uh, Jensen is right, Cybil. They died out eons ago," Luca said, trying to reassure her.

"I'm surrounded by idiots!" she muttered. Then, she shook her head and looked at me. "The answer you need is..." she trailed off. After looking into the distance for a few seconds, she flicked her eyes back to me. Confusion was etched into her wrinkles as she tried to remember what she was about to say. Her brows furrowed more as she eyed me up and down, creeping me out. Finally, she sighed and closed her eyes as if having fallen asleep.

"I think we should go." Luca grunted after a few minutes. I nodded and proceeded toward the door.

"You're in love with her, aren't you?" Cybil asked me as I stepped across the threshold. I spun back and looked at the kooky old lady.

"Yes." I nodded.

"Then I will pray for you. This isn't over yet. Seek the broken wolf northwest of here. Only she can tell you what you need. And please watch out for Jensen. That stupid boy is going to get himself killed. Although, I think many will be dead before long."

Broken wolf.

Out west.

No, she couldn't possibly mean... could she?

I hurried out the door to catch up with Luca. I wasn't going to be home in time for the pack run. If the crazy old lady's information was correct, the rogue army was west.

CHAPTER 57
ROMAN

I should have been going to visit my sister. The morning after the pack run, I should have packed my overnight bag and driven to the group home to spend much-needed time with her, before heading back home. I was sure my sister appreciated the routine just as much as I did. Yet, I couldn't make myself go. I looked out my window—and waited.

I knew why I was waiting, and it was pathetic. Rue had her head between her paws, not offering any pearls of wisdom as I began scrubbing the countertops to distract myself.

Vinny had disappeared. Gone radio silent. It was strange not having him around. I knew he wasn't going to be around for the pack run, but I had no idea what he was doing or if he was safe. When lunchtime rolled around the day after the pack run, my fingers had itched over my keypad, wanting to ask him when he was due back or whether he was okay, but pride stopped me from doing so.

By dinnertime, I had given in and sent him a text message. He'd responded instantly even though it had been a single line:

ASSHOLE

Told you you would miss me! Be back soon.

The moving dots told me that he was writing something else, but then, after a moment, they stopped, leaving my brain to wonder what might have happened. But my pride refused to let me message him again.

I finished wiping the counter before putting the cleaning products away. This was only the second day of no contact since that quip about me missing him. There was no reason to worry, I told myself and Rue, who was beginning to pace erratically thanks to my wayward thoughts.

Her ennui was morphing back into the rabid emotion I was used to. She was incessantly pacing within the hollow of my mind, each step spiralling a new emotion. An uncontrollable, feral tailspin was starting. Her mouth started to foam as she snapped and snarled in my mind. Blood red tinged my vision as my teeth elongated, and the thumping of my heart sent acid through my blood. My arms started to burn with her mood swings.

And then a knock at my door startled me.

Was Vinny back? And why was he knocking?

No matter who it was, Rue's tailspin was momentarily sidetracked.

I growled inwardly as my heart did a dance. I was acting like a silly schoolgirl. I sniffed the air curiously, but all I could smell was the gentle fragrance of the "fragrance-free" kitchen spray I'd been using. The aerosol itched my nose, making me twitch it like a rabbit as I made my way to the front door.

Murdoch was standing on my doorstep, running a hand nervously over the back of his head, making his brown hair stick up in all directions.

"Hey," I said with surprise as I stepped out into the cold air and closed the door behind me, frightened that Murdoch would smell Vinny. I was sure I was being paranoid, as it had been a while since Vinny had been over, but I hadn't been actively eliminating his scent like I should have been. And with the irritant of cleaning product inhabiting my nostrils, there was no way I would be able to confirm if Vinny's scent was present or not.

"Hey." He gave me a once-over before offering me a small smile.

"What brings you all the way out here?"

"I was hoping we could talk?"

"Okay." I nodded for him to continue. He looked toward my door.

"Do you have coffee?"

"Uh, sure."

I walked back into my house and called over my shoulder as he followed me inside. "What did you want to talk about?" I filled the kettle with water and turned it on.

"You've been cleaning?" I looked back at him and noted that he wasn't actively sniffing or being accusatory. He was making awkward small talk. Rue was no longer having a meltdown. Instead, her mood shifted, and she grinned maliciously, instantly causing distrust between my crazy wolf and myself. I shot her a warning glare while being prepared to push her back.

"I've been known to clean my house on occasion." I smiled playfully, trying to ease his nervousness.

"And here I thought your sister was your hired help."

"Hired implies that I pay her. Not everyone can afford hired help, rich boy."

"Yeah, but she still cleans your house, even though she has those pups to look after." *Ouch.* Was that a dig? I kept my tone friendly.

"I take no responsibility for my sister's persistent need to pick up after me. Besides, she comes here to feed me, not clean for me. That's just a bonus." I placed the last of my coffee in front of him—none of the fancy crap he was used to, just plain old instant coffee.

"Are you not having one?"

"I don't actually like coffee," I admitted.

"Since when?"

"Since always. I just drank it out of necessity."

"I never realized."

"I've been trying alternatives, but I haven't found anything I like. I guess I'm sort of on a detox now."

"Well, you look good," he said sweetly. I smiled and redirected the conversation.

"What did you want to talk about?" Rue tilted her head in morbid interest. She was basically salivating at the humiliation that was about to unfold. We both were about ninety per cent sure what he had come all this way to talk about.

He took a deep breath, steadying his nerves and readying himself for the bombshell he was about to deliver. He opened his mouth to speak, then stopped instantly. A choking sound emitted before he snapped his mouth shut. His jaw clenched as he sniffed. He spun around. His mouth opened and closed a few times as his brain started to digest the information his senses were telling him. He stood up and walked to the couch, moving a cushion and glaring at me as he pulled out a piece of clothing. But the clothing wasn't mine. Murdoch was holding a pair of Vinny's boxer briefs.

I opened my mouth to explain, but all that came out was a squeak. I knew I needed to explain, but how could I explain it? Murdoch would never understand it. Fuck, I didn't even understand it.

He shook his head, his face contorted with anger. I opened and closed my mouth a few times in a panic. He waited and waited, expecting me to start a dialogue, but I couldn't get my mouth to speak. I needed him to say something—he obliged.

"So, the rumours are true." His voice was deceptively soft as he closed his eyes momentarily, the hurt evident on his face. His jaw was rigid, and his eyes glowed with barely controlled rage. "I need to hear you say it. Did you fuck Vinny?" I nodded, guilt washing over me. But when I opened my mouth all that came out was another *squeak*.

"How many times?" *Squeak*.

"How could you do it, Roman?" Murdoch looked disgusted. "How could you degrade yourself to that? Did you just conveniently forget that your sister is in a care home because of him?" The waspish tone bit into my soul. Rue's hackles rose defensively, but before I could find my voice, he stomped toward the door. I stood up quickly to stop him, his coffee cup tipping over in the process. Coffee poured over the breakfast bar and onto the floor as Murdoch stormed out, slamming my front door.

I left the coffee pooling on the floor as I chased him outside, following him out to his car as I called his name and banging on the window, but he swerved out of the driveway, almost running over my foot in his escape. Guilty tears streamed down my face, and I collapsed onto the driveway.

Murdoch's outrage was justified.

I was left weeping. And not just a few measly tears, but big, ugly crying where my tears mixed with my snot.

I had agreed to Vinny's demands. Hell, I had wanted it. And I'd understood the consequences. Yet, I couldn't stop the tears. It was done, and as much as Rue didn't think we had lost much, I did. Murdoch had always been there for me. He was the constant that I could rely on. He was my friend, and I had ruined everything.

Eventually, I picked myself up off the cold gravel, and without checking the state of my appearance, I hopped into my car, letting Rue's instincts lead the way.

CHAPTER 58
ROMAN

Nerves were heavy in my stomach as I walked into the group home. While I wept uncontrollably in the car, Rue directed me to the care home, indicating in her eerie wolfy way that I needed to be here to become whole again. Gone was the crazy wolf who, only hours before, was intent on ripping everything to shreds, replaced with one whose instincts were finally to protect me—to heal me. A warmth ran through my chilled cells, much like a loving embrace. Maybe she was right; maybe seeing my sister would make the world make sense again.

A kind carer smiled as I walked past. "Two visitors in one day. She will be thrilled."

"Is one of my siblings here?" I asked as I started toward the communal living area.

A scent caught on a breeze, and my heart revved and stalled at the same time, pounding loudly in my ears. Peppermint swirled my nostrils, and I didn't hear the answer she gave me. I didn't need it. My blood ran ice cold before boiling over.

Rue's hackles exploded skywards. My nails were elongating and thickening within my closed fists. I was already on edge from the situation with Murdoch and the warm comfort that Rue had supplied earlier now burned into excruciatingly hot anger. The little sliver of tame wolf was gone now, slipping right through my frayed nerves. Her feral nature was coming forward.

"What the fuck are you doing here?" Her voice bled with mine.

"Visiting Indiana." Vinny stared me down. His chiselled face was etched into a state of righteousness.

"Get out!" I spat.

"Is everything okay here?" The carer looked between us anxiously.

"He is not welcome here." My voice sounded animalistic—hollow. Snip. Snip. Snip. The last threads of control were breaking one by one.

Suddenly, Vinny's hands were encasing my wrists, and he was forcing me out the side door onto the patio. The nurse looked on curiously as he led me away from prying eyes.

He stopped near a large hedge and let go of me, placing his hands in a gentle, nonthreatening gesture. He was saying something, but a piercing noise in my ears drowned out his words. He watched as my body started to shift. My skin itched and bubbled. My eyes were flashing purple, and the venom on my tongue was frothing.

Indiana was off-limits. Surely, he knew this. I didn't think I would have had to put this into the agreement. I assumed it was just understood. Then, the need to shift stopped. A cool trickle ran down my spine. I was human, but Rue was entirely in control.

No!

She sneered at me as I tried in vain to find something to grasp onto.

It was pointless. There was absolutely nothing I could do to push her back. I was going to watch her kill him. I was going to watch her kill any witness to her murder. It was going to be a bloodbath.

Her emotions were sluicing through me, each one scarier

than the last. At this moment, she didn't care that he was a phenomenal kisser, and she made me feel things I didn't know I could feel. Or that up until this point, we were both missing him.

Gone was the rabid wolf feeling like she was backed into a corner. Instead, she was deathly calm, and her instincts were telling her to take him out—to protect Indiana. She wanted him deader than dead. She stared at him with cold calculation, her eyes full of bloodlust.

She was going to kill him.

Yet, she didn't go for the kill. She watched him curiously, a perfect predator stalking her prey, and like the master marauder she had become, she put on the perfect impression of me.

"What are you doing here?" she gritted out, acid rolling through her speech.

"I told you, visiting Indi." The way her nickname rolled off his tongue revved up Rue's anger, but she didn't let her perfect mirage waver. She was pretending to be me.

"How did you even know she was here?" My voice wavered on a whisper. He didn't answer. He didn't have to. I knew it the second Rue opened my mouth, "Clem."

A fresh wave of white-hot anger exploded behind my eyes as Rue's acting continued, hot tears burned. "She had no right. I don't give a shit that she's luna. This is my fucking family."

"She only told me after I begged her. I hounded her for months after the accident to let me see her. She only agreed *after* she spoke to your mom and dad about it, and they developed ground rules. The biggest rule was to tread carefully around you, to avoid you entirely. It wasn't hard, considering I had already left Blackfern Valley." My neglectful parents had allowed Vinny to visit her? The man who imprisoned her in here? Not only that, but all of them had agreed to keep it from me?

"Why?" I asked at the same time Rue did. "Why keep this from me?"

"I assumed because you were hurting over our...departing." He shrugged.

Rue scoffed, her voice like poison-dipped barbed wire. "Best thing I ever did."

He shook his head, his long blond hair flopping into his eyes. He pushed it back, and I saw the pain he was trying to hide. It was so fleeting I thought I'd imagined it, but the words had hit their mark, and Vinny's eyes flashed with agony before frosting over. Rue sneered at me as she shook my head, pretending to be heartbroken as she let fake tears roll down my face. "In fact, this just reinforces why I did it in the first place. We're done. This is over."

He blinked at me stupidly as if the words were lagging his brain.

"You need to leave," she screeched dramatically. The silver in his eyes flashed as tears continued to roll down my cheeks. He went to reach out, and then, as if he thought better of it, he shoved his hands into the pockets of his pants. The way his large, rough hands had pawed at me seemed in the distant past. Any warmth was now effectively frozen under a big slab of ice and barricaded by the polar bear that was Rue.

He opened his mouth and closed it again. Opened it. Closed it. For once, he'd been rendered speechless.

Tears continued to leak, and his quiet, defeated expression snapped something deep inside me. My heart plummeted. I realized, in that excruciating second, that I cared for Vinny a lot more than our agreement dictated.

Rue sneered back at me, her expression dripping with contempt. She was cruel in her affirmations that we would never be together; that being with him would destroy me like it had destroyed Indiana. Now, she was in control. He would never hurt me again.

Horrifying images flashed before my eyes, and I let out a

panicked cry within my mind. I desperately tried to reach out and grab her fur. She flexed a muscle, pushing the body weight of a wolf down on my subconscious. I felt like a pup being reprimanded. This was the Rue show, and I was all but a spectator and Rue wasn't finished.

"Is this some kind of sick joke? Are you visiting your trophy, letting her know you've tasted my cunt too? That you've had me on my knees, begging for your cock in my mouth?" The voice was salaciously sultry, with the exact amount of disdain that I would put into my words.

I took a step toward him, close enough to kiss him. Near enough to slide my fingers into his beard and tug. *Close enough to slit his throat.* And while the thought terrified me, Rue was basking in the idea,. His saddened eyes sharpened as his nostrils flared as he watched the contradiction unfold—tears of anguish, yet scent of arousal. Yes, the idea of soaking in his blood turned Rue on.

I saw his hand twitch, desperate to reach for me, embrace me and run his nose through my heat, lapping up whatever angry arousal I could give him. He wanted me to pound out my anger and use him for release. Anger was better than my defeated, broken sadness. Anger he could deal with. He would allow me to use him, and in doing so, it would fix whatever was broken.

I could feel his desperate emotions as though they were my own, but they weren't even tempting Rue. Orgasms would no longer satiate her. She lusted for something else. But first, she was going to play for a little while. That way, her kill would be a lot more satisfying.

"You complete jackass! You fucking hurt her!" My mouth moved—a puppet of her master. I thrashed under the weight of her hold, screaming in quiet torment, unable to break through.

His eyes flashed in angry disbelief and instantly hardened. "Pull your head out of your ass. I didn't fucking touch Indiana, Roman! She was my best friend! I had nothing to do with this."

He waved his hand back toward the group home. Rue bared my teeth at him in response, my wolf canines extended and dripped with saliva. She made it look like I was losing control, whereas, in reality, I had lost it the second I'd seen him here. And he had no idea. He still thought I was battling to keep my wolf back. He still hadn't worked out that it wasn't me he was speaking with.

Rue grinned back at me as his desperation revved up. His emotions were disjointedly fuzzy. "You've never believed me. How many times must I say it? I wasn't even there that da—"

"She was pregnant. Did you know that?" Rue's voice was cold. His face blanched. He hadn't known. "She told me she was going to meet with you. She said she needed to tell you. That was the last time I saw her."

"She didn't meet with me, Roman! The baby wasn't mine."

Rue scoffed. "Yeah, right."

"Honestly. I didn't know she was pregnant. I never was with her that day. I told you this after it happened. I told everyone. But you still don't believe me, do you? You want it to be me so you can have a reason to hate me—to avoid your attraction toward me. It gave you an excuse to reject our mate bond. This is bullshit, Roman. The only one who knows what happened is Indiana."

"And Murdoch. He saw you in the forest near Plymouth Point, and then twenty minutes later, he found Indiana."

"But he didn't see me with Indiana because I wasn't with her."

"She smelled like you, even crumpled on the rocks, she smelled like you! No one else."

"Are you shitting me right now? You have circumstantial evidence at best!" His desperation was warring with his anger, and Rue smiled softly, winning her game. "You believe Murdoch over me."

"Why wouldn't I? You're a liar. You always have been—"

"I have never lied to you!" he snapped.

"You've never told me the truth," I countered.

"I have always told you the truth." I made a scoffing noise. He hadn't outright lied to me, but an omission was also considered lying in my mind. He stared in silence at me, waiting for me to contradict him. The silence between us lengthened. We'd come to an impasse. Rue fidgeted internally as if she was getting bored. She wanted his anger. She wanted him to lose control; wanted him to attack her, whether out of passion or anger. And then she was going to bust her claws out and remove his favourite appendage.

He didn't make a move, though. He refused to offer me comfort. My heart galloped. Maybe he did know it wasn't me. Maybe there was hope. Or maybe he had no idea. After another minute, he rubbed his face in frustration, his eyes as hard as they'd been the day he rolled back into my life.

"Murdoch likes to blame me for everything, doesn't he? And you just lap it up. You always have. Why haven't you questioned him about that day? Why don't you ask Murdoch if he was the father of the baby? They were fucking each other at the time. Did we fight about it? Yes. All we ever seemed to do was fight about it. Indi was my best friend. She was like a fucking sister to me, and she was in love with that total dick!" He shook his head frustratedly. "Did she spend the night at my house the night before? Yes. Was I sleeping with her? No, and I never have. Did I push her off Plymouth Point? Fuck no! I wasn't there. I was on duty running with Sean, and next thing I knew, the warriors were yelling '*Indi is at the bottom of Plymouth Point*' through the mind-link. Murdoch told everyone I was with her. It's horse shit. I could easily have turned around and passed the blame onto him. Could have said he had something to do with it back then, but at the end of the day, Indi made her own decision, and there was no point in blaming anyone but her."

I shook my head vehemently, trying to process the bullshit he was spouting as I tried to push through again. Rue rolled her eyes at me before turning back to listen to what Vinny was saying.

"—for trying to end it all." Something vibrated in my mind as I gaped at him. My thrashing stopped.

"She didn't!" Rue snapped, her calm composure breaking slightly as she looked back at me.

"How can you be so sure?" The softness of his words sliced deep.

"Because I know Indi!"

"A werewolf with heightened reflexes and healing abilities is found hurt on jagged rocks, and your first instinct is that she was pushed by yours truly. Even though she was training to be a warrior and would have sensed that a mile away. No one pushed her, Roman, she simply gave up."

"You would say anything to appease your guilt." Rue snarled through my voice. "And she didn't try to kill herself! She wouldn't do that!"

"Yes, I want to appease my guilt. But not because I hurt her, Rome. It's because I wasn't there for her when she needed me to be. Much like you, I guess."

"What is that supposed to mean? I had nothing to do with this!" Rue's voice was icy.

"That's not what I meant."

"What did you mean then?"

He stared at me quietly, indicating we had reached another impasse.

CHAPTER 59
VINNY

WHEN DID this all go so wrong?

Vali was edgy as we watched Roman take an astonishing level of control back over her wolf. That's when I noticed that the purple rings around her eyes were full and bright, indicating she had merged while I was away. It explained her control, but it didn't explain the goosebumps prickling over the back of my neck. Vali said nothing but watched Roman with piqued interest.

There was a fiery anger emitting from Roman. I could taste the heat on my tongue as her delicious scent swirled around me. I itched to hold her, to kiss her and take away her pain, but Vali's instincts were holding me back.

His instincts were my instincts, and they caused me to pause as I looked her over again, trying to ignore my frantically beating heart as my eyes roamed over her. What was Vali seeing that I wasn't? I looked at the dark hair piled in a messy bun on top of her head, her purple and brown eyes shooting sparks at me, her soft mouth over her ridiculously thick jacket which covered the delectable curves I knew lay underneath. If she weren't so angry, I would have made a joke that she looked like a marshmallow, but now wasn't the time.

A low buzz started within me as broken threads started to repair. They were too weak to grasp, but I instinctively knew what they were. I couldn't explain how it had happened or why, but our mate bond was now flickering. The threads burned bright before dampening, the connection weak. The mate bond had been brutally severed years ago, so why was it back now? I looked at Roman suddenly with hope.

No, something was off. Something made Vali wary nevertheless. Roman's voice sounded hollow, angry tears were streaming down her face, but beneath her perfectly controlled rage, I could feel her fear. It was clear to me that she didn't feel our bond, but something inside her was charging it.

"*Vali,*" I grunted as pieces of the puzzle started clicking together. "*What is wrong with Roman?*"

"*I don't know.*" He shook his head. "*She feels different.*"

"*How?*"

"*I can't explain it. I feel Rue's anger.*" Vali fidgeted, his feelings encasing me, warring with Roman's. There was something he wasn't saying.

"*And Roman?*" I prodded as I looked at my mate's beautiful face.

"*I'm... I'm not sure.*"

Sticky dark tar melted onto the flickering light of the mate bond, and Vali shivered and growled at the sensation. Sudden, icy fear encased my body.

"*We need to go,*" Vali commanded.

"*We can't leave Roman.*"

"*I don't think that's Roman.*"

"*What are you talking about?*"

The tar continued to move down our thread and Vali started to cough badly. My heart thundered as unimaginable pain shot through my mind. I clutched my head in agony as the threads of the mate bond started to glow brighter. Each pulse impregnated the tar-like substance deeper. And each time that happened, Vali would dry heave and shudder with pain.

"That's Rue." Vali coughed weakly. *"She's going to kill us. Now fucking run!"*

I gave Roman one last pained look, the browns of her eyes shadowed by the bright purple rings. I took a step back and tried to mask my fear.

"Okay, Roman, you win. I'm going."

I took a step back. She took a step forward, an evil smile spreading over her kissable mouth. I took another step back. She mirrored the action. Vali sent out a warning growl toward Roman, and she broke into a sinister cackle. The sound rained over me as I turned and ran, but I was going to be too slow on two legs, especially if she shifted.

"Vali, can we shift?"

"No." He shook his head. *"That might kill us. Get to the car."* He coughed harder.

I sprinted to the parking lot, searching for the black SUV. After our search for the camp was a bust and letting Balls escape, I decided to come here and discover if Indi was the broken wolf Cybil had referred to. Instead, I'd found Roman. My heart thundered as the black tar settled deep. Did I get the wrong broken wolf?

"Drive!" I shouted, throwing myself across the backseat and coughing. Luca was startled awake but didn't need an explanation. He threw the car into drive, squealing the tires as he raced out of the parking lot. Roman leaned cavalierly against the entrance sign of the group home, giving us a little wave as we screamed past her. I collapsed in agony, clutching my chest, over my heart, as I lay on the backseat, weaving in an out of consciousness.

"What the hell was that?"

"The blackness, it was her. The mate bond, it was her. I don't know how, but Rue has turned it back on." He shook his head. *"Rue has turned it back on, and the black crap that was covering it was immobilizing me."*

"Why?"

"To weaken me so she could kill us."
"Roman wouldn't kill anyone."
"No, but Rue would. She's feral. And Roman's given into her bloodlust."

There was just no way. There was no way Roman would do that. No way this prophecy was real. Was it? I blinked back the tears that misted my vision. I was sure I could make a weak connection to my alpha and luna with this distance, but I couldn't while Vali was incapacitated.

"The minute we are strong enough to handle it, we need to reach out to Clem and Liam. Warn them."

And then darkness overtook me.

My sister gave me a side glance as we walked. She didn't offer any conversation but eyed me repeatedly, waiting for me to start the dialogue. I didn't want to talk; conversation would make me want to rehash the fact that the love of my life was prophesized to kill my niece—her daughter—and there was no way I was going to let that happen.

If the prophecy foretold that she was going to kill Lacey, I was going to have to kill Roman first. Same went for anyone who was deluded enough to try and help her. Vali, still affected by the black tar, nodded in sombre agreement. I shook my head, perplexed. *Did I honestly believe in this crackpot prophecy now?*

After Luca and I had made our getaway, I had told Clem and Liam that he and I had gone searching for answers only to find Roman had given into her darkness. After three days of painful debriefing, speculating and arguing, I excused myself. I needed time to mourn and prepare my soul for what needed to be done. So naturally, my sister was now following me everywhere to keep an eye on me.

Still, she said nothing as I plotted. The first that had to die was the rogue. The only reason he was still alive was because of the she-wolf walking next to me. He should be dead, but a fight between alpha and luna had broken out, and she'd somehow convinced her mate to keep him alive.

Her human compassion was not considered a bad thing, not even among werewolves. Werewolves had a human side, too, after all. The difference was that both my sister and I had been raised for a large portion of our lives in the human world, and although I had dropped a lot of my human culture the moment I found Vali, it was evident my sister had kept a larger portion of hers. Making us in disagreement over the fate of the rogue.

She believed it was inhumane to keep torturing him, especially if he had nothing new to give us. She did, however, allow us to keep his body weakened. She wasn't stupid enough to leave a full-strength rogue in the cells.

Unfortunately, he hadn't died with the amount of torture we had put him through already. Werewolves, as a species, were a lot more durable, having the stamina to withstand hours of torture, never getting sick, healing from wounds, and ironically, considering the vast quantities we ate—lasting a long time without food and water. While a normal human could barely last a week without either, a werewolf could last months.

As long as a wolf spirit wasn't fully debilitated, the body would simply remain in a status of constant healing. The stomach would eat itself, heal and eat itself again. The werewolf would be cranky and savage as fuck, but, theoretically, he could survive for a really long time. I hadn't heard of anyone who'd tested to see for how long, though—not even in some of the nastier packs I had come across.

"Do you want to tell me what you're planning?" she prodded gently after sixty minutes of aimless wandering on two feet. Vali was still too weak to shift.

"You know what I'm planning," I grunted, stepping on a thick root.

"You can't do it, Vinny. It will destroy your soul."

"My soul was destroyed the moment she rejected me," I admitted the truth for the first time out loud.

"As was hers." There was only the sound of the surrounding forest for a few moments. "You could have told me."

"I know." More silence. I gave into a question that had been haunting me. "Do you think her rejection of our bond turned her wolf feral?"

"I still don't believe she's feral, Vin."

"How can you say that? Look at the evidence. She did something I didn't even know was possible. She revived our bond and contaminated it. Without Vali, I wouldn't have stood a chance against her. She would have slit my throat and let me bleed out."

"I get that, but that still doesn't mean she's the wolf from the prophecy."

"Please don't tell me you're that dim!" I snapped. "How many signs do you need? Something big and flashing, saying *'feral wolf here'* with arrows and shit?"

She frowned. "If she were the feral wolf, she would be joining the rogues as their queen, but she hasn't. I can still feel her connection to this pack. She hasn't gone rogue."

Angrily, I kicked a stone into a small creek. "She'll go there eventually. The rogues probably don't even know that she's given into her bloodlust. Our friend in chains told us he was there to find her. As soon as our back is turned, she'll free him, and then we're all fucked. You need to allow the execution order go through." I kicked another rock.

"She's not going to commit treason." Clementine rolled her eyes, ignoring my stance on the rogue for the umpteenth time. "That would be a death sentence."

"Having a feral wolf should've been a death sentence!" I barked at my sister.

"Are you even listening to yourself? This is your true mate! What the hell would that have done to you if we murdered her?" She shook her head at me sadly. "I love you, Vin, and I know you're grieving, but what you're spouting is utter bullshit and you know it. No one in this pack would've ever been able to kill Roman." She looked at me pointedly. "Especially not you."

"I don't have a choice!"

"There is always a choice!"

"This is your daughter. Your first instinct should be to protect her." Clem's eyes flashed dangerously at my insult.

"I am protecting her." Her voice was stern. Guilt washed over me, and I hung my head in submission. My comment had been uncalled for. After a few moments, Clementine wrapped her small, chubby arms around me. "Don't do anything stupid. If she is the feral wolf of this stupid, so-called prophecy. There still might be a way to stop her. Help her."

"Why do you care about her so much?" my voice broke with the strain of holding back unshed tears.

"Because, five years ago, I watched your soul shatter in front of me when you were begging me for permission to leave. You had barely left town, and the very same day, I saw Roman up there." She nodded to a sharp ridge in the distance. "Her grief overwhelmed her, and as soon as I saw her, I knew. Your attitude and her despair. All the pieces clicked together. She not only lost her sister, but she'd also lost her true mate. She had spiralled in her grief, and her wolf had taken over completely. Her family were no help. I was the only one who managed to bring her back. And I think it was because of a connection through your mate bond. I was the closest thing to her mate. She healed, but it was a Band-Aid and a fragile one at that. Why, do you think, when you asked for permission to see Indiana, I told you to tread carefully? One misstep, and I was worried all the effort to keep Roman's wolf controlled would come undone." Clem took a deep breath. "You don't understand what it was like in the first year after you were gone. She changed, redirected her focus and isolated herself to protect everyone." Clementine shook her head remorsefully. "She still has a few close friends who understand the issues with her wolf, who refused to be chased away, but she's never really repaired the damage with her family. She never repaired the damage within herself."

She paused and twisted her head, looking upwards, frowning at the bluff edge of Plymouth Point.

I mimicked her posture as the sound echoed with my advanced hearing. Someone was having a lovers spat, and it was very heated one. Where Clementine shook her head and evidently told herself that eavesdropping was inappropriate, I had the reverse notion. I focused my ears and noted the tones of the voices instead of focusing on what was being said. Ask Fate, and she will deliver. Fuck me. Vali growled low, but it didn't take much to convince me that we needed to investigate.

"I'm going to go check it out." She made a motion to follow. "You go to Dad's and go spend time with Lacey."

"I don't think you should be alone with her."

"She's my mate. I need to do this," I whispered sadly. "And I need to do it alone. But I'll call if I need backup."

Clementine looked as though she was going to argue, then she snapped her mouth shut and nodded sadly, giving me a slight squeeze before pivoting on her heel before heading in the opposite direction.

CHAPTER 60
VINNY

I stalked up the path that led uphill to Plymouth Point. I didn't need to know where or how, I just followed the gravitational tug that urged me forward—the corrupted mate bond had pulled me upwards.

"Oh, here he comes! Your delusional knight in shining armour." Murdoch looked murderous. Roman looked exhausted, almost forlorn, until her eyes met mine. The purple flashed, and she gave me a sly smile. What game was she playing?

Her hand ripped away from Murdoch's arm as if she had been burned. Then, she angled herself delicately as if she was slotting between Murdoch and myself. I tried to ignore Vali's uneasy rumble in my chest and looked directly into Murdoch's livid face. *"Get away from her right now!"*

His eyes flashed to mine, his jaw tightening before the idiot took a step closer to Roman and a step closer to the edge.

"What's going on?" I asked in a non-suspecting friendly tone.

"Nothing." Roman shook her head with a slightly panicked performance. Her eyes darted between me and Murdoch as if she was worried a fight would break out. Vali growled low. Rue had Roman's mannerisms perfected.

"Well, it's obviously something," I grunted, rolling my eyes and playing along.

"Just a discussion—" Roman started, her icy attitude adding to the chill in the air.

"A discussion?" I scoffed. "You could hear your argument from the pack house," I exaggerated. "Hell, any louder, and you could have heard it from Lupus'."

"Fuck off, Stevens," Murdoch spat. "You've done enough damage to last a lifetime." I angled my body toward Murdoch's, taking in his aggressive posture, knowing he was moments from snapping. Whatever Roman had been doing or saying, it was evident that she had purposely been riling him up.

Murdoch had no idea what werewolf fuckery he had just stepped into, and as much as the concept of him trying to take on her insane wolf usually would have amused me, there was a more profound need to divert his attention—to save him—purely because he had shit instincts and couldn't sense that Rue was in control. His rose-tinted glasses had taken away his self-preservation to such a degree that he couldn't differentiate between the girl and the beast. I couldn't understand why his wolf would let him play right into her immoral claws.

Roman placed her hands on his chest, begging and acting suddenly naïve and sweet. I could taste the vulgar faux-saccharinity of her words. Vali choked on it. Murdoch, however, did the opposite and looked momentarily swept up in her drama, determined to be her saviour no matter the cost.

Nervous bubbles trickled over my skin, and I knew I needed to move his focus back to me, not on the deranged she-wolf in front of him. Desperately, I grabbed onto his argument in an effort to move him away from her. "What damage are you referring to, Murdoch? I can assure you that Roman enjoyed me damaging her." The rings of his eyes flashed dangerously. I kept eye contact with Murdoch, giving him a smarmy smile. I refused to acknowledge Roman, but I felt her eyes boring into me. Her curiosity piqued and pinged against our blackened bond.

"You're fucking scum. You always have been. You don't fucking deserve her," Murdoch said in a deadly quiet tone, the sound of his wolf vibrating in his throat.

"We can agree on that." I chuckled. "But Roman is a grown woman and can make her own mistakes."

"So you admit you are a mistake."

"Full heartedly. But she's a slow fucking learner. Come to think of it, I haven't fucked her slow yet." I flicked my head over and gave Roman a wink. "Maybe next time." Her irises flashed purple, and despite herself, a small smile flickered at the edge of her mouth. Vali hummed with an unsettling, puzzled pride.

Murdoch, on the other hand, had stepped a safer distance from Roman, simmering with jealous rage. I glanced at his arm and noticed the thickening of his hair. Being a merged wolf didn't mean he didn't lose control; I knew that firsthand, especially if both beast and man were losing it.

By the cruel, hungry look in Roman's eyes, it was time to put the final nail into the proverbial coffin.

"I think I finally see what you see in this dick. He's as unhinged as you are. He's going to shift at a little competition. You two are a match made by Fate." Roman's eyes were slitted with callousness before a clawed hand tried to swipe at me. I dodged it by the breadth of my nose.

Pivoting on my heel, I watched as Murdoch fought for control over his wolf. His spine was cracking back and forth as he forced the transformation to stop. I instantly felt terrible for him. It was excruciating to fight a transformation. However, if it moved him away from Roman, it had to be a good thing.

A sinisterly joyful emotion swamped the mate bond, followed by a strategic notion. Roman had wanted him to lose it, but I wasn't supposed to be here. Now, she was trying to figure out how to turn this in her favour.

I refused to look at Roman and attempted to ignore the conflicting, confused emotions of my wolf as evil stratagem flooded the mate bond. I needed to concentrate on getting Murdoch a safer distance away. He was still too close to Roman. She stalked him with a predatory grace. My body buzzed with her anticipation for the moment she would try to sink her claws into him and end his life.

Finally, after a few seconds, Murdoch was in control, away from the edge and right in my face. When he spoke, his words were aimed at Roman, but his spittle sprinkled my skin. "He will fucking hurt you, just like you hurt Indi."

"On that fucking train again, are we? For fuck sake. I didn't do it," I growled, pushing against the mate bond to test its reactions. She didn't so much as flinch at my prod. Her mood remained patiently observant, the perfect predator.

"So that's how you convinced Roman to fuck you. You somehow convinced her you were innocent?"

"I am fucking innocent. I told everyone the truth five years ago. I never saw her that day. Maybe if I had stuck around five years ago, Roman would've finally gotten the full story because you haven't told her all the details, have you, *Murdick*? Why don't you admit that you were the father of Indi's baby?"

Murdoch's face drained of colour. His eyes danced over to Roman. From the petrified look on his face, he hadn't known that Roman knew about Indiana being pregnant, but he had definitely known. His eyes darted anxiously over Roman, nervous of her reaction.

Roman thought I was the father and wouldn't entertain spreading pregnancy rumours about her invalid sister. She would've never stooped that low. But why had he kept that piece of information from her?

Anger flooded through me. Had Murdoch done something to Indi? It wasn't as though the thought hadn't crossed my mind previously, but I had always reminded myself that there was no way Indi would let someone push her off the cliff. And even if, by some miracle, he had surprised her, that fall shouldn't have been enough to put her in the state that she was now in. She should have healed. Unless he hadn't surprise her. Unless he'd used her love for him to put her into a false sense of security about the baby and—

"Why don't you admit that you fucking pushed her off Plymouth Point, you sack of shit."

In a blink of an eye, Murdoch lunged at me. Dust flew up as I landed in the dirt, the sound of hits and grunts echoed around us as punches and kicks were landed. I feigned shock for a few seconds to let him think he had the upper hand, but I wasn't shocked. This was Murdoch: he jumped to the bait every—single—time. This time, I wasn't baiting him, though. I wasn't trying to show him up. I wasn't playing a game.

I let myself feel the emotions that had been brewing deep within me, and redirected their energy into my fists. Indiana. Roman. Rue. Roman's rejection. The love of my life was trying to kill me. Rue. *Fucking Rue!* Even through the anger, the sorrow and pain I felt should have crippled me and rendered me sloppy and useless even though I was trained. Instead, every feeling was directed into my attack with precision. My emotions made me stronger, more accurate, more...deadly.

Roman needed the truth to come out. She needed to find the strength to battle Rue. Murdoch had been lying to her for years and, even after all of this, if Roman didn't return and I had to take her out, at least she would finally know the truth of what happened to Indiana. We both would.

I tackled Murdoch with a sinister smile as I felt his rib pop. His head crashed against a rock and bounced with a satisfying crack. Murdoch wasn't deterred, and he charged forward again. My knee collided with his stomach as my fist pulled back.

Roman's bloodlust singed my senses as my fist hit his jaw with a triumphant crunch. I collapsed, coughing and choking, the blackened tar was infiltrating my system again. Roman smirked from behind him. A feather touch tickled the mate bond, though. What was she doing now? The feathery touch morphed into a thorn, followed by strong intent. Before I could warn him, small hands had reached around Murdoch in what one would have considered a loving embrace. The scent of blood was in the air, followed by a sharp gasp before Murdoch twisted to look at Roman as blood splattered on the dusty ground.

CHAPTER 61
ROMAN

"Still haven't learned to guard your face, I see." Vinny sounded amused through his anger. Murdoch doubled over, pushed himself up onto all fours and spat at the ground before lunging again. A blue tinge was already forming under his left eye, and the blood was drying on his lip. A look of pure hatred was exchanged between the two, then the fists were flying again. My lips twisted with Rue's malevolent smile as she watched with morbid interest and strategized on how to use this latest development to her advantage.

Rue took a stealthy step closer to Murdoch, claws extended. Her game had been thwarted the moment we had smelled my mate walking up the hill. My heart somersaulted and thumped rapidly at the warmth of that repaired connection. I instinctively reached out, and for the briefest second, I could touch it, even from the confines of my mind. The silky rope brushed my fingertips, but when I went to grasp it, it was gone.

Sticky, warm wetness covered my fingertips, and a strong metallic scent reached my nose—blood. I scrambled within my mind, trying to will Rue to withdraw her claws, but all she did was cackle loudly in my head.

"Rue, don't!" Vinny shouted. "Please don't!" His eyes were

brimming with emotion as he panted with exertion. Hope welled in my chest. He knew it wasn't me. His eyes bore into my soul, pleading with my insane wolf.

Her claws pressed harder, and Murdoch groaned in pain, slipping onto his knees. The claw marks were deep within his abdomen, raking upwards with the movement.

"You can't kill him!" Vinny's voice vibrated into me as Murdoch's pulse hammered against my claws. I pushed all my thoughts into retracting my fingers. There wasn't even a timbre of being able to shift.

"Why?" she laughed, a musical carefree laughter that made Murdoch's eyes snap open. His eyes were full of hurt as he looked up at me.

"Because, Roman doesn't want you to. If she's still in there, listen to her."

"She's weak!" Rue screeched in my voice. "Always has been!"

A buzzing irritation came down the mate bond, like a swarm of angry bees, but it was directed toward my wolf rather than me. He didn't think I was weak at all—the complete opposite it seemed. More feelings were being thrust my way—empathy, followed by unsurmountable pride. Something warm rumbled deep within my chest, and then there was a sad desperation. Finally, settling on a sliver of hope, I tried to grasp onto that feeling, to embellish it and project it back. My hand swiped into the void, but there was nothing to grab hold of.

"Stop trying to find Roman down the mate bond," Rue snapped. "Or I'll poison it again."

"That's the only way you can take me out, Rue? By weakening Vali?" His voice sluiced through me as gruff desperation leaked through his speech. "Let Murdoch go and come get me then, you psychotic bitch. You and me, baby, once and for all!"

She released Murdoch and edged toward Vinny, running my tongue over the sharpened points of my teeth before my voice danced sweetly on the breeze.

"Didn't know you cared for him, Vinny. Thought you hated the guy."

"I don't want him dead, Rue."

"Even after Roman used him to get you off her mind? Repeatedly?" His eyes narrowed at her words. "Oh, she'd convinced herself I was breaking free and she was losing control. That was easier than admitting she had been thinking of you." My feet moved forward as Rue changed her prey from Murdoch to Vinny. Vinny didn't move a muscle but watched me with intense scrutiny. "She thrashed in the sheets with him, your arch-nemesis. One word, baby, and I'll end him for both of us."

"He's not worth it, but you and I are endgame, babe." His signature smirk made my heart flip. Was he talking to me? The mate bond was quiet.

"We are. We always have been. It was always going to end like this—fucking or killing. So why not both?" My blood-drenched claw swept down the soft cotton over Vinny's hard chest. She glanced back at Murdoch and sneered. "We can start with Murdoch and have a celebratory rut in his blood. You did mention you wanted to take me slow. How about it, baby?"

Murdoch stayed down, weak in submission, his hands clutching his slowly healing abdomen. Then, his pattern wavered cautiously over the mind-link as if he were testing it. However, no connection was made. My mind-link was still broken. Vinny's clouded eyes made it evident that he and Murdoch were talking.

"Nuh-uh, baby! No mind-linking. That's cheating. You mind-link, you die. More importantly, they die." There was an almost childish glee to my voice that made me shiver. I felt my fingers press into Vinny's chest.

"Fine, you sadistic bitch," he grunted but otherwise ignored the sharp pinpricks in his shirt.

"Is that a way to talk to your true mate?" she crowed in my

voice before stepping back toward Murdoch and crouching to watch the colour drain from his already pale face. Another evil cackle escaped my mouth. "That's why you never stood a chance, Murdoch. Even rejected, the pull between Vinny and me was phenomenal. Every fuck blasted every cell with energy. Every orgasm both killed and energized her at the same time. But hey, you were sort of fun, too. There was potential there." She stepped back from Vinny and gazed playfully at Murdoch as if he were another toy in her deranged game. "Once I kill Vinny, I can teach you how to please me. To worship me." My boot flattened against his chest, pushing him back into a submissive position.

"You were mated to him." Murdoch's voice broke.

She smiled softly at him. "Fate is funny like that."

"I never fucking stood a chance," he mumbled as he closed his eyes in realization.

"Well, I did reject him. Spoiler alert: apparently, our mate bond is repaired." She flashed Vinny a sharp-toothed smile before continuing her conversation in a coy voice. "It's okay, Murdoch, baby. A mate bond can't be reactivated if he's dead. There's no coming back from that."

"You can't, Roman!" Murdoch's eyes were wide with panic. "Just reject him again, and we can be together." Rue looked back at me with an astonished expression. I shook my head in disbelief. He still thought there was a chance. She had just tried to kill him, and she was casually talking about murdering him, then Vinny, and he still wasn't running.

"Run!" I screamed from inside my head. Rue gave me a toothy grin.

"But where is the fun in that? Don't you want me to kill him? Then we can fuck in celebration that your rival is finally six-feet under," she said, batting my eyelids at him like a sociopath. "We can only be together if he's dead."

"You're true mates, Ro." His voice broke. "I love you too much to let you kill yourself like that."

"Oh, baby, it won't kill me because Roman is already dead." Her voice cut precisely where it was meant to.

I screamed at Rue, slamming against the impenetrable block in my mind. Grief wavered over the mate bond as Vinny registered her words. It was thick, heavy, and choking me.

"No, Vinny! I'm not dead. I'm right here!"

Vinny's howl vibrated into my soul and caused me to collapse onto my hands and knees within my mind. Another howl jolted into me. Then another. I gritted my teeth against the agony. And in the brief second that he stopped howling, I grabbed and pulled at the mate bond. He had to know I was still here!

I looked at the cream wolf that stood before me, saliva dripping from his mouth. His hackles rose seconds before he lunged at me. Rue cackled and pirouetted away from the edge of the cliff. Vinny didn't go over but lunged for me again.

Rue danced out of his way, cruel laughter joining the symphony of ripping clothes as she twisted and morphed, fighting him in both forms. I couldn't understand where she had learned this control or speed. But it wasn't important right now. What was important was making sure Vinny knew I was still alive.

The smell of burned rubber infiltrated my nose as thick, black tar started to make its way down the mate bond. I panicked. She was trying to weaken Vinny like she had done before. If only he would turn off his connection, it might buy him some time.

Pain erupted as Vinny sliced my Achilles tendon before carving up my calf, rendering me immobile. I cried torrents of tears as I watched the face of my half-shifted true mate—my executioner—the pure loathing in his eyes, bearing down on me. It was a look I hadn't seen since he'd walked into my hospital months ago. No, that wasn't quite right. I shuddered. I had never seen this expression on his face—this look was murderous—the thing of nightmares.

He was about to deliver a fatal blow when a brown wolf knocked him down. Rue grinned as Murdoch snarled and snapped at Vinny. She pushed her healing power into my leg, laughing maniacally as she watched the two wolves brawl.

I couldn't let her fix my leg, but I still couldn't break free of her cage. Inspiration hit. It was my last shot. Would it work? With one last burst of energy, I simultaneously focused on my mate bond and on Vinny, trying to find his pattern scent. I felt the painful shards of the bridge connect and gritted my teeth at the agony as it tried to open. I focused on connecting the mind-link and the mate bond together, praying the bond would heal and boost the connection long enough for him to hear me.

"Vinny, I'm alive. Help me!" I shouted over and over. The pain ricocheted and split my mind.

Everything went black.

CHAPTER 62
VINNY

I GRITTED my teeth against the pain as my head split open. I could feel Roman—her agony. Giving Murdoch the slip, I watched as Rue took a step toward us before collapsing into a heap inches away from the bluff's edge.

"Roman!" I shouted, sprinting over to her. "Roman!" I threw my arms around her unconscious body. *"Murdoch, help me!"* I screamed down the mind-link as I ran my hands all over my mate's body, checking her for injury, trying to sense her. She was alive. I had felt her. Had she managed to break Rue's hold? Was she back in control? I couldn't feel anything now.

"What the hell is going on?" he snarled, baring his teeth and putting his head low between his front legs in an aggressive manner.

"Roman is alive!"

"No thanks to you. Get away from her!"

"No, you fuckwit, that was all Rue! It wasn't Roman. Rue was in control! Rue said she was dead, but I felt her. She's alive." I kissed Roman's forehead. *Please be okay, Ro!* Tears spilled from my eyes. I was going to kill her. I was seconds away from killing her. I looked at Murdoch, a man I owed my life to. He stopped me from making the biggest mistake of my life.

"*We need to lock her up.*" My eyes snapped up at the furry beast of Murdoch's wolf as he shifted into a man. Deep gashes covered his torso, and his face was bruised, but he mostly looked exhausted. "We need to lock Roman up, Vinny. For everyone's safety."

"You think she could still be Rue?"

"I think we would be stupid to risk it."

"There's only one place that will hold her, but it's too risky."

"Just for a day or two, man. Until we can be sure she's back in control." He looked down at Roman. "I couldn't even tell she wasn't herself. How could I not tell? I've helped her back from the brink so many times over the years."

I slinked my arms under Roman's naked, unconscious body and walked back toward the pack house, Vali pushing his healing abilities gently down the mate bond, pulling back whenever she stirred. He didn't want to wake her yet, but he couldn't help himself from healing her.

By the time we got to the pack house, she was free from many of her superficial cuts and scrapes. However, the injury in her leg was going to take a little longer. Guilt washed through me again. I would've killed her without hesitation.

Alpha Liam jogged down the porch steps with Beta Ryan, whose eyes raked over Murdoch's excessive injuries as he handed him a spare pair of shorts. Alpha Liam kept his eyes on the unconscious she-wolf in my arms. "We'll need to put her in a cell."

"We can't," I said, my voice gruff with emotion.

"It's the only place safe enough to hold her."

"Don't make it easy for Fate. The rogue is down there. Send me in to kill the rogue, and then I'll happily lock her in her temporary cage."

"I can't do that." Alpha Liam closed his eyes in annoyance. "Look, we'll keep her as far from his cell as possible and leave a guard with her at all times."

"Me."

"Not you," he said, meeting my gaze.

"Me."

"You're too close to this."

"No, I'm fucking not. This is my family, my niece, my mate. It has to be me."

"That's why you are too close to this. You won't do what is necessary."

"I almost did!"

"So why is she alive?"

"Because Murdoch stopped me." My heart jolted as I peered down at Roman's face. "And then... I felt her. Roman is still in there."

"And that's why you won't be able to do it now. You hesitated once, you're likely to do it again. You love her."

"Wait! Alpha." Murdoch stepped forward. "You can't actually be suggesting we kill Roman."

"Of course he isn't!" My sister's voice vibrated toward us as she walked in our direction, my niece on her hip and my dad frowning in tow behind her. "Our first priority is to help her, Murdoch."

Alpha Liam nodded. "We wait and see. I know you love her, but if she's a threat, it's one we can't have in this pack. If it comes to it, we will remove *every* threat. For now, let's put her in the cells, then we can discuss it.

Vali snarled in warning as Ryan made his way to remove Roman from my hold. I took a step back, away from his outreached arms. His eyebrows shot upwards as he calmly said, "Bro, let me take her to the cell."

"Don't fucking touch her," Vali growled through my teeth. Ryan's eyes widened at my blatant insubordination.

"Vinny," Dad said, taking a step forward. "Let me take her for a minute. You get some pants on. Then we can both make sure she's comfortable."

I weighed my options and grudgingly slid my mate into my father's arms before snatching a pair of track pants and yanking them on, keeping my eyes on my dozing mate the entire time. Vali grumbled with determination. She wasn't going to be executed. He needed to save her.

Her cell was in the farthest corner of the building, six cells away from the rogue and still not far enough for my liking. I twitched nervously. It would be so easy just to walk in there and slit his throat. Vali rumbled at the thought. I lay Roman on the small cot as my father donned some gloves, before removing the chains from the wall, looping them three times for easier handling. I knew he was removing them for my benefit. It proved they wouldn't chain and torture her nor give her a weapon to hurt herself or someone else—keeping everyone protected—including Roman.

He stepped out of the cell to dispose of the chains and grimaced when the chain accidentally hit his bare flesh. Pure silver chains and bars, which seemed necessary when dealing with a rogue, now made my stomach churn.

I swiped her hair from her face and gave her a gentle kiss on the forehead as Ryan dropped a threadbare blanket over her body. I shook my head at him. "That won't do. She'll freeze. Her wolf doesn't heat her."

"It's all they had in the cupboard," he mumbled, looking apprehensive as he saw the first signs of her shivering now that she wasn't in my arms. "I'll see if I can find her something warmer. And I'll send the pack doctor in to make sure she's okay." I didn't reply but listened to the sounds of his retreating footsteps.

Dad returned and gave my shoulder a squeeze. I knew he wanted to help me; my entire family did. But they didn't know how. I had never told them I was mated, then rejected. To find this out at the same time they discovered that my mate was the feral wolf in the prophecy, I couldn't imagine what was going through their minds. Yet, it didn't stop him from wanting to support me. Tears welled behind my eyes, and I blew out a heavy breath, wishing I could just collapse into my dad and take his support. But now wasn't the time to break. I shrugged him off gently before I shuffled Roman, sitting on the cot and resting her head on my lap. I tucked the blanket around her and then proceeded to run my hands down her body in an attempt to keep her warm.

"Do you want to come to the inner circle meet? I think you should be there."

"I need to be here for Roman. She's cold."

"Ryan will be back soon with a blanket and warm clothes." I said nothing. "The doctor will be here soon, too. She won't be alone, Vinny."

"I'll stay, too." I glanced up at Murdoch, who was leaning against the stone wall of the cell. I hadn't even noticed he had followed us. He met my gaze with a solid sincerity. "Nothing will happen to her, I promise."

CHAPTER 63
VINNY

THE VOICES WERE harsh as I stepped onto the first step that led up to the pack house. I gave Dad a sideways glance as the words floated into my ears—words like prophecy, rogue, destruction. Vali growled low as I forced myself into the alpha's office with pent-up aggression.

"Anyone touches her, they die," I growled. Clem looked up at me with a frown before she returned her attention to the circle of wolves debating loudly.

"No one is going to touch her," Dad whispered. "They just need to discuss all the possibilities. Everything needs to be out in the open. It's the diplomatic way."

"It's wasting time," I grunted back.

Alpha Liam put up his hand in a gesture for silence. A small amount of power waved through the room, and the conversation immediately ceased.

"Now that we're all here, we can discuss this properly."

"I thought we were discussing this, Alpha," Milo said. "We were discussing that this is too fucking close for comfort. The fact of the matter is we all thought this prophecy was bullshit until Roman went feral."

I glared at Milo. "And now?"

He glanced at me. "And now, too many stars are aligning."

"The prophecy is still bullshit," I said with false bravado. I was still debating things myself. "Look, I've been battling with this for days –"

"Days! You knew about this for *days*?" Milo looked livid. "You knew about this and kept it to yourself. Even though it could endanger the whole pack?"

"Of course he didn't," Dad cut across, defending me.

"Then why are we all just hearing about it now, after she's tried to take out a member of this pack?"

"She tried to take me out too," I muttered under my breath, which, of course, everyone heard.

"Just brilliant," Milo snapped, throwing his hands in the air. "All of this information would have been good to have days ago!"

"Milo," Alpha Liam said calmly. "Vinny brought this to my attention before this even happened. We knew his theory, and I chose to keep it from this council. Fear-mongering and pitchforking have never helped anyone in this pack." He glanced at his mate. "This pack lived in prejudicial fear for years. We have only just started getting rid of the blood-hate, and people have only just started trusting again. What do you think the pack is going to do if rumour spreads of this prophecy? Why the hell do you think I kept everything about this quiet? If information got out that there was a prophecy, and now everything about Roman, we would have a coup on our hands on top of everything else. People would demand execution. She would get worse treatment than half-breeds have ever gotten."

"I'm sorry, Alpha, but the pack has a right to know," Milo disagreed. "They already know the rogues are attacking."

My sister piped up, "Do you remember when we met, why you were on the enemy's side? I was Roman, Milo. I was being targeted. It's scary having an entire pack hate you because of what you are born into. What if everyone hated you because of something they perceived you to be, without any proof or full understanding?"

"I told you I wasn't a blood-hater. I wasn't there for that reason. I earned my pardon."

She gave him a sad smile. "You did. So why haven't you learned from it?"

Milo looked ashamed, and in his moment of quiet solitude, Alpha Liam took charge. The discussion circled the rogues, who quickly moved back into prophecy territory. After another thirty minutes of solid arguing, my sister spoke up again.

Everyone stopped and looked down at her, tiny but in control of the room. "Your alpha and I don't believe in this prophecy. Roman is troubled, but that doesn't make her feral." She gave me a sympathetic look. "I believe she was just reacting to horrible circumstances that plagued her life. We have to prove that Roman isn't a threat."

"There's only one way to prove that." A voice piped up. "Put her with the rogue in the cell."

"You have got to be fucking kidding me!" I snapped, my fur itching to burst out. I was going to take that fucker out. Circle member or not. Dad squeezed my shoulder again.

"We won't be doing that. She will remain in a cell until we can determine if she's back in control of her wolf," Alpha Liam declared to the room.

"Alpha, may I have a word?" Doctor Todd cleared his throat from the doorway and looked nervously around at the group. "Alone?" he added.

This had to be about Roman. I was desperate to see her, but I needed to hear what the doctor had to say. I looked to Alpha Liam, desperation written all over my face. He looked around the room before singling out his father, my father and myself. "Dad, Patrick and Vinny will remain behind. The rest of you will head to the amphitheatre, and I will call you back when we've finished."

The circle gave the doctor a curious look, knowing it had to be an update on Roman, but said nothing as they filed out of the pack house. When the sounds of the wolves disappeared, and only Clem, Josiah, Dad and myself were left in the room, Alpha Liam turned his attention to the doctor. "How is she?"

"Still unconscious." He cleared his throat. "She's frail, but I think she will be okay. Honestly, I won't know more until she wakes up." He fumbled a little awkwardly. "May I speak frankly?"

"Please." Alpha Liam nodded.

"I heard some of the discussion between your inner circle as I was coming over. I didn't mean to eavesdrop, but I think you need to know something." Alpha Liam nodded, indicating that the doctor should continue. "I don't want to break patient-doctor confidence, but I feel this is important to Roman's fate within this pack."

Alpha Liam gestured for the doctor to sit, and he settled into a plush armchair, stretching his legs out. My father and sister also took their seats, while Alpha Liam positioned himself in his chair behind the desk, and Josiah leaned casually against the wall. I, however, was too restless to sit and twitched anxiously.

"When she was sixteen years old, she came to me concerned that her wolf was rabid. Those were her exact words. She was terrified of what that could mean, and after running through unnecessary tests to help ease her anxiety, I reassured her that her wolf wasn't rabid. Her anxiety wasn't new to me. Before she gained her wolf, on the brink of puberty, she started to suffer from anxiety and clinical depression."

I grunted my disbelief, causing the doctor to snap his attention toward me. There was no way Roman suffered from that. "She hid it well, but it was there. She was medicated on a low-dose mood stabilizer, and she went to a therapist for a couple of years, getting the help she needed until she met her wolf. Then, medication stopped working." He paused. "When her wolf manifested, the beast was highly strung. I believe her wolf was feeding off her anxiety, her needs. With every year that passed, a different major event brought her back to see me. She was convinced her wolf was rabid and kept asking me to fix her wolf. There was nothing to fix. It would just take time. I told her this time and time again. Her therapist told her the same thing—it was all normal. Her wolf was a little more energetic than the average wolf, but I reinforced that she was not diseased or, as you have been saying, feral. I truly believe that even though the evidence is showing the contrary."

He took a deep breath. "There hasn't been enough research into mental health in werewolves. There never has been any reason to. At sixteen, the wolf gene repairs all damage—no more sickness, physical or mental. However, I've been thinking she's in her mid-twenties now and still battling this. I'm convinced she has been battling a mental illness, and what you're seeing is her wolf's reaction to that." He had a thoughtful expression on his face, as he hypothesized. "What if the reason we have these so-called feral wolves is that the wolf spirit can't fix the problem, and it gets drowned in the brain chemicals? I would wager to say that most of these feral wolves aren't truly feral. I would say they are just reacting to brain chemistry."

"But what about the fact that her wolf can't keep her warm? She has no instinct to protect her?" I asked guiltily. It felt wrong to talk about Roman this way.

"I believe it could be a physical manifestation of her mental condition. The same as not being able to mind-link."

I gave Doctor Todd a confused expression. "Wait, she can't mind-link?"

"Have you not noticed? She can only mind-link in wolf form. When her human side is mostly dormant."

I blinked a few times, thinking back to all the times I'd tried to mind-link her.

"What's next, doctor?" asked Clementine while I struggled to come to grips with just how broken my mate was.

"We need her to wake up. We need to assess her mental state. There is nothing to be done until then."

"And if it's still Rue?" Josiah asked in a soft, paternal tone.

The doctor sighed a heavy breath. "That's not a decision for me. But in my professional opinion, mental health is a tricky thing, and no one should be punished for having mental health issues."

CHAPTER 64
VINNY

THREE DAYS HAD PASSED, and Roman still hadn't stirred. The doctor visited every day to assess her state, but there was no change. He just said there was no reason why she shouldn't be awake. It was a matter of time. Alpha Liam had agreed to let me sit with her in the cell, hoping the mate bond would heal her enough to wake her up.

But so far, she just slept like the dead, covered in thick track pants, a hoodie and a thick blanket. The cells had no heating, and there was never any need to heat them. I pulled a purple toque out of my pocket and gently put it on her head, brushing my hand over her face.

Come on, Roman, wake up.

"You getting any sleep?" Liv asked as she peered into the cell. Out of all her friends, Liv was the only one who knew where she was and why. Murdoch raged about how all her friends would like to be there for her, but Alpha Liam reminded him it was a cell, not a hospital wing. They couldn't just sit around her bedside and bring her flowers. Her family hadn't even been informed as it was currently too risky to tell them.

There was an argument before Alpha Liam commanded

that the only people allowed to know and visit her were the inner circle, a few warriors, Murdoch, and me.

I grunted in response to her enquiry.

"Any change?" I shook my head and sagged onto my three-legged stool. Liv opened the door with a whinny. "Go home and sleep." I looked up at her, her fiery mane barely contained within her ponytail, her eyes just as tired as mine.

"Were you working a triple shift? You look like shit," I grumbled at her.

"Pot, meet kettle." She rolled her eyes at me. "Go home. Get sleep. Shower, using soap preferably, and then go and enjoy your niece's first birthday."

I FUMBLED INTO MY BED, realizing it was the early hours of the morning. I swear it had been dawn when I entered the cells. *How long have I been in there for?* I set an alarm on my phone, allowing myself to catch up on a few hours of sleep before I meandered to the pack house to do the dutiful uncle thing of being there for Lacey's first birthday and debriefing with the alpha on Roman's latest update. Four words: Nothing new to report. It should be the shortest situation report ever.

Exhausted and wishing I could have tucked up with Roman instead, I folded into my pillow and drifted into a restless sleep, Vali pacing out his agitation in my mind. When the alarm blared only minutes later, I groaned and rolled myself into the shower, knowing that getting through today would require a lot of coffee.

True to form, when I walked up to the pack house, there were no balloons, no bouncy castle, and nothing else that would resemble a kid's party. It was just a regular day. I opened the door to much of the same. The pack house was quiet. I sat down on the couch and closed my eyes for a moment. I opened them again when I felt tiny hands pulling at my leg. Lacey was pulling herself up to stand.

"Happy birthday, kid," I said as I patted her head awkwardly.

"She didn't mean to wake you," My sister said from the open-plan kitchen, taking a swig from a coffee cup and placing ingredients inside a large bowl.

"I wasn't asleep."

"Your snoring said otherwise."

I grunted in response, stood up and went into the kitchen, where my sister was making a chocolate cake.

"Where is everyone?" I asked, sticking my finger into the batter. She whacked my hand before I licked the goo off my finger without a care.

"Liam and Dad have gone scouting with the warriors this morning. Most warriors have been doing overtime, feeling that this is the day shit is going to go down. Liam was getting antsy and pissing me off, so I sent him out, and Dad smartly followed."

"When are they due back?" I asked, taking my sister's cup of coffee and giving it a large sip. She scowled and pointed to the coffee pot before taking her own cup back. I grudgingly grabbed a *World's Best Dad* mug from the cupboard and poured coffee to the brim.

"Should be soon," she said, continuing to mix her batter a little more aggressively than was needed.

"You realize there is a big party planned anyway." Her eyes snapped to mine, and I knew I hit the nail on the head.

"I'm aware. Liam isn't going to stop the pack from having fun. Just his own daughter."

"She won't remember this, Clem," I said kindly.

"I know." She sighed. "Family afternoon tea will be fine."

"Speaking of family, have you heard from Sean?"

"Liam talked to him a few days ago. He said he was going to try and make it back."

"And how was he?" I really hoped that the reason he had stayed away so long wasn't because his mate had rejected him.

She gave me a sad look as if she mirrored my thoughts. "I don't know, but he knows we're here if he needs us."

Sean didn't show up to the afternoon tea, and I tried not to add the worry I had for my friend to the worry I was consumed with over my mate. If he had been rejected, I knew firsthand how much that sucked and how much time it took before you could feel some semblance of normal. So, even though I wasn't feeling it, I decided to be the doubly attentive uncle.

I smiled at the giggling baby as I blew bubbles through a wand. The bubbles, I was told, were to add to the aesthetic of the thousand photos being taken as Lacey enjoyed smashing her cake with her tiny fists. She was unsure at first, but after some encouragement from her dad, she started punching into it with the enthusiasm of a heavyweight boxer.

The small party went off without a hitch, and soon, I was helping load dishes into the dishwasher. I was hoping that the party at Lupus' tonight would also be an uneventful success, even though, in reality, we were all waiting for the other shoe to drop.

The minute I could leave the pack house, I made my way down the path to the stone cells. Voices travelled down the path to meet me. My heart constricted, then thundered in my chest, and I threw my head back, closing my eyes in thankful prayer as I instantly recognized one of the voices.

I approached the warrior, who gave me a small smile as he said, "She's awake." Instead of rushing through the corridor, I stopped to eavesdrop.

"You just don't get it!" Murdoch's exasperated voice bounced off the walls.

"No, I don't, so explain it to me." There was a second of silence, then there was a stammer as Murdoch started speaking again.

"I-I remember the first time I saw you. You were walking

Indiana into kindergarten class with this massive toothy smile and larger-than-life personality. You were a little bossy, but always full of laughter." His voice was gruff. "As time went on, I was so sure we were mated. Everything about you made me spin out of control. Even after I turned twenty, every full moon, I was hoping that the moon would link us. I was so sure there had to be some kind of mistake when three moons had passed and nothing had happened. I confided in Indi." There was a pause, then a strain in Murdoch's voice. "Indi had always been infatuated with me." Another pause as if he was struggling to find his next words. "I was depressed, and she was there." He shook his head. "It was just supposed to be the one time, but you know how these things spin out of control. She was with Vinny, and I sort of liked the idea of fucking him over." I rolled my eyes but still didn't move from the entrance.

He released a deep breath. "Fate is cruel, you know? I was infatuated with you, and we're not mated. Indiana was infatuated with me, and we also were not mates. I think she was devastated, but she pushed it down deep and even though she knew I was in love with you, we started seeing each other."

There was another long pause. Vali was itching to see his girl, but I knew the moment I started walking down the cells, Murdoch would stop speaking. I needed to hear this just as much as Roman did.

"And five years ago?" Roman's soft voice prompted.

"Five years ago," his voice wavered and he sighed heavily. "Five years ago, Indiana informed me that she was pregnant. She was sure the baby was mine." His heart rate increased as he started to ramble. "She'd just dropped this bombshell on me. Even though I knew there was no way to determine if the pup was mine, I tried to scent her in vain to see if I could figure out whose pup it was. All I could smell was her, Vincent Stevens, and me. His scent was fresh. She had just been with him while she was supposedly pregnant with my pup. I saw red, Roman. Here she was, trying to tell me she was in love with me, that we were having a pup, and she smelled like that fucker. We got into a fight and I told her I didn't want it. She only wanted it to be mine 'cause Vinny was trash. I accused her of being a gold digger. I called her some other horrible names, then I told her that I was certain you and I would be chosen mates and that her spreading illegitimate rumours was just a ruse to sabotage my being with you."

There was another few seconds of silence. I couldn't imagine what Roman was thinking. I reached out to gently stroke the mate bond, surprised to hit an abyss. She was blocking me. I didn't like the uneasy feeling it left me with, so I took a step into the stone corridor and started toward her cell in the back.

"—Indi and I had started something, but it wasn't her I wanted, Ro. It was you! I'm ashamed, Roman. I shouldn't have said any of that to her, but I was in love with you, and she was going to ruin it. I told her I hoped that she and the baby died."

Vali growled angrily, and then I finally saw him. He had collapsed against the stone wall opposite the cell door, with his knees propped up, his arms slung overtop, and his head lowered in shame. Roman stood close to the silver bars but not touching them. She still couldn't see me at this angle, and she still hadn't sensed me. I stopped to take her in.

"In a matter of seconds, I had destroyed her, Roman. As she was running away, I screamed at her that maybe Vincent would be a bigger sucker than I was. That's the last I saw of her. I shifted and went for a run to clear my head, and a couple of hours later, I found her at the bottom of the ridge." He pressed his eyes with the rough pads of his hands as if he were trying to push the memory of finding her out of his mind. "I found her, but I never lay a finger on her."

Roman's mouth parted into a soft circle before she spoke in a soft, foreign, icy voice. One that she used with me so many times before. "So you used my known hatred for Vinny and the grief over my sister to your advantage! What was the plan,

Murdoch, that I would be your damsel in distress and turn to you in my angsty grief for closure? Or was it that I would fuck out my anger and eventually fall in love with you?"

Vali growled with possessiveness, and Roman looked instantly in my direction. And right then, I knew—I knew that it wasn't Roman. Fuck.

"Yes, I was hoping for that. I've always hoped for that. It was easy to blame Vinny."

"So you made out that you had seen him push her off the cliff."

"No, I never actually said I had seen them together. I only said she was covered in his scent. You made that connection by yourself, and I never corrected you, nor was I going to. You hated him even more than you already did, and that was bound to work in my favour." He lifted his head, still not noticing me standing in the shadows, trying to focus on the conversation as my heart was ripped from my chest, beating hard as it shattered. She wasn't my Roman. What the fuck was I going to do?

"But I did wonder if she'd told him, and he reacted worse than I had. All I know was Vincent wasn't in the cells. He was walking around as if shit couldn't touch him. Your whole family was grieving, so instead of hashing it out with him, I dutifully stayed by your fucking side. Then, the coward ran away. You were hurting, Indi was in a coma, and finally, when it came time to ask questions, his sister gave him a fucking out instead of punishing him."

"She gave me an out because my true mate had rejected me, and the pain of that was crippling," I said, stepping out of the shadow and looking directly at Roman, watching her brown and purple eyes attempt to act remorseful.

"Hello, Rue. Where's Roman?"

CHAPTER 65
ROMAN

"Why did you have to do that?" Rue snarled through my voice, no longer acting as me. I keeled over in distress. How had my plan failed? "Twenty more minutes, and I would have convinced him that we could be chosen mates. Twenty more minutes, and I would have been out of this cell."

"And here I thought you were trying to get Murdoch to tell you the truth."

"Oh, that? Nah. That sap started spouting out his truth the moment I opened my eyes. Relief and guilt spilled out of him like vomit. It was all very Hallmark." I studied Vinny as she continued. I had no strength to stop her; she was me, and I was her. "Besides, we all know what happened, even if Roman won't admit it to herself." Rue flashed Murdoch a snide smile. "Indiana got knocked up by a guy, wishing she was her sister. Then, when she thought he would play happy family, she saw his true colours. Then, in some post-traumatic, pre-partum depression, she flung herself from Plymouth Point, Isis doing nothing to help her. Honestly, she may have the name of a queen, but she was a weak fucking wolf." My mouth continued to move. "Anyone who tried to imply or tell Roman outright what had happened, she went into heavy denial, pushing the information into the back of her mind and making me deal with it. That's what led her to cut off poor Mom and Dad. They tried to tell her, and as usual, a fight broke out. It started off about Indi, then quickly turned into a fight about how I was out of control. Bitch, my sister just tried to off herself, and Fate decided it would be funny to mate me—"

"You knew about it, and you didn't tell her?" Vinny asked incredulously. She stopped her blustering rant and laughed at him before giving him a sweet smile.

"It was my job to protect and heal her. So, I took all her pain and hid it from her, then gave her another to blame. You were pretty convenient, so thanks for that."

"Where is Roman?" Murdoch snarled angrily, jumping to his feet, his eyes flashing.

"Don't worry, Murdoch, she heard your heartfelt confession. She's just too weak to move from behind my block."

"Your block? You pushed her behind your mental block? No human can go back there!" Murdoch exclaimed.

"Not without consequences, no." I gave him a toothy smile. "Unfortunately, it's all I can do to detain her. I wish I could kill her, but that would kill me, and you know, I actually like living. Especially now that I'm finally free. I never did thank you, Vinny. You're the one that gave me the strength to push her back. Kudos for visiting Indi by the way. That opened up the floodgates, and all the emotions I've been suppressing for her overflooded the control she had on me. It weakened her enough that I could push her back and lock her in a place she can never leave."

"I'll get her out." Vinny snarled, the silver of his eyes brightening in promise. My heart flipped with hope as Rue cackled maniacally.

"Oh darling, how heroic of you." My face pressed against the bars, searing my skin. Rue didn't even flinch as the smell of burning flesh sizzled the air. "But she can't get rid of me either, so even if you manage. How will you keep me back? Roman tried to fight back and weakened herself even more." She looked between Vinny and Murdoch, running my tongue over the sharpening tips of my protruding canines. "In fact, it was very rude of her. We were in the middle of trying to figure out who I was going to kill first." My voice lit up as Rue came up with another sadistic idea. "Does anyone have a loonie? Since we couldn't decide, let's leave it up to Fate. I'll flip a coin. If it lands on heads, I kill Vinny because he gives great head. Damn, that'll kind of suck, but Fate would have spoken. But..." she dragged out the word excitedly. "If it lands on tails, I kill Murdoch and still have the opportunity to get great head."

I looked at Vinny and felt his mind whirring as he talked to his wolf. I waited to see what genius idea he was going to come up with. He was my mate. He had to be able to save me. But after a few more seconds of him just staring at me, my body slumped, and Rue's disinterest flooded my mind. I crumpled in defeat.

"The mate bond can heal anything. The mate bond will keep her under control," Murdoch said with desperation. He may hate Vinny, but the idea of losing me was worse. Then, I realized that he had said it through the mind-link. I gasped from behind my wall. I could hear them. I could feel their patterns. But from the looks of it, they couldn't feel me.

"You have to mark her on the next full moon. That way, she's fully tethered to you," Murdoch continued desperately.

"You want me to mark myself to a feral fucking wolf?" Vinny raised his eyebrow at Murdoch.

"Hear me out. If you mark her, you'll have a direct link to her. You may be able to unlock the cage where she's keeping Roman."

"There's no guarantee that will work. Even if she doesn't try to kill me as it's happening, she could do so much more damage being mated to me. What if she turns around afterwards and instantly rejects me? You know that would be worse than death. Or I could be linked to a feral and sadistic wolf, wondering when and how she was planning on killing me and my loved ones. Don't you realize

her vicious form of pleasure is torture? She thrives on torturing me, you, everyone. Ever since the mate bond was repaired, she's been trying to poison it, choking Vali and killing him slowly, loving the pain she's been inflicting. What if she just traps me, poisoning me daily, but not enough to kill me, just enough to make me wish for death, while she kills everyone I care about? I wouldn't be strong enough to stop her. There are many things that could go wrong with this plan."

"But it might be the only way to save her!" Murdoch shouted. Vinny shook his head, torment and anger warring within his eyes. *"If you won't try, then I will!"* Murdoch's eyes found mine, and behind the anger in his voice, there was a glimmer of hope in his eyes, but it was nothing to the instant rage that glowed in Vinny's.

"She's mine!"

"Then mark her!"

"We just had the full moon," he reminded Murdoch in an annoyed tone.

"So we keep her locked up until the next one, then you mark her."

"She's already rejected me. Sure, it feels like our bond has been repaired, but who knows if that's normal or if marking would even work?"

"You have to try!"

"Look at you two bickering like an old mated couple!" My voice shocked them into silence.

"Oh look, I have your attention again! Good. You know I'm not going to let you mark me. Although, the idea of Vinny breaking into my cell, pinning me against the wall and biting me as he fucks me senseless is arousing. And Vinny was right in saying I would kill him before the bond took hold, if it even fucking worked. The way I see it is that you only have two options: set me free or kill me. We all know neither of you will kill me, so I guess option one it is."

"Or option three: you come find me and fulfill your destiny," a gruff voice sounded down the cells, one that made me shiver.

She snapped my face back from the door, skin sticking to the bars.

"Who's that?" Rues excitement over the newcomer ignited on my tongue. Rue looked back at me as I realized it could only be one person. That would explain why everything went quiet after he hurt Vinny, but surely he wouldn't still be here? How was he still alive?

"No one." Vinny snapped, trying to block the corridor with his body.

A soft chuckle echoed off the walls.

Rue craned my neck to look down the hall, seeing nothing but darkened stone. She turned back and scrutinized Vinny carefully, assessing his mannerism. He was hiding something from me. I took a deep sniff, my nose twitching as a musty jail cell infiltrated my nose.

"I told you, half-breed; I told you that your feral mate would be mine," the voice coughed again. "Don't worry, sweetheart, now that I've found you, the next phase can start."

"You haven't found shit!" she called back before rolling my eyes at the two wolves in front of me. Then my mouth cracked with a grin as her attention turned back toward Vinny. "Is this where you throw all the loonies?"

"It's just the two of you."

"Ah! Toonies then," she said with a wink. If he appreciated her joke, he never let on. Instead, he stared at me with a blank expression.

"Tell me, sweetheart," the rogue called again. "Have you given into your bloodlust yet? The prophecy won't be fulfilled until you do."

She rolled my eyes again and decided to play along. "I tell you what, you find a way to get me out of this cell, and you can watch my first kill." I heard the low grumble from within his cell. "Then, if you're a good little wolf, I'll let you claim me however you wish."

"Sounds good to me, sweetheart."

She shook her head in amusement and turned her attention back to Vinny and Murdoch. My mouth curved into a dangerously seductive smile. Before Rue could continue her torment, a loud explosion echoed throughout Blackfern Valley. The ground rumbled, and my ears pinged with an annoying high-pitched sound. *What the hell was that?* Vinny froze before looking around in shock as another loud explosion sounded in the distance.

Then I heard it: the alpha command that sounded across the pack like a civil defence siren.

The rogues had arrived.

CHAPTER 66
ROMAN

I CRUMBLED under the weight of the alpha's voice coming through my mind-link. Somehow, I had managed to hear Vinny and Murdoch's inner conversation without pain, but it was like my mind was cracking and splitting across fine fissures and pumping them full of hot, searing lava. Rue snarled and whimpered, frothing at the mouth as the excruciating lava solidified into heavy molten rock, weighing her and me down. I tried to ignore the excruciating ache and focused on what was being said. Words jumbled deeply, shaking my core and submitting me into a crouching position as I clung to the hair at my temples.

Snippets of information were filtering through my broken brain. Somehow, the rogues had blown up the elementary school. *Holy crap!* We were under attack, and our enemy had taken out our main assembly area for the young and the old. With a final howl in my head, the terror subsided, and my body shifted into fur and teeth.

I pushed against the wall separating me from Rue and felt it give. Gasping, I pushed as hard as I could, desperately before Rue gained control. I panted as I pushed forward, occupying the space with my wolf spirit. She snarled menacingly at me before

I tackled her to the ground. I had never been able to touch her before. Her fur was silky soft under my fingertips, and her teeth were agonizingly close to my throat. We had merged, but we were not one.

"Rue!" I shouted. She wriggled and bit my arm, puncturing the skin deep to the bone. It didn't hurt. Should it have hurt? Confused, I shoved her off and tried again. *"Rue, why are you like this? Rue, stop fighting me, Blackfern Valley is under attack! I don't care if you hate me. I don't care about any of it. We can sort through our issues later. Right now, your pack is under attack."*

Did she even care about her pack? I had no idea. Yes, she was crazy, but at the end of the day, she was a pack wolf. And until she abandoned her pack and went rogue, she would still have pack instincts. Right?

She snarled menacingly and pushed herself away from me. I watched anxiously for the fake-out. She growled low, keeping an eye on me as much as I was keeping an eye on her—an impasse.

I looked out into the corridor and only saw Vinny, indicating that Murdoch had already run out into the fight. *"Vinny!"* I called. *"Vinny, it's me, I promise. Please let me out."*

"Roman?" His voice wavered.

"Yeah, let me out. We are under attack." His human eyes looked deep into my wolf ones.

"No."

"No?"

"No."

"Vinny! Let me out!"

"I can't, Ro. I'm sorry. You're safer here. Everyone is safer with you here." My heart shattered into glass; tiny shards entering my bloodstream, slicing throughout my body. I saw the regret in Vinny's eyes before the gorgeous green steeled over and became frosty. He pulled off his clothes and shifted, leaving me alone in my cell, leaving me alone with Rue.

"Don't worry, sweetheart, help will soon arrive," the voice

called. Rue flicked her tail, seemingly ignoring the voice though a minuscule amount of interest trickled around me.

I looked at the cell door and withered in defeat. I was a threat because Rue was a threat. My family and pack were fighting for their lives, and I was stuck behind bars because my wolf had decided to go full-crazy. I had always known she was rabid. I had always known not to trust her. Gentle apprehension tickled my senses as I looked over at the black wolf in my mind with purple and brown eyes. I didn't think she was strong enough to push me back behind the wall again, but I kept an eye on her regardless. She tilted her head at me which I met with a glare. For the first time in my life, I wanted to give into my anger, my hatred and my bloodlust. For the first time, I really wanted to end Rue's existence. She chuckled at my train of thought.

"You need me."

"Doesn't mean I have to like you." She shrugged without a care.

I stayed in wolf form, pacing the cell as I listened to the sounds of battle throughout the forest. Ten minutes passed, then fifteen, then thirty as I paced, desperate to get out. I tried to mind-link Vinny, to beg for my release again, but he had turned his connection off. I could still feel him, though. The mate bond allowed me to trace his moods and keep tabs on whether he was hurt or not, but shortly after that, it went dark, too. The isolation was suffocating, although my instincts told me he wasn't doing anything malicious. My nerves prickled against my fur, zinging uncontrollably like a thousand fire ants running under my skin.

I needed out of here. I reached out to my friends. Surely, someone would help, right?

I opened my connection to three of them at a time. That was all I could manage. All of them were distracted, battling droves of unwelcomed wolves. No one would answer me, not even Liv, who seemed to be in the thick of it but was always there for me no matter what. It was finally Murdoch who answered my pleas.

"*Roman, you are safe there.*"

"*I want to help.*"

"*You can't.*"

"*I have to!*"

"*No, I mean, you can't. We can't let you out. Alpha Liam commanded it. The minute the rogues attacked, the elderly and the pups were to barricade themselves somewhere safe. Anyone who could fight needed to fight, and no one was to enter the cells. Meaning that once I left, I couldn't get back in, even if I wanted to.*"

"Shit," I cried. I really was stuck. "*Be careful!*"

Had Vinny been staying for me? But then, why had he suddenly changed his mind and leave?

Loud footsteps broke my thoughts as someone started walking through the corridor of the stone cells.

Shuffling footsteps followed by the creak of a door, were then met with the sound of chains rattling. Someone was setting the rogue free. But no one could enter the cells, right? Unless they weren't pack.

I tried to scent the air, but all I could make out was the stench of a dirty, musty jail cell.

"End cell," the rogue's voice coughed. "I'll join you in a moment."

Footsteps echoed through the hall again. Rue's hackles edged up as we prepared for whoever it was. Then he came into view.

Simon.

I bared my teeth, growling menacingly, my ears flat against my skull as he took a step forward.

"You'll need to shift," he said unperturbed, looking directly at my black wolf form standing aggressively in the middle of the cell. "I can't talk to you in this form, Roman."

I looked warily at Rue, and she gave me a quick nod. Shocked as we both were to see Simon there, knowing about werewolves, we were both sure we could take out one human if we needed to. Any werewolf could overpower a human.

"There she is." Simon's eyes travelled my naked body as I stretched upwards onto two legs. I shivered at the cold—not the greedy, predatory look in Simon's eyes, a contrast to his usual, gentle demeanour.

"What the hell are you doing here?"

"Orchestrating the big escape," he said, easily placing his hands on the bars without so much as a burn. He was human, after all. My mind buzzed.

"Sorry it took me so long to get to you. We needed to make sure it was you. I only got the confirmation an hour ago. Let's get you out of here."

"I'm not going anywhere with you," my voice came out squeaky instead of firm like I intended. He rolled his eyes as he examined the door. I studied him as he studied the door. Questions pinging through my mind.

"You know about werewolves." There was no panic in my voice this time.

"Obviously." He grinned at me as he popped the door open.

"H-how did you even know about me? Cybil?"

"Really? I live in a town full of werewolves, and your first thought is that a crazy old bat told me? I've been watching you for years. *You* told me about werewolves." He opened the door wide and gestured for me to follow. I remained still.

"So, you thought you would, what? Get yourself involved with shit you couldn't possibly comprehend?"

"Oh, I comprehend it fine. Come."

I glared at him and crossed my arms. "Why on earth would I go anywhere with you?"

"Don't be like that, sweetheart," the rogue's voice taunted as he shouldered past Simon and entered my cell. His entire frame took up the doorway. Simon, I could take, but this rogue was monstrous. If anyone had hoped his strength would have been weakened in the cell, they were sorely mistaken. He seemed larger, more unhinged.

The scent of sweat, sour milk and musty rogue choked me as he took another step toward me. I froze as his nose traced down my neck and rested on my collarbone.

"Delicious," he growled. The sound vibrated into my core, and I felt myself dampen. He grinned at me as the scent of my arousal rose. Rue was practically purring at the size of the rogue, thrilled at the thought of ravishing him, while I was left terrified.

"Tell me, sweetheart, are you ready to fulfil your prophecy? Are you ready to give into the bloodlust and fuck on the corpses of your enemies?"

Rue cackled but didn't even attempt to push me out of the way. She was intrigued by this rogue but also cautious of him. She definitely wanted to fuck around with him for a bit, and even though it was dangerous and would probably lead to my death, her thoughts were drowning me, and I couldn't help but want the same.

I stepped back from the rogue and gave him a sultry look before running a finger down his chest and onto the engorged package between his legs, making him hiss as his icy eyes darkened with lust. "What are you planning exactly?"

He thrust his dick into my hand before slamming me against the wall, canines extended as he sniffed my neck again. My heart pounded in my neck. His hands made quick work of his pants. His hot cock slapped my ass as he centred himself. His teeth grazed the space between my neck and shoulder.

Alarm bells instantly rang out. Rue thrashed him off before his teeth could snap down before his dick entered me without permission. As turned on as she was, there was no way she would allow herself to be taken like that. There was no chance in hell she would let him mark her like a prize either. My heart clapped with thunder as anger stormed my bloodstream. She snarled, her mania showing through my eyes. He grinned playfully as if my crazy wolf didn't scare him in the slightest.

"Alpha Jackson, stop the foreplay. There is no time for this." Simon snapped. Jackson looked momentarily disgusted at the title bestowed onto him. Rogues didn't have alphas—because rogues didn't have packs. He turned to me, and the repugnant look was replaced with a sinister smile.

"Your work is done, human."

"*Our work*. And it's not until the kid is dead."

Jackson chuckled and stepped away from me toward Simon, who hadn't registered the threat in the air. "The pup will die because my mate will kill her."

I looked back at Rue in astonishment. *This guy has a mate?* Then what the fuck was he just trying to do to me? She shrugged, disinterested in my thought and more aroused by the scene unfolding in front of us.

"Yeah, well, we should probably get a move on. You and Roman can fuck around later. I want to get back to Nola." He gave me a wink. "And then maybe I will finally get a turn with you."

It wasn't his admission to wanting to have sex with me that had me blinking repeatedly. Had he said Nola? As in Nola Lawson? As in the blood-hating, ex-pack-wolf who disappeared during Lincoln's coup? There was no way Nola would date a human; she hated humans. My mind whirred; the straw-coloured wolf on the security feed. Cybil's warning. The fact that Blackfern Elementary was now rubble. *Fuck!* That's how Simon knew about werewolves. He'd been sleeping with Nola, and Nola had entangled him in the largest, most lethal game of werewolf fuckery. He didn't stand a chance.

"I said," Jackson annunciated as he took a step closer to Simon, "your work is done."

His words were immediately followed by a horrible, raw, ripping sound as Simon's head was torn from his body, spraying the room with blood. Jackson dropped the head unceremoniously to the ground as the prick returned his gaze to me, smiling coyly beneath the glitter of blood across his face.

CHAPTER 67
VINNY

INFORMATION RUSHED at me through the mind-link while instinct and infrared senses controlled my movements. It was information overload, but I allowed Vali to channel it where appropriate, slashing our way through rogues as I kept tabs on my pack.

Werewolves were racing through the forest in a blur of fur and speed. I ran forward and took out the nearest rogue I could, biting into his flank and rolling with him, his teeth snapping audibly, struggling to get the upper hand as I quickly sliced my claws down his abdomen, disembowelling him. Without blinking, I was back in the thicket. Wolves were dancing all around us as the battle continued.

I had no idea who was winning and if this was just the beginning. Were we about to head into decades of pack war—a never-ending battle thanks to a some bedtime folk tale? And it may not only be rogues who constantly attacked but also any wolf pack who believed in some idiotic prophecy. A prophecy that put a one-year-old infant at risk. I took the anger and channelled it toward the next rogue, shifting and snapping his neck as I raced past.

Four other rogues stampeded around me, closing in. I tracked their movements through the forest, *my* forest. I skidded to a stop, my heart thundering in my chest as I braced myself in a low position for the attack. Within seconds, my wish was granted as dirty, swamp-smelling rogues cantered through the trees.

Before I could launch off my haunches, a sizeable tawny wolf slammed into the biggest rogue as a small black wolf ran behind him, snapping her teeth at their heels like she was herding sheep. Their combined power was crippling as they directed their alpha waves toward the four herded rogues. I could feel the rage and protective instinct in each precise move. They would die before they let the rogues anywhere close to the town.

Happy they didn't need my help, I took off adjacently, disappearing behind a tree, watching a light-coloured plume of a tail vanish into the thicket. My nose followed a scent that registered somewhere back in the corner of my mind—a smell I couldn't place.

I took three steps in the direction of the light-coloured wolf when one of the rogues Clem and Liam were managing broke rank. His momentum threw me sideways as he barrelled past me. I rolled, and half expected his halitosis and rotting teeth to be inches from my face. Instead, I saw his tail flick behind a tree as he charged in the direction of the pack house. I was sure Lacey wasn't hidden at her house, but that didn't matter. I still needed to take him out.

I spun, chasing him and snapping my teeth, trying to deter him back. It did nothing. He raced onwards, faster, more determined. I dug my claws in and tried to increase my speed. A rust-coloured wolf burst from a hidden location and tackled him to the ground.

There were a few wolves acting as sentries all along the town perimeter. Most gathered around the pack house as the last line of defence. The mutt had no idea until Cassie was on top of him. One loud snap and a rough canine shake ended the mutt's life quickly and quietly. It must have been the easiest kill

I had seen. Déjà vu hit me hard as I watched Cassie throw the rogue away like the garbage he was. Blue eyes found mine, a stiff nod, and then Cassie bounded off again, back toward town, disappearing behind the trees.

Roman kept attempting to reach me, and as much as I wanted to go back and be with her, I'd made my decision when I left the cells earlier. As horrible as it sounded, I didn't trust her. I didn't know if I could ever trust her. As much as Vali was convinced it was Roman, I knew I needed to protect my pack, my niece and myself from her.

Vali reluctantly agreed and reached into the depths of my mind, placing her in darkness. This way, I could focus on the task at hand and not the desperate need to return to the cells to be with her—to guard the cells from the outside if I couldn't find a way in. The alpha command was direct. No one was to enter those cells.

I could feel the adrenaline bubbling through my veins as I returned to my hunt, taking out rogue after rogue, instinctually missing my own pack members. How many wolves were attacking? It felt like thousands. And then a movement caught my eye. A wolf the colour of spun straw came barrelling through the woods in the direction of the town. *The elusive light-coloured wolf!* She didn't look rogue, but she didn't feel like pack either. I sprinted and bounced off my hind legs, ready to tackle the bitch when her scent enveloped me.

"*Nola!*" Vali growled in warning. I pivoted on my heel as she dodged my advance. I was right. I had seen Nola on the first full moon just after I'd come back, and here she was again, infiltrating my pack.

I ran and pounced, springboarding off a log, allowing Vali's speed and agility to dominate my senses before my body twisted into a half-shift. But Nola was ready; she scraped her claws deeply against my exposed human belly. Each claw slicing my skin felt hot and sharp. I hissed against the pain before I contorted once more, moving out of her reach and repositioning myself for an attack.

My hackles shot skywards as I landed on four paws, growling lowly at her. Nola was a blood-hater who made our lives a living hell. Before, she was a useless she-wolf with a vendetta, but now, she was evidently trained as she mirrored each move with deadly precision. The Nola I remembered was not much for fighting, always allowing others to do her dirty work for her. This only led to the question, who trained silly, blonde, vapid Nola?

She was here because of Lacey—her training was targeting my niece. I bared my teeth and growled again. Anger enveloped me. She knew these pack lands like the back of her hand. She knew where we would assemble the old and young. She hadn't come back to rejoin the pack and was evidently the biggest threat in these woods. Her fate was sealed, and I needed to take her out quickly.

Another pack wolf came closer. Perfect. I had backup. I leaped at the same time Sean did.

Sean. He was a sight for sore eyes, but I had no time to play fight or roughhouse with him. There was a battle going on. He had come back to our pack at the perfect time. We needed as many strong warriors as we could, to take out Nola and her rogue army.

Sean landed lithely before barrelling toward Nola on the right while I took the left flank. She sneered at him before charging into me, sending me careening into a tree trunk. I grunted in pain and shook myself off.

Sean's attention was briefly distracted, and he turned back to Nola, his shoulders low and his hackles high. She huffed in general annoyance before her claws dug into the dirt, and she launched herself at him. He snarled and rolled with her, pinning her down, but instead of going for the kill shot, he held her throat and rumbled lowly. I skidded to a stop, confused that he was re-enacting a training class rather than dispatching her.

She broke his hold, piercing into his ankle before shaking her head viciously, feral saliva dripping along with Sean's blood. Tendons severed under her canines, with a horrible ripping sound. He roared in pain as he tried to fight her, but she dashed out of his reach, snapping at his other ankle and repeating the process. Shit, Sean was out! How had he let her get the jump on him?

I pivoted angrily, but Nola was gone. She hadn't stuck around, but she hadn't gone too far. Vali had triangulated on her within minutes. Nola sneered as I tackled her to the ground. The deadly dance started again. Wherever she had been, and whoever had been training her had built her into the perfect weapon.

Guttural sounds echoed around us as we both battled for our lives, knowing only one of us was going to survive. Nola was too equally matched. No, I wasn't ashamed to admit it, she was better. She hadn't even tired. It was apparent she was just getting started on her agenda.

Even though we were close to town, no one was coming past this way. I had no idea where the sentries were, but it had become pretty obvious that no one else was around to help me take her out. I didn't think I could take her out on my own, but at the very least, if I died, I was going to try my damndest to take her out with me.

Desperately, I snapped and snarled at Nola, realizing that even though she was partially shifting, her fighting style was eerily similar to the rogue we'd imprisoned, although she didn't have his brute strength. He had almost killed me, too. The only thing that saved me had been my pack, who were still nowhere to be seen.

Nola's teeth snapped at my furry forearm, clamping down hard. I grunted in pain under her latch. I tried to partially shift, hoping to force her jaws open and release myself from her hold. It did the opposite. Her fangs sank deeper, and the motion of my shift caused them to move downward, dragging through the skin as they ripped and shredded the muscle underneath. Warm blood oozed onto my fingertips, which refused to flex. When I tried to shift it back into wolf form, I was met with excruciating pain. Something was wrong—my wolf couldn't take over.

Nola had done more than just wound me; I don't know how, but she'd severed the flow of energy between human and wolf, locking my arm in its broken human state while the rest of me remained fully wolf. Vali focused on forcing me to stay in wolf form, as shifting fully back into a human would be a death sentence.

My mate bond opened to Roman momentarily as Vali lost focus on keeping her out. I fixated on her tether, sending as much love and regret down it as I could before sealing it shut again.

I looked into Nola's cold blue eyes, realizing that her tactic revolved heavily around immobilizing her opponent. She just needed to take out another arm or leg, and I would be submissive to her every whim.

With every last breath of energy I could muster, I fought Nola. Blood slicked over us both as the wound in my arm kept oozing. It was awkward to fight like this, but I had no choice. It was this or death.

An eery howl sounded in the distance, and Nola snapped her head up. I took advantage of her distraction and grabbed her human throat in my wolf mouth. My teeth punctured her jugular as she helplessly clawed at me. I started shaking her neck like a rabid animal; a sickening crunch telling me that her neck was broken. I shook again for good measure and ripped out her throat, sinew and blood splattering the dirt beneath us.

Sean let out a long, agonized howl that vibrated into my soul and gave me goosebumps. He released another, which, with his alpha power, rendered me flat against the forest floor, forcing me to shift into my human skin. I whimpered in pain, my body overcome with anguish as he howled again. The weight of the howl crushed my heart, and the answering howls echoing through the forest told me I wasn't the only one who felt his pain. There was only one thing that could cause that amount of turmoil.

"Mate." Vali choked. *"We killed his mate."*

Suddenly, Sean's body was towering over me, his tendons only partially mended. When his canines encased my throat, I knew my life was forfeit. Cold shock ran through me. I had killed his mate. I had taken the one she-wolf that had been made for him. Right then, I didn't fight, and neither did Vali. This was an acceptable way to die. In the jaws of my best friend —the best friend I had unwittingly betrayed.

I thought of my mom. I thought of my dad. I thought of my sister and my niece. My last thought was of Roman, but I didn't reach out, not even to say goodbye. There was no time to say all I wanted to say to each of them. I closed my eyes and waited for the final chomp. I gave Vali one last stroke within the hollow space of my mind and sent him unwavering gratitude for always being there for me.

The uncomfortable pressure on my throat released, and I opened one eye, scared yet curious about his play. Sean was gone. I sat up slightly and watched as his sandy brown tail disappeared into the trees.

CHAPTER 68
ROMAN

I felt a wave of emotion come down the mate bond before it was shut off. *What the hell was that?* I looked briefly at Rue, who, for the first time in a very long time, looked petrified instead of delirious. Without saying a word to me, she attempted to reach him and hit the cold abyss he had shrouded us in.

The interlude was brief, and shortly, I was jolted back to reality where Simon's head was a mere foot away from me, staring up with lifeless eyes, and the rogue's nose was running all over me like I was the most delectable treat he needed to savour.

"So, let me get this straight, you're attacking my pack because of a bedtime story," I asked, kicking Simon's head away and looking distastefully at the rogue. My voice oozed contempt. I willed him not to see through my façade. If Rue could pretend to be me, surely, I could pretend to be his feral wolf.

"I'm here for you," he said earnestly. "The rogues are just a distraction so we can do what we need to do. At first, we were looking for weak points in the half-breed runt, but then your delectable scent wafted into my path, and I knew there was no need to see the little bitch first-hand. I could smell the truth in your tones—the way your wolf needed to be freed. So, I had to go away and think about how to get to you instead. I knew I needed to get caught, to find out as much as I could about you. Position myself for when you really needed me. Then you were delivered right onto my doorstep, twisted and beautifully insane. Oh, baby, we are going to have so much fun together."

His eyes raked me again, threatening sex and violence. For a second, I almost let Rue take control, nearly desperate enough to let her handle him entirely. But the memory of what it felt like when she trapped me—the powerlessness—made me hesitate. I was terrified of being locked away again, of giving her that chance. But was I better at this game than she was?

Being merged with her wasn't what I thought it would be. My entire life, I was told that we would sync into one soul, that my wants and needs would become hers, and that her feelings and my feelings would be one and the same. Instead, we still felt like two separate entities, worlds apart. I was the Doctor Jekyll to her Mister Hyde.

A sick grin spread over my face, and I barely recognized it as my own. "And what if I don't need your help?" I said, forcing saccharine venom into my words. Rue snickered in my head, amused at my weak attempt, but I gripped tighter to the role, refusing to give her complete control

Jackson joined Rue's laughter, his breath fanned across my face, and I fought back a tremor.

"You're the one who said if I set you free, I could watch your first kill. Then claim your pert ass in the aftermath." I shivered involuntarily. Jackson's cock twitched against my leg in response. I wasn't aroused. I was disgusted and terrified. However, Rue was aroused at the thought of the bloodbath and by her thought process, I knew she was at least a little intrigued by the weapon between his legs. I knew he must scent my arousal and my disgusted terror, but the mixture seemed to fascinate him.

His tongue laved the column of my neck as I curled my fingers flirtatiously around his bicep.

"But you didn't set me free. The virgin sacrifice did," Rue said through my voice, laughing manically toward Simon's bloody bust. I pushed her back again, and she huffed in amusement.

"You're not free yet," he grumbled against my throat.

"Am I not?" I challenged, stepping away from him toward the door. He watched me, a hunter willing me to run. *I didn't stand a chance.*

"Oh darling, you're never going to be free again." The thought made me quake, and Rue snarled her displeasure. She wasn't a kept wolf. She surged forward, causing my eyes to narrow at the rogue.

"Come on, Roman," she rasped. *"Let me play—I'll show him what he's dealing with."*

Jackson's eyes were now suspicious as they watched me, and I knew at that moment that I was too weak of an actress to play the feral wolf in his story.

Reluctantly, I loosened my grip, allowing Rue the reins just enough to keep us both alive. She pushed forward, her fur sliding over me as she pushed me aside, giving me a canine smile in the process.

Her malicious nature oiled me as her laugh tore from my throat, low and wild, her fingers winding possessively through his dirty, matted hair. I stood on the edge, barely in control, trapped in my fear of him killing me and her taking over completely.

"You really think you can keep me? Oh honey, you have no idea who you're dealing with. You want to kill the little pack princess? Fine, let's go kill the fucking pack princess. I'll give you her entrails as an appetizer. But make no mistake, there will be no chains." She released his hair and pushed him playfully away, then made a show of looking at his throbbing dick. "Well, unless they're tied to a bed." She gave a saucy wink before pivoting on my heel and shifting.

Turning my back on him was a disrespectful and perilous move. I half expected him to attack, but instead, Jackson's monstrous wolf paced my flank as we padded out of the stone cells and emerged into the woods. The sounds of battle echoed all around us.

Rue led the way, keeping quiet as we moved, using the infra-red and wolf senses to locate members of our pack, and stealthily avoiding them, finally showing me what her instincts were capable of. She was scarily good at this.

My ears twitched at the sounds of battle, and the stench of metallic blood infiltrated my nostrils. Rue glowed and purred as we weaved around a tree, diving deeper into the forest. If she weren't on a mission, she would be enjoying this, dancing in the killing fields like the crazy wolf she was.

I thought of what Jackson had said about the prophecy. Did people honestly believe that it was real? Jackson thought it was —obviously. According to him, allowing Rue to kill would trigger her bloodlust, and her conscience would be lost. She would be truly feral and packless.

The prophecy also told of an alpha of alphas bringing down the world. The anti-messiah of the modern world. It was hard to believe that people could believe that shit. There had been no evidence of magic in the world: no witches, no faeries, no vampires. I couldn't explain why werewolves were the only alleged magical creatures in the world, but werewolves only had the power to shift, not to cause natural disasters.

The rogues believed the folk tale, though, so intently that they were out there warring on my pack. Was this going to be the life of Blackfern Valley from now on? Would we constantly be on edge. Always at war? Rue grinned at me, making me pause in my thoughts. The thought of constantly killing made my tongue salivate with her anticipation. If it came to war, I would have to leave. It was the only way I could keep Rue out of it. Being around a constant bloodbath would only trigger her.

It was the only way to keep my friends safe. I thought of Vinny, knowing his cream-coloured wolf was out there, battling for his life, the life of his pack and the life of his niece. The niece Rue had just agreed to kill—a piercing pain shot through my heart. I tried to feel for Vinny but was met with emptiness.

Rue chuckled as she danced around the next tree. Her desire to kill flooded through me as we passed something that looked like a large intestine hanging from a lower tree branch.

She stopped to scent the ground, figuring out where to go next. I noticed that Liv had been through here recently. Did I push Rue back and follow Liv's scent, leading Jackson to the trained warriors? Hadn't it taken six warriors to take him down that first time? The smart thing would be to lead Jackson to Alpha Liam to deal with, and hopefully, at the same time, he could deal with Rue. Instinct was telling me to trust her, but how could I trust my instincts when they were her instincts, too? She could have been planting this intuition as a red herring. Rue scoffed at the paranoid thought, pushing me back as she moved us back in the direction of town.

We came to a clearing as greens and reds danced across the skies, and she shifted us back into human form. I looked up toward the northern lights, but I could barely see them with my human eyes. Jackson rubbed his fur possessively all over my naked body before he shifted back.

His eyes dragged from my naked body up to the sky. "The auroras are out. Everything is aligning."

"Lacey is about a click that way." Rue pointed my finger toward the town that lay just beyond the trees as she buzzed with excitement. We had gotten this far without being caught.

"I don't believe she is. You have been zigzagging me all over this forest," he said with deathly softness. She started to laugh, tinkly and unhinged. She stepped forward, running a finger down his broad chest.

"I've been avoiding the guards on the town line. Trying to find a way in. Do you really think I'm going to be stupid enough to trip the town alarm?"

"You should be taking them out, ripping them from head to toe."

"As exciting as that would be, the more noise I create now, the less likely we will be able to get to your alpha of alphas."

"*Our* alpha of alphas." He looked around the clearing. "Now, where?"

"We follow that creek, and it leads to a small path that heads into town." She turned my back on him and meandered up the path next to the creek.

"Why aren't we going to the pack house?"

"Do you honestly think they would hide the children at the pack house?" She asked over my shoulder. "Alpha Liam is smart. He's put guards around the pack house to encourage rogues to go there. But that's not where the non-fighters are."

"Where are they?"

"Well, usually at the school, but someone got all bomb-happy and blew that up." She laughed gleefully, flipping my hair over my shoulder. "So now they are scattered among the houses. People are hiding in the basements." She leaned against a tree, sizing him up, making it look as though I was interested in being debauched against the trunk but, in reality, I was trying to find a weakness. "But we are going to Lupus'," she added in the same bright tone. I looked at her in panic. Her eery wolf sense told her where to find her alpha's bloodline, even though Lacey didn't have a wolf yet. And she had just told the rogue who wanted her dead. I just hoped she had a plan. His face snapped out of whatever brief trance he was in.

"What the fuck is a Lupus?"

"The town bar."

"The town bar?" he snarled angrily.

"Sure, I need a drink. And after the time you spent in the cells, I would think you would too." She winked at him playfully. His hand encased my throat, pushing me hard against the trunk and cutting off my air supply. Rue grinned at his reaction, not in the least bit afraid.

"She's hiding with her grandfather at Lupus'." He released my throat and bared his teeth at me. Before sniffing my neck again, scenting for something. He pulled away and gave me a soft, dangerous smile.

"Lead the way."

CHAPTER 69
ROMAN

I stepped out of the trees and into the parking lot of Lupus', looking around at the desolate town. I padded down the side path next to the dumpsters and opened the back door—it was unlocked. Jackson slid up beside me and grinned evilly as we walked directly into the storeroom. A low baby's cry sounded, which we followed into the main bar area. In a porta-cot, between the dining hall and the bar, lay baby Lacey fast asleep but obviously dreaming as she flailed her arms. A big black wolf launched on top of the bar top, snarling low.

Patrick's massive salt and peppered wolf towered over us, muscles rippling under his sleek fur, his low growl reverberating through the room. Another light brown wolf skulked from the other side of the bar. Alpha aura filled the room, but Jackson seemed unbothered by Josiah's presence, and it was the same with Rue.

Jackson's eyes gleamed with malice. I turned and gave Jackson a cheeky wink before shifting into my wolf. I barely finished sprouting a tail before Jackson, Josiah, and Patrick clashed with vicious-sounding snarls.

But Rue's focus wasn't on the brawl. It was on the porta-cot ten feet away. I gazed at the tiny, sleeping form of Lacey, her small chest rising and falling. I stalked closer, the steady thrum of her heartbeat drawing me in. A table shattered under the weight of the wolves behind me, but I didn't even flinch. Both pack wolves were too busy trying to take down Jackson to split their attention to me.

Rue smiled through me, her predatory thoughts bleeding into mine. *One bite. One snap of our jaws. She won't even scream.*

My mind started to blend and haze as if in a trance, Rue's insane desires becoming mine. We were merging into one mind, a primal, unstoppable force. I felt her anticipation—how easy it would be, how natural. I felt the bloodlust rush through my heart like a second, sinister heartbeat.

I faltered, torn between Rue's insanity and my own logic. I knew I shouldn't have trusted her. The wolf wanted to kill. She thrived on it, fed on the chaos. My control slipped, just for a moment, as Rue pushed me harder, taking us a step closer to the baby.

"*No,*" I cried, fighting to regain control. I could feel her claws digging into my mind, pulling me under, forcing me backward. But I dug my heels in, refusing to let Rue take over completely. Never again. "*Jackson is the real threat. He's the one who needs to die. Not her!*"

Rue snarled as she fought for dominance. Outside my mind, the sound of glass breaking acted as a symphony to the anarchy inside my head.

"*The pup is innocent. How could you think of killing her? What threat does an* infant *pose? The prophecy is bullshit, Rue. You know it. There is no world-bending messiah. There is, however, a very dangerous wolf in our midst. Jackson is the threat. Jackson wants to imprison us, rape us, and use us for his own agenda. We will be powerless, Rue.*"

She stopped fighting me, blinking as my words reached her ears. We turned as one toward Jackson, whose eyes were now burning with desperation as a wobbly Josiah remained between him and his prey. Patrick charged at Jackson from the side, snarling and snapping his jaws aggressively, smashing him into the pool table with such force the coin container burst open and gold and silver clinked onto the floor. There was a yelp, and then a strong metallic scent of blood permeated the air. Jackson jumped over the pool table and bared his teeth at Josiah.

I didn't want Patrick or Josiah to die, and from the looks of it, they were about to use their last breath of strength to defend their granddaughter until further help arrived. But they had help—they had me! I launched toward Josiah, pushing him aside as Jackson broke free from his mouth. In doing so, I put Jackson dangerously close to Lacey.

"Keep away from her!" Josiah mind-linked me. *"Alpha and Luna are on their way—you're dead. I suggest running now."*

"I'm not going to hurt her, I promise! You two have to trust me and keep him distracted." Josiah looked at me for a long second, weighing my command, weighing whether he could blindly trust me.

"Whatever you're going to do, do it fast. Even drugged, he's too fucking strong," Patrick answered for Josiah as he charged forward again, a flash of teeth, blood and fur.

His voice echoed through my mind. *Too fucking strong.* It took six trained warriors to capture him that first time. And now, it was up to me. *Fuck! What the hell am I going to do?* I'd told him to trust me, but I didn't have a plan. I was just making it up on the fly.

Jackson's eyes burned with rage and desperation as he looked at Lacey, who was now sitting up and screaming angrily at being woken.

Jackson turned just in time to see Patrick attack and, in one swift move, sent Vinny's dad flying through the glass front of the restaurant. Josiah threw a chair at him, momentarily breaking his concentration, distracting him further, and giving me an idea at the same time. Would he expect a wolf to use a weapon?

In one fluid movement, I shifted my paw into a hand and

snatched the paring knife from behind the bar. Rue's instincts flared, eager for the kill. I let her guide us this time, letting her give in to savagery. With lightning-fast precision, we slashed across Jackson's throat deeply with the small blade.

Jackson's eyes widened as he barked out a cough. His hands became human as they moved to his wolfy throat. He grasped and pulled at the hemorrhaging wound as though he could pull it away from him. I scurried off the ground out of his reach. He looked enraged and full of panic, shifting grotesquely between human and wolfman.

I took a frightened step back and allowed the knife to clatter to the floor. We both looked down at it, stunned. Had I really gotten that lucky? Six warriors were required to capture him, and I incapacitated him with a knife Liv used to cut lemons for drinks. A gurgling sound made me look up. In those seconds, he could have snapped my neck, but looking at him, I realized killing me was the last thing on his mind.

I pitied the rogue—he was going to die painfully slow. No one deserved that. Rue smiled silkily as I stepped forward in my full human skin. I mirrored Rue's smile before I slammed my fingers, tipped with wolf claws, deep within his neck—exploding through the remains of the artery and severing his vocal cords. He slumped over and closed his eyes.

There was a seismic shift within my body as I suddenly was forced back into my wolf. A predatory thrill rushed through me as the scent of Jackson's pooling blood added to the frenzy. Rue took charge, snarling and swiping her claws at his face.

I started to sway with vertigo as I fought to surface. All I could hear was the final heartbeats from Jackson as Rue bit into his soft underbelly, ripping through his flesh.

"Rue, enough, he's dead." I fought her for control. She pushed me back and growled as she rolled onto his corpse and bathed us in his blood. *"Rue!"* I screamed at her. *"Rue, stop! Rue!"* I tried to force the shift.

She roared psychotically at me. Oh, god. Jackson had been

right, I was the feral wolf from the prophecy. She was out of control, and I couldn't shift back. Cold panic washed over me as I continued to struggle. My bloodstream burned like lava, and my brain felt like it was going to rip apart as I pushed forward. Rue flicked her tail in annoyance and huffed at me, seemingly unperturbed by my attempts. I heaved and twisted, pushing against the beastly feeling within my chest.

The cold panic magnified. She didn't care about the war that was ongoing or that there were two wounded werewolves and their granddaughter who probably needed medical attention. She was having too much fun dancing on the entrails of her victim.

The only way to get her to retreat would be if someone knocked me out, and even though I was safely inside Lupus', getting knocked out in the middle of a werewolf war didn't feel like the best idea. Besides, I had been knocked out before, and when I woke up, she was still too powerful to control. Just as I was about to reach down the mind-link and yell at someone to come and kill me, a medium-sized black wolf with an alpha aura came racing through the patio doors at the other end of the bar.

"Rue! Give Roman control back, now!" The command vibrated my entire body as Luna Clementine leaped toward her pup.

Rue trembled and whimpered as the command rolled onto her. She retreated into my mind, and I was finally back in control. Clementine had saved me after I put her daughter in danger. I took a moment to gather my breath and force down the guilt threatening to overcome me. I needed to help my pack. I needed to find Vinny. I pivoted on my heel and ran out the patio doors back toward the battlegrounds. For the first time, I could actually take in the entire scene around me.

The pure carnage excited Rue. This was her land, her kin, but the pure bloodbath it was turning into was her ecstasy. She stayed back in my mind, allowing me to navigate the forest while she just enjoyed the film. I saw my brothers roaring ahead as droves of rogues seemed to break through the frontline again and again. It was a deluge of dirty mutts, and we were drowning. There had to be hundreds of wolves. It was hard to tell where the pack ended and where the rogues began. When I'd directed Jackson here, there'd been no wolves, and within the twenty minutes it took to assassinate him inside Lupus', it was like the rogues had overrun this part of the forest.

I couldn't see any of my friends. Something told me I would know if any of them were hurt, so I just kept an eye out for them as I charged forward, avoiding the teeth of a dark grey wolf that came out of nowhere. He was massive. I took a tentative step back in our mind and let Rue temporarily free, praying that I could rein her back in.

Pure, evil emotion raged through my veins as my teeth sank into his cruciate ligament, the sickening snap echoing in the chaos. He roared in agony, his knees collapsing under him, but I wasn't done. My claws raked across his flank, shredding muscle and tendon in calculated precision. Every move was surgical, deliberate—a violent symphony composed by years of nursing knowledge and sharpened by Rue's natural instincts. Techniques for immobilization, suffocation, and total evisceration played through my mind like a textbook turned warfare.

He spun, enraged, and large drops of saliva were flicked in my face. I lunged, my jaws snapping down on his shoulder, grinding through mangey fur and flesh until the bitter tang of blood flooded my mouth. My teeth scraped bone, and I wrenched back with all my strength, ripping apart his deltoid and leaving his arm hanging limp and useless. His howl rattled my ears, but it only fueled Rue's excitement.

Blood dripped down my muzzle as Rue stared at his weakened husk of a body. She didn't deliver the final blow. Instead, she watched him as the life started to leave his body at an excruciatingly painfully slow rate. She had allowed me to take pity on Jackson. She had allowed my brief humanity to trickle into her and take him out. But Jackson had been a more significant threat, and now she wanted to have fun.

Beta Ryan's voice sounded down the mind-link. A small number of rogues had made it into the town from another location. He didn't say what would happen if the rogues managed to break through in full force or which location the rogues were heading in. He didn't need to. Jackson somehow got the message to his rogues about Lacey's location. I would have said it was a mind-link, but everyone knows only pack can mind-link.

This was all my fault. I debated heading back into town to cut them off before they could even make it to Lupus'. Rue shook her head at me and pushed me forward, slamming into another rogue who was trying to sneak past quietly. Rue grinned as she swiped my paw out, shifting it at the last second, punching through his sternum—something I had no idea we could do—it was a lot harder tissue than the neck. I felt his heart quiver as she wrapped my fingers around it, squeezing as hard as she could before turning my fingertips into claws and puncturing it.

I couldn't understand how she was so good at this. She possessed the instincts of a pack warrior despite having no formal training. It was all pure intuition for her—and the idea of her unleashed in the world, unchecked and uncontrollable, was utterly terrifying. She was destined to become a killing machine, and I wasn't sure if I had the strength to stop her.

I snarled and yelped as teeth met my skin. A wolf had barrelled into me and pushed me down into a muddy puddle. I didn't register to see if the wolf was friendly; I just registered the attack. Getting hit unexpectedly by a wolf at full speed still felt like a freighter, even with Rue's combat knowledge. My body ached and burned, but I pushed myself up, frothing at the mouth. A second rogue rumbled menacingly at me, his putrid stench encasing me.

Two against Rue. Seemed fair. She was far too excited by the prospect, and I was sure we were going to die.

I stood up a little wobbly, ready to meet my maker. Everything happened quickly. Rue let out a battle cry as we pounced, aiming for the femoral artery of rogue number one. I knew the second mutt would take me out, but I wasn't going to die without attempting to kill at least one of them. My teeth sliced the artery, and warm blood trickled into my mouth and over my muzzle. The second wolf slammed into me from the side with bone-crushing force, driving me into a tree. Flesh ripped free in my jaws, leaving a gaping wound in his companion as I collided hard against the trunk. Pain seared through my body as the mutt appeared triumphant before me.

"*Roman!*" shouted a voice down the mind-link. Liv. I blinked as Murdoch and Liv came galloping through the brush. Liv leaped into the air as Murdoch went low, both taking on the wolf that was about to finish me off.

"*More are incoming. Get the fuck out of here, Roman.*" Murdoch shouted as he leaped off his hindquarters and took off to the side, landing on top of another rogue. Rue was now frothing rabidly, giving into her bloodlust. If she gave in to it, I would be lost forever. I had to get Rue away from here. I turned tail and ran. I sprinted deep into the forest, thankful that I hadn't run into any more rogues yet. Rue kept fighting me to head back toward the battle, and it was taking all my power to resist her as my mind started to blend and haze again. I just needed to get to my house. I needed to get away—as far away from here as I could.

It was a hard slog, but the further I got away from the battle, the easier it was to subdue her. Less than a kilometre out, I got a whiff of icy peppermint. My heart started hammering in my chest. He was okay. I had shut down my brain and heart to Vinny while I was fighting, as he had done to me, but now I was more than grateful for the scent. I was thankful he was far away from the battle. Rue stopped fighting me long enough to allow me to race toward Vinny, the gravitational pull guiding me over rough terrain.

CHAPTER 70
VINNY

"Vinny!" she cried as she sprinted toward me. My heart split with relief as I hobbled toward her. The mate bond started humming, pulling me in. Then, I scented the metallic tones of blood. Vali grumbled low.

"Roman! You're covered in blood." I anxiously sniffed at her fur and muzzled into her side, trying to find the source of the scent.

"Not mine!"

"Whose?" A soft rumbling vibrated from my body, responding to her gentle hum as I flanked her, still checking for injury. I felt her inner torment as she battled on whether she trusted me enough to tell me whatever had happened to her out there. I knew I deserved her distrust. I mean, I didn't fully trust her either, but that didn't make witnessing it any easier.

"In case you didn't notice, there's a war going on right now!" she quipped. *"I got lucky."*

"The other guy didn't." I grinned down at her before I dipped my muzzle into her neck and sighed. Her jasmine scent made everything better, and all I wanted to do was shift so I could hold her, kiss her and be with her in the moment. But her

distrust and inner battle were raging on, thrumming against the mate bond, making me sick with guilt.

"*You're hurt too*," she exclaimed, noticing my injuries, her aura sending a smidgen of worry toward me.

"*I'll live*," I grunted. She stared at me, her eyes and mood steeling over. She nodded before proceeding toward her house. "*What are you doing here?*"

"*Clementine said she saw you in the fight. I was worried,*" I mumbled guiltily as I tailed her up the porch steps. She shifted when she reached the top. Roman was standing, blood-covered and naked. Her hair was tangled and knotted with twigs and leaves, and her brown eyes were wide. I was momentarily distracted by her blood-matted hair and skin. But she was right; she didn't have a serious scratch on her. Somehow, she had managed to stay safe.

I shifted with a loud, agonizing sound. I took in the extent of my healing injuries. I was definitely in a bad way. Vali had been right; it wasn't a good idea to stay in the fight. We were about to bow out and find somewhere safe to hide when Clementine mind-linked and said Roman was battling rogues. Panic had washed over me. I wanted to go find her and keep her safe, but Vali told me to come here to rest and wait for Roman. His eerie wolfy sense told me that she was okay and on her way here. He would know the second she was in danger. I argued that we would be too far away. He was adamant we needed to stay put. The debate continued for forty minutes before I finally scented her on the breeze.

"Worried for the rogues? Or worried for your niece?" Her tone was waspish, bringing me to a halt.

"What—"

"I know you came back because the rogues are after Lacey."

I stopped walking and gaped at her. "You knew?"

"For months." She shrugged as my eyes narrowed. "Nothing stays secret in this place, Vinny."

"You kept it a secret for months. You didn't even mention it to me."

"When was I supposed to mention it? In between orgasms?" she snapped irritably. "But it was the rogue who told me the rest. You should have told me about the prophecy."

"The prophecy is bullshit!"

"Is it?"

"Yes."

"Then why did you keep me locked up?" she snarled angrily, her eyes full of hurt. The rings of purple flashed brilliantly with her rage.

I looked down at my feet, guilt washing through me before looking up and remembering that she had been in the cell with the rogue. My heart raced uncomfortably at the danger I put her in. She had been safe in her cell, hadn't she? But where was the rogue now? "How did you get out of the cell? What about the rogue? Are you okay?"

"I killed him." she shrugged nonchalantly, throwing on her silk housecoat over her dirty body before pulling a suitcase out of her closet.

"You killed him?"

"Yes. I did." Her voice wobbled, her eyes were soft and expressive. "He was after Lacey. I needed to take him out."

"You saved Lacey."

"From one rogue, yes. But the war is still going on. There are many more who are trying to kill her, Vinny." She took a deep breath as if steeling her emotions away again. She looked at me with unyielding eyes, her voice hard. "But if we believe the prophecy. I'm the one who is meant to kill her."

"I don't believe that," I whispered.

"Don't you?" she challenged. I blinked a few times as I watched her shoving clothes haphazardly into the case.

"Where are you going? What happened out there?" Her throat bobbed as she swallowed roughly. Tears escaped, and I instinctually captured them, licking the sweet, saltiness off my finger. I was rewarded with a warm buzz. "Talk to me, Ro."

"Simon. Simon got me out."

"Simon? Wait, you don't mean," I tried to catch up. *Surely not!* "*Simple Simon?*"

"Yeah." She choked on her tears and took a shuddering breath as she tried to regain her icy composure. It took every part of me not to lap at her face directly. Instead, I tucked her into me, giving her permission to fall apart. I knew she wouldn't cry long; she wouldn't want to show me weakness. Vali rumbled within, wishing he could heal her pain.

"I don't know how it happened. He was in league with the rogue. The rogue somehow summoned him, I guess. The school blew up, and you ran off. I screamed at anyone to help me. No one could. I was stuck. Then the next thing I know, Simon was releasing Jackson and me."

That smarmy little weasel, I rumbled in anger. *What the hell is that little prick doing here? How the hell did he know about werewolves?* I knew I didn't voice this out loud, but Roman answered my questions anyway.

"I don't know how he even knew about werewolves or the prophecy. Or how he got involved with any of this. Apparently, he had been watching me. I think he was dating Nola, but Jackson ripped off his head before I could ask any more questions. Jackson said his part in this was done and just popped off his head like it was a cork in a wine bottle. I can still hear his head being ripped from his shoulders. It excites Rue, but it sickens me." She gasped, taking a panicked step backward. "Nola has infiltrated our pack, Vinny. You have to mind-link Alpha Liam. You have to warn him. Mine is still broken."

"Nola is dead." I shuffled my feet. "I killed her."

"What is it?" she asked me, sensing my dread.

"Sean was there too."

"He's back?" Her eyes looked momentarily relieved before she saw my expression. "Is he okay?"

"He and Nola were true mates, and I killed her in front of him." I choked.

"Oh, Vinny." She wrapped her arms around me as tears started to form behind my eyes.

"I thought he was going to kill me, Rome. I was ready for him to kill me. His teeth were at my throat." *My last thoughts were of you.* "But then he just left."

"I'm sorry, Vinny. Maybe, when this is all over, you can find him and—"

"Say what? Sorry for killing your mate who orchestrated a coup on our pack to murder your infant niece?" I snarled. Roman sighed and shook her head, unable to offer words of comfort. There was nothing she could say, regardless of Nola's intent. True mates were one of the most sacred bonds in our culture, and I had killed her.

I avoided her eyes, noting the messy suitcase on her bed. "Where are you going?"

"I have to get out of here." Vali snarled unhappily within my mind.

"Why?"

"Because I'm a feral wolf, Vinny."

"The prophecy is bullshit, Roman."

"Maybe. But feral wolves aren't Vinny."

"You're not feral," I growled at her, Vali's voice joining my own.

"Rue and I are merged, but we aren't connected. Something went wrong. She's more unstable than ever; she's bloodthirsty. You heard her when she had me trapped. You felt the things that she was going to put you and Murdoch through. And just for sport!"

"But you're back in control of her!"

"For how long, Vincent? She's strong, and I can't keep her where there will be constant temptation to kill."

"What are you talking about?"

"Feral wolves eventually give into the bloodlust, and when

they do, they become unstoppable killing machines. You didn't feel her out there in the war zone. She was elated and aroused over the death and blood. When I killed Jackson, I thought it was all over for me. Rue was rolling on his corpse, and I couldn't stop her. Each kill quickened her heartbeat like she was an addict getting a fix." She took a breath and shook her head. "This was only one war. How many wars is Blackfern Valley going to have due to this prophecy? How much more bloodshed is on the horizon? I'm scared that if I stay here, I will turn fully feral and hell, I might even kill Lacey."

"But you saved her tonight."

"That was only because Rue thought it would be more in her favour to take out Jackson than it would be to kill an infant. I'm not going to pretend she has a redeeming quality, Vinny. I'm not going to tempt Fate either."

"So you're leaving?"

She nodded. "To keep the pack safe."

"Where are you going to go?"

"I don't know."

"If you just leave, you could turn rogue."

"I need to keep Rue away from everything, Vinny. You must realize that it's too high of a risk."

"I know that! I understand that! Trust me, I do, but we have to do it smartly. If you abandon this pack, over time, your scent will change, and you will be packless," I whispered. "Rue is more likely to be feral without a link to her pack."

"What am I meant to do then?"

"Ask for permission. Liam will grant you leave."

"I'm a threat to his daughter. He's more likely to kill me on the spot."

"Please trust me."

"Trust you? You locked me up! You left me! And now you want me to trust you?"

"Yes!" I shouted angrily. "Because, if you become rogue, you *will* die! And I can't lose you like that!"

I slammed my mouth over hers, kissing her deeply. I pushed all my love for her through the kiss, nipping desperately at her mouth. The sweet, nutty flavour exploded over my tongue as she melted into my frenzied attack. She was mine! She couldn't leave me! Vali rumbled possessively as I gripped her matted hair and twisted it around my fist. She moaned against my lips before pushing me off, then lowered her eyes back to her suitcase. I could feel her inner turmoil, and as much as I wanted to rage, shout and make her submit to me, I softened my approach.

"It's too risky for you to leave now. The battle is still going on. You have to wait until Blackfern Valley is rogue-free."

She shook her head stubbornly. "The commotion could help me escape."

"Or a rogue could find you and kill you before you make it five kilometres."

"Rue won't let that happen. She's excited over the prospect of killing some more." Roman looked horrified at the admission.

I looked at her, marvelling at how, even layered in blood and dirt and as terrified as she was, she stroked my insides in a way that I never wanted it to stop. It wasn't sexual desire; I just needed her. I needed her more than air. Vali whimpered with concern. She was going to run to protect her pack and I was going to lose her.

I needed to get to my sister and brother-in-law fast; there was no time to waste. Vali stretched, testing his strength before nodding. We would be okay with shifting again, but I knew the fight was still out of us. We had to be careful.

"Promise me you won't leave until I come back."

"Where are you going?" she whispered.

"I'm going to ask our Alpha for an audience."

"Um, you really think he's going to grant an audience in the middle of a battle?" she asked me ludicrously. I turned and gave her a chaste kiss on her puffy lips. "Wait for me."

CHAPTER 71
VINNY

The second I left Roman's porch, I wanted to turn back. The instinct to return to her was overwhelming, but I pushed my paws harder into the forest floor. I knew deep down the reason I wanted to turn back was to stop her from leaving, to beg her to be with me.

The thought of her leaving me tightened my throat like a vice. Her decision to leave was the most selfless thing she could do, meaning that I, too, had to be selfless, and if she were granted this, I would have to let her go. But I knew I couldn't just *let her go*; I would tail behind her. I would chase her to the end of the earth if I had to. I couldn't lose her a second time.

Vali whimpered, whipping his head back toward her cabin. I shook my head and pressed on. I wouldn't be gone long. I wasn't stupid; I knew Roman wouldn't wait for me. She had no reason to, so the quicker I could get to Alpha Liam, the better.

I approached the boundary of Blackfern Valley and barrelled through the trees, stalling momentarily to take in the bloodbath around me. Low shrubs that should have been green were covered in blood, so rich they looked black. The smell of death coagulated the air.

Vali whimpered as I slowed my pace to a trot. Pack members

were embracing both in wolf and human form, huddled over their dead friends and family. I wanted to offer my condolences and help with the cleanup, but my time was precious.

I ran past a small mound of corpses. The pack had already started collecting the rogues into a burn pile. Luca and Milo swung a rogue between them, tossing it on the heap. Before moving over and letting Sophie and Cassie do the same. Cassie caught my eye and gave me a grim smile. I nodded my furry head at her. She may do daft, naïve and downright stupid things regularly, but she really was loyal to this pack and the members in it.

I continued on, weaving through the forest, mentally ticking people off in my mind as I found them alive. Sending a wave of gratitude every time I spotted someone I cared for. Not only that, I found myself looking for Roman's friends and family so that I could report back to her and let her know who was safe. Speaking of friends...

I spotted her red hair and instantly triangulated in on it. I splashed through a stream toward the fiery beacon.

But she wasn't alone. Israel was wrapped around her, their arms tightly intertwined in an embrace.

It wasn't just a quick hug—it was one of those desperate, unspoken moments of relief and shared grief, the kind that clings to the soul in the aftermath of battle. Liv's fingers curled into Israel's hair, both of them clinging to each other like they'd lost too much already.

Then Liv sniffed the air and turned toward me with a curious expression. I felt as though I had interrupted an intimate moment, but I pushed that thought away as Israel gave Liv a brief brotherly kiss on her forehead. He stepped back toward another deceased pack member in the distance, his head hanging sadly. She watched him with a soft expression.

"*I need your help.*"

"*Hello to you, too.*" Her voice was silky as she snapped her head back at me, her eyebrows arched.

"Sorry, I really don't have time for pleasantries. I need you to go to Roman."

"Why?" Her brown furrowed into concern as she looked around for her best friend.

"She's spiralling. Rue is out of control, and Roman's just learned about this bullshit prophecy. She's going to run, Liv, and if she runs, it will be a death sentence for her. I need you to go stop her from leaving until I get back."

"Where are you going?"

"To get help. Please, Liv, you're the only one I can trust with this. You're a warrior—you can handle it if Rue tries anything."

"What the hell has been going on, Vinny?"

"So much. There is so much that has been going on. I don't have time to explain right now. Please, Liv, if Roman runs, she'll do something we can't undo. I'm asking you—begging you—to keep her safe until I get back. I need you to save my mate from herself."

Liv opened her mouth to say something, then grinned at me. "Wait, did you just say 'mate'? As in true mate?"

"Yes," I grumbled. I was sure she already knew the truth about Roman and me, but apparently, Roman had kept this secret from her best friend.

"I knew there was something between you two! I mean, I knew you guys had been doing the horizontal tango a lot recently, but I always wondered if you were destined to be together. There was even a small betting pool on it when we were teenagers. One that you weren't involved in for obvious reasons. Oh, this is so good!" she hopped around, dancing on her feet excitedly, her mouth speaking at a hundred kilometres an hour.

I groaned deeply. "Liv, focus! Get to her now. She's at her house. Keep her there, keep her safe. Please, do this for me. Please."

"Fine." She launched one last gaze in the direction Israel had gone, with an expression that made me wonder, but before I could question it, she stripped her tank top and shorts off and shifted into her rust-coloured wolf before cantering off in the direction I came.

Half an hour later, I bounced up the pack house steps, shifting and snatching a pair of shorts from the basket beside the door before I stepped into the living area. Hot relief burst out of me when I saw my dad sitting on the couch, tears burning in my vision. Vali pushed me forward, eager to get to our kin. As soon as Dad saw me, he stood up and wobbled over.

"How are you doing, old man?" I asked, taking in his pale complexion and sunken eyes.

"I'm far too old for this shit," he smiled. "Glad to see you're in one piece." I nodded as I was pulled in for a rough hug. I held him there for a good few seconds, breathing in his familiar scent and supporting Vali's familial needs. I tried to break the hug, but Dad gripped me again. "Your Roman really is something. Hold onto her," he whispered in my ear before pushing me away, his eyes as wet as my own.

I looked around the pack house, noting that the office door was shut. Shit. I was going to have to knock and interrupt whatever pack business he was dealing with.

A noise on the stairs pulled my attention. Clementine came down the stairs from the alpha quarters, freshly showered and holding little Lacey. Without even asking Clem for permission, I tucked Lacey into my arms and sniffed her head, squeezing her against me. Vali rumbled contentedly as he watched her. I pulled my sister in with my other hand, giving her a brotherly kiss on top of her head.

"Glad you're safe," she mumbled into my side.

"You too," I grunted, looking at my niece's cherub face. "Have you heard from Sean?" I didn't look around for the man in question. Vali could sense he wasn't here, but from the way Clementine's eyes filled with tears, I knew she had felt Sean's pain the moment Nola died. I didn't envy her and Liam's ability to feel the intense emotions of their pack members. I couldn't imagine it; it was hard enough dealing with my own pain.

The door to the office swung open. Alpha Liam and Beta Ryan came out of the alpha's office, their expressions sombre.

The war might be over, but there was still a lot to do. Alpha Liam scented his mate's tears and instantly walked over and folded her into an embrace before he spotted me holding his daughter with a special fondness. I cleared my throat, still refusing to let go of the pup that was at the epicentre of this trainwreck.

"Alpha Liam, may I have a word?"

CHAPTER 72
ROMAN

Vinny left in a blur of fur, and worry immediately gripped me. I couldn't hear the battle sounds this far out, but there was no indication that it was over.

I looked down at my dirty, blood-covered skin. I needed to wash, so I stepped into the bathroom and turned the shower on. As soon as I was clean, I could throw my suitcase in the trunk of my car and get out of British Columbia. But where would I go? Down to the US border? Up to the Artic Circle? How far would I need to go? Jackson had indicated that once Rue had murdered someone, she would become unstoppable, that all feral wolves were the same. Then she killed him and rolled all over his dead body, claiming her first kill's scent. I waited for the proverbial shoe to drop and for her essence to override me, but so far, she still seemed much the same. Yet, who's to say the uncontrollable bloodlust wasn't lurking beneath the surface?

Maybe I wasn't the wolf in the prophecy, or maybe there was part of the prophecy that I hadn't heard, which would be explained when the wolf became psychotically murderous. Regardless, the risk was too high. Feral wolves were bloodthirsty, and with the threat of constant war and the threat of having a feral wolf that was close to Lacey and the pack, it was all too much and too perilous.

Dark, browny-red water washed down the drain as I scrubbed my skin, washing away rogue blood, dirt and tears. Vinny had asked me to wait, but I couldn't. I needed to go as soon as I could.

Rue smiled with an evil softness. *"It's better this way. He's only going to hold us back. We will be better off on our own, and I can kill any dirty rogues we come across who thinks they can challenge me. He's being a prima donna. We won't die. I will be having too much fun to die."*

I dried myself off, getting changed into sweatpants and a hoodie. I looped my wet hair on top of my head when I heard the sound of my front door.

"I knew it! I've always known that you and Vinny were fated to be together," Liv's voice called out as she stomped into the house. I stared at her dirty, naked body. There was a deep scratch down her cheek, but other than that, she was okay. Tears welled in my eyes as she made her way toward me. Hugging me into a chokehold against her warm, naked body.

"You knew we were true mates?" I choked, wondering what the hell she was doing here. "Did Murdoch tell you?"

"What? Murdoch knows?" Her eyes sparkled. "No, *that* discussion can wait. Yes, I knew. Of course, I knew!" She gave an exaggerated shrug. "I've known for ages."

"You *knew*?" I whispered, stunned.

"Obviously." She released me and strolled into my room, yanking open my dresser drawers like she owned the place. "But I didn't bring it up because you had enough on your plate. Rejecting your mate is already brutal—I didn't see the point of rubbing salt in the wound." She quickly doned a pair of denim shorts she had pulled from the drawer. "Even when you finally admitted you two were boning, I didn't want to make it harder by making you relive it, so I let it go." She gave a flippant wave of her hand before putting on a t-shirt. "I'm magnanimous that way." When she pulled her fiery mane through the t-shirt I opened my mouth again.

"Why are you here?"

"Your mate told me that you were going to run and that I was to stay with you until he got back."

"Vinny asked you to babysit?"

"He asked me to help you. He was like, *'Please, Liv, if Roman runs, she'll do something we can't undo. I'm begging you to keep her safe until I get back. I need you to save my mate from herself.'* Then he gave me an 'oh shit' look—like he thought I knew about your true mate status already. I mean, I *did* know, even though no one actually told me." She cackled and then clasped her hands together. "Oh, I love a happy ending. Especially after all the shit we've been dealing with lately."

"How did you know?" I whispered, unable to grasp the fact that she knew my biggest secret. I had kept that information buried within the depths of my soul. I hadn't told anyone.

She gave me a sombre smile and directed me to cuddle with her on my bed, her flippant attitude changing automatically to a softer one. I tucked my head onto her shoulder and wiped a few tears that had escaped.

"How could I not know? I've always known. The air could combust between you two even before that fated full moon. Sean and I even had a betting pool going through most of our teenage years. We tried to figure out how to get you two to hook up, thinking maybe if you just gave in, it would just burn out, which was the other favoured option in the betting pool. But then Vinny disappeared, and you changed."

My chest tightened at the memories, but I let her continue.

"Your romantic, bubbly nature was shadowed by something painfully dark, and Rue started getting progressively worse. She wasn't nearly as aggressive before he suddenly left. Two things immediately became very clear. One: it was never going to burn out between the two of you. If anything, it was going to burn even brighter. And two: when you rejected Vinny, he ran. Little is known about the mate bond and even less is known about what happens when you reject it. But from what I witnessed with Rue, I would say that *this* is what happens when you reject the bond." She gestured at me in from head to toe.

"No. She was feral before that, before I rejected him." Rue rolled her eyes in a bored fashion. She was over this conversation already and was itching to get on the road.

"So, this is to do with Indiana? You don't still think Vinny had a part in that do you?"

"No, I know he had nothing to do with that."

"You finally believe us?" Liv took my hand and gave it a squeeze. "We've always tried to tell you, but you kind of closed down, and eventually, it was easier just to let you believe whatever you believed."

"Rue was trying to protect me in her own twisted way," I said defensively. Liv looked at me as tears welled up in my eyes. "It doesn't matter anyway. I rejected Vinny, and our bond is severed," I fibbed, but before she could question it, I added, "I have to leave Blackfern Valley."

"Why?"

"Because of the prophecy."

"You don't honestly believe that pile of horse shit, do you?"

"I can't risk it. Even if the prophecy isn't real, Rue is too dangerous. I barely have her under control as it is. She's feral, Liv, and feral wolves give into bloodlust."

"Then seal your mate bond with Vinny. That will chill her out." Rue flattened her ears in horror.

"We don't know that. It could make it worse. I wouldn't want to condemn anyone to that fate, let alone, Vinny. No, we can't be together," I whispered.

"Why the fuck not?"

"We just can't!" I shook my head. "There's too much damage and history between us. Not even world-shattering sex can fix that."

"I don't see why you're holding back. This could fix everything. You love him, even if you're too pigheaded to admit it. He definitely loves you and always has. What the fuck do you have to lose?" She sat up on the bed next to me. "Most people would kill for the chance to be with their mate—"

"We are not mates anymore. I rejected the bond," I interrupted her.

"Potato, Potahto." I frowned at her, and she sighed. "I love you, but if you don't go for it, I will."

Rue snarled in my mind, green with jealousy and threatening to retake control. Just because she didn't want him didn't mean she wanted someone else to have him. I glared softly at Liv.

"What? He is a catch. If you don't mate with him, someone else is going to realize it and do it. It may as well be me," she said with an irritating brightness. Rue flashed forward, growling through my teeth.

"Why are you pushing this?" I pushed away from her, irritation bubbling through my skin as I tried to control the inner wolf. I knew she wasn't serious, but Rue was frothing at the mouth, imagining all the ways she could skin Liv.

"Why *aren't* you pushing this?" Her blue eyes implored mine. "I think he's good for you. You don't need him to be happy, Roman, but you are happier with him."

"We constantly argue."

"No, you constantly challenge each other."

"He's an asshole!"

"But he's *your* asshole." I looked back at Rue's stoic face. Her ears were still lowered in disgust, but her emotions were blending with my emotions; they were as confusing as my own. As much as she hated him and wanted to wear his entrails as a garter, she annoyingly loved him, too. It was in that instance I knew she would never hurt him. Or at least I strongly hoped she wouldn't. Rue sneered at me. I bit my lip and looked at my best friend.

My lips trembled. "I'm terrified."

"I know."

"But I have to do this, don't I?"

"Yeah, you do!"

"Do you think he'll come with me?"

"You're still planning on leaving?"

"Yeah, that plan hasn't changed."

Liv gave me a soft smile. "I think that wolf would follow you to the ends of the earth."

After Liv took a shower, she decided to help me pack, resigned to the fact that I was leaving her, too. The shoe I had been holding slipped from my fingers and hit the floor with a clatter. It wasn't just Liv I would be leaving behind, it was everyone. And the worst part? I didn't even know if anyone had been seriously hurt—or worse.

Liv must have noticed the turmoil in my expression because she quickly reassured me that, thankfully, our friends were okay. Her words brought me to tears again, a bittersweet wave of relief washing over me as I thought about the people I couldn't bear to say goodbye to. She promised to explain everything to them, including my parents. I nodded, though Rue scoffed indignantly in the back of my mind, her energy restless and volatile.

Liv gave me a small smile as she refolded the clothes I'd carelessly tossed toward the suitcase, her movements calm and deliberate. She filled the silence with fragments of the battle, recounting her own role in it. When Vinny had reached her, she'd been helping my brother with the grim task of tending to the fallen. Yet, she had dropped everything to come check on me.

I couldn't help but protest, telling her she should be out there, scouting for stray rogues or helping others. But deep down, I was glad she had stayed. Even if I couldn't say goodbye to everyone else, I had this time with her. I told myself they would all understand. *I hope they will.* Goodbyes were hard on me emotionally, and I couldn't afford to let the added stress aggravate Rue's already fragile state.

Rue paced in the back of my mind, her impatience to leave radiating through me as we waited for Vinny to return. Her insistent inner monologue reminded me of the fact we should just go; we didn't need him. I shook my head. I would touch her every now and again, hoping I could reassure her, but I was met with hostility and the occasional snap of her teeth every time.

The last time we were on the same page had been when I was drenched in Jackson's blood, and that was only momentarily. I wondered if we would ever be on the same page about anything normal.

I WOKE up with Liv's arms wrapped around me. Vinny hadn't come back, and by the light streaming through my window, it was well into the next day. Panic choked me as I reached for the mate bond. It was still there, warm and humming like a gentle caress. I felt him stroke back, soothing my sudden spazzing heart, although he didn't attempt to mind-link me. Or if he did, he couldn't access my broken brain.

Liv sighed and rolled over, the flames on her neck licking under her fiery bird's nest. She sat up and looked around anxiously as if she had forgotten where she was.

"Coffee," she demanded sleepily.

I kicked my legs over the edge of the bed and went to the kitchen to see if there was any coffee hidden anywhere, but thinking she would have to settle for a disgusting energy drink instead.

Before I moved off the carpet and onto the laminate floor, I heard a car come up the driveway. I walked to the front and saw a black half-tonne truck parked behind my crappy sedan.

CHAPTER 73
ROMAN

Alpha Liam climbed down from the cab, and Vinny followed from the passenger side. Liv nodded toward them before she stripped and bounded into the forest on all fours, leaving my Fate in the hands of my Alpha.

"Alpha Liam," I greeted, opening the door and lowering my head. Rue paced anxiously in my mind. She may be feral, but she still was naturally subservient to this wolf. This man had the power to end her, and she knew it.

"Roman." He nodded.

I stood back and allowed him entry into my home. He stepped over the threshold before sitting at the dining table I never used. I took a seat across from him, glancing back at Vinny, who placed a dusty-looking rucksack behind the couch, before closing the front door and hovering in the doorway. Alpha Liam started to speak again, and I instantly gave him my full attention.

"Vinny asked me to grant you an urgent audience at your place. He thought it would be safer than bringing you to the pack house."

"The rogues," I croaked. Although I already knew the answer, I needed to hear him say it. "Are they—"

"We've won this battle," he said, his voice steady and grounding. "There's a huge mess to clean up, pack to bury, rogues to burn. But it's over."

"It's really over?" I asked desperately.

"For now." He sounded exhausted but gave me a levelling stare. "I know what you did for my daughter."

"I wasn't going to let Jackson kill her," I croaked, praying that he believed me. I wouldn't have. I would have stopped Rue somehow until my dying breath.

"He thought you were the feral wolf from the prophecy."

"I know."

"Are you?"

"Am I a feral wolf? Or am I the feral wolf from the prophecy?"

"I don't believe in the prophecy, Roman." Alpha Liam sighed and rubbed his tired face. "I believe other wolves believe in the prophecy, and that creates a problem for us that I'm unsure how to fix. We've won this battle—all the rogues are dead—but I'm unsure how long our peace will last."

"I'm sorry, Alpha," I whispered again, feeling sympathetic for the massive responsibility on his shoulders.

"So, I'll ask again. Are you a feral wolf?"

I struggled with my following words. "I honestly don't know, Alpha."

He gave me an appraisal, but I couldn't read him. "But you want to leave."

"Yes, Sir."

"Explain that to me."

"Rue is dangerous, which means I'm dangerous. She protected Lacey once, but I'm not convinced it was out of kindness or pack obligation. I don't believe she's redeemable." I took a deep breath. "The reason I need to go is because I don't trust her. I don't trust her around my friends...my family." I looked at Vinny, blinking back the tears. Rue, on the other hand, rolled her eyes dramatically. I ignored her and continued. "I don't know if she's truly feral because she hasn't given into bloodlust. I don't trust that she won't give in to the bloodlust, and if she does, that could be very dangerous for everyone. If I'm feral, I have a death sentence. If I stay here, someone, at some point, may have to kill me—"

"No one will touch you," Vinny growled. Alpha Liam shot him a look, and his lips pinched into a tight line. His eyes blazed with a protective need, but he stayed quiet, so I kept going.

"I can't put that responsibility on my pack mates. And I can't put my pack mates at risk from me."

"You've had control of her. You can learn control again." Rue glared at the suggestion, growling low.

"Barely. Right now, she's calm, but she's not happy with me. She's itching to take things into her own paws, but she's not going to try anything in front of you because she's submissive to you—for now. I don't mean any disrespect by that, Alpha." I lowered my head respectfully. "If you put her in a killing field, all she'll see is prey. She's a perfect huntress with no moral compass."

"We could train you with the warriors," Alpha Liam pressed.

"I don't think that'll work. She's never allowed me to gain an advantage at training. I've been to so many trainings that I should be at Liv's level by now, but she doesn't allow me to advance. She somehow holds me back like she's afraid that I would overpower her." I shook my head quickly while Rue laughed maliciously at me. "But even if she miraculously allowed the training at your request, even if you could mould me into a weapon, there is always the chance that she will turn and attack this pack instead." Alpha Liam said nothing for a few moments. The glow of his golden rings brightened briefly, before his gaze turned vacant as he conversed with his wolf. "I honestly think you only have two options: let me go or kill me."

"Over my dead body," Vinny spat angrily, moving away

from the doorway and stalking over to me. "No one is killing you."

If Alpha Liam decided my life was forfeit, there was nothing anyone could do. Vinny knew that. His emerald eyes glowed with silver rings. I tried to send calming tones down our mate bond. I didn't need him making a scene right now. As moving as it was, his overreaction could seal my fate.

"You know, I truly believe that my uncle Jed was actually feral," Alpha Liam said in a conversational tone. "Most people thought he was just a sick fuck, but after finding out as much as I could about this prophecy and feral wolves, it makes sense. He must've given in to his bloodlust. He lived off torture and killed his pups before they were born. He nearly wiped out entire family bloodlines for no reason, often leaving only one or two so he could torment them some more. That was the only reason he let my father live and bear pups. He killed for sport, boredom, or if someone decided to wear the colour blue that day. He was insane." Alpha Liam looked over at Vinny. "He killed Vinny's grandparents the day Patrick ran away, purely to bait him into returning with his human bride. Then, he repeatedly tormented him for years, even though he had granted his expression of leave to the pack. Patrick obviously never found another pack and was always connected to Blackfern Valley, but Jed didn't care about the fact he could have commanded him back at any point. He only cared about torturing his pack for sport, that was, until eventually my father put him down. That's the thing with feral wolves. All the research shows they need to be put down. There is no other option. There is no cure." Alpha Liam watched Vinny hover over me protectively before letting out a heavy sigh. "For your sake, I hope that's not true, Vinny."

He shifted his gaze back to me. "I'm not going to kill you, Roman. Losing one's true mate is soul-destroying. But I am granting you permission to leave. There is no need to turn rogue. Vinny's right, without a pack, you'll be more likely to go fully feral. So, you will still be a member of this pack. Although, out there, you will be on your own. No one will come to rescue you. So please don't start any pack wars because you will find you have no aid."

I swallowed hard, nodding in thanks.

"One more thing," Liam added, his voice carrying the weight of authority. "If you run into rogues or packs who believe in this prophecy—who think you're the feral wolf—do everything in your power to convince them otherwise. Then, report back to me immediately. You'll be my eyes and ears—my sentry. You're my first line of defence, Roman, and because of this, there will be no turning rogue, denouncing this pack, or joining a new one."

The command in his tone was unmistakable—it wasn't a request, it was law. Even if I ended up alone and Rue went feral, I'd have to report it to Blackfern Valley. He had granted me permission and protected his pack in one fell swoop.

"I accept! Thank you, Alpha." I bowed in gratitude as he scraped the dining chair back, ready to leave. Rue rumbled again, sifting through the alpha command, breaking it down piece by piece.

Alpha Liam placed a firm hand on my shoulder. "Thank you, Roman. Thank you for doing everything to keep my daughter safe. You will always be a member of this pack. Even as a nomad."

Alpha Liam exited without another word, the rumble of his truck echoing as he went to deal with whatever shitshow was left, thanks to the rogue attack.

"So that's that, then." Vinny pulled me into his arms, pressing a kiss to my forehead. His emotions washed over me—a kaleidoscope of longing, sorrow, and fear—before retreating into a carefully blank façade. His voice cracked as though he was holding back tears, but I couldn't smell any. "You don't know how hard it's going to be to let you go. I did this for you so you could have your freedom and be safe, but all I want to do is tie you up and never let you leave."

"Aren't you coming with me?" The words came out so fast I was worried they were incomprehensible.

"What?"

"You don't have to come if—"

"You want me to come with you?" He grinned at me, looping his fingers into the hem of my sweatpants as he encircled me in his large arms. He made a humming noise as if he was thinking about it. "Do you still hate me?"

"With every fibre of my being." I smiled softly.

"Do you love me?"

"With every fibre of my being," I admitted without a second thought, his eyes widening at my words.

He swallowed hard. "You love me?" he croaked.

"Yeah, I do." I gave him a small smile and tried to push back the building tears. "You know, when you're not being an ass."

"I see." His expression was blank. One Mississippi. Two Mississippi. Three Mississippi. I got to twelve Mississippi, and he'd still said nothing.

"You're such an asshole!" I grumbled. "Are you coming or not?"

He chuckled softly, giving me a chaste kiss. "If you can stand taking a trip with a world-class grade-A asshole, then yes, I'll come with you." He flashed me a grin, which I couldn't help but return before lifting me off my feet, squeezing me hard enough to cut off my air supply. Happiness flooded our bond. He let out a relieved-sounding laugh. "I will follow you anywhere, Roman. I had already decided that if you wanted to do this alone, I was going to secretly stalk you to ensure your safety—even if that meant stealing a car and following you. That's the sort of hold you have on me. Ever since I met you, you've had a hold on me." He shook his head, his eyes dancing with amusement. "My bag is packed. I've already said goodbye to my family. Did you honestly think I would let the woman I love walk out the door and never see her again? I said I wanted to tie you up and never let you leave, and I wasn't kidding." He grinned mischievously. "I would never kid about tying you up."

He lowered me to the ground and brushed his lips against mine, followed by a little lick to ask for entry. My heart galloped as I melted against him. A mewl escaped as I opened my mouth, allowing his tongue to dominate mine. The subtle nutty flavour made my gums itch, and a low growl escaped my throat as he pulled away, and Rue grumbled in annoyance.

"This is going to be fun. How long do you think we can go without killing each other?" he asked playfully. His happy mood was contagious, and his eyes twinkled with a glint I had once mistrusted. Now, the mischievous spark caused my lips to contort into an overjoyed smile.

"At least until the next town over," I joked.

"I was hoping a little longer than that." He said it so earnestly that my heart spasmed.

"Oh?"

"Yeah, I was hoping for forever."

"Forever I can do." I nodded. "Forever definitely works." I kissed him deeply again and began pushing him toward the bedroom. Rue's ears perked with untamed interest as my intent flooded around her. She wasn't going to get to kill again any time soon, but this was the next best thing.

"I thought we were going," he mumbled against my lips as I reached for the hem of his shirt. I lifted the garment upwards over his chiselled body and tossed it onto the floor.

"We are, but there's something we must do first."

"And what's that?" he rumbled as I kissed his scab-covered scratches on his hard chest before running my fingers playfully down the muscular plains, toward the sexy V that led toward his pants.

"We must say goodbye to this house properly. Starting with the bed. Then, there's the shower, and the kitchen counter, maybe even the couch. I don't have rope, but the tie from my housecoat should work."

"Insatiable little she-wolf, aren't you?"

"What?" I fluttered my eyelashes innocently. "Worried you can't keep up?"

Vinny growled and tossed me over his shoulder, carrying me to the first place on my list. Rue grinned excitedly, ready for the amazing, hate-filled sex that made my toes curl. But this time, it wasn't hate sex—and it wasn't rough and desperate. He had promised to fuck me slowly when he had taunted Murdoch, and now he was making good on his promise.

But he wasn't just fucking me slowly. No, for the first time, he was making love to me. He entered me slowly, taking every cell I owned, claiming it, and changing it. I smiled softly at him and felt the magnetic pull solidify into a bridge between our souls. His facial expression showed that he was feeling the same thing. Neither of us said anything. We both just marvelled at the thickening mate bond rippling between us, repairing itself into something amazing.

I could feel his emotions as he watched me with utter reverence, memorizing every second. Every inch of him inside me was an unspoken vow. Each motion, slow and measured, had me burning with desire—only for him.

Suddenly, something shifted inside me. It was a whisper, a call from Rue, whose instincts had always fought this. I'd always fought him, but now, as I lay beneath him, feeling him in every part of me, those instincts were becoming undeniable. It wasn't just passion, it was the primal urge of the wolf within me, urging me to claim him. To mark him.

I could feel Rue's desperate restlessness, the ancient pull that ran too deep for even her to ignore. I felt my canines lengthen, Rue's instincts pushing me to do what had always been unthinkable. My lips found the soft, vulnerable flesh between his neck and collarbone, and before I could even stop myself, my teeth sank into his skin.

The sharp, intoxicating taste of almond and honey filled my mouth as I marked him, causing another quiver and tightening inside me. My tongue laved the mark I left, sealing my venom inside and earning me a sexy moan from Vinny. His eyes were bright and lustful as it dawned on both of us what I had just done, but he didn't look mad—he looked at me with a deep, primal satisfaction.

"My turn." His voice was full of guttural promise as he changed position again, running his nose down my neck before his teeth snapped down on the identical soft spot, our scents fusing and mixing stronger than ever before as we imprinted on each other's souls.

Vinny smiled at me before brushing his lips softly against mine as he continued to make love to me. Both of us knew that if we made it to the next full moon without killing each other, we would make our bond permanent. I had to have faith that both our marks would work. Why else would the bond start to repair itself if Vinny and I weren't meant to be together? Rue rumbled deep within, too exhausted and satiated to argue with my thoughts.

This was the man I loved. The man who loved me in return. This was my forever, however long that would be.

Several hours later, I sighed as I locked my door for the first time in my life, diving into the passenger seat of my car and turning to face Vinny as he drove it with ease out of the drive, turning and twisting his way out of my secluded part of the snow-dusted woods. He paused at the crossroads, giving me a gorgeously loving look before turning away from Blackfern Valley, directing us toward our nomadic life together.

"So, forever?" I mind-linked him, and was met with his infamous, panty-dropping, crooked grin.

"Forever."

About the Author

Anna Elle is a romance author from Aotearoa, New Zealand, who has been making up stories for as long as she can remember—often getting lost for hours in worlds she either found or created herself.

Now based somewhere between reality and her next daydream, Anna writes moody, emotional stories laced with fierce characters, sharp banter, and just enough chaos to feel real. She's married to a wonderfully patient Canadian and has two wild sons who have lovingly helped turn her hair grey ahead of schedule.

A little chaotic, a lot determined, and always chasing the next story, Anna is still figuring out the dark arts of social media (so take pity and follow along). You can find her latest work, updates, and ramblings through her website: http://annaellewrites.com.

Loved this story?

Curious about Clem and Liam's journey?

Be sure to check out *Enlightened by the Eclipse* — available now!

instagram.com/annaelle.writes

tiktok.com/@annaelle.writes

www.ingramcontent.com/pod-product-compliance
Lightning Source LLC
Chambersburg PA
CBHW022024290426
44109CB00014B/735